D1559604

Campus-Wide Information Systems and Networks

Supplements to Computers in Libraries

1. Essential Guide to dBase III+ in Libraries
   Karl Beiser
   ISBN 0-88736-064-5   1987
2. Essential Guide to Bulletin Board Systems
   Patrick R. Dewey
   ISBN 0-88736-066-1   1987
3. Microcomputers for the Online Searcher
   Ralph Alberico
   ISBN 0-88736-093-9   1987
4. Printers for Use with OCLC Workstations
   James Speed Hensinger
   ISBN 0-88736-180-3   1987
5. Developing Microcomputer Work Areas in
   Academic Libraries
   Jeannine Uppgard
   ISBN 0-88736-233-8   1988
6. Microcomputers and the Reference Librarian
   Patrick R. Dewey
   ISBN 0-88736-234-6   1988
7. Retrospective Conversion: A Practical Guide for
   Libraries
   Jane Beaumont and Joseph P. Cox
   ISBN 0-88736-352-0   1988
8. Connecting with Technology 1988:
   Microcomputers in Libraries
   Nancy Melin Nelson, ed.
   ISBN 0-88736-330-X   1989
9. The Macintosh ® Press:
   Desktop Publishing for Libraries
   Richard D. Johnson and Harriett H. Johnson
   ISBN 0-88736-287-7   1989
10. Expert Systems for Reference and
    Information Retrieval
    Ralph Alberico and Mary Micco
    ISBN 0-88736-232-X   1990
11. EMail for Libraries
    Patrick R. Dewey
    ISBN 0-88736-327-X   1989
12. 101 Uses of dBase in Libraries
    Lynne Hayman, ed.
    ISBN 0-88736-427-6   1990
13. FAX for Libraries
    Patrick R. Dewey
    ISBN 0-88736-480-2   1990
14. The Librarian's Guide to WordPerfect 5.0
    Cynthia LaPier
    ISBN 0-88736-493-4   1990
15. Technology for the 90's
    Nancy Melin Nelson, ed.
    ISBN 0-88736-487-X   1990
16. Microcomputer Management and Maintenance
    for Libraries
    Elizabeth S. Lane
    ISBN 0-88736-522-1   1990
17. Public Access CD-ROMS in Libraries:
    Case Studies
    Linda Stewart, Kathy Chiang, & Bill Coons, eds.
    ISBN 0-88736-516-7   1990
18. The Systems Librarian Guide to Computers
    Michael Schuyler and Elliott Swanson
    ISBN 0-88736-580-9   1990
19. Essential Guide to dBase IV in Libraries
    Karl Beiser
    ISBN 0-88736-530-2   1991
20. UNIX and Libraries
    D. Scott Brandt
    ISBN 0-88736-541-8   1991
21. Integrated Online Library Catalogs
    Jennifer Cargill, ed.
    ISBN 0-88736-675-9   1990

22. CD-ROM Retrieval Software: An Overview
    Blaine Victor Morrow
    ISBN 0-88736-667-8   1992
23. CD-ROM Licensing and Copyright Issues for
    Libraries
    Meta Nissley and Nancy Melin Nelson, editors
    ISBN 0-88736-701-1   1990
24. CD-ROM Local Area Networks: A User's Guide
    Norman Desmarais, ed.
    ISBN 0-88736-700-3   1991
25. Library Technology 1970-1990:
    Shaping the Library of the Future
    Nancy Melin Nelson, ed.
    ISBN 0-88736-695-3   1991
26. Library Technology for Visually and
    Physically Impaired Patrons
    Barbara T. Mates
    ISBN 0-88736-704-6   1991
27. Local Area Networks in Libraries
    Kenneth Marks and Steven Nielsen
    ISBN 0-88736-705-4   1991
28. Small Project Automation for Libraries and
    Information Centers
    Jane Mandelbaum
    ISBN 0-88736-731-3   1992
29. Text Management for Libraries and Information
    Centers: Tools and Techniques
    Erwin K. Welsch and Kurt F. Welsch
    ISBN 0-88736-737-2   1992
30. Library Systems Migration:
    Changing Automated Systems
    in Libraries and Information Centers
    Gary M. Pitkin, ed.
    ISBN 0-88736-738-0   1991
31. From A - Z39.50: A Networking Primer
    James J. Michael
    ISBN 0-88736-766-6   1992
32. Search Sheets for OPACs on the Internet
    Marcia Henry, Linda Keenan, Michael Reagan
    ISBN 0-88736-767-4   1991
33. Directory of Directories on the Internet
    Ray Metz
    ISBN 0-88736-768-2   1992
34. Building Blocks for the National Network:
    Initiatives and Individuals
    Nancy Melin Nelson
    ISBN 0-88736-769-0   1992
35. Public Institutions: Capitalizing on the Internet
    Charles Worsley
    ISBN 0-88736-770-4   1992
36. Directory of Computer Conferencing in
    Libraries
    Brian Williams
    ISBN 0-88736-771-2   1992
37. Optical Character Recognition:
    A Librarian's Guide
    Marlene Ogg and Harold Ogg
    ISBN 0-88736-778-X   1991
38. CD-ROM Research Collections
    Pat Ensor
    ISBN 0-88736-779-8   1991
39. Library LANs: Case Studies in Practice
    and Application
    Marshall Breeding
    ISBN 0-88736-786-0   1992
40. 101 Uses of Lotus in Libraries
    Robert Machalow
    ISBN 0-88736-791-7   1992
41. Library Computing in Canada: Bilingualism,
    Multiculturalism, and Transborder Connections
    Nancy Melin Nelson and Eric Flower, eds.
    ISBN 0-88736-792-5   1991

42. CD-ROM in Libraries: A Reader
    Susan Adkins, ed.
    ISBN 0-88736-800-X   1992
43. Automating the Library with AskSam:
    A Practical Handbook
    Marcia D. Talley and Virginia A. McNitt
    ISBN 0-88736-801-8   1991
44. The Evolution of Library Automation:
    Management Issues
    and Future Perspectives
    Gary M. Pitkin, editor
    ISBN 0-88736-811-5   1991
45. Electronic Information Networking
    Nancy Nelson and Eric FLower, eds.
    ISBN 0-88736-815-8   1992
46. Networking Information: Issues for Action
    Elaine Albright, ed.
    ISBN 0-88736-823-9   1992
47. Windows for Libraries
    Dan Marmion
    ISBN 0-88736-827-1   1992
48. CD-ROM Periodical Index
    Pat Ensor and Steve Hardin
    ISBN 0-88736-803-4   1992
49. Libraries, Networks, and OSI
    Lorcan Dempsey
    ISBN 0-88736-818-2   1992
50. Unix-Based Network Communications
    D. Scott Brandt
    ISBN 0-88736-816-6   1992
51. The Role of Libraries in a National Research
    and Education Network
    Charles R. McClure
    ISBN 0-88736-824-7   1992
52. Using Windows for Library Administration
    Kenneth Marks and Steven Nielsen
    ISBN 0-88736-829-8   1992
53. Electronic Collection Maintenance and
    Video Archiving
    Kenneth Marks, Steven Nielsen, and
    Gary Weathersbee
    ISBN 0-88736-830-1   1993
54. An Internet Primer for Librarians and Educators
    Elizabeth Lane and Craig Summerhill
    ISBN 0-88736-831-X   1992
55. Directory to Fulltext Online Resources 1992
    Jack Kessler
    ISBN 0-88736-833-6   1992
56. Campus-Wide Information Systems and
    Networks: Case Studies in Design
    and Implementation
    Les Lloyd, ed.
    ISBN 0-88736-834-4   1992
57. DOS 5.0 for Libraries
    Karl Beiser
    ISBN 0-88736-835-2   1992
58. Wide-Area Network Applications
    in Libraries
    Gregory Zuck and Bruce Flanders
    ISBN 0-88736-841-7   1992
59. Information Management and
    Organizational Change
    Gary M. Pitkin, ed.
    ISBN 0-88736-842-5   1992
60. The Inlosphere Project:
    Public Access to
    Computer-Mediated Communications
    and Information Resources
    Thomas M. Grundner and Susan E. Anderson
    ISBN 0-88736-843-3   1992

Campus-Wide Information Systems and Networks

Case Studies in Design and Implementation

edited by Les Lloyd

Meckler

Westport ▪ London

378.0028
C1992

Library of Congress Cataloging-in-Publication Data

Campus-wide information systems and networks : case studies in design
and implementation / edited by Les Lloyd.
  p. cm. -- (Supplements to Computers in libraries ; 56)
  Includes bibliographical references and index.
  ISBN 0-88736-834-4 (acid-free paper) : $
  1. Universities and colleges -- United States -- Communication
systems -- Case studies.   2. Computer networks -- United States -- Case
studies.   I. Lloyd, Les.   II. Series
LB2342.75.C37   1992
378'.00285'4--dc20   92-8985
                                                              CIP

British Library Cataloguing-in-Publication Data

Campus-wide Information Systems and
Networks: Case Studies in Design and
Implementation. - (Supplements to
Computers in Libraries Series)
  I. Lloyd, Les   II. Series
  004.6

  ISBN 0-88736-834-4

Meckler Publishing, the publishing division of Meckler Corporation,
  11 Ferry Lane West, Westport, CT 06880.
Meckler Ltd., 247-249 Vauxhall Bridge Road, London SW1V 1HQ, U.K.

Printed on acid free paper.
Printed and bound in the United States of America.

This book is dedicated to PT and Bill Farinon, whose generous contribution to Lafayette enabled our networking project to commence.

"The exciting promise of technology must be kept in perspective. In the mastery of our machines, we must remember that the right decision is seldom based on quantitative factors alone. In the end, the only worthy purpose of technology is to advance the human endeavor, never to replace it."

—*Bill Farinon, 1988*

Contents

Part 2: Campus-Wide Information Systems

Part 3: Library and Administrative Networks

Introduction

This book was developed as a result of queries and comments I received through Lafayette College's *Using Computer Networks on Campus* conference series. Many schools are in the process of designing and/or implementing campus networks and seek the input and experience of other schools that have undertaken such projects. Over thirty schools from throughout the United States and the United Kingdom have contributed chapters to this volume on *Campus-Wide Information Systems and Networks*.

Chapters within contain information on several networking topics: campus networks, campus-wide information systems, and library and administrative networks. For the purposes of this book, I will define the first two terms as follows:

Campus network: The physical structure and configuration of the cable plant and equipment connected to form the local or wide area network providing connectivity to PC servers, multi-user systems, and external networks such as the Internet. In many cases, a campus-wide network is used to provide connections to faculty, staff, and students to access a campus-wide information system as well as academic, administrative, and library computer systems.

Campus-wide information system: A single system (or network of systems that appear to be one) that provides common, non-discipline specific functions to a campus. These might include, but are not limited to: budget information; bulletin boards; campus policies; campus schedules; electronic mail; library catalog access; registration information; other local databases.

Computer Networking at the American University: On the Road to AU2000

BJ Gleason and Gene McGuire
Computer Science and Information Systems
The American University

THE AMERICAN UNIVERSITY

The American University is a privately endowed, doctoral-granting university with an international student body located in a residential section of northwest Washington, D.C. The university's 78-acre main campus and 8-acre Tenley satellite campus are located within one mile of each other.

The University draws students from all 50 states and more than 125 nations. The student body and faculty reflect the international and multi-cultural character of Washington, D.C., and the university's programs take advantage of the unique resources of the nation's capital.

The American University consists of five principal academic divisions: the College of Arts and Sciences, with more than 20 teaching units, including the School of Communication and the School of Education; the Kogod College of Business Administration; the School of International Service; the School of Public Affairs; and the Washington College of Law. The university also provides undergraduate study-abroad programs in China, Mexico, South America, and Europe.

The university's current enrollment is approximately 11,600 students in 64 bachelor's programs, 79 master's programs, 17 doctoral programs and J.D. and L.L.M. programs. The enrollment includes approximately 5,500 full-time undergraduates and 600 part-time undergraduates. Other large enrollment categories include 1,200 Washington College of Law students, 1,500 nondegree students, 3,800 graduate students, and 500 Washington semester students. Approximately 60 percent of the students receive some form of financial aid.

THE COMPUTING CENTER

The Computer Center operates 24 hours a day throughout the year, serving the research and instructional needs of both faculty and students. The central processing unit is an IBM 4381 computer with 16 MB of memory, capable of performing 3.6 million instructions per second. The processor is compatible with the System/370 architecture of older IBM computers, as well as the newest extended architecture (XA) designs of the 3080 series processors.

Other major hardware components of the center include: a Wang VS80 minicomputer to support word processing and data interchange, IBM 3380 and IBM 3350 disk storage devices, six Memorex tape drives, three high-speed printers, 320 terminals locally connected to the system, and 50 teleprocessing lines supported by a Memorex 1270 terminal control unit.

OS/VSI (Operating System/Virtual Storage One) is the primary operating system at the university. MUSIC/SP (Multi-User System for Interactive Computing/System Product) is the primary time-sharing operating system. VM/SP or VM/370 (Virtual Machine/System Product) permits concurrent operation of several operating systems necessary to support the academic and administrative computing needs of the university community—including OS/VSI, MUSIC/SP, CMS (Conversational Monitoring System), and RSCS (Remote Spooling Communications Subsystem).

BITNET , an educational computing network, is available for faculty and administrative use. BITNET users can communicate with other universities, sharing information via electronic mail, text files, and computer programs.

The computer center supports more than 15 programming languages, including COBOL, FORTRAN, BASIC, Pascal, and PL/I. Other software packages available for general use include: SPSS (Statistical Package for the Social Sciences), SAS (Statistical Analysis System), GPSS (General Purpose Simulation System), BMD (Biomedical Statistical Program), MPS (Mathematical Programming System), and SCRIPT (text processing). Graphics support is provided by SASGRAPH running under CMS.

CURRENT EQUIPMENT CONFIGURATION

Here is a brief list of all the general-purpose labs distributed across the campus:

> *Advanced Technology Lab (ATL):* Located in the Mary Graydon center, this lab has a very eclectic collection of computer equipment: a NeXT machine, Mac II, several personal computers (PCs), CD-ROM, Color Printer, Kurzweil text scanner, and a SCANTRON optical mark reader. This lab is reserved for faculty, staff, and graduate students. It is designed as a resource to access computer equipment too expensive for any single department.

> *Anderson Computing Lab:* This is perhaps the most popular computing center for students. Comprised of several rooms in the basement of Anderson Hall, it features 23 PCs and 13 PS/2s on a No-

vell Network, 25 Mac SEs on an AppleTalk Network, several dot matrix printers, 5 Image Writers, and 2 laser printers. This facility also houses a Consensor Laboratory, an interactive classroom environment.

McCabe Computer Assisted Writing Center: This lab is designed to help students improve their writing skills. It has 19 PCs and a PS/2 on a Novell network, several letter quality printers, and a laser printer. This lab features a number of software applications to check student writing and provides student tutors to proofread and make suggestions.

Social Science Research Lab: This lab has 22 PCs on a Novell Network, as well as 7 terminals to the mainframe. Printing resources include 8 dot matrix printers and a letter-quality printer.

Mainframe Lab: 23 terminals are connected to the IBM 3090 and ES/9000-210. This center provides access to BITNET , Internet, and campus e-mail.

Information Technology Resource Center: Part of the Kogod College of Business Administration, this lab features 24 PS/2s on a Novell network, several wide-carriage printers and a laser printer. It also has a page scanner and a color printer.

Language Resources Center: Located in the lower level of the Asbury Building, this lab has 10 MAC LC computers on an AppleTalk network. A wide variety of language packages for English, French, German, Hebrew, Italian, Russian, and Spanish are offered. This newly renovated laboratory also houses a Consensor Lab.

Computer Science and Information Systems Lab: Located adjacent to the Anderson Lab, these two labs are reserved for graduate students and classroom activities. The lab has 42 PCs on a Starlan Network. An ATT 3B2 acts as the server.

CSIS/Math/Stat Lab: Located in the upper level of Clark Hall, this lab is shared by both departments. It contains several machines, including: NeXT, Sun, Amiga, PCs, and Macs. They are connected via an Ethernet backbone running both Novell and TCP/IP.

CSIS Hardware Lab: Reserved for graduate and advanced undergraduate students, this lab space is used in conjunction with the computer architecture courses. It houses two NeXT machines, three Macs, two Sun workstations, and several PCs. The machines are connected via an Ethernet backbone running Novell and TCP/IP.

Washington Semester Lab: A small lab located at the Tenley Circle campus, it contains ten PCs and a laser printer.

Learning Services Lab: A computer center designed for learning disabled students.

Library: The library has a large number of mainframe terminals to access the ALADIN system, as well as a number of PCs accessing CD-ROM collections.

In addition, each department on campus has its own independent Novell network. Most departments use PCs, but a small handful use Macs and run the AppleTalk network.

The most complex local are network (LAN) supports both the CSIS and Math/Stat departments, and is located in Clark Hall. Most departmental computer requirements are homogeneous—all PCs or all Macs. The CSIS Department has a wide range of machines connected to the network. A thin wire Ethernet backbone supports both Novell and TCP/IP, which in turn supports the PCs, Macs, Suns, and NeXT machines used in the department.

A listing of the AU LANs supported by the University Computing Center follows:

Location	Number of Network Drops	Number of Workstations
Admissions and Financial Aid	5	4
Anderson Hall Macintosh Lab	28	27
Anderson Hall PC Lab	65	65
Budget Office	10	9
School of Comm. Lab	23	22
Comp. Sci & Info. Systems	40	27
Hurst Hall Lab	24	23
Leonard Hall (dorm)	206	0
Language & Foreign Studies	4	4
National Center Health Fitness	5	5
Parking & Traffic	4	4
President's Building	19	13
Student Health Center	2	2
University Computing Center	45	41
Washington College of Law	79	75
Writing Lab	23	22
Total	582	343

AU'S CAMPUS NETWORK PLAN

The American University is planning to install a fiber-optic communications backbone to all buildings on the main campus and a satellite campus located one mile away. The immediate plans are for this fiber to be used as a data communications system to tie the seventeen existing Novell Ethernet LANs to the backbone along with the IBM 3090 and the ES/9000 mainframe computers. Future plans call for this backbone to be used for data communications including high-speed image and multimedia applications, voice, video broadcasting, and video conferencing. The network is planned to meet current needs and be adaptable to emerging and future communications standards in these areas.

A fiber-optic backbone is being installed in four phases:

- Phase 1 was the installation of extra conduits to all buildings. This phase was completed in the fall of 1990.
- Phase 2 is the installation, terminating and testing of the fiber-optic cable through the conduits. An RFP for this phase was issued in December of 1991 with a projected completion date of spring, 1992.
- Phase 3 will be the installation of electronic equipment necessary to connect the seventeen existing local area networks to the backbone along with the mainframe computer and Internet. This phase will begin immediately following the completion of the backbone installation.
- Phase 4 will be the installation in campus buildings of any wiring necessary to fully network the campus.

The fiber backbone is expected to grow quickly to meet all the data communications needs of the campus. Initially, it is expected that Ethernet and TCP/IP will be the two protocols supported on the backbone, but future growth in imaging technology and the need for university personnel to access research databases indicate an increase in bandwidth requiring a mode to FDDI (Fiber Distributed Data Interface) or other high-speed data protocols within approximately five years.

The university's networking plan also calls for the centralization of server management, maintenance, and backup functions by housing all existing and future building LAN servers in the university's existing computing center. In the immediate future, the servers will be connected to the building LAN they serve by Ethernet connections. Access to the university's mainframe computer will be through a 3270 gateway server running McGill University's NET3270 program and using the existing coax cable plant to attach to a 3174 controller. Access to the Internet will be accomplished either indirectly by accessing the mainframe and using the AUINET menu, or directly by running the NCSA/Clarkson University TCP/IP software on the local PC.

Necessary security for administrative data will be provided by separating student academic labs and dormitory LANs from administrative and faculty LANs; these two networks will, however, be bridged to allow electronic mail and file transfers to occur from any user to any user.

Immediately following installation of the backbone fiber, Phases 3 and 4 will begin, and major efforts will be directed toward the completion of a campus-wide data network. Present voice (telephone) and video communications will be unaffected by the fiber backbone installation and can continue operating on their existing cable plants. As the formats of voice and video increasingly become indistinguishable from data communications, the opportunity to utilize the data network to transmit voice and video without major conversion costs will be presented. Also, to the extent that voice and video producers are willing to provide the necessary end equipment, the fiber plant is sized such that fiber strands will be available for these applications from the beginning.

The primary goal of Phases 3 and 4 is to have every building on campus wired for a LAN and then connected to the fiber-optic backbone. Wiring every building for network connectivity will, of course, give every faculty member the capability to access the mainframe and use Internet and BITNET Currently, most, but not all, faculty offices have computers and/or connections to the mainframe at AU. Results of an informal survey done in November 1991 show the following:

Teaching Unit/Dept.	Number of Offices	Number with Computers	Number with Mainframe Connection
College of Arts and Sciences			
American Studies	2	2	0
Anthropology	8	7	1
Art	1	1	1
Biology	11	11	2
Chemistry	15	10	6
Communication	20	3	0
Community Studies	8	8	0
Comp. Sci. & Info. Sys.	12	12	0
Economics	24	24	7
Education	10	5	1
Health & Fitness	6	4	2
History	15	13	1
Jewish Studies	2	2	1

Languages	12	5	2
Literature	22	18	1
Mathematics & Statistics	15	15	13
Media	2	2	1
Performing Arts	15	4	1
Philosophy & Religion	7	6	1
Physics	6	6	6
Psychology	12	10	6
School of Int'l. Studies	42	32	21
Kogod College of Bus. Admin.			
Accounting	18	16	5
Finance and Real Estate	12	12	2
Int'l. Business	9	8	2
Management	19	19	6
Marketing	10	9	3
School of Public Affairs			
Government	24	21	5
Justice, Law and Society	19	19	2
Public Administration	19	11	3

SUBTOTALS

Arts and Sciences	247	178	56
		72.06%	22.67%
International Service	42	32	21
		76.19%	22.67%
Kogod College of Business	68	64	18
		94.12%	26.47%
School of Public Affairs	62	51	10
		82.26%	16.13%
TOTAL	357	274	95
		76.75%	26.61%

THE ROAD TO AU2000

In the past, the university Computing Center has supported the traditional users of computers: mainframe and PC users. In the past four years, the university Computing Center has made considerable progress in supporting these traditional users. During this time, the number of PCs in public labs available for student and faculty use has quadrupled and services have been expanded to offer advanced demonstration equipment, writing services to students, and statistical support for faculty. The mainframe has been upgraded for present usage levels and placed on a two-year upgrade cycle.

These traditional services will continue to be supported but are expected to continually evolve. The university's overall vision for the year 2000 encompasses much more than technology; computers and networking play a key role in transforming the university workplace. Some of the planning assumptions concerning the workplace of the year 2000 are listed below.

The American University is moving toward a future where there will be:

1. Offices and dorm rooms with
    a. a computer on every desktop (students may bring their own)
    b. local area network connections within the department or work group
    c. a connection to the campus backbone network

2. Dedicated classrooms with
    a. desktop computers, or hookups for students' computers
    b. multimedia podia for the faculty
    c. connections between the podia and classroom desktops
    d. a connection to the campus backbone network

3. Desktop computers featuring
    a. a graphical user interface (GUI) to be replaced eventually by voice interface
    c. a Windows (or OS/2 or UNIX) environment
    d. a customized AU software "toolset" including e-mail, voice mail, file transfer, and remote log-in
    e. a connection to the campus backbone network

4. A mainframe computer with
    a. a graphical user interface (GUI)
    b. state-of-the-art database software
    c. an integrated, institution-wide database
    d. simple, common reporting tools
    e. a connection to the campus backbone network
    f. connection to Internet, BITNET, and ALADIN (temporary)
    g. target response time for all categories of users

5. A campus backbone network with
    a. FDDI compatibility
    b. high-speed (bandwidth) capacity
    c. voice, data and video (digital) signal integration
    d. connections to each campus building LAN
    e. connections to Internet, BITNET, and ALADIN (to replace the mainframe connection)

6. Services that offer all campus users
    a. phone help lines (for computing and network questions)
    b. training classes (on computing and network subjects)
    c. 24-hour mainframe services
    d. PC maintenance services
    e. PC software and hardware installation
    f. Departmental LAN costs, installation, and management

7. Services for special groups of users
    a. 24-hour public lab management (students)
    b. electronic classroom scheduling (faculty)
    c. system design and programming (departments)
    d. statistical consulting services (faculty & students)
    e. equipment compatible with the needs of physically/mentally challenged individuals

8. Capacity planning for growth such that
    a. mainframe CMS use will grow at 30% per year
    b. mainframe MVS use will grow at 60% per year
    c. mainframe disk usage will grow at 25% per year
    d. PC lab usage will grow at 20% per year
    e. network growth to be determined
    f. planned replacement of desktop workstations at 20% per year

The items in this list have not yet been prioritized. It is anticipated that priorities for a given budget cycle will be proposed by the University Computing Center's management in consultation with the Faculty Senate's Computer Resources Committee (for academically related proposals) and the Administrative Computing Committee (for administratively related proposals).

This list was distributed in November 1991 to all AU faculty by the Long-Range Planning Subcommittee of the Computer Resources Committee. Faculty were asked to respond with comments agreeing or disagreeing with this vision of the future. They were also asked to provide comments on any specific feature(s) they found particularly necessary or desirable.

SUMMARY

The American University is in the midst of a large-scale network implementation effort. The objectives of this effort are to wire every building on the main campus and the satellite campus for network connectivity. The fiber-optical backbone network is scheduled to be installed during the first part of 1992. Existing building LANs will be connected to this backbone giving the building occupants network access to the campus mainframe, as well as Internet, BITNET, and ALADIN. Buildings that do not currently have LANs will be wired and connected to the backbone.

A fully networked campus where faculty, administration, and students have access to each other and centralized databases both on- and off-campus is one of the goals of AU2000. By planning for a world and workplace transformed by technology, the University Computing Center plans to successfully guide The American University along the road to AU2000.

ACKNOWLEDGMENTS

The information in this case study has been obtained from documents at The American University as follow: the University Computer Center's Long-Range Plan; the University Computer Center's Annual Report, Academic Year 1991; the American University's Request for Proposal on a Fiber-optic Cable Installation. The information contained in these documents is the result of the efforts of Mark V. Reed, Executive Director of University Computing; Frank Connolly, Director of Academic Computing; and Tom Southall, Manager of User Services & Training, among others. Their cooperation in sharing this information is appreciated.

An Academic Computing Perspective of Networking at Bloomsburg University

Robert Abbott
Director of Academic Computing
Bloomsburg University

Robert Parrish
Vice President for Administration and University Treasurer
Bloomsburg University

David Heffner
Academic Computer Administrator for Networking and File Servers
Bloomsburg University

This chapter presents an overview of the networking evolution, the present state, and the implementation of a relatively comprehensive strategy for full campus networking at Bloomsburg University. It is presented from the perspective of academic computing on the Bloomsburg University campus.

ASPECTS OF THE ENVIRONMENT

Bloomsburg University is a middle-sized state university with a strong emphasis on teaching. It is the third largest of the 14 universities in the Pennsylvania State System of Higher Education. Student full-time equivalent population is 7,400 with 375 faculty and 450 staff. The university's current Strategic Directions Statements call for the integration of technology into the curricula. Computers and networking are considered an important technology which the University has recently committed itself to significantly increase in 1992.

DIVERSITY OF COMPUTERS

There are over 1,000 personal computers (PCs)on campus, with well over half being used by students and faculty. The personal computers used are IBM and compatibles (AT&T, Zenith, Gateways, and others), Apple IIGS/ IIe, and Apple Macintosh. There are 11 host/file server computers used in the academic area and 2 in the administrative area. Of these 13 hosts, 12 are UNIX-based. In addition, there are 8 Macintosh Appleshare file servers in the academic area and 4 in administrative areas. Administrative computing is centered on the Unisys 2200/402 mainframe computer with an extensive system of terminals and PCs in campus offices that are now primarily connected to the mainframe by copper wire cables and multiplexors.

DECENTRALIZATION OF PC ACQUISITION AND OF LAN NETWORK DEVELOPMENT

Bloomsburg University has a decentralized process for acquiring computer equipment. Acquisitions in the administrative area are coordinated by Computer Services. Acquisition in the academic area involves the Center for Academic Computing and the various departments and colleges. The process of acquiring academic equipment begins in the departments, goes through the deans to the Provost, who refers the requests to a faculty equipment committee. This committee prioritizes requests for the Provost as an advisory committee. It is a bottom-up approach that allows for a high degree of direction from the faculty at several key points, but also can result in the procurement of a variety of hardware and applications.

Departments and colleges can establish local area networks (LANs) and have done so in the past. Some of the first steps in networking originate at this level. Networked computer classrooms have begun as departmental computer classrooms. In the case of both the LANs and the classrooms, the support for these facilities has shifted from departments or colleges to the Center for Academic Computing. This evolutionary process has brought us to the point of having essentially LANs to work with—AT&T Starlan and Apple's AppleTalk.

We do expect, however, to have some other very small, standalone, specialized networks that we may or may not integrate into the broad campus network. One of these will be a four-station IBM token-ring network that delivers K-12 educational programs for teacher training. Initially, it will be a standalone network, but plans are being made to bridge it to the Ethernet network.

CAMPUS NETWORKING GOALS AND PLANS

In 1989 the Academic Computer Advisory Committee recommended three broad goals to the Provost for academic computing at Bloomsburg University. These were endorsed by the Provost and several planning committees. Two of these goals are directly related to networking:

1. Provide for every faculty member a workstation that has adequate printing and communication capability necessary for their activities at Bloomsburg University.

2. Provide connection of faculty workstations, host computers, file servers, classrooms, labs and student work areas, and access to off-campus networks.

A PLAN IS DEVELOPED

In 1991, at the initiative of the Vice President for Administration and with his direction, a comprehensive plan to provide basic campus-wide networking for voice, data, and video was developed and financing established. The University has now made a major commitment to networking the campus. This plan has widespread support and the financial commitment to see it through.

Later that same year a plan for financing the Provost's goal of providing a computer for every permanent faculty who desires one was developed and approved by the planning and budget committees. As part of the project, a network board will be purchased with each new computer. Thus, Bloomsburg University is approaching the mid-1990s committed to campus networking and providing computers for every faculty who requests one.

The basic goal of the network will be to allow faculty and staff to access any academic or administrative resource on the network from their office or from off campus and to allow students to access academic and appropriate administrative resources from all computer labs and classrooms. Some of these resources are word processors, graphics programs, spreadsheets, and discipline-specific programs on MS-DOS and Macintosh file servers; terminal access to host computers for programming languages and statistical analysis; the PALS Library systems, a BBS, and online databases; the student course scheduling and registration system, and other administrative functions; and Internet and BITNET connections off campus.

OFF CAMPUS NETWORK CONNECTION

In the spring of 1992, the Pennsylvania State System of Higher Education (SSHE) will be implementing a telecommunications network that will connect the 14 state universities having a present total of twenty-three campus, branch, and central office locations. This system-wide network will allow faculty, staff, and students to communicate with each other via voice, data, and television signal and will provide a gateway to Internet and other national/international networks. It is based on the TCP/IP protocol.

FROM THE PAST

Like most colleges and universities, all computing on campus was done initially on one large mainframe; first with card input, then progressing to paper terminals, and next, CRT terminals located near the computer. The mainframe was shared by administrative and academic users. As interactive programs developed, CRT terminals were located in offices in other buildings, connected by copper cabling running underground. In the early 1980s we began to replace CRTs with PC microcomputers for academic computing. PCs supported both DOS programs and asynchronous terminal connection to the mainframe. Later PCs with synchronous capability began to replace administrative terminals.

With the addition of an academic minicomputer in 1985, the greater portion of the academic instructional functions moved onto a separate machine in a separate building. PC microcomputers again served the dual function of terminal and standalone computers. These were located near the UNIX minicomputer, an AT&T 3B5, and were directly connected to it via serial cable.

FIBER—EARLY GROUNDWORK

The campus will build on and add to existing fiber connections between buildings. In 1984 the university decided that fiber-optic cables would be important cabling in any future telecommunication infrastructure. Thus, in 1985 when the university purchased and installed an AT&T System 85 digital phone switch, it took the opportunity to lay 108 fiber strands between five of the central campus buildings to provide the nucleus of a multimedia telecommunications network.

As buildings have undergone major renovation, they have been wired internally to facilitate voice, data and video in classrooms and most offices. This has been done to two classroom buildings over the last several years. In addition, a complex of six new student apartments on the upper campus has telecommunications wiring built into each residence. Fiber now connects these apartments and the other upper campus facilities to the lower campus.

Since the original five buildings in 1985, fiber has been extended to nine more buildings. The fiber cabling was laid, anticipating the growth of campus networking. The telecommunications networking, voice, data and video are now being extended on this interbuilding fiber backbone. Fiber is generally considered to be an inexpensive, high-capacity, and low-maintenance cabling medium today. We feel fortunate to have come to that conclusion seven years ago and have had the opportunity to add fiber cabling, so that today it is available between most of the major campus buildings.

DEVELOPMENT OF LOCAL AREA NETWORKING

Local area networking for file and print serving began in 1987 with an Apple-Talk network serving a small cluster of Macintosh computers in a public lab. This was followed quickly by a 1MB Ethernet LAN using two AT&T Starlan file servers to provide services for a College of Business classroom/lab, and an AppleTalk LAN for Macintoshes serving a Psychology and Sociology classroom/lab, during the 1987-88 academic year.

ETHERNET

Most of the College of Business classrooms and faculty offices are located in one building. This was one of the buildings recently renovated which had cabling built into it. This provided the opportunity to network all offices and most classrooms as the building was being reoccupied. While this area was being networked, the technology changed from the 1MB Starlan over Ethernet to the standard 10MB Ethernet. A mix of the two speeds exists, with a second classroom/lab and some faculty offices connected over a 10MB Starlan Ethernet segment. With an AT&T bridge between these two segments, it is functionally transparent to users. The network includes two AT&T 3B2/500 file servers, an AT&T 386 file server, and two AT&T 3B2/310 print servers. The College of Business performed networking under the direction of one faculty member who worked on a voluntary basis to establish and provide support for it. It is now maintained by Academic Computing.

EXTENDING THE ETHERNET NETWORK

As noted, interbuilding computing began with multiplexors and copper wire connecting terminals to the administrative mainframe. The first interbuilding Ethernet connections came about in 1989, primarily to provide the College of Business faculty and students a synchronous connection to the administrative mainframe. This was done by extending the Ethernet over the interbuilding fiber-optic cable. The synchronous protocol conversion needed by the Unisys 2200 mainframe was provided by a product from CHI Corporation and Control Logic.

As part of this project, an asynchronous, non-Ethernet link was also established connecting the academic minicomputer, the administrative mainframe, and the Ethernet network extending from the College of Business. It was provided by an AT&T ISN switching box that gave terminal connections between the academic minicomputer, the administrative mainframe and a UNIX 386 server on the Starlan network. These were single-user lines at 9600 baud.

Both of these efforts were pursued as pilot projects. The subsequent extension of the Ethernet network to the academic minicomputer obviated the need for the asynchronous link. Future synchronous connections to the Unisys will be through a software protocol conversion program running on a UNIX minicomputer that is accessed using TCP/IP, rather than the CHI gateway. PC and Macintosh network users, as well as dial-in users, will have synchronous-emulation access to the administrative functions on the Unisys 2200 mainframe.

APPLETALK

The number of AppleTalk networks has increased from the two first established in 1987 to the present seven that support students and faculty. There are an additional four that are primarily supporting administrative functions for a total of eleven AppleTalk networks. Within a single building several of these have been linked by bridges to form larger, segmented networks with multiple file servers, printers, and zones. AppleTalk network size is controlled by the use of bridges (Shiva Netbridges) that create zones within segments or link separate networks. This isolates traffic to the zones and allows for access control across the bridges as needed.

EXTENDING THE DEPARTMENTAL APPLETALK NETWORKS

In 1991-92 we took our first step in creating a campus-wide AppleTalk network by connecting three AppleTalk networks located in three different buildings. This was done with Cayman Gatorboxes connected to the Ethernet network in each building. A "tunnel" was established which effectively makes this one single network with multiple zones. In 1992 two other buildings will be connected to the AppleTalk network in the same way. The broad campus-wide AppleTalk network, which will eventually bring in all Macintosh network users, provides academic computing with applications available on multiple file servers and with remote administration capabilities.

The use of a Gatorbox provides us with an additional function, for it allows Macintosh users on the AppleTalk network to connect to host computers via TCP/IP. As TCP/IP is our standard for connecting host computers, this gives AppleTalk network users access to all campus and external telecommunications features.

MACINTOSHES OVER ETHERNET

Some Macintosh SEs and Macintosh II are being connected to the Ethernet network directly via Ethernet boards. They have the same network functions as those going through the Gatorbox but operate at the 10BaseT speed of 10MB per second when on the Ethernet segment. Access to the Appleshare file server drops the speed down to the 230KB per second speed of Local-Talk. This is not the case when accessing the Appleshare server running on the AT&T Starlan Server S. This single server handles both Appleshare and Starlan clients in their appropriate modes. For the Mac, as well as the DOS users, it provides server access at 10MB per second.

ACCESS TO HOST COMPUTERS AND FILE SERVERS

By 1991 the number of Starlan file servers had increased to eight. Each of these is also a UNIX system that allows for terminal access by users. In addition, there are three other UNIX-based systems on the network—a Unisys U6000, a DEC 5000 system, and an IBM 6000 RISC system. The Unisys 2200, though not a UNIX system, is also connected to the Ethernet network as discussed previously. Of these, seven are presently running TCP/IP.

Starlan users can use UNIX and the services of the other Starlan servers by running a version of Kermit, provided as part of Starlan. Kermit provides a terminal connection for the client PC to the AT&T UNIX Starlan server allowing access to UNIX as a VT 102 terminal. Once on any of the AT&T UNIX systems, the user can connect and log in to any of the other AT&T UNIX systems through the basic UNIX "cu" command. Once on an AT&T UNIX system that is running TCP/IP, the user can use "Telnet" to connect to other TCP/IP host computers such as the Unisys U6000, the IBM 6000, the DEC 5000, or any other host on- or off-campus that is running TCP/IP. Access for users is further enhanced by enabling dialing into any one of several minicomputers with modems attached from off-campus; then they can connect to the UNIX system that they must be on to do their work.

For access to the TCP/IP host, the Starlan user can run a program called TAP which provides TCP/IP access to a host, such as the U 6000, without first having to log in to an AT&T UNIX system. Offices in the College of Business use this program to access the U 6000 and through it administrative applications on the Unisys mainframe. Non-Starlan network users can run a TCP/IP program on the PC which permit direct access to any TCP/IP host.

Macintosh users who are directly connected to the Ethernet network operate the same as PCs with the TCP/IP program. Macintosh users who are only connected to the AppleTalk network will get access to the host computers on the network through a TCP/IP program, but this involves a transparent link through the Gatorbox gateway. Macintosh users, as with the PC users, can have Telnet terminal sessions and use FTP for file transfer.

MS-DOS client workstations that have Starlan software installed have networked DOS services available. A menu provides options for selecting general-use programs such as WordPerfect or specific course-related programs such as an accounting publication search program. Selections are made to use MS-DOS or UNIX software that is directly available either from the local server or from a remote server located in another building. A distinct advantage of this is that a faculty person can give instruction in a classroom in one building using a computer server that services a student lab located in another building. Instructional flexibility is enhanced for both room scheduling and for demonstration and training. This same advantage holds for Macintosh users.

CAMPUS-WIDE NETWORKING

By early 1991 four buildings were connected via Ethernet over fiber-optic cables. This supports Starlan file serving, connection to the mainframe, mini-computers, and AppleTalk networking. The PC computers connected were a mix of 8088, 8086, and 80286 using Starlan 8-bit Ethernet boards. The Protocols used are Starlan, TCP/IP, and Apple File Protocol. Kermit, VT100, and AT&T 4410 are the primary emulators used for academic functions. Synchronous terminal emulation for the Unisys is provided by a mix of hardware and software solutions. TN3270 protocol will also be available in the future. Links were made between the AppleTalk network and the Ethernet network. Individual Macintosh computers had been connected directly to the Ethernet network using both Apple File Protocol and TCP/IP.

A COORDINATED AND COMPREHENSIVE PLAN

It was again with the need to upgrade the telephone switch that we took the opportunity to assess our overall telecommunications needs and provide the first comprehensive campus-wide plan that includes voice, data and video. In 1991 a plan to provide the basic network infrastructure for voice, data and video was developed based on plans from the telecommunications, TV/radio, administrative computing, and academic computing areas. The plan received the endorsement of the various committees, and funds were allocated for the project.

The plan builds on the existing structure that had emerged through the evolutionary process of satisfying demands of various areas on campus at different times over the previous five years. This structure allows connection and communication between the different established networks and protocols. It is committed to protecting and integrating the existing networks and existing PC users.

The plan provides for additional fiber between buildings, hubs, concentrators, wiring within the buildings, a large number of Ethernet boards to connect existing faculty and office PCs and Macintosh computers, network management software, a central router, and a central concentrator that will link 50 dial-in users to the network.

As it expands networking will build on the existing base of 10BaseT cabling, with new cabling being unshielded twisted pair IEEE 802.5 rated at 16MB. Fiber cabling between buildings will be 62.5 multimedia. A central router will be used to provide network segmentation for the campus. Concentrators and hubs will have Simple Network Management Protocol (SNMP) capability and will be located on each floor of every building. This will permit localization of data broadcast, remote network management and multiple data paths. TCP/IP running on the various host computers will allow for telnet terminal communication, FTP file transfer and Simple Mail Transfer Protocol (SMTP) for e-mail communications between host computers.

Implementation of the plan will involve connecting existing faculty PCs that are not on the network. During the first phase, two administrative computers in each office area will be moved from the existing copper wire/ multiplexor route to Ethernet. The plan for administrative network conversion calls for the remaining office PCs to be moved to Ethernet at the rate of 20 percent a year.

SOME PROBLEMS, ISSUES , AND EVENTS

Computers for Every Faculty Member

The university's project of providing a computer for each faculty member who requests one will be implemented in 1992. This plan also calls for the purchase of a network board for each of the new computers. The computers will be 386SX or above for MS-DOS users, and Macintosh LC or above for Macintosh users. This will immediately have an impact on the campus networking project since these new users will soon want to have their computers attached to the network. Adequate hubs and concentrators will be in place, but additional twisted-pair cables have to be run for the new users.

E-mail Across the Various Platforms

One of the major uses of a campus-wide network will be electronic mail (e-mail). Presently, there are two parallel groups of e-mail users—those connected to the administrative Unisys 2200 using its office mail system; and the second is the College of Business which connects faculty and secretarial users using Starmail. These two mail systems cannot communicate. Add to this the pockets of Macintosh e-mail users who are using CE Software's Quickmail and one has a significant task of integrating e-mail. Presently, we are working to link the Macintosh Quickmail users to the UNIX e-mail system using Cayman's GatorMail-Q to bridge two of the platforms.

Accessing the Library's CD-ROM Over the Network

The university library is in the process of implementing CD-ROM databases and indexes to replace or supplement the paper volumes and microfilm/ fiche holding. Questions that we are confronting are whether to use standalone PCs for accessing the CDs or to provide network access. Network access raises questions of how widely the access can and should be. Should it be a small network operating only in the library, or one connected to the campus network? Is there a way to provide access to all network users, Macintoshes as well as PC, and in the future to sister institutions across the state?

Most of the standard CD-ROM databases, indexes, atlases, and references are formatted for either MS-DOS or Macintosh systems At this point we have been successful in a test project using Starlan network connections to network a CD-ROM server running OptiNet on a PC. Thus, an MS-DOS solution for network access is available for our Starlan users.

We would like broader access over the network allowing the Macintosh users and anyone with TCP/IP access to the campus network to use the CD ROM resources. We are presently exploring this approach.

Client Security, Virus Protection and Menu Control for User Interfacing

For LANs there are three basic ways to establish a session with the file server. The first does not require any software to reside in the PC. The basic programs to make network connection are on the network board and on the server; thus there is an auto-boot from ROM. Second, some of the systems allow for a floppy disk to be used to start the client workstation, with the remainder of the network client software downloaded from the server. The third method requires the software to be present on the PC hard drive. Having a hard drive is very useful, if not necessary, in this scheme. If the hard drive approach is chosen, it provides a set of problems that become very important as networks grow large, especially as it becomes campus-wide. The latest version of Starlan available at this time does not allow a floppy disk to start the client's server connection. For some of our applications we have found it necessary to have a hard disk because they will not run from the network. In addition, there are a number of important large programs, such as PageMaker, that are best run from a local hard drive to attain acceptable performance.

When software to access the network must be installed on each client hard drive, all the problems of having to maintain the integrity of the hard drive are now added to the basic network responsibilities. Each PC must have a file security program to prevent tampering with the programs if they are in public access areas. An antivirus program must be in place to protect from plagues. Menus, whether part of the security program or a separate software, must be installed and maintained. Problems of RAM cram often emerge as you try to put all these pieces together.

RAM Cram and Configuration Problems

A somewhat new term that all too quickly has become a major topic in client-server networking is RAM cram. The problem arises when one adds network drivers to the client PCs that are using relatively large programs, which in combination with the operating system are already using most of the available 640K of RAM. Adding a 60-80K RAM resident device driver is often not possible. One then has to enter the realm of expanded, extended and high memory. This will add a new dimension to configuring PCs. It will necessitate the staff quickly becoming adept in the tools and arts of memory management. Having 1 or 2MB of RAM does not necessarily solve the memory problem. One must learn to use memory management tools such as QEMM to move programs into extended and expanded memory areas, and investigate the newer version of MS-DOS and its competitors to determine if the new features can help solve the memory problem. Additional costs are involved in the use of memory management software. The push to the 386SX-type of computers becomes even more acute, since higher memory cannot be used on the older 8088 and 80286 machines.

In DOS machines, many e-mail programs and TCP/IP programs reside as terminal-stay-resident (TSR) in memory. Security software and virus programs use memory for their device drivers or as TSRs. As campus solutions are sought for communications, software and memory factors must be kept constantly in mind. In configuring individual client workstations, one must monitor memory as menu options are selected and deselected. In software acquisition, it will become more important that the software can be used in high or extended memory or that it can be loaded and unloaded from precious base memory.

The increased popularity of Windows brings up questions of the availability of disk space, memory, and security. Software selection must be able to be secured in a read-only mode from either the server or the workstation. Coordination between Academic Computing and faculty becomes very important to select not only the best software for instruction, but also software that fits with the campus network and access desired. Faculty selection of programs must take into account whether the program will run efficiently over the network or will have to run off the hard drive of the individual PC. This will determine whether we will have to purchase a network version or multiple single-user copies as well as how many stations on which it will be available.

Before the RAM cram becomes a problem, there may be the problem of having a conflict of interrupts. Each board on a PC must use a unique interrupt. Many of these are already being used before putting in a network board. One must also be aware of what memory areas are reserved for the network and video boards, depending on what high-memory segments are needed. Working out solutions for these puzzles has been one of the more difficult and time-consuming tasks associated with networking. This problem becomes particularly acute when it is coupled with the RAM cram problem.

Training and Supporting a Greatly Expanded Set of Computer Users

Networks provide new functions or change how old ones are performed. At the most basic level, users will be introduced to a new interface that provides the options for network connection. This may be simplified to a menu, but users will still need some support in understanding the menu navigation and options. The new functions that will come with the network will require more than basic training in many areas. E-mail, no matter how easy to use, will take some training in the basic concepts and the use of functions.

As off-campus links become available, this again will require support for the user. Users will need to become proficient in sending mail to colleagues around the state and world, as well as around campus. Users will need to know how to establish terminal sessions using the Telnet component of the TCP/IP suite. The same will be the case for the FTP component for file transfers.

Our network will present a tremendous index of resources; the users will need to know not only how to use the network but also what is available and how it is found. We have to begin to prepare ourselves to introduce the campus community to a much expanded world of computing. It can be expected to create a significant new set of demands on the computing staff of the university.

We are working on plans to utilize remote access programs, such as pc-Anywhere for DOS users and Timbuktu for Macintosh users, in order to allow support staff to provide help to users without the need to leave their offices. These programs, which work over the network, allow us to see the user's screen from our office computer and actually to take control of it if necessary.

Establishing Stable and Manageable LANs with Redundancy, Recovery, and Backup

In the academic area, one of the earliest reasons for LAN networking was to provide students access to programs and shared printing services. The problems of giving students disks with programs on them or having them buy their own copies was solved by locating the software on a file server that could be accessed by all connected computers. This satisfied the user's requirements quite well, but it did create another task for those who have to maintain the network. Although it was a minor problem when one or even several PCs went down, it is now a major undertaking when a file server serving 25, 50, or 100 users goes down; it is the same as when a minicomputer or a mainframe goes down. The networks, with all their components, have become critical service elements in the academic function. As campus networking becomes a reality, this becomes an increasing concern with each new server, host, router, and expanded network segment.

Many potential problems can be avoided by planning for redundancy of services and procedures to provide remote administration and backup. The network itself is becoming very important in providing solutions in this area.

The individual file servers that existed when we had isolated networks now are becoming backups for each other, providing a degree of redundancy where none had existed. Plans are being developed to take advantage of UNIX's "cron" feature to have some of the individual systems automatically backed up to tape over the network in off-hours. For some of our systems with the relatively small 60MB tape drives, the ability to back up over the network to 320MB tapes provides a savings in personnel time and in the number of tapes needed and stored. Remote file-sharing software allows us to locally mount remote file systems, and then use the tape drive on the local machine to back up the file systems. All Starlan and UNIX administrative tasks can be handled remotely with the basic network software. The AT&T 486 StarServer S's Appleshare component can also back up files from remote Appleshare servers onto this system, and then archive them on 320MB tapes; with Timbuktu we are able to remotely do the administrative work on the AppleTalk network. Routine administrative tasks such as adding accounts, adding and removing files, as well as emergencies can be handled over the network with a considerable savings of time.

The workstation capacity of the campus network does not appear to be limited by the Ethernet bandwidth. Of growing concern is the ability of the existing servers to handle future computer sessions on the servers. Servers used as TCP gateways for administrative functions use sessions that compete with MS-DOS and UNIX sessions on the servers. With only a limited amount available, server usage must be closely monitored.

Developing the Tools and Skills for Network Management, Efficiency and Diagnostics

Network traffic may not be a problem in the early phases, but it is wise to develop both the tools and the skills needed to analyze usage patterns and solve problems at concentrators, hubs, bridges, routers, boards and wiring. With SNMP implemented on newer components of the network, we will have a network analyzer to monitor and analyze basic network activity and component functions.

For the Starlan network components we have available an AT&T network management program that runs on one of the servers. This is an additional tool for monitoring network activity down to the individual board level. For the AppleTalk network on the LocalTalk wiring (the standard AppleTalk network) we are using two network tools for monitoring and troubleshooting—Apple's InterPoll and AG's NetWatch.

Providing Personnel Support in a Time of Growth Restrictions

As has been indicated a number of times, the growth of networking provides new functions, but also creates new demands and responsibilities for staff . They must install and maintain the full range of equipment from the PC and its software through the wiring, hubs, concentrators, and routers to the hosts/file servers and its hardware and software . User support requires a considerable initial investment in personnel time. This continues as users come to rely on the network for new services and engage in new activities such as off-campus mail and file transfer. With network access becoming more critical for the end user, parameters need to be set, defining what are reasonable responses to various network problems. Academic Computing's limited staff normally work Monday through Friday from 8 A.M. until 4:30 P.M. By comparison, labs and classroom activities function over 95 hours per week including weekends.

As with most institutions of our size and type, personnel resources in general are a step or two below what we need, and quite a few behind what we want in order to improve our services. We will be incurring significant increases in campus computer activity in 1992 as we implement networking into new areas on campus. We will be adding 50 current faculty who now have computers but no network connections; the next phase will come as we purchase new computers for 150 faculty who now have none. These users will be calling on the network to perform both academic and administrative functions. For many of them these will be new activities that require training and support. We expect to have to devote an increasing amount of staff time in this support area. A new range of network support activities will essentially have to be provided by a staff that is essentially fully engaged in handling existing responsibilities.

PLANNING AND EVOLUTION

Bloomsburg University's history and experience are typical of many state universities and private colleges regarding campus networking. Until recently there was no University campus-wide plan. There was a significant amount of networking taking place in spots about campus before developing and funding a campus-wide network. The process of network development at Bloomsburg could be called evolutionary—evolutionary, but not without consideration of and in anticipation of the probable future directions.

By focusing on the MS-DOS and Macintosh computers, by starting with Ethernet, AppleTalk, and UNIX, we provided solutions to the needs of the time. The personal computer provided the solution for a variety of academic needs, including word processing, CAI, spreadsheets, graphics, programming and terminal emulation. Five years ago these were basic needs. The demands were for local file serving and print sharing; these were satisfied by installing local area networks. We did not have significant demand for full campus networking, even though some would have liked to have had it at that time, nor were funds available in the past. By purchasing computers incrementally and developing local area networks to solve specific needs we were both experimenting on a small scale and gaining experience in the process.

Needs, technology, standards, and funding have converged to allow us to implement a campus-wide network that builds on what we have and what we have learned. Technological changes have provided the means for connecting and communicating between diverse systems. Our network as defined protects our existing base while providing for anticipated growth.

With the diversity that was introduced by the microcomputer, a central concern for networking became interconnectivity. This has essentially been solved; connections can be made between nearly every network type, minicomputer and mainframe, and the mainstream personal computers (MS-DOS and Apple Macintosh) via gateways, protocol converters, and emulators. Therefore, as we plan to add more RISC workstations for high-end users, we expect no problems in physically connecting them to the network with Ethernet and functionally communicating with TCP/IP.

New challenges in the 1990s are in the general realm of interoperability. For us, as discussed earlier, electronic mail is a problem to be solved. While document sharing across platforms is done, it is usually via floppy disks. Word, Works, WordPerfect, Pagemaker and documents can move between MS-DOS and Macintosh OS. Some vendors are providing solutions, but for us, sharing documents over the network is only at the beginning stage. The direction of many developers is in providing this interoperability. We will likely see some major new solutions come to market in 1992-93. Developers, as well as users, must live in a diversified environment.

SUMMARY

Within the next year Bloomsburg University expects to establish a campus-wide network utilizing TCP/IP, interfacing as well with the telecommunication network of the Pennsylvania System of Higher Education. The campus network will transmit over fiber between buildings, use a central router, have a hub for each building, and a concentrator on each floor. This topology will allow approximately 1,000 connections in each building.

By providing personal computers to the permanent faculty and networking current PC users, the demands on the networks and support staff will materially increase. While we are agreed on the network architecture, much remains to be addressed in the areas of interoperability and file server/database security.

The comprehensive plan also includes administrative computing, voice communication, and television signal networking. This chapter is presented from the perspective of academic computing on the Bloomsburg University campus.

ACKNOWLEDGMENTS

This chapter has benefited from comments and suggestions from Harold Frey of the Computer and Information Systems Department.

Boise State University Campus Network

Alex Feldman
Assistant Professor Mathematics
Boise State University

INTRODUCTION

Boise State University is a state institution in an urban setting; Boise is both the capital and the largest city in Idaho. The student population of approximately 14,000 is comprised mostly of undergraduates. Boise State has the largest enrollment, both on an FTE (full-time equivalent) and total student basis, of any university in Idaho. The Center for Data Processing provides centralized computing resources, administers the campus network, provides consulting services to departments all around campus, and writes software for the administrative branch of the university. Most of the campus occupies a contiguous plot of about 110 acres, but like many urban campuses it has buildings sprinkled about the neighborhood, with private and municipal land separating them from the main campus. This presents potential problems with building a campus-wide network.

HISTORY

The entire campus—both the academic and administrative branches—has been using IBM 360/370 type mainframes since 1970, the current incarnation of this being an ES9000(1912). These machines have been used all over campus; access has been principally via synchronous terminals, each connected directly through its own coaxial cable to the computer. Printers connected to this system were only available at four locations on campus, with only one of these providing batch print services. Minicomputers have never really gotten established at Boise State; the College of Business has used HP-3000s and an HP-2000 for many years, but other machines from Data General, Datapoint, Digital Equipment Corporation, NCR, and IBM have come and gone over the years without generally having been replaced. The only "networking" that involved any of these machines was that several of them were connected to the IBM mainframe via serial lines that were used to permit batch job entry or for printouts to be sent to remote locations. Some minicomputers that have survived on campus, albeit nomadically, are a small collection of ATT-3B2s; presently, two of them are being used as file servers for DOS machines, while

27

one is providing some minor services to dialup users, and three others have been retired. Like many institutions, Boise State experienced the microcomputer boom of the late 1980s, and as a result there are presently well over a thousand microcomputers on campus. However, it is only in the past two years that they have begun to be networked in any volume.

It is difficult to cite the first network on campus, since opinions will vary regarding what constitutes a network and hence which agglomeration of machines and wires was the first true network. Arguably, the first "networks" on campus showed up in 1985: a small Intel network connecting a few 8086-based microcomputers, and a small AppleTalk network connecting two Macintoshes and a Laserwriter. Some more AppleTalk networks followed, as well as two Ethernets, each connecting two ATT 3B2 computers and running a proprietary protocol. One of those networks was then expanded to include three 3B2s and a terminal server, followed shortly by a DECStation 3100. This TCP/IP network was located in the Math-Geology building, where it served both departments and was the first truly ``heterogeneous" network on campus. (Throughout this chapter, "ethernet" will improperly be used to refer to both the IEEE 802.3 standard and the trademark "Ethernet," since in many cases it is actually difficult to tell them apart; hardware and software advertised to be one often works perfectly well as the other). Meanwhile, efforts had been underway for several years to install the physical media to connect the various buildings on the campus. For several years, that item in the budget was cut, but in 1986 a feasibility study was done and the following year bids were solicited to install a broadband backbone. Vendor protests lodged with the State Purchasing Department interfered with the award of the contract and killed the project, causing the money to be spent elsewhere. In retrospect, this was probably serendipitous, since the wait may have led to a superior system. (Of course, it is almost always true in the computer arena that waiting a few years will yield better products at a lower price, and thus taken to its logical conclusion one should never spend any money on a computer.)

In 1988 a few faculty members became particularly concerned about the lack of an Internet connection at Boise State. Two new faculty members needed the connection to do their work, and the existing Bitnet connection was not adequate (remote log in is not available on Bitnet). As a result, Boise State joined Westnet, one of the regional NSFNet networks. In order to serve the faculty who needed the connection, as well as the professional staff of the Center for Data Processing, a coaxial cable was strung through the steam tunnels to connect three buildings via an ethernet. Thus was born the Boise State Campus Network. At about the same time a "Computer Task Force" comprised almost entirely of faculty was formally convened by the Executive Vice President to propose improvements to the university's academic computing infrastructure. The participants agreed that a network was a top priority and drew up a plan for a fiber-optic based network, which would connect all the buildings on campus and be expandable in the event of new construction.

In the following year, partial construction of the new network was funded; not all buildings were connected, but enough were to provide connections to all those departments that were ready for them. The timing of the Task Force's recommendations was auspicious; they came out only a few months before the State Legislature approved some one-time money for higher education. The need for the network was established beforehand and well placed in the rush for those funds. Prior to the approval of the one-time money, some inquiries had been made regarding private foundation funding, which is another kind of one-time funding. Normally, using one-time funds for computer purchases is perilous since the rapid advances in the field make equipment obsolete within a few years, when the one-time money may not be available. It seems reasonable to expect, however, that the fiber plant will have a life cycle several times as long as that of an average piece of computer equipment.

At this point an interesting, if unintended, experiment took place, and is in fact still taking place.

The Center for Data Processing decided to concentrate its networking resources in a few selected areas: maintaining and expanding the inter-building network, providing diagnostic and troubleshooting services, and setting up intrabuilding networks for its own internal needs and a few other administrative units. Intrabuilding networking, for the most part, was left to the academic departments within those buildings, with the Center for Data Processing available for consulting and help with some of the setup. As a result, most departments have still not been connected to the network. In some buildings, no reasonable wiring scheme exists, and thus building an intra-building network itself would require a significant amount of new wiring. Money for this kind of thing can be difficult to find in a department budget, but even in buildings where the wiring plant is essentially in place, use of the network has been slow to take hold. The details of this situation are discussed later in this chapter.

THE CAMPUS NETWORK TODAY

The reward of the delay in installing the network was the emergence of a *de facto* standard in fiber hardware (size of the fiber and the style of connector) as well as a decline in the price of fiber to where it became feasible to network the campus that way. Although a broadband system would undoubtedly have been almost indistinguishable from the present one at the user level, the fiber will almost surely be a worthwhile investment in the long run.

A broadband backbone is a conductor, and as such would be vulnerable to lightning and ground loops. Although lightning is not much of a problem in Boise, especially given that the cable would be run underground anyway, the certainty of avoiding ground loops is a benefit of fiber. Fiber also requires a modified star topology. (The campus was done with three "hubs" that should be adequate for the foreseeable future.) While that is initially more expensive than the modified bus that is used by broadband, it has the advantage of permitting the concentration of most of the "smart" network equipment at the hubs. Boise State has taken advantage of this situation by installing a router at one of the hubs; this concentration of equipment would have been all but impossible with a broadband. Finally, even though the full bandwidth of the fiber is not being used presently, it is substantially higher than that of broadband and may very well become necessary in the future.

Presently, there are two "data link layer" protocols running on the fiber backbone. Most building connections are made via ethernet, but there is also a token-ring connecting the three hubs. The fiber plant is also presently being used to run some multiplexed synchronous terminal connections to the IBM mainframe, but this is a temporary measure. With the relatively light use that the network is presently getting, ethernet has been an adequate backbone, and there are presently no plans to upgrade to Fiber Distributed Data Interface (FDDI). Although it is certain that sooner or later the backbone protocol will have to be upgraded, right now this is a low priority since the cost of upgrading will likely go down, and until the ethernet has been saturated there are plenty of other things to do. The token-ring is being used primarily to connect the College of Technology—which has an IBM minicomputer, several microcomputers, and lots of terminals— to the mainframe in the Center for Data Processing. The Administration building, which is the one presently served by the multiplexed terminal connections, will probably also get a token-ring in order to serve all the IBM equipment that is located there.

The Center for Data Processing, in addition to the token-ring connection, serves as the principal ethernet hub. As part of the connection to Westnet, the Center maintains a router to act as a gateway to the world. This same router has fourteen ethernet ports on it, which are enough to connect all the buildings and departments that are presently connected to the network via ethernet. As more connections are made, additional ports can be installed in the existing router, or more routers can be purchased. The latter course may be required, as departments saturate their own networks and decide to invest in their own local routers. The Center also owns a fiber ethernet concentrator (really a multiport repeater) that can be used to connect these "remote routers" to the campus network, so that the existing configuration may serve as the principal ethernet hub until we upgrade the backbone protocol.

The router that serves as a nerve center in this way is more than just an IP (Internet protocol) router; it can route AppleTalk packets and some other proprietary protocols. It can also act as a bridge and so accept any protocol that might be present. Presently eleven of the fourteen ports are in use, some of which are bridged in order to handle Novell networks.

AppleTalk, IP, Starlan, and Novell are presently the most active protocols on the network. There are no restrictions on protocols; this has not been necessary given the relatively low level of activity on campus. Whether or not to restrict the Campus Network to a fixed set of protocols is a question that won't go away. Although it is generally accepted that some day it will be necessary to limit the number of protocols that will be permitted on the network, that day has not yet arrived and a laissez-faire, first-come first-served policy has prevailed. This is certainly one of the areas in which policy is still in flux.

The Mathematics (which includes Computer Science) and Geosciences departments were the first departments on the network and still account for the majority of the traffic. Although these two departments share one building, each has its own subnet and router port; theirs is the only building with more than one subnet. The Geosciences Department has a cluster of DECstations, a Sparcstation, several X-terminals, and a Stardent P-3 minisupercomputer, as well as a few networked IBM-compatible microcomputers. This department often works with large data sets which can put a strain on the network, so they were isolated. Similarly, the Mathematics Department has a cluster of HP workstations, several X-terminals, three NeXT stations, an AppleTalk network, and two terminal servers. These last serve a terminal room that provides net access to students, and it is now the only generally available direct terminal access to the network on campus. Some other departments do have labs with microcomputers in them which are connected to the network, but any other terminals on campus are connected directly to computers. The Math Department uses the network not only to provide access to its own machines, but also to connect to a computer in the Center for Data Processing on which some introductory Computer Science courses are taught. This also creates a lot of network traffic (in fact, the most of any subnet) and requires an individual subnet. The first "remote" router to be introduced on campus will probably be in one of these departments.

Everywhere else on campus, the subnets are coextensive with buildings, regardless of how much use each subnet makes of the network.

Virtually everything that happens in these other subnets falls into two categories: AppleTalk networks and networks of IBM-compatible microcomputers (hereafter referred to as "PCs"). Although they did crop up elsewhere first, the first AppleTalk network to survive and prosper was set up in the Physics Department. Computers used in measurement applications were attached to instrument busses for some time in the sciences, but the more generic AppleTalk network has turned out to be quite popular on campus. The popularity begins with the popularity of the Macintosh computer. Many academic departments have purchased Macintoshes, and the university maintains a Faculty Computer Lab, which contains four Macintoshes and a Laserwriter. This lab provides laser printing, mail service, and file service to any (faculty) Macintosh users on the network, and it also has Macintoshes available for faculty who do not have their own computer; the former encourages acquisition of Macintoshes, and the latter encourages connections to the network. By far the most popular way to connect Macintoshes to the network at Boise State has been the Cayman Systems' Gatorbox. This device allows the connection of an AppleTalk network to an ethernet, so it is well suited to connecting an existing AppleTalk network to the campus ethernet. There are other devices that can serve this purpose, but the Gatorbox established itself at Boise State early and has had all the functionality that anyone here requires. There are presently eight Gatorboxes at Boise State, four of which are in academic departments and four of which are in various administrative departments (including the aforementioned faculty lab). Since each Gatorbox is capable of connecting 31 computers to the network, this represents substantial capacity that will never be used; right now the AppleTalk networks average about five computers each. Only five Macintoshes connected directly to an ethernet. MacIP has been installed on almost all are the machines on the network, so they can use Internet services as well as local network services. On the other hand, virtually all the networked PCs on campus are connected directly to an ethernet, with Novell NetWare and ATT's Starlan being the principal local networks that are used. Novell is found mostly on the administrative side of the university, whereas the Starlan networks predominate on the academic side.

The oldest Starlan network on campus is in the College of Health Science, which maintains a lab with 25 networked PCs in it and 65 more PCs in offices, along with 6 file servers. Almost all of these machines have TCP/IP software installed on them. Presently, this network is used to share printers and software, and to make use of the Library's automated systems. To the extent that in the future a state-wide network makes connections to area hospitals possible, the college will be well placed to expand its network to make use of interactive connections with remote sites and to share databases. The College of Business has the largest Starlan network on campus, comprised of 4 file servers, 61 PCs in two student labs, and approximately 100 other PCs. Because the entire college is in one building, the principal impetus to connect to the campus network is for Internet services and access to the Library. The college has generally accomplished this by installing TCP/IP on individual PCs, although the TCP/IP on the file servers makes connections through these possible as well. Shared printers, file service, access to the mainframe, access to the Library, and general Internet access are the two most used features of this network. The College of Business has no immediate plans to connect its HP 3000 to the network, since the current uses for this machine are somewhat specialized and would not be significantly enhanced with a network connection. Expansion plans within the college are centered on networked PCs and applications such as hypertext, multimedia and workgroup systems.

The Library installed a computer to maintain its catalogue just as the campus network was being installed. The vendor supplied an ethernet port and TCP/IP software so that network connections to the machine would be possible. Although there was a certain amount of difficulty with the network software at first, it is working now and may yet prove to be one of the more significant incentives for connecting to the network. People who are able to log in from their offices rapidly get accustomed to doing so. The incentive will increase as the Library's system grows to include circulation and serials information. The Library also has a small network of PCs which are used to access databases on compact disk, and this may in the future be accessible via the campus network.

THE FUTURE: IMPEDIMENTS AND INCENTIVES

With academic departments left to their own initiative to build their own networks and connect them to the campus network, the progress in this area has been spotty, at best. As described above, some academic units have substantial networks that connect all their faculty and provide access for all their students, not only internally but to the rest of the campus and the Internet as well. Others have small networks that are limited to a cluster of offices, and still others have no networks at all. While the latter group is rapidly diminishing, there is still only a moderate amount of interest in connecting to the campus network.

By far the largest impediment to connecting academic departments to the network, besides the ever-present budget considerations, is the fact that they have to do it themselves. Although numerous faculty who do not have connections to the network claim to want such a connection, few are willing to look at how other departments have done it and learn enough that they might be able to configure a network themselves. This is not surprising; there is nothing new or unreasonable about faculty members being jealous of their time, but it does indicate that if this do-it-yourself system is to work, significant and visible incentives must exist.

Providing and advertising incentives to use the network has also proven rather tricky. The faculty lab with its laser printers provides one for Macintosh users, but since they have to walk over to the lab anyway to pick up their output, many just carry a floppy disk over with them. One person has even pointed out that this has the added benefit that one can make changes to a document after seeing how it looks on paper. Even though laser printers are also connected to networked PCs in that same lab, it is a Novell network and as such is not accessible from most of the networked PCs on campus. The file servers in the same lab provide another benefit, but the ever-decreasing costs of disk space have blunted that incentive. The mail server for Macintosh users is a small incentive, but anyone who was interested in receiving mail from the world would have connected to the network anyway. In fact, most Macintosh users in academic departments have connected to the network, partly because of the incentives but probably mostly because of one professor who secured grant money to make a lot of that networking possible, and one employee in the Center for Data Processing who helped to make those connections work. The result was a local standard for connecting Appletalk networks to the campus network (the Cayman Systems Gatorbox mentioned above) which could be duplicated in many locations. While there are presently far fewer Macintoshes connected to the network than there are PCs, a higher proportion of the Macintoshes are networked. The Gatorbox may not be the best solution for everyone on campus, but the concentration on one solution seems to be the best way to get people actually connected to the network.

Some PC users on campus have installed TCP/IP software in their networked machines so as to have access to the world. This seems mostly to be used as a way to run tn3270 and use the PC as a connection to the IBM mainframe on campus. Some people are so used to the notion of having the mainframe as the only window to the world that they will need some help discovering that other machines can provide these services as well.

The Center for Data Processing has made available some modest incentives for generic (usually Unix-based) TCP/IP networking available, but this is still a small program. Name-service and network news service have been available for some time now, but relatively little use is made of these. A protocol translator to make heterogeneous connections easier is in the works, and someday general mail service and other centralized services may be added. This would seem to be an area where a centralized facility could make a contribution quite easily, since a low-end workstation with some extra disk space is all that is needed to accomplish all these things, provided that the staff are familiar with the problems associated with installing and customizing the requisite software.

EPILOGUE

Boise State University uses its network primarily to connect microcomputers. Other than PCs, Macintoshes and their servers there are only a dozen Unix machines in the Math and Geosciences departments, the IBM mainframe, the

Library's machine and an AS/400 owned by the College of Technology. The primary uses of the network are local, workgroup-related tasks. Many longer haul tasks, such as electronic mail, continue to be done in the old way if at all, with the university mainframe. There are some incentives in place to expand network access, but they do not appear to be taking hold very quickly. Most of the academic use of the network has been spearheaded by faculty members who have had experience with computer networks elsewhere. This is a positive sign, as it indicates that to whatever extent networks are useful but are impeded by the sort of momentum that impedes everything new, the use of networks in the academy will feed on itself. The problem that is faced by those who would like to speed up the process is to create the proper incentives.

The relatively meager involvement of the Center for Data Processing in getting individual departments networked has its bright side. Although the Gatorbox has so far proved to be an effective one-size-fits-all solution for connecting Macintosh users to the network, it is far from clear that the rest of the campus would fit into one mold so nicely. Indeed, the two departments that have done the most with networks to date (measured by traffic if nothing else), Mathematics and Geosciences, have built networks that would almost surely not have been developed by anyone in the Center for Data Processing. A few nonacademic personnel cannot be expected to be up to date on the computing nuances of all the fields that are represented in an academic institution, and may well be best advised to follow rather than lead. This leads to a certain amount of frustration among departments who know that they want a network connection but do not know how to go about it. However, in order to make use of the network the departments will have to learn why they want the connection anyway, so it is not all bad that this learning has to go on first. There is no question that the Boise State University Campus Network will continue to grow, both in physical size and traffic. The former will happen as a natural outgrowth of remodeling and new construction, with some unpleasant but not insurmountable problems when a city street or private property lies in the way. The latter will occur as the joys of networking become apparent to the community, and as networked solutions turn out to be cheaper and better than individual serial lines running between buildings, or other outdated configurations.

Denison University Campus Technology Overview

Joseph L. Fleming
Director of Computing Services
Denison University

INTRODUCTION

Denison is a selective liberal arts college with 2,000 students and 160 faculty. It is coeducational, undergraduate only, and essentially 100% residential. It is located in Granville, Ohio, a New England town transplanted to the boundary between the Appalachian and Midwest regions of the country. Denison is one of the nation's "Science-50," a group of 50 liberal arts colleges that distinguished themselves, according to a 1985 study, by producing disproportionately large numbers of scientists. In 1991 it was identified as one of the International-50, a select group of colleges that produce a disproportionate number of graduates with connections to international interests.

Denison has a tradition of strength in computing. It achieved some fame for development of minicomputer-based instructional applications in the late 1970s and early 1980s. Its 13-member Computing Services staff supports both academic and administrative computing, and is responsible for the campus data network (but not for telecommunication; there is no broadband/video network).

COMPUTING GOALS

In 1988 Denison's Information Technology Committee, which advises the Provost on information technology issues, formulated a statement of goals and objectives for campus computing. Among those with highest priority were:

1. Desktop computers for all faculty.
2. Open access student computing facilities sufficient in capacity and functionality to meet the needs of students.
3. A megabit-speed data network for the central campus, including fiber-optic cable between buildings.

4. Network Services, including access to
   a. on-campus computing resources, especially multiuser
      VAX/VMS and UNIX systems
   b. external networks
   c. the Library's online catalog
   d. appropriate on-campus data

FUNDING PLAN

As the Information Technology Committee reviewed its goal list, it articulated a capital equipment funding plan that is currently in use. A "big bang" approach, with one-time blocks of funds targeted at specific objectives, was deemed inappropriate. Instead, continuous funding was proposed, covering general budget categories such as Faculty Computers, Student Facilities and Campus Network. The amounts in each area would be subject to priority setting by the Information Technology Committee and other advisory committees, but the total each year would be, insofar as financially possible, constant. Under the continuous funding plan, discrete projects with objectives, target dates and cost totals could be planned and implemented within the continuing budget categories. The particular benefit of this approach is that planning beyond the project level becomes possible. Another advantage is that the process of setting priorities can continue after funds are committed. On-the-fly adjustments can be made as needed, yet the cost of any tradeoff, in both dollars and time of completion, is easily determined.

FACULTY COMPUTERS

In 1988 about 15% of the faculty had terminals in their offices with access to a multiuser computer, usually "the academic VAX." Another 10% had either DOS PCs or Macintosh microcomputers in their offices. Alhough the number of microcomputers was small, user loyalty was established; there was no attempt to select or enforce a single microcomputer standard for the campus. Two ad hoc committees (PC and Macintosh) were formed to select microcomputers for distribution to the rest of the faculty. Each recipient was given a choice of platform. The Faculty Microcomputer Distribution process became a distinct project with a budget and a three-year completion target. The project was accelerated with an infusion of additional funds shortly after it began, owing to higher than anticipated interest from faculty and the need to complete the faculty project so that resources could be directed toward the improvement of student facilities. The three-year project was within a few units of being complete in two years. About 60% of the faculty chose DOS PCs, and 35% chose Macintosh; in the meantime the Mathematical Sciences

Department received a grant that provided the remaining 5% with UNIX workstations.

STUDENT FACILITIES

In 1987, student computing facilities consisted of two public computing clusters in academic buildings, three in residence halls, and two computing labs run by academic departments. The clusters were equipped with VAX terminals and DECmate word processors. The Mathematical Science Department had a lab of DOS-based PCs, and the Economics Department had a lab full of Macintoshes. The total number of stations for student use was 91.

Since student clusters had not been updated with newer technology for some time, there was pressure from students for better access to microcomputers in the two department labs. The Math Department offered its "Computer Science 101" course (an introduction to word processing, spreadsheets, databases, and a little programming) to at least four sections every semester. The course was so successful it created a problem. Because enrollment was always full, the lab was available only to current students. Former students had no place to apply what they had learned in CS-101. The Economics Department was equally successful in saturating its facilities with current enrollees. Although the Economics curriculum had been revised to integrate computing in to the first three courses in the major sequence, the Macintosh lab was so busy that upperclass students were effectively denied access to tools they had come to depend on in previous courses.

The Information Technology Committee's plan had given faculty desktop computers and the campus network priority over student facilities. However, pressure from frustrated students and faculty was one of the forces behind extra funds for, and early completion of, the faculty desktop project. As the last round of faculty computers was being delivered (1990), one of the larger student clusters was gutted of DECmates and video terminals, and refurnished with networked PCs. Another cluster was converted to Macintoshes the following summer. By the next summer (1991) all stations in student clusters and labs were PCs or Macintoshes; most of those were connected to each other in local area networks. About half of the total were also connected to the campus backbone network and could access the applications on the academic VAX or the Math Department's UNIX minicomputers.

CAMPUS NETWORK—ARCHITECTURE

A campus network has been emerging since copper wires first began to spread from academic and administrative miniframes, through buried conduits, to remote terminals in faculty and administrative offices. The first "real" network was a DECnet-Ethernet, installed in 1984 as a cost-effective way to connect central hosts to terminals. Interbuilding segments of that network were changed to fiber-optic media in 1986; since that time all network media installed between campus buildings has been fiber.

As the Information Technology Committee developed its list of goals in 1988, it was apparent that the architecture of a campus network had implications well beyond carrying terminal traffic. Consequently, the committee undertook a review of campus network strategy. Fortunately, the time of the review coincided with the emergence of the national Internet and its regional affiliate, the Ohio Academic Resources Network (OARnet). Because connection to external networks was recognized as a strategic plus, and because it was in Denison's interest to be as technologically compatible with other networks as possible, Ethernet was chosen as the campus network "method" and TCP/IP as the standard protocol. That was a doubly advantageous choice because the investment to that time in DECnet-Ethernet equipment was, for the most part, preserved. Following the choice of a network standard, a Central Campus Network Project was initiated; it was to be a five-year $500,000 plan to provide megabit-speed connections (1) to all faculty desktop computers in central campus buildings, and (2) to all or most of the student lab and cluster computers in academic buildings.

The Central Campus Network Project was not a complete campus plan: it left out communication to two "downhill" campuses and to any of the residence halls. Denison's campus is on a hill. A compact academic quad is in the middle of the hilltop, including the Library, six academic buildings, one administration building, and the student center. Most of the university's classroom space and 80% of faculty offices are on the central quad. The Central Campus Network Project includes only buildings on this quad. Residence halls are at either end of the hilltop. Down the hill a few hundred yards in one direction is a mini-campus that houses the Fine Arts departments (Art, Dance, Music, and Theatre & Cinema). Athletic facilities, including offices of the Athletics/PE Department, are down the hillside several hundred yards in the other direction. The two downhill campuses are far enough from the center, and have used traditional miniframe computing services so little, that networking to them has never been a priority. When the Central Campus Network Project was conceived, extension of network connections to residence halls and to the downhill campuses was deferred since anticipated demand for services was minimal.

In 1991 the Central Campus Network Project was modified owing to progress on a related front. A plan was adopted that called for the Library's catalog to be online from local terminals or via the campus network by the fall semester of 1992. Consequently, extension of the campus network to all faculty offices was assigned a higher priority than increasing the network connection speed from kilobits to megabits for the 80% of faculty whose offices were in central campus locations. As this is written, extension of the fiber-optic plant to the downhill campuses is being planned. Kilobit-speed terminal server connections to faculty computers are proving to be satisfactory for the moment.

CAMPUS NETWORK SERVICES

The Denison computing goal list includes four subcategories under network services. They are access to

1. On-campus computing resources, especially multiuser VAX/ VMS and UNIX systems
2. External networks
3. The Library's online catalog
4. Appropriate on-campus data

Meeting the first two network services goals has been straightforward. By providing network connections and software, each of these stations is able to access "traditional" minicomputer applications. Initially, minicomputer connections were of the serial port-terminal server variety. The process of converting student clusters and labs to a faster and more flexible LAN-gateway link has begun. About 60% of the central campus student computers are now connected that way. However, few of the faculty connections will be converted until the campus network has been extended to reach the downhill campuses.

The need to access external networks was one of the principal motivations behind the Central Campus Network Project. The first subproject to be completed was connection to Bitnet in the fall of 1988. As arrangements were being finalized for connection to Ohio University in Athens, Ohio, discussions about a faster link to OARnet and the Internet via the Ohio Supercomputer Center in Columbus began. Denison joined OARnet and began exchanging Internet packets in the fall of 1990. Bitnet traffic was subsequently rerouted over the OARnet link.

On Denison's scale of information technology priorities, automation of the Library is unequivocally first. After the Information Technology Committee discussed campus network services in 1988, library automation became a free-standing project, with separate funding from the university's capital campaign and with priority higher than any of the projects covered by the Computing Services budget. Implementation was delayed by participation in an attempt to form an Ohio small college library consortium which, in the end, did not materialize. In the interim, the projects for faculty desktop com-

puters and the campus network moved forward. That progress proved fortui-
tous; it was feasible to go from the inception of the Library Automation Project to a network accessible online catalog in about one year. The project was
begun in the summer of 1991; the online catalog should be available by
means of the campus network to all faculty and most student clusters and labs
in the fall of 1992.

As a result of a 1987 report by the Ohio Board of Regents, 15 state universities and 2 of Ohio's larger private universities formed the Ohio Library
and Information Network (OhioLINK) to share library resources throughout
the state. According to the plan, community colleges, smaller private colleges
and public libraries will be welcomed as members in the future. OARnet will
provide OhioLINK's statewide network infrastructure. In the spring of 1990,
OhioLINK chose Innovative Interfaces, Inc., and Digital Equipment Corporation as its system software and hardware providers. Since Denison was already connected to OARnet, full OhioLINK compatibility seemed to be an attractive next step; Innovative, already a leading contender for automation
software, and Digital, a vendor with a well-established presence on campus,
were selected to provide Denison's automated library system.

The Library computer will be housed in Computing Services' main
computer room where it will be protected from environmental hazards such
as temperature excursions, dust and electric power anomalies. The computer
will be connected to terminals and microcomputers in the adjacent Library
building by a subnetwork of the campus backbone. As in other locations, the
link between buildings will be fiber optic. The network medium inside the
building will be primarily 10baseT (twisted pair ethernet). Initial connections
will go to approximately 55 stations (more than half of which are public access terminals) within the Library.

The online catalog is only the beginning of the list of library services to
be made available over the campus network. The automated system will grow
to provide circulation, periodical and acquisitions information. CD-ROM service is being planned. Access to other off-campus library systems both within
OhioLINK and beyond will offer a range of services which by today's standards are difficult to comprehend. It is the expectation of both the Library
and Computing Services organizations, however, that providing these services and supporting them at the level appropriate for students and faculty will
be one of the greatest challenges of the next decade.

The last of the network services to appear on Denison's goal list is access to "appropriate on-campus data." The item has proved to be last in priority as well as order of appearance. A campus-wide information system has
been a frequent topic of discussion, which always gets favorable review.
However, available resources have consistently been allocated to other areas.
It was surely the intent of the Information Technology Committee to support

an on-campus data system when the item was included on the goal list. When a fourth-generation language was selected in late 1988 for the university's administrative computing systems, one of the strong points in its favor was that it would simplify the process of creating and maintaining an on-campus data system. Yet, there are no projects. No funds have been allocated. On-campus data remain effectively under the control of, and must be dispensed by, the office that owns it.

There are probably several reasons why the on-campus data effort has never taken off. One is that the financial resources available for computing projects are, though substantial, limited. In some of the areas competing with an on-campus data system for priority (e.g., library automation, faculty desktop computers and student facilities), those finite resources have been called on to make up for lost momentum; major objectives have been pursued over compressed time intervals. Other priorities won out over on-campus data. Another reason for inaction on the campus data front has been personnel. It is not feasible to assign portions of a campus-wide data project to already harried Computing Services and administrative office staff, nor is it likely, given the current financial climate, that additional highly skilled people will be hired for that purpose. Finally, I detect from talking to faculty (the primary clients for an on-campus data system) a sense that the profound potential of computing and networks will be realized in instructional and research applications; ready access to on-campus data would be neat, but academic applications are more important.

FINAL NOTE

This account of computing and network decisions has been deliberately oriented toward an environmental rather than a technical point of view. It is about the expression of institutional priorities and values through the process of resource allocation. The process is important because new technologies are engines of change not only for higher education; our entire culture, perhaps the world culture, will also be transformed. Liberal arts colleges like Denison are well positioned to play a "disproportionately large" role (as they already have in science and international studies) in that transformation. We are advantaged because we are small and agile, because people with ideas are closely connected to decisions about uses of information technology and because our principal line of business is learning and teaching.

Drew University: A Case Study in Challenging the Conventional Wisdom

Richard A. Detweiler
Vice President and Professor of Psychology
Drew University

Ellen F. Falduto
University and Institutional Research
Drew University

INTRODUCTION

The history of technology in education is one of transitions—some successful, others less so. Conventional wisdom has suggested that the successful transitions are the impressive initiatives that have occurred at large, research-oriented universities, whereas the less successful transitions more often than not are the attempts by smaller, nontechnical institutions to implement information technology on their campuses.

Drew University has challenged the conventional wisdom. This institution—an independent university of 2,200 students including an undergraduate college, a theological school and a graduate school—has a reputation for innovation in higher education, and its emphasis on "technology in service to the liberal arts" is one of these innovations. Indeed, Drew University has demonstrated that a university need not be a large technical or research institution to effectively employ information technology in its educational program.

Drew has been described as "militantly liberal arts." Thus, it seems surprising that in 1983 the College of Liberal Arts faculty voted overwhelmingly to institute the "Computer Initiative" (CI), a program that led every undergraduate and graduate student and faculty member to have his or her own complete personal computer system. Drew quickly became one of the very few schools with a one-to-one ratio of computers to people. In 1988 the "Knowledge Initiative" (KI) added a campus-wide voice/data/video network that provides access to computing systems on campus as well as national and international networks and that provides extensive voice communications and video transmission capabilities.

43

This pervasiveness has resulted in technology becoming a part of everyday life at Drew and in the natural development of applications of this technology within Drew's educational program. The applications are as varied as the academic disciplines and the components of Drew's technology infrastructure. These applications and initiatives have not been without significant outcomes which have been recognized within the campus community and outside its borders.

THE CONTEXT

Drew's information technology initiatives were conceived within the context of the liberal arts, focusing on the potential of information technology to support or enhance the goals of liberal education. The fundamental goal of a liberal education is to teach people to think. A liberally educated person systematically, logically, and creatively accesses available information, develops understanding and insight, and communicates this knowledge to others. From this perspective, computers and networks are information processing tools and can be used to substantially enhance this thinking process. Indeed, given the massive amounts of information available as a byproduct of the information age, these tools can help to avoid the narrowness and specialization that are so much a part of contemporary education.

Therefore, the potential for impact on liberal arts education through computer and network technology is substantial. Unlike the efforts behind previous technology-based near-revolutions, Drew chose to focus on the integrated use of computer and networking technology to access, process and communicate information. The goal was not to make liberal arts and theological students technologists, but, rather, to make them capable, thinking people who can make use of technological tools in their everyday lives. It is worth noting that this is a controversial approach for some people—those who are already the campus "techies" argue that "high-tech" rather than "functional effectiveness" be the standard. Given economic realities, this also means the continued centralization of technology in their hands rather than having effective technology fully accessible to all people in their own living and working environments.

The philosophical basis for the Computer and Knowledge Initiatives provides for a unique case study. In addition, practical factors helped make them possible. In the case of the CI, the impact of the demographic slide on admissions made it clear that Drew needed to develop a more distinctive educational program, and the CI was part of this effort. Subsequently, the timing of the KI was facilitated by an obsolete and inadequate telephone system, the desire of the campus community for a communications and information processing system centered around a library automation system and the continuing need to maintain a distinctive educational program. Thus, Drew's campus technology efforts were developed within the philosophy of the liberal arts, helped accomplish educational objectives and met practical needs.

PLANNING AND IMPLEMENTING THE KNOWLEDGE INITIATIVE

In 1987 two planning activities were occurring simultaneously. In the first, the campus community was undertaking a capital campaign needs assessment. In the second, administrators were considering alternatives to an obsolete telephone system. The initial thinking was that Drew would replace its telephone system in the near term, and in the longer term would install a campus-wide network and library automation system. However, as system design was being developed, it became apparent that Drew had an opportunity not only to replace its telephone system, but also to simultaneously install a campus-wide communications systems and data network.

In the planning for the KI, it became evident that the traditional definition of "networks" was visually based data (text and graphics). Computer data networks overlook a fact that is obvious: that spoken language is an important, rich, and essential form of communication. At the time, with the application of computer technology to voice communication, it was possible to integrate this form of communication into communications into a single network design. Rather than having computer communications carried by voice lines (analog service with modems), the decision was to use newer technology to have computer lines carry voice service (by digitizing voice signals).

Drew's general concept for the KI was twofold: first, information processing and exchange is the most fundamental activity of an educational institution; and second, one should be free to choose the information exchange method (voice or data, immediate or delayed) which best fits the communication need.

Thus, typical educational activities could be described in terms of an information exchange method—for example, a library search would be an interactive data session; the submission of a student paper would be a delayed (electronically mailed) data session; a clarification of a course assignment would be a simultaneous voice communication; and a message from a professor to students in an international relations course to watch a late-breaking news story later in the day on video service would be a delayed (voice mail) communication. The ability to have simultaneous voice and data communications would be a real value in some contexts, such as for a faculty member and student to be discussing a library automation search reference list on-screen via telephone.

As we examined communication network alternatives, we were guided by both educational and technological principles. Rather than beginning with the technology, we began with our needs. We projected that, for data, a relatively high proportion of our 2,200 users would be active at one time, but that each user would be carrying out relatively low-volume data transfer tasks (e.g., smaller text files rather than multiple screens of high-resolution graphics). Our ultimate design need was to allow all 2,200 users to simultaneously send several thousand bytes without system response degradation. A packet-based data network (e.g., Ethernet) would not adequately meet our needs since such networks are better suited to handling relatively few users and larger volumes of data. A switched network design better met Drew's needs since such networks can handle the many user/moderate traffic scenarios easily. In addition, because current technology voice systems also use digital switched network technology, we had an opportunity to develop the integration of voice and data services in a way that would not be possible with a separate voice and data network. We chose not to make video service a part of this initial design and installation, although recently we have added that capacity.

After successfully completing a lengthy national search for telecommunications/network consultant support (with the selection of Telegistics, Inc.), serious planning for the system began. The first step was the development of a Request for Information (RFI). Rather than invest heavily in the development of detailed technical specifications, we issued an RFI that described what we wanted to accomplish and what our concerns were (e.g., a digital system capable of handling both data and voice, high-level use without performance degradation, needs for integration of voice and data, installation timeline, etc.), and had vendors inform us of what they had to offer and recommend optimal design scenarios. From these responses we examined hardware and software options, and we issued Requests for Proposals (RFPs) to those vendors that appeared to have the technical capability and support services necessary to implement the project. The RFI responses were a binding part of all following RFP responses.

Evaluation of the responses to our RFPs and selection of the vendor were based on a number of factors. Three primary factors were used as evaluation criteria:

1. *User Interface.* Of primary concern to us was the "humanness" of the system. Although there are many aspects of this critical dimension, one example of it is that people are not effective users of "pound/star" commands on telephones (e.g., "to pick up a call dial *6"). For this reason, we specified that telephone station equipment must have software defined and labeled feature keys (e.g., a separate button on the phone labeled "transfer"). We concluded that there must be at least ten such keys available. Similar-

ly, establishing a network data connection had to be not much more complicated than turning on a personal computer (PC) with communications software running.

2. *System Performance.* In this category we considered the technology itself: data throughput rate, number of simultaneous users of voice and data services, degree to which system balancing or engineering had to be done to maintain adequate performance, the ease of use and effectiveness of network management software, and so on. We were less interested in specifying the technical attributes of the system than specifying the performance standards of the system.

3. *Future Potential.* In this category we considered two factors: the adequacy of the design for the middle-term future (e.g., the ease of ability to support integrated services digital network [ISDN], availability of software development tools on the switch, etc.) and the service and maintenance availability, longevity and cost. We required evidence of a prior history of satisfied customers, guarantees of long-term availability of parts for expansion or enhancement and repair and provisos on maintenance cost escalation.

For the five top-rated RFP respondents, fourth and fifth evaluation factors were applied:

4. *Partnership Potential.* We knew that we would need an active and ongoing relationship with the vendor(s) to develop system enhancements appropriately and keep the system reasonably current for the longer term. We could not afford to support the needed development activities alone but wanted a vendor who would be willing to use our system as a site to cooperatively develop and test software and hardware. We described this as an interest in partnership.

5. *Price.* As is the case at any educational institution, price matters; moreover, we needed a system that optimized the price/ performance/humanness tradeoff. We were not willing to make significant concessions on any of these factors for the sake of short-term savings.

Proposals from 14 corporations were evaluated. Ultimately, Drew chose to forge a partnership with Bell Atlanticom, Intecom, Octel, and Digital, and later with Data Research Associates for library automation. All were committed to creating a one-of-a-kind national showcase demonstrating a fully integrated educational data and voice communications network. While many very visible high technology universities have implemented components of this system, no school has to date implemented a completely pervasive system that provides full functionality to every student, faculty member and staff office.

The switched network system we installed is a simultaneous voice/data network that is fully nonblocking (that is, all 2,200 people can have a simultaneous voice and data connection with no network performance degradation), and that provides a "connection" for every person on campus. There are four functional components of this system:

1. A data network linking the three computing centers (academic, administrative, library), all PCs on campus, and external networks (BITNET, Internet, etc.).
2. A network server providing electronic mail, database, and information services.
3. A voice system that provides direct inward dial capabilities, improved call forwarding/answering, conferencing, etc.; and full call accounting.
4. A voice processing facility including voice mail, audiotext, and automated call routing.

In very concrete terms this system is visible to the individual on campus through a station that includes a "fancy" phone with function buttons and the individual's personal computer. The phone is, in fact, digital and uses the same binary communication method that computers use. It gives the student full-featured voice capability (e.g., conference calling, forwarding, etc.) and voice mail. It plugs into a digital data interface that also contains a standard RS-232C jack for connection to the serial port on the personal computer. This interface, with 128KB bandwidth, provides simultaneous voice and data service with connections to the PC to every other PC on campus, to a data network that includes All-in-1 as the e-mail system, library automation and network connections to other campuses around the world.

In the summer of 1990, Drew's partnership with Bell Atlantic provided the university with the opportunity to install a broadband network. The broadband network component of the KI is an extension of the switched network and provides a "two-way" high-speed data and video transmission network. It has nearly one gigabit bandwidth. Currently, less than one quarter of this capacity is used for internal educational video broadcasts and providing access to 25 television channels. Future use will include high-speed mainframe computer links, and transmitting alarm and electronic door lock signals. Connections have been provided to every student room as well as every major building and selected classrooms.

Because of Drew's integrated approach to providing services, this technology has been provided at low cost compared to industry standards: digital voice service and data network connections at about $900 per voice/data connection (inclusive of all computer, switch, telephone, and voice mail hardware and software and with all new interior and exterior wiring for 54 buildings); and the broadband network at about $140 per connection (with all new interior and exterior wiring, nine nodes, and one head-end; and for video service a four-dish satellite ground station, video distribution equipment, and automated internal broadcast equipment).

The switched network system, including an entirely new cable plant, all new building wiring, building of a new network center, installation of all hardware and software was completed in ten weeks through the heroic efforts of all involved, beginning on about May 25, 1988. We began the training of faculty and staff on about August 15, 1988, and with all students on about September 1, 1988. In all cases, voice and voice mail were taught first, followed by network services. The installation of the broadband system—which included wiring the campus with coaxial cable, classroom and residence hall wiring, and installation of satellite dishes, hardware, and software—began in June 1990 and was completed in early September.

A schematic of the system is shown in Figure 1, and includes an Intecom S80 with about 5,000 ports (2,500 flex-IM ports), an Octel Aspen voice mail system with 48 ports and 100 hours storage; a VAX 6330 running

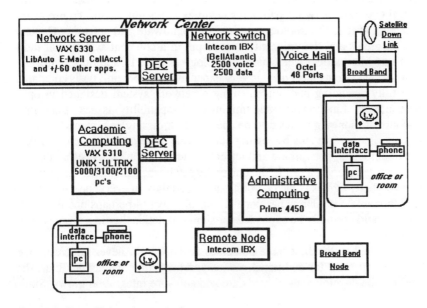

Figure 1. Drew University network system.

All-in-1, DRA library automation software, Alexis call accounting software, and other network services; and a dual cable broadband with a single head end, 9 nodes, and 1,000 ports.

IMPACT AND IMPLICATIONS

There are five outcomes of this system that merit special note. First, the system has further blurred the distinction between academic and administrative technology services. Although the extremes can still be identified (e.g., the payroll database is clearly administrative and the use of symbolic equation manipulation software is clearly academic), most technology services (networking, PCs, etc.) are used by all faculty, staff, and students. Although traditional organizational distinctions among areas exist by virtue of a recent administrative restructuring, the staff in the technology areas (academic computing, administrative computing, technology systems, and telecommunications) often collaborate on projects.

Second, the system at this time may be regarded as a fairly complete roadway with many vehicles on it. Clearly, Drew has hardly begun the process of putting up the roadsigns (appropriate software applications) and building exit ramps (to special purpose processors, e.g., UNIX or graphic stations). This will develop with time, out of the imaginations of faculty, students and staff.

Third, one should anticipate demand and put in hardware and software before it is universally demanded. This is important for two reasons. In the typical case one or two departments begin experimenting with the use of information systems technology and invest in hardware and software. General interest grows and the university tries to put in a coherent system, but must fight turf-like battles over which technology is best. In addition, putting in networking systems piecemeal is very expensive on a per unit basis compared with fully designing and implementing a network system designed to optimize needed functionality and minimize compatibility issues. Enormous amounts of money may need to be spent to link dissimilar systems or throw away earlier investments by tossing out existing systems. Drew acted on personal computers, networking and telecommunications systems before the demand curve rose. As a result, the university established standards that, though not everybody agrees is the one best one, is certainly in everyone's interest to be compatible with. Drew has done all this at a cost of perhaps one third that which would normally be expended for similar functionality in a more typical situation.

Related to the first three outcomes is the fourth: never underestimate the potential need for additional staff support. As line distinctions blur, the need for the development of hardware and software integration grows. Similarly, given a versatile network, the opportunities for new applications to make more effective use of the network grows. Both of these are natural and important. One must then balance the new unmet need against the potential cost of development. Drew has tremendous demand for software development that cannot be met without a number of staff additions that it cannot now afford. However, this problem would not exist if we had a less capable network. Should Drew, therefore, have put in a less complete network? That could have been done but at significant longer term cost. Must all needs be met immediately? As long as everyone recognizes that the current system accomplishes much that was never before possible and that there will be systematic development of software over time, then the answer is no. However, this is a nontrivial credibility and political issue that must be attentively managed.

Fifth, the system is complex and expensive to run; on the other hand, these expenses were largely anticipated and, because of the inclusion of phone service in the network system, self-amortizing by the application of phone use fees. Drew would not have been able to afford to put in and maintain a data-only system because fees for its use would not have been appropriate within the context of the philosophy underlying Drew's efforts. However, by applying normal residential rates to telephone service sufficient revenues are generated to largely cover system cost that is not covered through existing budget or capital campaign priorities.

Most importantly, as with any effort to introduce change, the key to the successful integration of technology into an educational environment lies not with the technology but with people. Drew's greatest challenge has been in getting faculty and staff involved in using technology for curricular and academic support purposes. Those involved in planning such a technology implementation may be well advised to avoid being unduly excited by technology itself. Rather, they should become very excited by what technology can do for the educational process within their institution and for the preparation of educated people. More attention should be paid to preparing people through information, accessible training, ready support, and incentives to use the technology. The important factors are not ease of use or the sophistication of the technology; rather they relate to how educated people think and approach information. This is not to say that the technology is irrelevant, but that the key to success is to look at all technological endeavors as human endeavors.

TOOLS PROVIDED THROUGH DREW UNIVERSITY'S KNOWLEDGE INITIATIVE

In principle the installed system provides every person with access to every other person, every significant database, every major computer resource, every external network connection, and every personal computer productivity tool. These tools and their uses are as follows:

TOOL	USE
1. Personal computer or workstation	Word processing and other software; data networking; printer; software applications.
2. Digital voice service	"Real-time" voice connections to all people on and off campus with enhanced features; voice mail connections to all people on campus; voice menuing and information providing services.
3. Data network connection (19,200MB async)	"Real-time" access to all other PCs, central computers, external networks, library, network services, etc.; electronic mail.
4. Broadband network	9-node dual cable broadband system with a single (1 gigabit) head end and about 1,000 ports; currently providing 24 video channels; unused bandwidth of about 800 megabits for high-speed data, signaling, alarms, and so on.

SERVICES PROVIDED THROUGH DREW UNIVERSITY'S KNOWLEDGE INITIATIVE

The following information/computing system services are available through the use of these tools:

Academic Computing	Programming languages, statistical packages, and other applications running on a VAX 6310 with 32 megabytes main memory, 2.4 gigabytes storage, and 72 ports; and a networked Digital ULTRIX system including 5000, 3100, and 2100 series systems.
Administrative Computing	A single, comprehensive, relational administrative information system including all facets of university operations. The system runs on a Prime 4450 with 16 megabytes main memory, 2.5 gigabytes storage, and 120 ports. (Available to administrative offices only.)

Network Services	Library automation for about 500,000 volumes and including acquisitions and circulation (approximately 240,000 bibliographic records are in the database at this time); electronic mail with about 70,000 active messages at any one time; about one-third million data network connections (150,000 hours log-on) per year; call accounting software handling about 1.3 million calls per year; external network connections; and about 60 other applications running on a VAX 6330 with 2,500 accounts, 64 megabytes main memory, 5 gigabytes storage, and 128 ports.
Voice Services	Voice and data switching system with 2,500 voice and 2,500 data ports, nearly $1 million per year Drew telephone company (about two thirds of this amount is billed out to students and offices) handling about 2.5 million external calls per year, running on a mixed fiber/copper switched network with 131 trunks and one T-1; and voice mail/voice processing handling about 5 million calls per year on an Octel system with 100 hours of storage and 48 ports.
Video Services	Four satellite dishes, antenna, tape broadcast systems providing foreign language broadcasts (SCOLA), internal broadcasts (educational, informational, entertainment), educational (CNN, C-SPAN, Discovery, Arts and Entertainment, etc.), and entertainment (broadcast TV, MTV).

In addition, the following support is provided to all users at no additional cost:

Training	Training for network and personal computer use for 450 new people an-

	nually plus ongoing training and support for 2,700 people.
Hardware	All hardware (2,500 voice systems, 2,500 data systems, 9 nodes and 1,000 broadband ports, 2,500 personal computers, 2,100 printers, and miscellaneous other devices) are repaired and supported by a repair staff; about $750,000 worth of personal computer hardware and software are ordered, processed, inventoried, and distributed annually.
Aide Station	Walk up and call-in support for all 2,700 users of network and academic services.

HARDWARE AND SOFTWARE CURRENTLY ON THE DREW UNIVERSITY CAMPUS

Hardware

Personal computer systems (approximately 2,500)
 • Zenith (most systems)
   Laptops (majority): Z-286 supersport (with 20 or 40MB hard drive); 8088 processors: Z-181, Z-184 supersport

   Desktops: 286 processors—LP-8 (mhz) with 20MB hard drive, LP-12(mhz) with 20 or 40MB hard drive; 386 processors 25 and 33 mhz units with 70-130MB hard drives; 8088 processors—Z-159, EZ-PC

 • Epson: (desktops) QX-16s, Equity I, II

 • PC printers
   Epson: majority are 80 column near-letter-quality Epson printers (LX-570, LX-510, LX-810, FX-85). There are also 24-pin letter-quality printers (LQ-510, LQ-1050, LQ-2550) and laser printers (EPL-6000).

   Hewlett-Packard: there are some Laserjet II and Laserjet III printers.

 • Scanners
   Xerox 750 page scanners and HP Scanjet

Minicomputer Systems
- Digital Equipment

    VAX 6330 (campus network server) with 128MB main memory, 128 ports, 5 gigabytes disk storage

    VAX 6310 (academic computing system) with 32MB main memory, 72 ports, 2.4 gigabytes disk storage

    ULTRIX (UNIX) system (academic computing system) comprised of a 5000/200 with 32MB main memory, 1.3 gigabytes disk storage, CD-ROM, DAT tape backup; 3-3100s with 16MB main memory, 332MB disk storage, tape backup; 7-2100s with 8MB main memory and 104MB swapping disk. All are Ethernet networked using the 5000/200 as a server and are linked to the campus-wide network via a DEC server.

- Prime

    4450 minicomputer (administrative computing with 16MB main memory, 120 ports, 2.5 gigabytes disk storage

Telecommunications
- Intecom

    S80+ digital switch with 2,500 voice and data ports, one T-1 circuit, 131 trunks, three RS-232 command links to the VAX 6330, voice mail system, and network menu processor. The system uses a combination of fiber-optic and twisted pair cable.

- Bell Atlanticom

    Broadband Network—a dual cable (coaxial) broadband system with approximately 1 gigabit bandwidth, an AMP headend and distribution system, nine nodes and 1,000 terminations. The system is designed to run a mix of video and high-speed data applications.

- Octel

    ASPEN voice mail and processing system with 48 ports and 100 hours storage; also includes directory and forms applications

Software

Minicomputer Software
- Digital

    All-in-1 electronic mail, file management, library automation access system running on the VAX 6330; a variety of network information applications; VMS operating system; programming languages (C, Pascal, etc.)

• Bell Atlantic
Alexis call accounting software (running on the VAX 6330)

• SPSS Inc.
SPSS running on the VAX 6310

• Data Research Associates
Online public access catalog system running on the VAX 6330 with approximately 500,000 records

• AIMS Group, Inc.
Academic Information Management Software running on the Prime 4450

• Prime
Primos Information (INFORM) database query/reporting software (running on the Prime 4450)

• Watchung Software Group
PARADEX, INFORM sentence management/advanced INFORM query processing compiler (running on the Prime 4450)

Drew-supported PC Software
• Standard Drew Software:
Pacific Crest Software
"PC-Solve" problem solving/analysis software (PC based), pilot use in certain courses by participating faculty

WordPerfect Corp.
WordPerfect 5.0, 5.1

Enable Corp.
Enable 2.0, 3.0

Zenith Data Systems
DOS 3.3+, 4.0; Microsoft Windows

MS-Kermit (communications software)

• Other Supported PC Software
Approximately 90 applications supported for class and administrative uses, 1,600+ titles available for use.

Building a School LAN: The Georgia College Experience

Richard Bialac
Department of Information Systems and Communications
Georgia College

ABSTRACT

In tough budget times, Georgia College integrated an archipelago of personal computing islands into a network that is a delivery service. It is generating demand for services for instruction and research as well as administrative communications. While strategies for planning a school LAN are well documented, few have been successfully implemented.

ENVIRONMENT

Milledgeville, Georgia, still thrives in its glories of old. It was the capital of the state from 1803 to 1868, and it survived through the War of Northern Aggression, when Atlanta grew out of the ashes of Terminus, the ending point for four railroads. Milledgeville does have the distinction of being the only city other than Washington, D.C., that was planned as a seat of government. It still maintains a colonial, "Old South" charm and mentality.

Back on Thanksgiving of 1864, Sherman visited Milledgeville. (Southern ladies and gentlemen do not address him by his Rank of General or by his first name.) Numerous are the stories about why he did not raze the town on his pyromanacal March to the Sea. The stories range from a love interest in town to the pleas of a Masonic brother.

The only scorch mark in Milledgeville was the prison. In 1889 that became the site of a college for women that went through a succession of names and gender admission requirements to become what is now Georgia College. It currently has 5,000 students on four campuses in central Georgia. Milledgeville is located in the geographic center of the state.

The campus is the oldest in the university system of Georgia, and the oldest building on the campus is Atkinson Hall, built in 1894. It was completely renovated in 1982 and is now home of the School of Business. At the time of renovation, other than providing space for typing and computer labs, no computer communications considerations were made. Still, it is the most modern academic building on campus, with a satellite dish on the roof and coaxial TV distribution in each office.

The story might have ended here, for Milledgeville is noted for historic preservation. People post the birthdate of their house on their front lawns, have yet to allow parking meters, and still hold balls in Civil War period costumes.

Georgia College may be among the most progressive change agents in central Georgia. Computing has been Personal Computing—based with 20 Apples, 60 IBM personal computer (PC) compatibles, and 8 MacIntoshes. As recently as 1989 each of the five departments had a PC for secretarial use, but faculty depended largely on their own personal computers. The School of Business supplied computers only to the newer faculty who negotiated one as a condition of employment. The Information Systems and Accounting departments had obtained their computers by forgoing some travel support to obtain hardware and software. There were also four hardwired dumb terminals in the computer lab and one dialup access to the statewide network for connections to the University of Georgia computers in Athens and other facilities in the state.

Meanwhile, in Atlanta, in the northern part of the state, the Office of Information Technology (OIT) of the Board of Regents was building a TCP/IP network to touch all 34 state institutions for administrative and academic uses. OIT also provided computer services through a CYBER 960, an IBM, and data switch connections to the University of Georgia, Georgia Tech, Georgia State, and other facilities.

THE SCHOOL PLAN

When I arrived in 1989, the School of Business was already established in computing academically with an undergraduate program in place since 1982 and Georgia's first master's of MIS program which started in 1987.

Two days after I arrived in Georgia, there was the first of several hurry-up projects. The Board of Regents had a matching funds project with a due date the end of my first week. As a result of this program, the Director of Academic Computing obtained a $25,000 grant. A faculty advisory committee decided to replace a TI 990 (circa 1972) used for C, RPG, and COBOL instruction.

That committee desired a resource of more generalized applicability, lower maintenance cost, and higher reliability. We selected a VAX, but with only $25,000 were limited to the smallest one, a 12MB Micro VAX 3100, 436MB of disk, a printer, and 8 CRTs. My personal knowledge of DEC went back to 1971 when I was in the private sector and one of the first commercial OEMs (Office and Electronic Machines). My back is a collection of old arrow wounds from being a pioneer.

While the VAX was an amazingly small but simple box, it was 2.4 times faster than the first VAX I bought for $300,000 in 1977. A big selection consideration on DEC is its connectivity. It used Ethernet to a terminal server that would allow PCs in the lab and faculty offices to connect.

In November, three months after my arrival, my dean asked me to prepare a request for the next budget cycle for a local area network (LAN). There was a previous experiment with an NCR peer-to-peer LAN on twisted pair cable which had a good user interface but was very "fragile" when it came to physical changes in the connections. This would be a renovation project to get on a seemingly endless queue of projects on the oldest campus in the university system. Most projects remained on the list for years, with annual revision of the cost, to allow for inflation and other increases by not acting on the project.

In addition to the renovation project, I prepared for the dean an inventory of the 42 faculty and department offices' computing resources. This was the basis of a request to yet another budget, the QIPs (Quality Improvement Project). Several irons were now in the fire. Now follow this carefully: the LAN became the justification for the faculty hardware request, and the faculty hardware was part of the justification for the LAN.

The Dean took the initiative to equip the entire faculty with computers that could access the building network and help to increase faculty morale. It also reflected changing expectations of intellectual activity in the school, a march as determined as Sherman's, towards accreditation of the business program.

While working with the Digital Equipment Corporation (DEC) systems engineers on the VAX configuration, a relationship had been started. My personal experience with LANs was limited to the 16-station Novell ARCnet and a 4-station IBM PCnet. The Atkinson Hall LAN would be a very high-visibility project to connect 100 nodes: every faculty and administrative office, and each classroom, not only to Georgia College computing, but also to the statewide TCP/IP network and all sister institutions and via BITNET to the world beyond.

My limited experience, although I was well read, gave me an un-Southern sensation. I felt as if I were treading on ice that seemed to be holding other people bigger than I. I had the same sensation in 1978 when the Ohio River froze. Cars drove across it, yet there was a silent fear that you were approaching a hidden thin spot.

I decided to use the expertise of the DEC engineers we met from our VAX experience. A site visit and followups at their office provided an equipment list and allowance for installation cost of $23,000. This was to be an internal network that excluded equipment for any connection to outside campus or statewide networks, or even a bridge to keep our traffic internal. It also excluded the network cards for each PC.

They estimated 4,000 feet of Ethernet cable and three multiport repeaters, and thickwire backbone spiraling up the elevator shaft. An allowance of $12 per node was allowed for a box and faceplate, and $15 was allowed for installation. We used DEC list prices for everything including cable with no discounts. I knew that surprises happen and that this would provide a buffer.

I also visited reference sites and sister institutions. I was disheartened to find at that time that it appeared that the DEC Personal Computing Services Architecture (PCSA) and DEPCA cards (an Ethernet interface card) at $600 seemed to be the only way to reliably connect via the VAX. I felt this project could be years away and since the connection was the responsibility of the departments, the cost of the DEPCA cards did not impact this renovation project budget. I gave budgetary guidance of $600 per connection to the Dean.

THE CAMPUS MASTER PLAN

My experience in identifying the networking needs of the School of Business got me appointed to a campus-wide LAN committee. This committee would perform needs assessment and identify potential applications and benefits to both faculty and administrators.

A plan did develop, but with so many other projects needed on this old campus, the $750,000 estimated cost seemed unobtainable. The favored approach from the administration was to pay for the CAMPUS LAN with energy savings that would accrue from a centralized energy management system on campus. An academic and administrative LAN could piggyback on an energy management fiber-optic backbone. Contractors who would guarantee such savings existed in urban areas but were not willing to do so in Milledgeville.

IMPLEMENTATION

The faculty in the Computer Science and Information Systems departments could not wait for what looked like three-four years until the project percolated up the priority list of renovation projects. With the implementation of the VAX we ordered a spool of six conductor office cable. Armed with $239 worth of office cable and a DEC modular jack terminator, our physical plant people strung spokes from the VAX to each faculty office in those two departments. (See Figure 1.)

In the fall of 1990 we started using the Microvax in language instruction, e-mail, and database experimentation among Computer Science and Information Systems faculty and students. We used both the hardwired terminals and PROCOMM terminal emulation serially through the terminal server to the VAX. Connection to Novell servers, BITNET, and to the world beyond were still just dreams. These dreams were not those of pioneers, for we had

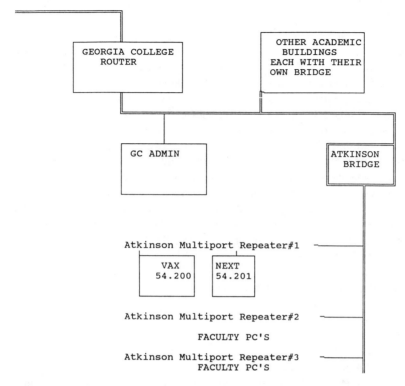

Figure 1. Schematic of Georgia College Campus LAN and Atkinson LAN.

colleagues who had come from schools that had such facilities. We would not be pioneers with the technology, but we would be the first to implement them on our campus.

In April 1991 we made our annual departmental presentation to the Vice President and Dean of Faculties at Georgia College. In that meeting a pitch was made for increased institutional support for computing. The VP/Academic Affairs informed us and our Dean that the building network had been removed from the renovation project list because it was reported that I had achieved the goal with the $239 of serial cable and the help of physical plant labor.

Having the reputation of miracle worker is appealing to one's ego. If I could install a 100-node network estimated at $23,000 for $239, I would be retired, esteemed, and as wellknown and wealthy as Mitch Kapor and Bill Gates. We immediately dismissed that mistaken opinion and followed up in writing. We reluctantly continued on our mission, assuming we were back at the end of the queue.

May 10 was my birthday. I received a call from the Dean. The VP approved the $23,000 project, but it was year-end money and had to be spent by June 21! Whether it was guilt, luck, or the recent re-queuing of the proposed project, I didn't care. I had a mandate from the Dean. I now had to make good on that November 1989 estimate, deliver the capability, and not ask for more money! This was also tied in with the last three weeks of school, Summer School starting, personnel issues, moving a new faculty member to town, graduation, and all the other year-end issues.

At the time of the project estimate, I had established contacts with both vendors and other institutions already into networking. I also had my initial design, equipment lists, and estimates from DEC. One caveat I had at that time was that while there were several ways to connect PCs to the VAX (PCSA, Ultrix-Vax Connection, serial terminal emulation) only the DEC DEPCA cards at $600 each would reliably work on Ethernet. The DEC design was a Thickwire Backbone snaked through the elevator shaft with a multiport repeater and multiple legs on each floor. The $23,000 was for all hardware for the network and an allowance of $12 per node for the connection box in each office, plus total labor of $1,500. It acknowledged that to be fully operational, it needed $600 per PC interface, and a bridge to isolate traffic from a Campus Backbone.

I contacted DEC as well as two firms with experience in wiring schools. Interface Electronics in Duluth, Georgia, was one of the firms. All three firms were invited for a site visit and a walkthrough of the facility. These meetings developed the final configuration. We chose a thin wire backbone of 20 feet with three multiport repeaters and the fiber-optic bridge in a wiring closet adjacent to the computer lab. The computers are on a leg of one repeater. On May 17, I released the RFP for the equipment and installation materials.

Equipment selection was based on equipment that must be on state contract because the last day for ordering off-contract had passed in April. Vendor reliability and support were judged by references. Supplier flexibility was also judged by commitments since equipment suppliers were not installing, but had to guarantee the success. They also would need to support the installation team and to allow the exchange of network interface cards if any additional parts or supplies were needed.

On June 7, our physical plant department released a Request for Quotation for the installation with a ten-day due date. Included was the materials list ordered from Interface Electronics. Bids were received for installation on June 17, 1991, and a purchase order was issued. The amount of the bid was $1400 under what was expected. Since the purchase order would release the commitment for the full estimated amount, additional purchase orders were prepared for Network Interface Cards (NI5210/8) to make up the "slack."

Our specifications included running telephone cable to each floor's telephone room and office cable from each classroom to the VAX computer. The telephone wire effectively makes available at low cost a modem connection for any faculty member whose computing needs are not satisfied by the network. The office cable will allow serial access for computers. I was also concerned about the security of students having access to outgoing phone lines, so that they only exist in faculty offices.

Con-optics, Inc. of Duluth, Georgia, installed the network in July. As with any installation, something new is always learned. They found that a 100-yea-old/8-year-old rehabilitated building offers many surprises in the area of insulation, conduits, secret passages, and false walls.

LESSONS AND LUCK

First, DEC was not the low bidder. And second, it was worth it to test "I can't say that will work."

We were able to work within a reasonable estimate at the list price without any discounts. We had cost savings from price declines for improved technology, non-DEC equipment, and intangible vendor/installer confidence. Even the proposal received from DEC was lower than their 1989 estimate based on their DEC-HUB-90 technology. These savings were offset by the initial way-too-low installation estimate of each node. The $1,500 total estimate was actually closer to $70 per node.

I did treat the installation crew to a cookout feast in my own form of Southern hospitality. We also supplied a student to assist in the wire pulling. The installation was completed and tested on target on July 31, 1991.

We use NCSA Telnet and FTP programs from the University of Illinois, a no-cost shareware program to drive the cards. The program's only deficiency was the inability to toggle a local printer on/off and the inability to transmit an ASCII file from the PC up to the host. (FTP is used to do that.)

Careful planning was not enough: we needed some luck. For example, we used much more wire than was originally estimated.

	Estimated Feet	Actually Used Feet
ThinNet	4,000	7,000
Telephone cable from faculty offices to phone room	10,000	12,000
Office cable Classroom to computer	2,000	4,000

The other lucky aspect that was part of this project was the timing. The $23,000 funding was out of year-end money that had to be spent by June 21.

Our new year money became available on July 1, and the equipment portion was frozen on July 3, and is frozen for the rest of this year. Had we not been able to acquire 18 network cards and the bridge before the freeze, or as part of the base project, we would have had a beautiful network and no way to connect to it.

EXPANSION

Earlier I mentioned that the faculty computers became the justification for the LAN. Having the LAN as a delivery service and demands for services not in our building became the justification for the bridge and fiber-optic link to Peachnet. That became the justification access to the campus administrative computer, and so on. At each growth phase the successes and cumulative investment make it easier to support requests for additional services.

BENEFITS

The first immediate benefit was e-mail capability within the School of Business. Second, BITNET users could now access the Cyber from their offices 24 hours a day instead of from the computer lab during its hours. They also had both printing and capturing to a disk file capability. Third, IBM and other users had access simultaneously in their office. Fourth, department chairs and deans could monitor Winter Quarter registration from their offices on demand instead of waiting for a closed course complaint. Fifth, dial-up access was provided to all services, including from faculty homes, or anywhere in the state or nation via Internet.

This last benefit has a significant impact on the cost of delivering our services. For example, adding a course at an external center can now be done with minimal new equipment because Telnet and FTP services allow access to the same mini at our main campus. We were just informed that our library will be connecting into the Campus LAN making their services available to us and the rest of the state for that matter.

TRAINING

Training was provided through faculty-led seminars and demonstrations. We provided a User's Guide but encouraged user experimentation.

Chairs and Secretaries   VAX and E-Mail
                                               Access to Administrative Computers
                                               for Course and Student Information

Faculty   VAX E-Mail Languages
                                      TCP access to other computing
                                      BITNET & TCP

A mandate from the Dean that department chairs and secretaries will check their e-mail daily assisted in the behavior modification desired. We checked daily for e-mail from the Dean when she was on a visit to Australia.

THE FUTURE

We are trying to anticipate growth areas for the future. The VAX seems to be very capable for us. We have requested adding a School of Business DOS-based server to accommodate scheduling, student information, WordPerfect document interchange, and budgets. We want to complete our program of providing a computer and network card for each faculty member. We see the disks on the VAX as being the first item that needs to grow, and again we hope to take advantage of price/performance increases in the newer hardware.

Like most campuses, we are educating the administration that LANs and minis are different from PCs. They cannot be self-maintained, and they have more expensive software. Computing at Georgia College is striving for increased institutional support.

Dreams are still there. We dream of access to an infinite stack of CD-ROMs with every journal article on them. We dream of an electronic replacement to faculty meetings. We dream of an infinitely friendly interface. Somehow dreams are turning into expectations, and then reality, faster these days.

One hundred years ago, an English professor on this campus complained because, while there were plenty of sewing machines and typewriters (we were high tech even then), there was no library on our campus. Now the technology has changed, but the need for information is still high. And we expect it to be here soon.

The University of Hartford Campus-Wide Network

David Kelley
VAX Systems and Network Manager
University of Hartford

INTRODUCTION

The University of Hartford is a four-year private university with an enrollment of 8,400 undergraduate and graduate students. The university consists of ten schools and colleges: the Hartford Art School, the College of Arts and Sciences, the Barney School of Business and Public Administration, the College of Basic Studies, the College of Education, Nursing and Health Professions, the College of Engineering, the Hartt School of Music, the Ward College of Technology, and Hartford College for Women. There are almost 20 buildings (not including student residences) on the university's 200-acre campus plus two remote sites. Over the past three years, the Computer Services Department, which provides both administrative and academic computing services and equipment, has installed a campus-wide network that now encompasses an IBM mainframe, 2 VAX 6000s, 2 MicroVAXs, 25 VAXstations, 12 Sun workstations, about 500 "dumb" terminals, about 100 personal computers (PCs), and connections to Internet and BITNET.

In 1988, Computer Services began planning the university's campus-wide network system. At that time, there were a few Ethernet-based local area networks (LANs) on campus in Computer Services, the business school and in the Computer Science Department, and an ARCnet/Ethernet hybrid in the engineering school. All of them ran different networking protocols (DECnet, Novell NetWare, TCP/IP, Banyan Vines). None of them were connected to each other. This document describes some of the challenges, both technical and political, that we encountered while building the network.

THE BEGINNING

Work on a campus-wide system started when the Alumni Relations/ Development Department decided to switch its computer operations from a VAX11/750 to the university's IBM mainframe. That department, located about a mile from the university's main campus, was connected to the VAX-

11/750 on campus via an eight-line statistical multiplexor utilizing a 9600 baud telephone link. The users experienced extremely slow terminal response time since all eight active terminal users were competing for time on that 9600 baud link. The problem was that they needed to be able to get to both the VAX and the IBM computers from their terminals while the conversion from one system to the other was in progress. Clearly the existing multiplexor would not do. The university had a long-standing relationship with IBM and Digital Equipment Corporation (DEC), and both vendors, as well as others, were invited to propose solutions to the problem. Some of the needs were identified as follows:

- The solution must provide easy access to both the IBM and DEC environments since access to both systems would be required during the conversion, as well as after it.
- The terminal response time must be substantially better than that of the existing multiplexor, especially because of the "screen-oriented" nature of the IBM.
- The solution must be affordable.
- The equipment should not become obsolete after the conversion was done.
- The equipment must operate over telephone lines since the university does not own the land between the campus and the remote building that houses the Alumni/Development Department.
- The equipment at the remote site must be remotely serviceable and configurable from the Computer Center.
- The architecture must be expandable without having to add more and more costly telephone lines and interface devices.
- The architecture must allow for microcomputer networking in addition to the terminal access.

DIGITAL AND IBM PROPOSED SOLUTIONS

IBM's scenario involved a large number of the (then new) IBM PS/2 computers whirring away in closets, complete with monitors, keyboards, mice, and hard disks. These PCs would have terminal port cards installed in them, and wires would be run from each ASCII terminal, or PC emulating a terminal, to the backs of these PS/2 machines. Several PS/2 machines would be required at each end (the campus and the remote building), and they would be linked together in small token-rings. A "token head" would act as the connection to some unnamed third-party telephone interface equipment that would make the connection to the other end. The net effect was a large, intelligent multiplexor with a few connections to the IBM and a few connections to the VAX-11/750 (but to no other VAXs on site).

Digital showed up with a DECserver 200 terminal server. It was compact and rather nondescript, with no keyboard, no monitor, no hard disk, no floppy drives, no mice. It ran on Ethernet, the most common network type already in use on campus, it provided access to all VAXs in Computer Services which were connected together in a small LAN, and it could provide outgoing connections to any non-Ethernet computer (i.e., IBM mainframe) that had RS-232 terminal ports.

Since both proposals involved some amount of real network equipment, subsequent discussions moved more toward the selection of networking protocol and topology for the campus. The issues discussed included:

- Cost
- Cabling distances and options
  a. Can a smaller, less expensive cable be used within offices?
  b. How long a cable is acceptable before a repeater has to be installed?
  c. Can the signal be sent over fiber, telephone, and twisted pair wires?

- Performance
  a. How well can it handle hundreds of interactive terminals?
  b. How fast is the terminal response?
  c. Do file transfers bog everything down?

- Flexibility
  a. Can we connect to machines that are not manufactured by the network vendor?
  b. Can we place VAX and IBM printers out on the network?
  c. Can PCs join the network?
  d. Can existing networks be connected?
  e. Can various machines from different vendors use the system simultaneously (i.e., Digital and Sun)?
  f. Can both the administrative (IBM mainframe) users and the academic (Digital VAX, PC, Sun) users share the same system?

- Maintainability
  a. Can the network devices (bridges and terminal servers) be remotely configured, tested, and examined?

Of the two proposals, Digital's terminal server solution was less expensive.

ETHERNET CAN RUN OVER A NUMBER
OF DIFFERENT MEDIA

Within a building, we would use fairly inexpensive "thin wire" coaxial cable to connect stations together, as had already been used in some of the small academic LANs. At this point in time, we do not use twisted pair Ethernet devices because we don't yet trust its resistance to ambient electromagnetic radiation noise such as that created by computers and fluorescent lights.

Each thinwire cable can be up to 600 feet long, and machines can be connected to it using a traditional "tee" or using a newer, "nonintrusive" wall jack.

Ethernet can also be repeated to remote, off-campus sites using T1 telephone lines and special bridges. We chose Vitalink's TransLAN bridge to connect the Alumni/Development people down the road to our existing Ethernet VAX LAN in the machine room. This provides excellent terminal performance (it is overkill for the more than 30 terminals we now have down there), but more importantly, it allows PCs to be connected to the LAN to retrieve data from the systems as if they were right on campus (as is now being done.)

For on-campus interbuilding connections, we wanted to avoid using copper cabling because of bad experiences with such links in the past. Most of the VAX terminals in a number of the buildings used to be directly wired to the VAX in the Computer Center using underground terminal wires with lightning arresters on them. However, every spring and fall, we could count on a number of terminals, and the VAX, being severely damaged, not by lightning, but just by the normal electrostatic charges that accumulate on buildings. The charges would build up and then look for a place to go. Underground copper wires leading back to nicely grounded terminals and the VAX were ideal candidates. The result was a lot of damaged equipment, despite the lightning arresters.

Fiber was the chosen medium for interbuilding links. There are now seven such links, and there has never been an equipment failure on them to date. Although installation of fiber cabling is very expensive, it is well worth the cost.

We also considered microwave links and laser links for interbuilding connections. Microwave links and their support equipment are fairly expensive, require FCC licensing, and are not looked on too highly by people in academia. Also, our campus is located in a residential area that we felt would add to microwave's unpopularity. Laser beam links were in their infancy at the time and seemed like a bit of a gamble—"what if a bird builds its nest in front of one?" Both microwave and laser devices have to be installed in such a way that they have line-of-sight access to each other, and they would be an eyesore sticking out of the tops of campus buildings. There would also be problems getting good line-of-site links on our heavily treed campus. If there was a problem, or we just wanted to check up on things, we would have to gain access to the rooftops, contend with weather, and so on. Also, both of these devices are designed to provide just one thing—the network link. For about the same cost, we were able to install lots of extra fibers for future use, such as the phone system, security cameras, extra data links if needed, and FDDI fiber networking in the future.

Ethernet was one of the best performing, most widely used networks available.

For a long time, we were unable to provide much terminal access to the IBM mainframe or to the VAXs—we just didn't have the wiring, ports, or equipment. Once the Alumni/Development Department was successfully connected with four times as many terminals as it originally had, and they had full access to all of the university's large systems, things would start to grow quickly all over campus. (Today we have over 500 terminal connections.) We also expected to be distributing data files across the network to microcomputers as well.

It was clear that we should provide as fast a network as possible to ensure that terminal performance would remain high for several years to come. Ethernet can transfer a theoretical maximum of 10 million bits of data per second. IBM token-ring, at that time, could transfer a theoretical maximum of 4 million bits of data per second. IBM contended that their 4MB token-ring network was faster than the 10MB Ethernet network supported by Digital— that is, 4 is greater than 10. While it is true that 40% (4MB) utilization on an Ethernet is considered "healthy," 70% (7MB) utilization is considered "heavy," and 80% (8MB) is "maxed-out," IBM token-ring throughput would never exceed 95% of 4MB (3.8MB). We chose to go with Ethernet, as has about 80% of the rest of the world. We now have over 500 terminals, 40 workstations, and 100 microcomputers connected to the campus-wide network (which we have configured carefully). Performance is excellent, even during peak usage times.

ETHERNET AND DIGITAL'S DECSERVERS PROVIDED THE MOST FLEXIBLE TERMINAL SYSTEM

Part of the decision to use Ethernet was based on the fact that we already had a substantial investment in Digital VAX computers and Sun workstations that were running on Ethernet. The business school also had a couple of Novell networks running on Ethernet. Digital VAXstations, to be installed later, also required Ethernet to operate in a Local Area VAXcluster. Ethernet allows all of these differing machines to share the same campus-wide network system. They operate independently of each other, and in cooperation with each other, and where necessary, software is installed to make them talk to each other.

Other things we were able to do with the Digital DECservers was to connect rather nonconnectable systems, such as the IBM mainframe (our first objective) and the engineering school's rather unusual combination ARCnet/Ethernet system. The DECservers can provide both incoming and outgoing connections through their data ports, and can offer any device connected to their ports as network services. This makes it possible for any user on a network terminal server to log onto the IBM mainframe which is connected to another terminal server by just typing "CONNECTIBM." All Digital VAXs are available directly through their Ethernet network ports without having to "go out" through a terminal server port and then back into a VAX port. In fact, no terminal ports at all need be provided on the back of the VAXs.

For "way out" devices, such as the engineering school's Banyan network, which has a mixture of wiring schemes and network protocols, the best way to connect was to provide terminal ports to the Banyan via a terminal server (similar to what we did for the IBM). Users on the Banyan network, regardless of the type of wiring or topology to which their PC is connected, establish an outgoing connection via their network to the back of the Banyan server box itself. Those ports are then connected to a terminal server. The net result is that the Banyan network acts as a data extension cord between a user's PC (which acts as a terminal) and the terminal server. The user then has full terminal access to everything on the campus-wide network.

A PC can be connected to the Ethernet as well, whether it just uses it to connect to its own local server, or, by running appropriate software, it can participate as a computer system on the network interacting with the VAXs, the IBM, the Suns, or the worldwide Internet network directly.

The network makes distributing IBM mainframe, VAX, and PC printers throughout campus relatively easy. Any terminal server port can be configured as a printer. Any printer, even 2,000 line per minute line printers, can be "hung" anywhere on the network.

Because of the network's high degree of flexibility, it can be shared by both academic and administrative users. Often, people use it for both academic and administrative purposes. An example is a faculty member who uses it both to access the IBM mainframe for student records and to access the VAXs or the Internet for academic purposes.

DIGITAL PROVIDES EASILY MANAGED HARDWARE AND SOFTWARE

Important factors in choosing the Ethernet devices to be used in the network were their performance, their network efficiency, and their maintainability. Network devices are distributed throughout the campus in wiring closets, basements, and equipment rooms. It is impractical to run out to the devices every time you need to change the configuration of a terminal port or check the status of a bridge. Digital's devices have a lot of built-in intelligence and diagnostic capabilities that can be accessed from any terminal anywhere on the network provided the device in question is functioning at all. This is important when you get a report of a problem and need to diagnose and solve it quickly. Any extra amount you pay for a device with this capability is more than made up for in personnel time savings. Also, quick solutions result in more satisfied users.

NETWORK POLITICS ON AN ACADEMIC CAMPUS

In an academic environment, setting up and enforcing network protocols and policies can be just as difficult, if not more so, than designing the hardware layout. It is precisely the openness and ease of use of Ethernet that makes it, and the various networking protocols that run on it, a controversial system. Issues to be decided included:

- What protocols are to be used (DECnet, LAT, TCP/IP, Novell, Banyan VINES)?
- How are subnetworks to be connected (make the connecting department buy a bridge)?
- What kinds of uses will be allowed (Is it okay to "test" the system with heavy looping traffic? Should file service across buildings be allowed? What if a user degrades network performance in such a way that it affects others?)

When the network was in its infancy, Computer Services approached the academic computing committee to share information and to work together to set up some networking standards for both the administrative and academic areas on campus. Computer Services presented a detailed outline of recommendations ranging from wiring schemes to protocols to usage policies. The committee, rather than discussing the issue, preferred instead to "take each individual case as it came up." Computer Services, faced with the task of immediately connecting 200 administrative users, did so using the guidelines in the proposed document.

Since then, one of the continuing debates on campus has been which network protocols—LAT (Local Area Transport) or TCP/IP (Telnet)—should be used, mainly for the purpose of terminal access. While all protocols are allowed, Computer Services chose to use the LAT terminal protocol for terminal access due to its very high performance and built-in efficiencies, and the fact that a majority of our users on the network are accessing VAXs, which speak LAT most efficiently, and the IBM via Digital devices (terminal servers and a MicroVAX-based gateway).

The administrative and academic users share the network, and we felt that it was important to choose the most efficient and natural protocol for the task in order to ensure that both areas would experience very fast terminal response time—often the most obvious indication of network performance to the users. As a policy, terminal access to multiuser systems on campus is done via LAT. When a LAT user needs to connect to a TCP/IP-based system on Internet, or a non-LAT speaking UNIX system on campus (both of which account for an extremely small percentage of our network usage), they can do so via a small VAX-based gateway on campus. At one point, we had installed a couple of different Telnet packages on our VAXs to allow those users to connect directly to them via TCP/IP. However, frequent software failures brought the whole system down, making it undesirable to use considering the small number of users requesting the Telnet access versus the large number of production users who were seriously affected by the system failures.

Another debatable topic is the physical connection, namely, how an existing LAN should be connected to the campus-wide LAN. Computer Services requires the use of a bridge to make these connections in order to protect the campus-wide system from being unnecessarily bogged down with local traffic, and to prevent the local network from being slowed by campus-wide traffic. Other departments agree with this arrangement in theory, but sometimes balk when faced with the reality of having to purchase the relatively expensive bridging device.

Computer Services' position is that all LANs, with a few exceptions, be connected to the network via bridges in order to protect the investment in the campus-wide system. As the campus-wide network was built, each building was bridged as it was added, in essence, keeping each building's local traffic local. There are some buildings on campus that house only one department. Therefore, the users in those buildings have the option of not using bridges when connecting their smaller local networks to the campus-wide system since they will affect no one on campus but themselves.

The next issue, which is probably more of an issue in academic environments than it is in the corporate world, concerns the right to "experiment with" or "test" the network. Examples of this type of usage are loopback tests and programs running in infinite loops that tie up the network unnecessarily. Computer Services prohibits this kind of "usage." Any testing or diagnostics that need to be run can be handled by authorized personnel in Computer Services.

There is also a question of allowing users access to file servers in remote buildings. While it is physically possible to access a PC file server in a remote building (loading WordPerfect, for example, many times from a machine across campus may conserve some hard disk space on a user's PC), it substantially slows down the networking equipment and fiber-optic links.

Therefore, Computer Services requires that applications be loaded only from local hard disks or servers in the same building as the client station.

There is also the question of "sniffing," that is, "eavesdropping" on the network. This occurs when a user obtains or writes a program that allows a view of all data passing on the network, instead of just those data that are normally destined for, and processed by, his or her local station. This activity is viewed in the same light as the tapping of telephone lines and is not allowed.

It is the responsibility of Computer Services to provide a reliable networking environment for the campus. The intent of the current networking policies is to encourage reasonable, cost-effective use of the network, conserving its bandwidth and high performance for legitimate data, resulting in equitable computing benefits for the entire university community.

Networking the Kent State University Geauga Campus

Larry Jones
Dean & Assistant Professor, Computer Technology
Kent State University

INTRODUCTION

Kent State University is a large, multicampus system covering seven counties of northeastern Ohio. The central campus is located in Kent. It offers degrees at the baccalaureate, master's, and doctoral levels and has an enrollment of approximately 23,000 students. Kent State's regional campus system includes seven campuses with a total enrollment of approximately 9,000 students. The sizes of these campuses range from credit enrollments of 600 to 2,400 students. The regional campuses offer two-year associate degrees and baccalaureate course work for programs at the Kent campus and transfer to other institutions. The profiles of the student body and the publics served are similar to those of community colleges.

COMPUTING AT THE GEAUGA CAMPUS

The Geauga Campus is the smallest two-year institution in the State of Ohio. It is a single-building facility that is located in a very rural section of northeast Ohio. At the associate degree level, it offers only four degrees: accounting, business, computer technology, and general studies. The enrollment dropped significantly during the early 1980s to a low of 225 in 1986. There were serious discussions about closing the campus at that time. However, the enrollment has since rebounded to an all-time high of 634 for the fall 1991 semester.

At the time of my arrival as Dean in January 1987, the campus had few computer resources. For instruction, there was a VAX 11/730 that was used for the Computer Technology courses, one 286, and about six personal computers (PCs) and XT class microcomputers. Those computers were all in one large classroom that also housed six dumb terminals for the VAX. For administration, there was one terminal to the VAX in the main office used to run an old COBOL program for registration that was written at another campus. There were no microcomputers for use in administration. The information system at the campus was, at best, in a shambles. Important data were not maintained or were all over the place, some on the VAX but mostly in unorganized paper files.

Five years later, the computing scene at the campus is dramatically different. The entire campus is networked with two Ethernet Novell local area networks (LANs) running NetWare 386 version 3.11 and using 486 tower systems as fileservers, one for academic use and the other for administration. They are bridged together to facilitate network management and to accommodate users who need access to both. There are three academic labs housing a total of forty-four 286 and 386 microcomputers, and another lab is devoted to computer-assisted instruction. Every administrator, full-time faculty, and staff member has a 286 or 386 class microcomputer on their desk.

We have standardized on WordPerfect 5.1 for word processing, WordPerfect Office 3.0 for e-mail, Lotus 1-2-3 3.1 for spreadsheets, and dBASE III Plus for databases. We recently purchased a site license from Borland, so all of their software is also on the LAN. Everyone has access to those and a variety of other application software packages. For output, there are eight laser printers located throughout the building in labs and general office areas. On the administrative network is a complete student information system application that was designed, developed using Clipper, and implemented in-house. The VAX has been upgraded to a 11/750, but it is used mostly as a communications conduit to the rest of the university and the outside world.

I believe that networking administrative and academic areas has allowed the campus to clean up its information act, maximize its yield rate with prospective students, target new markets within business and industry, and improve the retention rate through computer support of the entire curriculum. The enrollment has more than doubled, with a parallel increase in number of administrative, faculty, and staff positions to serve the additional students. The campus has gone from a deficit situation to having a budget that is solid and a fund balance that is increasing. Although I cannot tie all of this prosperity directly to the integration of computer technology, I can safely say that we have become much more efficient and effective in administration. Also, we are providing our students with an educational environment that integrates the use of microcomputers as productivity tools throughout the curriculum, thereby better preparing them to function in our technological society.

HOW WE DID IT

A Clear Priority

Because I have been teaching microcomputer applications in the graduate department of Educational Administration and in the Computer Technology associate degree program since the early 1980s, I have a distinct bias toward upgrading campus computing and networking. As a campus Dean, I was able to make that a high priority in planning efforts. I had been in other administrative positions within the Kent system and was also spearheading some projects to electronically link the regional campuses' libraries with the newly installed cataloging software on Kent's IBM mainframe and had started some pilot projects on administrative use of LANs. Because of those activities, I brought with me a 386 system for myself and a small Novell LAN with a 286 file server and four XT workstations. Therefore, on my first day as Dean, I greatly increased administrative computing at the campus.

From that day forward, the message was clear to all who worked or took classes at the Geauga Campus that microcomputers would become increasingly important in their daily lives. Over the past five years, three new full-time positions have been created to support that effort and "spread the word." The Computer Center Manager is responsible for networking all academic computers and establishing functional labs to support a variety of curriculum needs. The Coordinator of Computer Aided Instruction is responsible for integrating the use of microcomputers throughout the curriculum. He has been successful in convincing faculty in many disciplines that learning can be enhanced through the use of CAI software, videodisc technology, and productivity tools such as word processing with spelling and grammar checkers. Most of our English classes and several other disciplines schedule class sessions in the computer labs to hold in-class writing assignments and to use a variety of specific software packages.

A Programmer/Analyst position was added about two years ago to assume the responsibilities of managing the administrative network, a task I had been performing, and to develop a complete student information system. I call it a "cradle-to-grave" system because I want to use it to track all prospective students from first contact through admission, registration, graduation, and alumni followup. Although not finished, it now meets almost all the needs originally identified. Actually, it will probably never be finished because we are always discovering new needs and finding ways to improve the current system's modules.

Training and retraining has become an ongoing effort at the campus. Some of that training is done one-on-one, particularly with the faculty. Several of us develop and teach workshops to cover specific software and give employees release time to attend. I also encourage everyone to take some of our computer credit courses to gain more in-depth knowledge of applications.

Paying the Bill

Paying for the academic network was relatively painless because during Ohio's last three biennia there has been a great deal of support for enhancing existing high-quality programs. For that purpose, the state created Academic Challenge grants that provide each campus with $50,000 per year for each biennium, a total of $300,000 over six years. In addition, as each grant expired at the end of a biennium, moneys were rolled into the subsidy to further support identified programs for two more biennia. It is probably no surprise to the reader that the Geauga Campus chose, in part, to enhance its associate degree programs in business, computer technology, and general studies by integrating the use of microcomputers throughout the curricula. We were also fortunate to participate in a limited offer from Novell for a free license for Novell's NetWare LAN operating system to start an academic network. The only stipulation was that we post a big red sign that stated the NetWare was donated by Novell. Although we have paid for upgrades and purchased the 386 version of NetWare, that sign still hangs in a lab. Thanks Novell!

Initially, I could only get microcomputers into the offices when old equipment was replaced in the academic lab. Those were added as workstations on the LAN I originally brought to the campus. The major cost of upgrading that administrative LAN and providing microcomputers for all administrators, faculty, and staff was taken little by little out of the operating budget and, after the campus came out of a deficit situation, the fund balance. Fortunately, each of Kent State's regional campuses receives subsidy as a separate line item in the state budget and carries forward its own deficit or fund balance. A deficit for one campus is covered by the fund balances of other regional campuses, but the system as a whole must stay in the black. As long as the system is healthy, a campus may request to use part of its fund balance for various projects including computerization and renovations. A high priority for the Geauga Campus was to use a portion of those funds to complete the administrative LAN. With those resources, a 486 file server was purchased, NetWare 386 version 3.11 was installed, and all full-time personnel had their own microcomputers by spring of 1990.

Strategic Need for Networks

Microcomputers have changed the way institutions design and manage their information systems infrastructures. Once they experience the utility of a standalone microcomputer, users look for ways to share software, data, and peripherals. Since the early 1980s, many organizations have focused on exploiting LAN technology as a means to meet those needs.

LANs can enhance the quality of work life in areas of improved productivity, making jobs easier, more reliable data access, and improved efficiency. With the additional benefits of enhanced communications among all campus constituents, including faculty, a strong case can be made for implementing campus-wide LANs as productivity tools. This is particularly true at a small campus where limited resources should lead us to view information technology resources as a major strategic asset that can be utilized to maintain a competitive edge when recruiting students.

The common strategic objectives of higher educational institutions can be placed in three categories: recruitment, retention, and revenue generation. All areas require that institutions, particularly two-year institutions, must strive to become more dynamic, flexible, and responsive to the needs of prospective students, current students, and business and industry. LANs allow institutions to maintain centralized, accurate, nonredundant data in a cost-effective manner to facilitate that responsiveness. In that manner, LANs can greatly improve the success, or yield rate, of turning prospective students into enrollments.

LANs also reduce or eliminate the amount of paper floating around and among offices so efforts can be focused on activities that maximize the return on investment of time and resources. Using centralized databases, tracking systems, and automatic personalized inquiry response and followup materials, institutions can ensure that they hit the narrow window of opportunity when the prospective students' interest levels are at the peak. Similarly, those same tools can facilitate extensive tracking to minimize the loss of enrolled students owing to the lack of timely problem identification or simply the lack of adequate attention.

On the instructional side of the enterprise, LANs can greatly enhance communications among faculty and between faculty and students. Utilizing this technology will have an increasing impact on teaching and learning, as we prepare students in all disciplines to exist and prosper in a technological environment. Computer literacy is beginning to rank with the need to be able to read and write in our society and is fast becoming an assumed skill in the workplace. In fact, formalized life-long learning in technological areas is rapidly moving from an option for working people to a necessity. It is hope that students will come to view and use microcomputers and LANs as productivity tools that provide information, computation, and communication services and serve as vehicles for computer-assisted instruction (CAI).

Planning for Campus Networks

The typical life cycle of LAN implementation encompasses:

- Investigation and analysis of defined problems that LANs address, including feasibility studies
- Selection and design
- Implementation
- Maintenance and evaluation

The key to successful LAN implementation is planning. The planning process should involve every potential end user in exercises and discussions that assist them in thinking backwards from blue sky wants and wishes of potential output and uses of LANs to the realities of current LAN technology and budget constraints. The user's needs should be the driving force behind LAN implementation. The importance of total involvement in planning is to get disparate views out on the table for discussion. Also, personnel involvement in the planning stage can be a major motivating factor in acceptance of the LAN and its systems. If a thorough job is done at the planning stage, the selection of specific hardware, wiring scheme, operating system, and application software should be easier.

Implementation of the LAN solution, once again, requires total involvement of the end users. That involvement should involve sufficient training to facilitate the conversion from old work methods to the new automated environment. Once implemented, there needs to be an ongoing process of maintenance, evaluation, enhancement to meet newly defined problems, and planning for future growth.

RECOMMENDATIONS

The following recommendations are based on our campus experiences and my readings.

Planning

Dwight D. Eisenhower is credited with stating that "plans are nothing; planning is everything." The key to successful LAN implementation is that process of planning.

- Establish a central authority and support at a high level to coordinate all planning and implementation of campus-wide networks. At our campus, that central authority was held by myself as Dean.
- House responsibility for computing in a single unit and disseminate information to all members of the campus community. Although I eventually delegated the responsibility for academic and administrative LANs to separate individuals, central coordination was still maintained in my office.
- Involve all personnel continually in planning the campus information system. We often met with groups of personnel to identify needs and problems and develop alternative solutions.
- Develop an organizational infrastructure that supports campus-wide use of microcomputers and LANs. We created staff posi-

tions that were specifically responsible for that integration.

- Integrate all curricula within campus-wide networks with the support of requisite instructional software. This is the responsibility of the Coordinator of Computer Aided Instruction.
- Secure every method possible for long-range financial support for development, including federal, state, private, and local sources. The primary sources for our LAN efforts were state grants and local campus resources, although we must now turn to other sources.
- Integrate new LANs into existing information systems with bridges, gateways, and shared modems; one of the most significant technical issues will be connectivity. We connected our two LANs with a dedicated microcomputer serving as a bridge and provided access from the LANs to the VAX to communicate with the outside world. Do not forget such things as faculty access to BITNET and other academic networks.
- Do not skimp on file server and workstation capacity; plan for future growth and software requirements. For file servers, we bought top-of-the-line 486 towers with largest hard drives available and plenty of RAM. Although many staff members still only have 286 workstations, we have only been buying 386 25MHz and 486 machines for the past year and a half.

Implementation

- Train, train, and train all users as a continuous, centralized function with a budget allocation of institutional resources. All of our training is performed by myself, faculty, or peers, so there is no real cost. Whenever possible, I like to use peers as trainers because that activity becomes an ongoing process in the workplace. All our training is done on company time unless someone enrolls in a regularly scheduled credit course.
- Seek the involvement of top-level administration in training and use of system. Unless enthusiastic support and use of the LAN by those at the top are apparent, people will not jump on the LAN bandwagon quickly.
- Develop a mind-set of never typing anything twice (e.g., convert existing databases to word processing merge files for personalized letter generation). I have found this type of behavior modification to be the most difficult to implement among our office staff. Every once in awhile, I still find someone typing multiple mailing labels when the data are readily available to produce them.

- Use central, shared, nonredundant databases to ensure the maintenance of accurate data. Involve users in database design so that the structures of data are correct.
- Use e-mail as an ice breaker to get personnel on the LAN quickly; it provides immediate gratification. You may need to be a little autocratic; I gave everyone a month to become familiar with the software, and then stopped all in-house memos and post-it telephone messages. E-mail was adopted quickly at the Geauga Campus.
- Establish guest LAN accounts for part-time faculty and student help so that they can take advantage of the applications available.
- Create and use public directories for shared access to files. We have one in which everyone has full privileges. It is mapped as a logical drive "G:" that stands for "general." So, if I want to draft a letter and have someone else edit it, I copy it to G: drive and send an e-mail memo indicating its name to the person.
- Make synergy the goal for campus-wide networks to improve access to resources and universal use of information. With LANs, the whole is absolutely greater than the sum of its parts.

Maintenance and Evaluation

- Establish a detailed plan to continue LAN development, operate the system, address users' needs, and involve faculty and staff.
- Formalize LAN management responsibilities into new or existing positions. The LAN environment is much more complex than standalone microcomputers. Someone must be trained in the intricacies of LAN management.
- Select a LAN manager with excellent interpersonal and organizational skills; they are just as important as technical expertise, perhaps more so.
- Establish backup procedures for LAN data and stick with them. Again, this responsibility must be formalized. With improved tape backup drives and software, this can often be performed on an automatic, timed basis. However, even with that ideal setup, someone must still load and label tapes.
- Establish security measures appropriate to the environment and data.
- Protect your LAN and users from viruses. People still share floppies and, if your LAN is linked to other networks, unwanted

demon programs can come from anywhere. Develop policies and procedures that spell out safeguards and invest in virus protection software.

SUMMARY

Although not a panacea, LANs offer tremendous opportunities to maximize productivity and the efficient use of limited resources at small institutions of higher education. Most authors agree that LANs will be the computing platform of the 1990s and the most important technical issue will be connectivity. As educational institutions, we can greatly benefit from being part of these exciting changes. The integration of LAN technology throughout the Geauga Campus of Kent State University has had an extremely positive impact on our ability to deliver quality instruction and manage ourselves more efficiently and effectively.

Small College Networks in the 1990s: The Lafayette College Campus Network

Patrick Ciriello
Supervisor of Networking and Technical Services
Lafayette College

BACKGROUND

Lafayette College is a private, four-year, coeducational, liberal arts and engineering school of about 2,000 students and 175 faculty located about 90 minutes from both New York and Philadelphia. The unique combination of arts and sciences and the desire to integrate technology into the liberal arts curriculum led to the institutional commitment to upgrade Lafayette's computing facilities and to create a campus-wide network that would facilitate this integration for the present and foreseeable future.

Networking is becoming more of an issue in today's society. Businesses use networks so that they can better facilitate and manage the flow of information from one location to another, whether it is down the hall, across the street, or around the world. The same is true in the educational arena. Colleges are looking to networks to assist them with their administrative tasks and to create an environment that is more conducive to the educational goals of the institution.

The network initiative at Lafayette began in the mid-1980s. At that time, a committee was established to examine the needs of the college and recommend an appropriate method by which Lafayette should approach the issue of networking. By 1987 certain goals were defined: the first was to establish a "test" network, using one residence hall; the second was to begin the design of a network that would encompass the entire campus, including offices, classrooms, and student rooms.

To accomplish the first goal, Lafayette worked closely with IBM to design and install a token-ring network in Watson Hall, one of the larger residence halls on campus (and coincidentally named after IBM's founder). The goal of the study was to get students to use the computers and the network as much as possible. The Watson network had 72 student rooms (each had a workstation[1] connected to the network) and was serviced by three personal computer (PC)-local area network (LAN) servers and three public print stations.

To accomplish the second goal, several administrative steps needed to be taken. The first was the hiring of a new director for academic computing (it was decided that the network, although it was to be campus-wide, was to be administered by the Academic Computing Services division). This position was filled in August 1988. A second position, Supervisor of Networking and Technical Services, was filled in December 1988.

At the time the Watson study began, a donation from an alumnus of the college made it possible to begin the construction of the conduit system that would eventually house the cabling for the new network. IBM and Lafayette decided on a design that would essentially divide the campus into three rings, and the conduit paths were designed with this in mind. In the original planning, the design called for a fiber-based backbone, with each building bridged onto that backbone. However, as the planning and design of the network progressed, this path was abandoned.

In the summer of 1988, half of the conduit system was installed, based on the initial drawing provided by IBM. It was at this time that Watson Hall was wired, and in September the Watson Study began. Several months into the study, many of the original ideas about how the remainder of the campus would be networked were abandoned. One of the first ideas abandoned was that of public printer stations in each residence hall. Aside from the management and administrative hassle of having to maintain those sites, the potential for vandalism was quite high. The second idea abandoned was the use of Windows and HDC Express. The overhead of using those packages made the workstation intolerably slow. It was also decided that the use of the IBM Bridge program as a means of providing connectivity around campus was also an untenable solution. In fact, there was a question as to whether the IBM token-ring solution would be used at all as a campus solution.

Beginning in January 1989, the search began for a comprehensive solution and design that would provide full connectivity to the entire campus. One of the first decisions that was made was what services must people be able to access. It was decided that everyone should have access to LINC, the main application center for the campus. LINC (Lafayette's Integrated, Networked Campus) is an IBM 9375 running VM and MUSIC. Several of the college's more useful applications, including e-mail, reside on LINC. It was also decided that everyone should have access to the academic development system, which at that time was a VAX 11/750. In addition, the engineering division was in the process of designing and installing a SUN workstation lab, and that too required campus-wide accessibility.

Given the diverse nature of the resources that had to be accessible from the PC workstations, the decision was made to use TCP/IP as the campus standard for connectivity, in addition to IBM LAN-Manager. To support the IBM LAN-Manager protocol, the devices used to interconnect LANs had to support Source Route Bridging. The devices also had to support the TCP/IP routing protocols. In the early months of 1989, such a device did not yet exist.

Note, however, that the IBM bridge program would allow the TCP/IP protocol to operate across the bridge. But since it did not support IP subnetting, the entire campus would have to have been one flat subnet. With over 2,000 possible host addresses, this was not a feasible option.

Lafayette hired the consulting firm, TeleGistics, Inc., to assist with the selection of hardware and the engineering of the wiring project. The conduit system having already been installed based on the original IBM concept, it became necessary to find a way to make the conduit design support a much more flexible approach: multiple rings with a common intersection. Instead of having the internetwork device in each building, and using the fiber as a high-bandwidth backbone, the fiber would be utilized for its distance ability. The starting and ending point of each ring was extended via fiber to one central location, the Network Control Center (NCC). Under this scenario, it is possible to tap directly into each network on campus from one physical location. Therefore, all the routing/bridging devices could be centrally located, servers would also be located and maintained in the NCC, as well as any management facilities that would be used. In the case of the servers, it allows the server to be local to a network, thus increasing utilization, even though it is physically on the far side of campus.

As each network environment available was reviewed by Lafayette and TeleGistics, one critical point became very clear. The system had to be manageable with limited staffing. In fact, this aspect, and the support of then-current standards, became top priorities when the final selection process began. The two finalists were chosen because of their management ability. The final choice went to the vendor whose equipment had the necessary management capabilities, supported the required standards, and met the pricing needs of the college. One solution was a token-ring-based solution, and the other an Ethernet-based solution.

Up until this point, the only experience the college had with Ethernet was a small backbone cable that provided connectivity between the multi-user systems, and a small Star-Lan (1 Mbps) lab. There had been much greater experience with token-ring by then, including the Watson study, several public labs that were designed and installed by the staff, and an ongoing relationship with IBM. Eventually, we did decide on the token-ring vendor, and it might be argued that the deck was stacked. However, one of the important design concepts that the college wanted to preserve was that of centrally located equipment supporting the remote networks. The Ethernet vendor's solution was unable to support that type of physical topology. It was also uncertain how expansion would be done, given the need for several layers of bridging and the inherent limitations on Ethernet in this area.

In summary, the Lafayette network was to be a token-ring-based installation. The next step was to determine the type of cabling. Shielded twisted pair (IBM Type 1) was chosen because (1) it is supported by all the main network types (4/16 Mbps token-ring, Ethernet 10BaseT, PhoneNet, etc.), thus providing a high degree of flexibility for the future, and (2) any new technologies developed for twisted pair cabling will always have a distance advantage over shielded twisted pair. The idea of bringing fiber to the workstation was also investigated, but no compelling reason existed at that time to justify the added expense.

It was the beginning of summer 1990, and everything seemed to be in place. The physical access protocol, the cabling type, and the equipment vendor had all been decided on, and installation was "almost" on schedule. However, in the hustle and bustle of designing the physical side of the network, little thought was given to which network operating system would be used.

The assumption that had been made was that Lafayette would continue to use IBM PC-LAN Program and IBM OS/2 LAN Server. In July of 1990, a Network Technician was added to the Lafayette staff, one who had a great deal of experience working with Novell, IBM PC-LAN, and OS/2 LAN Server, as well as many other types of network operating systems. The staff members who were already familiar with PC-LAN, the new Network Technician, and several students tried for a month to get OS/2 LAN Server to work.[2] However, progress was slowed at several points. First, they were unable to use generic accounts on the servers. Each person, or at least each machine, had to have a separate account. This posed an administrative nightmare, as the desire was to make all the servers (at that time, four of them) identical. Second, there was no easy way to create the accounts; each had to be done by hand and took at least five minutes to create each one. There were 2000 students, and 600 employees for which to make accounts! Another "inconvenience" was the fact that the more user accounts OS/2 LAN server had, the longer it took to boot up. After about 100 accounts had been created, it took the server nearly 30 minutes to boot!

It was at this that time the switch to Novell was discussed. Soon after, the point was reached where OS/2 LAN Server just wouldn't do what was needed. Two weeks before the network was to go live, Lafayette ordered several copies of NetWare. One week later, the servers (all four of them) were installed and operational, running most of the required packages, and supporting three accounts for all the users. Currently, Lafayette has six NetWare 286 servers and one NetWare 386 server.[3] The four NetWare 286 servers provide 400 concurrent connections for the general campus population. The NetWare 386 server will be used for special applications, as well as being the only server onto which user may store data. The NetWare 386 server may, in the future, also support the Macintosh users on campus as well. There are two departments that use the IBM PC-LAN program; they will move to Novell during the summer of 1991.

There are a few other items of interest about the Lafayette network. In the campus-wide configuration, the network utilizes token-ring (STP [shielded twisted pair], UTP [unshielded twisted pair], and fiber), Ethernet (thick wire, thin wire, 10BaseT, and fiber), 56/64K synchronous DDS lines, and T1 lines. Each workstation on the network is configured as an IP host machine,[4] and thus has access to all the multiuser systems on campus. Most of the PC workstations are IBM PS/2s (Model 30/286 and higher) and Zenith (286 and 386) machines. All the high-powered UNIX-based workstations are SUN machines (Sun-3, Sun-4, Sparc-1, and Sparc-2).

Currently, the Lafayette network consists of 20 token-ring networks (see Figure 1), one Ethernet backbone, two extensions of the Ethernet back-

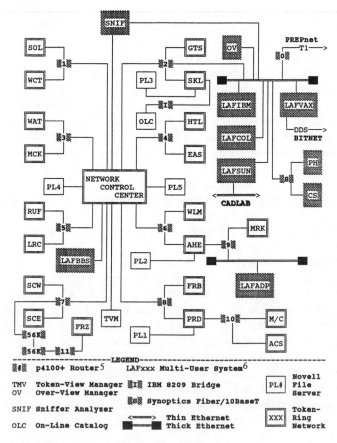

Figure 1. The Lafayette Network as it exists today.

bone that use 10BaseT and fiber, and one separate thin-net-based lab. All the segments of the network are connected via the Proteon routers or through Sun workstations running routed. One IBM 8209 token-ring/Ethernet bridge connects the library catalog system to the network. The network encompasses over 40 buildings and can support over 2,500 workstations.[7] Future expansion projects will include the installation of dedicated fiber and DDS lines[8] to off-campus buildings, including offices, student residences, and possibly faculty residences.

NOTES

1. During the 1988-89 school year, the workstations were IBM Model 25s with a single floppy drive using network boot proms. During the 1989-90 school year, the workstations were replaced with Model 25s equipped with 20 megabyte hard disks.
2. The college had PC-LAN already installed. However, there were features in the OS/2 LAN Server that made it more appealing than PC-LAN. Unfortunately, both systems suffered from similar drawbacks, and neither was a viable solution.
3. All the servers running NetWare 286 are IBM PS/2 Model 70s with 120MB internal ESDI drives, 1.2GB external SCSI drives, and 10-16MB of RAM. The NetWare 386 server is a Model 70/486, with 120MB internal, seven 330MB SCSI drives, and 16MB of RAM.
4. On the PCs, the MD/TCP package is used for IP connectivity to the IBM, VAX, and Sun machines. This package was developed by the University of Maryland with support from IBM. It is available through WISC-WARE, and is the only noncommercial TCP/IP package available for token-ring. Currently, no software is available to allow the Macintosh computers to user IP with the token-ring boards.
5. Router "0" is a Proteon p4200.
6. LAFBBS is an FTP server running the KAQ9 shareware package, using the MD/TCP device drivers for token-ring and a packet driver that makes the token-ring card look like an Ethernet card. LAFCOL is a Sun-Server.
7. There are approximately 1,400 outlets available on campus. Since a token-ring network can support 250 users, with the use of splitters and dedicated labs the Lafayette network could actually support over 4,000 stations.
8. Currently, planning calls for the use of 56/64K dedicated phone lines as a temporary measure to provide connectivity off-campus. The permanent solution will involve the installation of dedicated fiber cables from campus to those buildings.

University of Limerick: Network Systems and Resources

Gordon Young
Manager Information Technology Department
University of Limerick, Eire

Patrick Kelly
Director Information Systems and Librarian
University of Limerick, Eire

INTRODUCTION

The University of Limerick was founded in 1972 as the National Institute of Higher Education (NIHE, Limerick) with 113 students and 43 staff. It grew rapidly and acquired full independent university status in 1989. It currently has an enrollment of 5,444 students and 502 faculty and staff. Considerable capital money was invested during the period 1972-89, and a high percentage of this was invested in computing and network technology.

In 1983 the university decided to invest in distributed computing and to build a local area network using Ethernet technology. This investment was possible because of capital grants available from the Irish government and the European Investment Bank for the expansion of the university.

DEVELOPMENT OF THE LAN 1983-1987

In 1983 the university built an Ethernet network using thick-wire technology. Six segments were laid around the building, each linked to a backbone segment using repeaters. The thick wire cable was run in ceiling ducts along the corridors. This was the first large Ethernet installation in Ireland. One hundred Digital Equipment Corporation (DEC) professional computers were purchased, and each department received a MicroVax II computer for departmental computing, all being interconnected to the Ethernet. Terminals to the VAX computers were interconnected using either terminal servers or the direct ports available on the VAX computers.

The university's administrative computers were also interconnected to the same network (i.e., a separate secure Ethernet was not constructed). Although the potential security risk was recognized, it was envisaged that it would only be a short period of time before encryption would be available.

PHASE 1: FUNDING OF THE DEVELOPMENT

At this point it is worth reflecting on how the funding model affected the design and implementation of the network. The capital monies for computing were distributed both centrally and departmentally. The Computer Centre used its capital for the purchase of the network, repeaters, and so on, and to upgrade an existing VAX 11/780. Departments received funding for their own MicroVAX II computers and associated terminals. They were also responsible for funding the interconnection of these terminals to their own computers. The university made a decision very early in its development that faculty should not congregate in departmental ghettos but should be intermixed to allow "cross-fertilization" of ideas to occur. This meant that individual corridors in the building would have a mix of faculty from different departments. Since each department had the responsibility for funding its own connection, invariably the departments did this in the cheapest way possible, ignoring the fact that an Ethernet infrastructure was available and that adjacent offices belonging to other departments were wired back to other VAX computers/ terminal servers. What should have happened was for terminal servers to be provided in areas around the building and the ports on these servers made available to the different offices along the corridors regardless of the ownership of the offices. Since the capital funding had been distributed, this was not possible unless the departments wished to pool their monies. Without the necessary political support however, pooling was not possible. This infrastructure served the university well, supporting primarily DECnet and in particular DEC's Local Area Transport (LAT) protocol. A central VAX was interconnected to the public X25 network and through this network to the Irish Higher Education Network (HEANET) and to other research networks such as BITNET.

During this period the network was used primarily for terminal traffic and for file transfer between the different VAX computers and the DEC Professionals.

PHASE 2: 1986-90

The second phase of development coincided with the rise of the personal computer (PC) and Macintosh computers and the development of thin wire Ethernet. The first clusters of PCs started to appear in the university in 1984-85 in departments that had become considerably disillusioned with the DEC Professional. Indeed, the DEC Pros had become little more than very expensive terminals to the VAXs. These PCs were networked using the early IBM technology, for Ethernet interfaces were not available at this time.

In 1986 capital money was made available to purchase some clusters of IBM-compatible PCs. Thin wire technology was now available, and since it was considerably cheaper to interconnect a PC to thin-wire rather than the existing thick wire cabling it was decided to connect the PC clusters to the existing network using thin wire cabling and multiport repeaters. Unfortunately insufficient monies were available to replace the repeaters interconnecting the existing thick wire segments, and because of the "two repeater" rule these thin-wire clusters had to be connected to the university backbone segment, ignoring the fact that an existing Ethernet segment might be available immediately adjacent to a PC cluster!

Considerable pressure was applied to increase the number of PCs that could be purchased with the available money rather than spending the money on the network to support. It was the opinion of the Computer Centre that PCs could not be supported properly unless they were networked to a server. This was not the general view of faculty at that time. Consequently, as many PCs as possible were connected to each thin wire segment (30 per segment)—eventually causing reliability problems.

Early in 1988 3COM's 3+Share file servers were purchased to support the PCs. All the applications software was delivered via these servers with students maintaining their own disk space using the floppy drives on each PC. Making the applications' software available in this way has the following advantages:

- Only one copy of the software is needed to be maintained, saving considerable support time.
- Students can be certain that they are using the "official" software and that it is the most up-to-date version.
- The server software is virus free.
- Cheaper software licenses are available for network server rather than multiple individual copies.

PCs were also purchased by individual faculty members who also wished to gain access to these network servers and to their own department computers. The existing thick wire Ethernet cable was only available along corridors and not as access points in the individual offices. Since central monies were not available to provide an Ethernet connection in each office it was decided to charge individuals $900 for a network connection. This covered the cost of

- the Ethernet card for the PC
- contribution toward the multi/single port repeater used
- thin wire cabling

When a request came for a particular office connection, a thin wire segment was provided both to it and adjacent offices.

This was the first time that central services had increased computing costs, and it met with considerable resistance from faculty, for they felt that the Ethernet infrastructure had already been funded centrally back in 1983 and that therefore they should not have to pay to connect to it. However, it did avoid departments laying their own thin wire segments. Now all offices have a thin wire connect available. Responsibility for this whole infrastructure resides with central services.

Many faculty did not pay the connection charge, preferring to use a standalone PC. They felt that it was better to spend the money on individual software licenses rather than use the software available from the network servers. This has only changed recently with the provision of networked CD-ROM services.

During 1987 the university built its first student residence accommodation, and each bedroom was wired with a thin wire Ethernet connect. The residences were connected back to the university via a fiber-optic cable.

RELIABILITY OF THE INFRASTRUCTURE

As the number of individual PCs grew, the reliability of the infrastructure decreased. Central services soon experienced the same problems as other large sites in supporting a daisy-chained Ethernet infrastructure. It took too long to isolate faults, and access to individual offices was difficult. Consequently, steps were taken to reduce downtime, including

- The repeaters interconnecting the thick wire segments were replaced by bridges and the backbone segment by a short piece of thin wire interconnecting these bridges in a communications closet.
- The PC cluster segments were broken down so that no more that six PCs were on the one segment.
- Make-or-break Ethernet connecters were used as soon as they became available on the market.
- Time domain reflectometer (TDR) tools and network monitors were purchased.
- The individual thin wire segments were removed from the backbone and interconnected to the nearest thick wire segment.
- A secure segment was created for administrative computing.

1990 EXPANSION OF THE UNIVERSITY

The latest phase of the network development has been associated with the expansion of the university from a one-building to a "multibuilding" campus. It has also coincided with the development of twisted pair Ethernet.

In 1987 the Computer Centre grew to become the Information Technology Department, with responsibility for the university telephone service and media services as well as traditional computing and networking responsibilities.

The university has constructed two large new buildings (one of which contains the Department of Computer Science) and has absorbed a teacher training college located on the same campus. The Information Technology department was involved from the beginning with the design of these buildings and has strongly influenced the provision of service duct layout and false floors.

Learning from the experience in using daisy-chained Ethernet, and that information trade directory (ITD) was responsible for the provision of telephones, it was decided to use level 4 shielded twisted pair cabling for all data/ voice outlets in these buildings. The buildings have been cabled on a star basis, with no cable length greater than 100 meters and all cables wired back to communication cabinets (premises distribution services). Shielded twisted pair cable has been used because

- It is expected that emission control regulations will be higher in Europe than in the United States, and consequently it will be necessary to use shielded cable to meet these standards.
- At this stage it appears that it will be cheaper to support Fiber Distributed Data Interface (FDDI) across shielded twisted pair rather than unshielded twisted pair wiring.
- STP cabling can also be used for video and sound.
- The cost difference on an overall contract is only marginal.

All the new Ethernet components (including the communication hubs) support Simple Network Management Protocol (SNMP). The individual buildings are connected back to the existing central backbone using fiber-optic cables (62.5 micron) containing 24 fibers.

Using this infrastructure offers many advantages:

- Each individual PC is connected directly to a hub and is not dependent on any adjacent connections.
- It is expected that the twisted pair cabling will support 100 megabits/second.
- Individual ports on the communication hubs are controllable centrally.
- An outlet in an individual office can be used for voice/date/ video by simply patching on the communication panel.

At present a twisted pair infrastructure is slightly dearer than an equivalent thin wire Ethernet, but the advantages in using it far out weigh the additional costs.

ADDITIONAL TECHNICAL SERVICES

This period has seen a considerable growth in services and protocols supported. The 3+Share servers have been replaced with LAN Manager. Macintosh and UNIX servers have been added along with networked CD-ROM. Protocols now supported include:

- TCP/IP family
- DECnet
- NETBIOS
- XNS
- AppleTalk

NETWORK SIZE

The network supports over 700 nodes, including 19 workstations, 11 VAX minicomputers, 600 PCs, 40 Macs, and 33 terminal servers. The infrastructure includes 9 bridges, 9 multiport repeaters, 1 router, and 3 intelligent hubs.

The university has installed 3 kms of thick-wire, 10km of thin wire and 40kms of twisted pair Ethernet cabling.

STAFFING

The staffing numbers provided to support the infrastructure have remained static from the original provision of the network in 1983. ITD has four operations and two systems staff to support all the centrally provided servers, computers, and network infrastructure.

NETWORK SERVICES

The University of Limerick network now routinely provides a range of information resources, tools and services that can support many aspects of the teaching, learning, research, and management processes (see Figure 1). The challenge is now to make these facilities known to and easily usable by students, faculty, and staff. This will require a degree of organization of internal and external resources, which to date is not apparent. As the network resource grows to include multimedia documents, the necessity for a comprehensive and "open" means of identification and acquisition to the desktop will be of major importance.

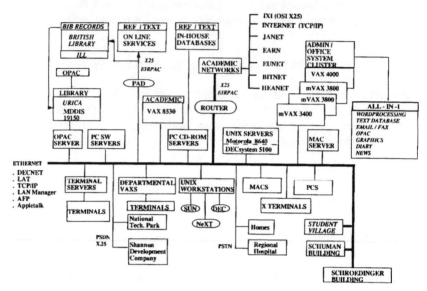

Figure 1. *University of Limerick ISSD network services.*

ORGANIZATION

In 1986 the University of Limerick integrated all areas of the organization with major information-handling responsibilities into one Division of Information Systems and Services. This included the Computer Centre, the Library, the Educational Technology Unit, office systems and services, telephone services, and printing.[1] The network underpins this structure, giving it current operational validity and provides the vehicle for the delivery of future innovative information services. This has already had major implications for the role of the Information Technology Department and is having similar implications for the role of the Library.

The development of a ubiquitous and genuinely useful network facility is much more than a technology issue. Its consequences are no less than a change of role and even culture for many involved, providers, and clients, and it is a powerful driver for organizational development and change for all.

USER SERVICES

The network now supports the information management needs of all sectors of the university. This includes academic facilities such as applications software, access to the Library OPAC, and a vast range of other information sources internally (through networked CD-ROMs) and externally, as well as gateway access to all major academic networks.

University management and administration are supported by a range of integrated office facilities such as word/document processing, e-mail/fax, text database, diary management, spreadsheet, and access to major internal databases.

The University of Limerick is truly a networked organization. If the network fails, the organization quickly comes to a halt. This is at once a major achievement and an awesome responsibility for information systems.

THE FUTURE

The university urgently requires good network management software. A number of products are currently under evaluation, and it is expected to make a purchase shortly.

The staffing levels are very low for supporting an infrastructure of this size. In particular, little preventive monitoring of the network is performed and problems are detected only after they have occurred. Since all university services are completely dependent on the network, much more monitoring of network performance and errors will have to be performed. The Information Technology Department has been trying to have the university recognize this need for some time. This recognition was recently achieved when all services were lost for an afternoon while a network fault was isolated and corrected.

The university is in a good position to move to a FDDI network when traffic levels dictate the need, for the backbone is completely contained within a communications closet.

Central capital funding from the government has now ceased and it is difficult to obtain monies for network infrastructure upgrades. The university has also moved very much to a cost-centered approach, allocating more monies to the departments than central services. This will make it difficult to extract the necessary finance from the system when upgrades are necessary because of performance problems. Indeed, it is likely that monies will only be forthcoming after severe network congestion problems have occurred. To avoid this type of scenario, it may well be necessary to charge departments an annual overhead for the different types of computers that they connect to the network. This is particularly the case for research-funded workstations and PCs because the government is very much of the opinion that the state funding for the university should be used primarily for undergraduate teaching.

NOTE

1. Patrick Kelly, "Information Management: An Academic Context," *British Journal of Academic Librarianship* 3, no. 3 (1988): 122-135.

Campus-Wide Information Systems: A View from Marist College

Onkar P. Sharma
Professor and Chair of the Division of
Computer Science and Mathematics
Marist College

Carl L. Gerberich
Vice President for Information Services
Marist College

HISTORY OF NETWORKING ON MARIST COLLEGE

Typically, networking on a campus is a bottom-up process. Some academic and/or administrative units configure and implement a networking environment that will best meet their needs. There is always a need for organizations to share information or expensive devices such as laser printers or plotters. They often don't want to wait for the computer centers that may have a backlog of projects. Moreover, developing their own systems gives them a sense of ownership and responsibility from the very beginning. Gradually, other departments build their own local area network, and later these different groups want to share information and connect them together. Thus, the network starts from the bottom and adds capacity incrementally. Later on, when they want to use the computing and storage capacity of a large mainframe available on the campus, the local area networks (LANS) are connected to this mainframe.

At Marist, it is actually the network that came first, and thus the way we are getting started is somewhat unique. About five years ago, Marist was experiencing a number of problems: growing pains caused by the rapid growth in student enrollment, an inadequate home-grown administrative system, an antiquated telephone system, and an inadequate library.

So in 1987, the President of the College, Dr. Dennis Murray, chartered a group to conduct an in-depth study of all the informational needs of the campus. The group was chaired by the Vice President of Information Services and comprised representatives of other administrative units such as Registrar, Bursar, Financial Aid, Institutional Research, and Admissions. This led to a series of meetings between IBM and the Marist staff, and the Marist/IBM

Joint Study was the outgrowth of this idea. The results of this effort will be discussed further in the section on the background to the Marist/IBM Joint Study. The Joint Study included provisions for the expansion of the campus network. In particular, the agreement provided for the residence halls and the classrooms to be connected to the mainframe computer, an IBM 3090 Model 200E.

The Joint Study provided a point of departure in terms of networking on Marist campus. First, the idea of networking came before the idea of developing and sharing applications as is usually the case. Second, these networks are being installed by the Computer Center, and the sense of ownership that normally comes from a bottom-up implementation does not yet exist at Marist. Third, the expertise to build and maintain the network is lacking at the local level. As a result, one of the biggest challenges at Marist is to transfer the sense of autonomy and responsibility to people who would be working with the networks. Moreover, because Marist is moving rapidly to network the campus and it may take some time before the faculty and students are ready to accept the ownership and responsibility for the network, it is planned in the interim to train and use Computer and Information Science graduate students as network administrators. These students, though trained by the Computer Center, would report and be responsible to the respective units where they would be working. Fourth, we don't have the problem of compatibility since all the hardware comes from the same manufacturer. Last, we don't have the problem of capacity because that is one of the main premises of the Joint Study.

MARIST/IBM JOINT STUDY

The use of technology has always been a goal of Marist College. The college seeks to apply technology across the curriculum to improve the learning process and to provide students with experience on the types of technology they will use after graduation. The Marist Mission Statement contains the following:

> The College seeks to explore ways in which academic excellence may be enhanced by state-of-the-art information and communications technology. While broadening intellectual horizons and developing skills, Marist at the same time provides opportunities, through its undergraduate and graduate programs, for career preparation and for entry into the world of work.

Shortly after the establishment of the first student terminal lab in 1983, Marist entered into a joint study with IBM to study the use of computers in a writing class. The class evaluated what was then IBM proprietary software. The class went on to test the use of word processing. In the years since the initial study, Print Journalism, Behavioral Science, and Art have incorporated the computer into their curriculum. Marist requires an Introduction to Computing course of all students except those majoring in Languages or Fashion. This course aims to prepare the student for the workplace by giving hands-on experience with both mainframe and personal computer applications. Special emphasis is given to word processing, spreadsheet, and database applications. One section of this introductory course is taught as an "electronic" classroom. All student assignments and the instructor's comments on those assignments are done through electronic mail.

As mentioned earlier, in 1987 Dr. Dennis Murray initiated a study of information needs at Marist College. Key faculty and administrators were a part of the committee. A survey was sent to all the faculty and staff. In addition, some faculty, staff, and students were asked to participate in detailed interviews. From these interviews, a range of problems were uncovered, related to the administrative system, the library, and the telephone system. The committee made recommendations for solutions to the most important problems. The final report was made to the President and to the Board of Trustees. A member of the Board of Trustees made the observation that the committee's recommendations were based on an assumption about the amount of resources available to the college. The committee was asked to consider how their recommendations would change if they assumed all the resources they needed were available.

Discussions with IBM followed. This was the beginning of the interactions that would finally culminate in the Marist/IBM Joint Study. The question asked by the Board of Trustees was intriguing: How would having infinite MIPS and infinite storage change the way a small customer used technology?

This became the premise on which the Joint Study was signed on June 22, 1988. Could a small customer, such as Marist College, employ computer power to enable the Marist community to use the computer without running into the bottleneck of limited resources? IBM selected Marist College because of Marist's long-term involvement with using technology across the curriculum. IBM stated very strongly: Don't try to be something you are not. Don't pretend you are a Stanford or MIT. Do the things you do best. Use technology to meet the needs of your students and faculty.

The introduction of advanced technology was not to be an end in itself, but instead technology was to be used to assist in reaching the goals of the Marist Strategic Plan. Technology was to be used to complement other activities to:

- Make Marist a unique institution in the highly competitive era of the 1990s.
- Provide Marist's graduates with an advantage in the job market because of the education they have received.
- Improve student retention by providing support services that are designed to meet the individual needs of our students.
- Maintain Marist's leadership position among small colleges in integration of leading computer technology into the curriculum and academic services.
- Expand on Marist's tradition of community service.

The Joint Study had three objectives:

- To improve the technological infrastructure at the college.
- To make the technological resources available anywhere on the campus.
- To build on Marist's tradition of community service by making the fruits of the technology available to schools and nonprofit organizations outside of Marist.

The improvements to the infrastructure included:

- The installation of a new administrative system to improve the services provided to our students.
- The installation of a Library automation package called DO-BIS.
- Supplying faculty members with personal computers (PCs) or terminals in their offices. When the project began in 1989, personal computers were not supplied for individual faculty use. This number has increased every year and now nearly 50% of the faculty have PCs in their offices provided by the college.

To make computing available across the campus, Marist developed an aggressive plan to cable the campus. A fiber-optic backbone was constructed linking the major buildings on the campus. The buildings themselves were wired with type 2 cabling. For the initial projects, Marist stayed with the technology it had been using and understood best. The Computer Science and Communication Arts faculty were connected into the mainframe using the fiber-optic cable to attach channel extenders. Study areas on each floor of the largest dorm were set up as student terminal rooms. The philosophy was still that of a centralized mainframe and computer center providing computational services.

JOINT STUDY ADDENDUM

In 1990 the Joint Study was expanded to include the telecommunications area. As part of that expansion, IBM set up a new telephone system for Marist which provided state-of-the-art telecommunications. In addition to such features as call forwarding and call waiting, the system also made available Phonemail.[1] Phonemail has drastically changed the way students, faculty, and staff communicate. During the summer of 1991, this telephone system was extended to the students in the dorms on the south end of the campus. They now have local, long distance service as well as Phonemail.

It became clear that a cultural change was taking place at Marist. The philosophy of centralized computing services was being replaced by a decentralized computing environment, and the role of the computing center was changing from providing all computing services to that of enabling its users to provide much of their own computing services.

INTEGRATION OF NETWORKING INTO THE EDUCATIONAL CURRICULUM

Marist has a vision of becoming as nearly as possible a paperless institution where faculty would send assignments and projects to students electronically and students, in turn, would return the completed work using the same media, and where students and faculty would be able to reach the library from their offices, laboratories, and dormitories at any hour of the day to reference, search, identify, and obtain materials from books, journals, periodicals, and abstracts for their research, assignments, and projects.

This vision is going to be accomplished by utilizing the resources made available through the Marist/IBM Joint Study in the area of telecommunications and networking and by extending it where necessary. The implementation is planned to be completed in several stages. First, all the classroom buildings and the majority of residential dorms have already been connected through fiber-optic backbone, thus providing the capacity to transmit audio and video signals and images between the buildings.

Second, the ROLM Corporation's telephone system has been installed on the campus with the Phonemail voice-messaging capability. This system runs on the network established by the fiber-optic cable and is extremely useful. Faculty are, of course, not available 24 hours a day. Since the dormitories are also connected, students can now call and leave messages for the faculty on such matters as seeking clarification on assignments and projects, setting up appointments, course scheduling, and a host of other academic matters. Faculty then respond when they are back in their office and either talk to students directly if they are present at the other end or leave messages the same way the students did.

Networking, telecommunications, and the power of the 3090 main-frame have all been combined to establish another form of communication between and among students and faculty. It is the electronic mail system. It is not as convenient as using the ROLM Phonemail system, but it is more versatile in the sense that it virtually does not place any limit on the size of the message and also produces a hard/soft copy of the message being transmitted back and forth.

The electronic mail system also enables faculty members to establish contacts with faculty on other campuses to facilitate and enhance their research. An interesting project that uses electronic mail system and involves students is the ICONS project. This project, initially developed at the University of Maryland, facilitates the exchange and discussion of ideas globally. This project is jointly supervised by faculty from the Political Science and Foreign Language departments.

The third form of communication, which is still in its infancy, will become possible through the linking of faculty offices, laboratories, classrooms, and dormitories through PCs, token-rings, servers, bridges, and cables. This will enormously expand the process of integrating computing in the curriculum. Although this discussion is perhaps typical of what most institutions do with networking, we still feel that its inclusion here is important because this discussion may tend to confirm what typically a small institution does with networking to improve the effectiveness of the teaching and the learning process on a small campus.

Currently, if faculty members have developed their own software for demonstration, then they use a roll-around cart to get their PC to the classroom. If the classroom, on the other hand, is equipped with a standalone PC, then the faculty members load their software on that PC in advance of the teaching time. This, at times, poses logistical problems. For example, the classroom may be occupied when a professor is free and vice-versa. However, once all the LANS are in place and connected, then the faculty will be able to create software on the PC in their offices and send it to be stored on the server. This will enable professors to demonstrate their application in the classroom without wheeling a cart to the classroom or storing the software on the standalone computer in the classroom.

Another scenario where networking will facilitate monitoring as well as sharing is in the area of students' projects and assignments. Currently, students completing programming assignments and projects hand over disks to faculty for evaluation and grading. On the other hand, if a professor needs to distribute materials to students, he or she prepares a disk for each student in the classroom or places this information on all the PCs in the laboratory. Once the LAN becomes fully operational, faculty members can develop the information on their PCs, transmit this information from their offices electronically, and store it on the server connected to the lab network, making the information accessible to every student without ever exchanging any disks. Moreover, the professors would then be able to communicate with students and monitor the progress of their work in an online environment.

It is also being planned to use the network as an instructional tool. Computer Science (CS) faculty are planning to have a network lab where students will gain hands-on experience. In this way different groups of students will be able to configure their own arrangement, make the corresponding hardware connections, and also develop their own application software. CS students taking operating systems and network courses will also be able to make small changes to the network operating systems and experiment with them.

There are also plans to facilitate software sharing on a larger scale. The college has purchased site licenses for Borland products, such as Turbo C, Turbo C++, Quattro Pro (spreadsheet package), Reflex and Paradox (database packages), and Turbo Pascal. Moreover, the computer center has installed several software packages such as Q&A (word and file processing package), WordPerfect (word processing), Lotus 1-2-3 (spreadsheet) and dBase IV on machines used in the lab for the computer literacy course. It is planned to take advantage of the network and make all these software packages, as well as some packages on the mainframe, available and accessible to students through the network installed in the dorms.

One of the most exciting applications, which has already been partially implemented, opens doors rather than windows of opportunities with respect to using library facilities. Recently, the library completed the installation of DOBIS/LIBIS, an integrated library system. This Software System consists of the following Subsystems: the Online Public Access Catalog (OPAC), Cataloging, Circulation, Acquisitions, Periodicals Control, Electronic Mail and Interlibrary Loan. The OPAC provides access by author, title, subject, publisher, call number, and abstract. Combined with the circulation module, OPAC enables users to determine whether the titles they want are available on the shelf. If a title has already been checked out of the library, it enables a patron to place a hold on that charged-out book.

In addition, Marist is one of the few schools in New York to maintain the ProQuest System. This contains compact disc databases with abstracts and full-text business and general periodicals. With the networking of the campus and installation of the DOBIS System in the library, members of the Marist community are now able to do a great deal of search and research from the comfort of their dorm, office, or home (through dial access from remote terminals).

FUNDING

Funding is always a concern. Marist has worked closely with IBM in setting up the Joint Study; it would have been impossible for Marist to reach this level of accomplishment without such support. The college has used its own capital funds to finance the fiber-optic backbone as well as the cabling and wiring of its buildings. To supply the computers for the faculty and to upgrade the computer classrooms and walk-in labs, Marist took advantage of the IBM Matching Gift Program. When IBM employees or retirees make a gift to the college, IBM will match the gift with a 5 to 1 voucher that can be used to purchase IBM products. During the last three years these vouchers have enabled Marist to purchase approximately $1 million worth of equipment.

PRESENT STATUS

The initial project was a local area network in the Personal Computer Support Center. The objective was to allow the sharing of letter-quality printers, plotters, and desktop publishing software in the Support Center. Much of the initial installation was done by students. It helped us to determine procedures to install, maintain, and manage local area networks. Marist established a LAN project team to implement further networking projects. The team included end users, telecommunications staff, and system programmers. When necessary, this team is enlarged to include additional end users who will be using a new LAN and specialists to address technical problem areas. The team approach has been highly successful and will be continued.

Next, the Dyson building, the first constructed since the beginning of the Joint Study, was totally wired for local area networks using the IBM token-ring technology. The requirements for these LANs were included in the original requirements for the building and in the architectural design of the building. The installation of the networks went smoothly, and service was available to the faculty and staff when they moved into the building in September 1990.

To gain additional experience with LANs, a LAN was established for the use of the Marist Information Services organization and was extended to include the members of the LAN project team. This LAN included a mixture of DOS and OS/2 requesters sharing a Postscript printer and various software applications. A major objective of this LAN was to determine what guidelines needed to be established to ensure that a new network could be incorporated into the campus networks. Marist wanted to make it possible for its more technologically advanced faculty and staff to implement their own networks without waiting for help from the computer center. It is important to provide the maximum local autonomy while minimizing the possibility of isolation. An initial version of these guidelines has been established. Student

Affairs is implementing a LAN independent of the computer center for inclusion into the campus network. During the summer of 1991, all of the south-end dorms were wired to permit students in their dorm rooms to have access to the mainframe and all local area networks on campus. (The plan is to complete the wiring of all campus dorms by September 1992.) Capabilities available to the students include the Library On-line Public Access Catalog, Electronic Mail, and access to BITNET and Internet. BITNET and Internet are international networks of higher education and research facilities.

Marist is currently installing the first of the student servers for the dorms. The students will have access to all software licensed by the college. Networking software will be provided by the college, and networking adapter cards will be leased to the students.

The Marist Institute of Public Opinion (MIPO) is a nationally known public opinion polling organization. A LAN being implemented for use by MIPO will use a network polling application. The objective of this LAN is to test the use of networking in the telephone survey interviewing process, streamlining data collection and analysis capabilities, as well as giving the institute an advanced state-of-the-art system. The LAN and its application software are now being tested and will be in operation in time for the early polls associated with the 1992 presidential election. This network is being expanded to include the Alumni and Development organization.

Examples of public service connections to the community would include the Small Business Institute, which makes databases available to small businesses in the area; and a project to permit students in the special education classes at the New Paltz Middle School to communicate with special education student teachers at Marist by electronic mail.

FUTURE PLANS

The faculty has increased the use of computing in the classroom as well as the number of assignments that require the computer. Additional classrooms have been set up to allow computer demonstrations in the classroom. The demand for walk-in labs has greatly increased since the beginning of the Joint Study. To adequately meet the needs for more and more software applications in our labs and classrooms, Marist will begin networking its computer classrooms. Servers will be provided for each of the computer classrooms to permit the specialized software of even the smallest class to be available to the students.

In a pilot project media specialists have began to work with Marist faculty to generate improved classroom demonstrations using the computer. Marist is providing faculty with resources to generate showcase projects using advanced technology. Future plans include establishing networks to connect the faculty offices, student dorms, instructional support centers, and classrooms containing a computer for demonstrations to make these classroom applications available to everyone on the campus who has need to use them.

A major effort will be made to equip the students, faculty, and staff to develop networking applications to meet their needs. Information Services and the Director of Academic Computing will concentrate on demonstrating what is possible and on training the end user to install or develop networks and applications. Guidelines and support will continue to be developed to minimize the work required to install a new network and to maximize its users' ability to access the network resources already available on the Marist Campus.

Marist is working closely with the Dutchess County Board of Cooperative Educational Services to investigate the possible extension of the Marist Campus Network to connect with a network in a local school.

APPLICATIONS

As we pointed out earlier, Marist College is building networking from the top down rather than from the bottom up. The college first installed the modern networking technology on the campus, thus opening doors to future applications. The college is now in the process of encouraging faculty and staff to develop appropriate applications. As an initial step in this process, the Executive Vice President, Dr. Mark Sullivan, invited faculty ad staff to submit proposals on the development of new information technology applications that feature innovative uses of Marist computer capabilities. Along with the description of the project/ application, the authors/investigators were requested to include an estimate of the resource requirements needed to support the project. The response was overwhelming, and about 30 proposals were received. A vast majority of these proposals came from the faculty, and although they were all interesting in their own right, the Executive Vice President, in consultation with the Academic Computing Committee, selected 12 proposals for further investigation. Those projects selected will be provided funding. Other proposals will be placed in a pending file to receive top consideration in the following fiscal year. Efforts have also been simultaneously initiated to obtain external funding for these proposals.

We would like to provide here a brief description of some of the projects that plan to use the network infrastructure in one way or the other.

Center for Mental Health Information Systems

As a first step in establishing the Center for Mental Health Information Systems, a Novell Network will be set up in the Computer Science Graphics Lab. This network will connect the existing Model 80s. As a second phase, this network will be connected to the optical-fiber backbone, giving access to the Marist LANS and to the mainframe. Students taking networking classes will be able to design and reconfigure the network as part of their class assignments. A later phase could be to include all the Computer and Information Science faculty in the network.

Distance Learning Utilizing Multimedia

An Introduction to a Computer Systems course will be offered as a distance learning experience to a pilot audience. A combination of videotaped lecture material, PS/2-based presentations using Toolbook, and online conferencing using the 3090 will be used for delivery. Students will download the PS/2-based materials from the mainframe.

Developing Group Discussion Skills

This proposal describes how computer-mediated communication (CMC) on the Marist mainframe could be used to augment an upper level group discussion skills course. The course objectives are to teach students Standard Agenda, a procedure for group problem solving, as well as communication skills for leadership, conflict resolution, and general participation in problem-solving and decision-making groups. CMC makes it possible for groups to function independently yet have access to the instructor without having to wait for class time or office hours for assistance.

Mathematics Education Enhancement

This project targets the enhancement of mathematics education by creating a community of local educators. Initially developed through personal contact, the community would be maintained and strengthened through technology by linking the local schools to Marist College. The community would then be extended to include students from the local schools. The link would allow all Marist facilities to be integrated into the daily teaching of mathematics in the schools. The link would also allow daily consulting between the Marist staff and the local teachers. Through the network, teachers could report on applications, get immediate support, and request supplemental materials or analysis of data. In addition, the schools would be linked to the Marist library and all the other resources in the network.

Paperless Classroom

This project demonstrates the use of the computer in the classroom to effect more efficient learning and interested students. It will test the hypothesis that students will become computer literate, faster, with a larger repertoire of skills, through an interactive process using the computer and minimizing the use of paper. All communication of student assignments, lab work completed by the students, evaluation by the professor, and tests will be done through the computer.

Link with Special Education Students

Using electronic mail, Marist student teachers in the special education program will communicate with children in special education classes in a local school. Students will be paired based on mutual interests and will correspond with each other several times each week. The children will benefit from contact with an interested adult and from additional practice in written communication. Student teachers will be given the opportunity to better understand the challenges they will face in teaching special education students. This will be an outreach to the surrounding community to assist in improving the quality of education and using computing and communications technology to enhance teaching and learning.

Strategic Economic Information Network

Marist has been designated as a State Data Center for the New York State Department of Economic Development. Marist will collect and provide information to the public in return for access to all federal and state economic and census data. The objectives of the Hudson Valley Strategic Economic Information Network are as follows:

1. To collect and compile economic and demographic data for the Hudson Valley Region.
2. To provide data in an accessible format for lay users in the Hudson Valley.
3. To access ability to the data for students and faculty at Marist for pedagogic and research purposes.

Based on the computing capacity of the IBM 3090, Marist will be able to serve as an important link in this statewide network and as the only university-based affiliate in the Hudson Valley. This data and computing capacity, along with Marist ties to the public and the business community, will provide an opportunity to catalyze a more coordinated approach to economic development efforts in the region.

Marist Institute for Public Opinion

MIPO surveys are cited by television, radio, and print media throughout the country. During the past year, print media coverage alone involved 303 different newspapers and magazines with a total of 1387 articles. The development of a local area network at the Institute for Public Opinion is an excellent opportunity to contribute to the developing application of computer capabilities in the survey research field. In addition, it provides a conduit to link the various activities: polling, training, and teaching at the Institute. Computer Assisted Telephone Interviewing (CATI) software will be installed on an OS/2 local area network. This step would

- Facilitate the instruction of students in class on the interview process and the use of computer applications in conducting interviews.
- Allow students to administer complex survey instruments by clarifying questionnaire branching and automating question skipping.
- Improve teacher-student interaction during the interview process so that students involved in collecting data might more easily ask questions through the network and obtain feedback from the faculty, thereby facilitating the learning process.
- Allow advanced students to learn to use this technology in the preparation of questionnaires, sampling, interviewing, and data analysis.

CONCLUSIONS

Marist has the network infrastructure in place. The students, faculty, and staff are becoming more aware of its potential for teaching and learning. The applications to exploit this technology are beginning to appear. There is no question that it will change the way we at Marist go about our work. It is opening new opportunities both on the campus and in our community.

NOTE

1. Phonemail is a registered trademark of the ROLM Corporation.

Networking at the University of Richmond

Tom White
Data Communications Technician
University of Richmond

BACKGROUND

The University of Richmond is a small, private institution located in Richmond, Virginia. The university is comprised of 3,500 full-time students and 1,500 additional evening and part-time students. It's schools include T. C. Williams School of Law, the E. Clayborn Robins School of Business, and several other important schools of study. The Jepson School of Leadership Studies will open in the fall of 1992. The Jepson building will also house our Academic Computing Department.

Networking at the University of Richmond got its start in the mid-1980s with the addition of an AT&T Information Systems Network (ISN) packet switch. The ISN has been used as an asynchronous switch to connect dumb terminals and personal computers emulating dumb terminals to host systems. A main node was installed in the campus telephone room at Richmond Hall. Copper wire connects most campus buildings to Richmond Hall in a hub configuration. This cable is owned by the university. Fiber-optic cable connects Richmond Hall to Academic Computing, the Science Center, the Business School, and to the Administrative Computing Center, where other ISN nodes are installed. Wiring to student dorms is owned by Bell Atlantic, the local Bell Operating System, and student telephone service is provided by Bell Atlantic. Network access from the dorms is possible only by dialup modems via our modem pool, which is connected to the ISN network.

By the end of the 1980s, the need for access to our mainframe computers had grown from a few select users and student labs to a necessary tool for administrative as well as academic purposes. A connection to the Internet produced a larger need for computer connections to the network. The beginning of the 1990s saw the addition of the University of Richmond library catalog to the network. This proved to be a very desirable resource, and requests for network connections poured in. While the library system was creating a need for data connections in the academic world, the Administrative Computing Department was busy installing a new student information system that would bring many administrative departments on line. In a period of just a few weeks, the number of requested new data connections amounted to a 33% growth in our network, with many more requests predicted. Our once small network had become a necessary tool as mandatory as a telephone and with almost as many users.

THE NEED FOR A NETWORK

We were soon faced with a major dilemma. The number of requests exceeded the physical capacity of our network. Additional equipment could be added, but the copper wall field in the campus telephone room was completely filled. Most of the asynchronous connections were over copper cable from the remote buildings to the main telephone room. Not only were we out of wall field space, but we were out of copper between buildings as well. A few of the more data-intensive buildings made use of remote data nodes connected via fiber-optic cable, but these, too, were full and there was no spare fiber for additional remote nodes.

In early 1991 several individuals from academic and administrative departments spent many hours in meetings and discussions to try to solve our problem. One of the issues we faced was the relatively slow speed of the ISN network. Most of the terminals operate at 9600 bytes per second (BPS). The maximum asynchronous line speed of the ISN packet switch is 19,200BPS, however some of the older mainframes had data loss problems at this speed, so 9600BPS has been the default setting. Several departments found these speeds inadequate for their needs. The Physics Department is involved in several projects around the country and found it impossible to transfer the massive files it required at ISN speeds over the Internet. Most of these transfers had to be spooled to tape in Academic Computing and physically carried to the Science building.

Our Math and Computer Science Department found the ISN so inadequate that it had a thick coaxial cable installed to tie its computer to the Internet. This cable runs out of windows, along the outside of buildings, and finally into the steam tunnel system to Academic Computing. The Math and Computer Department had a need that we were unable to fill in the time frame it required, so it did what was necessary to accomplish its work.

Obviously, this is not the type of solution that creates a manageable and reliable network, but it shows the length to which users will go if we do not provide for their needs. Since the Math and Computer Science Department, along with Academic Computing, will be moving to a new building in 1992, this is a temporary "patch" and will not adversely impact network integrity in the long run.

These problems were considered in the meetings, and it was very obvious that the ISN was not the best solution. The common denominator of most of the mainframes is TCP/IP, so an Ethernet backbone was considered the best alternative at this time. We don't have the high bandwidth requirements necessary for CAD/CAM applications, nor are we involved with video images, so Fiber Distributed Data Interface (FDDI) is beyond our present data needs. Representatives from Administrative Computing, Academic Computing, Math and Computer Science, Physics, Chemistry, University Services, and others agreed that a 10 megabit Ethernet was the way we should expand the network.

The ISN will continue to be adequate for much of our needs for many years. Many users require only e-mail and minimal file transfer activities, so ISN is a reasonable choice. Our decision was to install the Ethernet backbone and migrate the "power users" to the backbone; their ISN connections could be "recycled" to other users and possibly to student dormitories. Targeted ISN users also include users in buildings that are not yet connected to the backbone by fiber.

IMPLEMENTATION AND INSTALLATION

The next step in the process was to determine a network design and approximate costs involved in implementing our Ethernet network and submit the plan to the Vice Presidents for consideration. We had already decided that fiber was the desired medium for the backbone. The new Jepson Center was to get a remote voice node connected by fiber, so this much of the fiber needed was already budgeted as part of the construction. Copper to the Law School was fully utilized, and additional connections were required for both voice and data. Our main wiring field in Richmond Hall could not support additional copper connects, and the new remote node in Jepson Hall would have more than enough capacity to handle both buildings. Since the Law School and Jepson Hall are very near each other, I decided to include a copper run between the two buildings in the proposal. This will eventually allow the remote Jepson voice node to handle the Law School as well as Jepson, and will relieve an already overburdened wall field in Richmond Hall.

In addition to construction of the Jepson Center, a massive addition to the Law School was underway. Five hundred and fifty carrels were being installed in the new addition as an "office" for our law students. There are no plans for voice connections to the carrels, but network connections are planned for the future, so I added the Law School to the target areas for fiber installation. Our short-term requirements demanded that as many users as possible be moved off of the ISN and onto the Ethernet backbone to make room for many new "dumb" terminal connections required by the new Student Information System. By running a fiber connection to Maryland Hall, our administrative building, one of the two terminal servers in use in Administrative Computing, could be moved into Maryland Hall and 40 users could be removed from the ISN and placed on the terminal server (which users had previously accessed via the ISN, thus eliminating two hardware connects, one at the user end and the other in Administrative Computing—a net gain of 80 ISN connects). Several other buildings were targeted for initial installation based on terminals presently in use and accessibility to the steam tunnel system. Buildings not on the steam tunnel system may be added to the network at a later date, but were not included in this phase because of the expense of burying cable across campus.

After the locations were defined, the number of fibers needed at each site was determined. We added at least 24 fibers to each building, but only connected the number of fibers needed for the initial install plus two for growth and two as spares. With all the details worked out as far as where the fiber was to be installed, I next did an inventory of space available in the existing light guide connector boxes. A Request for Proposal was drafted and sent to several contractors.

I contacted several router and bridge manufacturing companies and requested information on their products and pricing information as well. I reviewed several articles and test result sheets on most of the major suppliers of networking equipment. Cisco and Wellfleet received top marks in my research, with Cisco a bit ahead for our needs and future projected growth path. I selected Cabletron to supply the bridges based on recommendations, published test results, and the fact that our Cisco sales team has a good working relationship with Cabletron (in our area).

There were still some concerns in our Administrative Computing Department, mostly security issues. We held one "open" meeting with Cisco and invited those involved with the network. This meeting had two purposes: first, to educate the users, most of whom had very little exposure to networking; and second, to include these key persons in the vendor selection process. No objections were voiced to the vendors I selected, so over the next few months, the network topology began to take shape on paper.

THE FINAL OUTCOME

Once we decided exactly what we needed to make the network a reality, we began to tally up the costs and put together a proposal to take to our Vice Presidents. These people are wizards of high finance and business, especially the business of operating a university. However, networking was a new and unfamiliar area to them. They spent the next few months asking questions and learning, in detail, every part of the proposal. We spent many hours preparing flip charts with diagrams and analogies of the network. Approval of this proposal also involved (and still involves) a bit of a change in philosophy: In the past, people were connected to the network on a need basis only, with small pockets of users scattered all over campus. With the new online Student Information System, the online Library catalog, Internet, Bitnet, Campus Calendars, registration, and more, almost everyone—students, faculty, and staff—will have a need to be on the network. If we are going to accommodate this need, a new network is required.

The network was approved during the summer of 1991. The installation is in progress and is a vast improvement for those already connected. A lot of people spent many hours planning this network. One aspect of this network that we can all feel good about will be the ease of expanding for future growth. The fiber in place now can be reconfigured for FDDI in the event we need the extra bandwidth. We can also run parallel fibers on heavy segments if needed. Our goal was to design a network that would serve our needs for decades to come, and I believe we have met that goal.

IGNET: Piecing Together the Future*

Jerome P. DeSanto
Assistant Provost for Information Technology
University of Scranton

OVERVIEW

The rapidly developing comprehensive telecommunications network at the University of Scranton in northeastern Pennsylvania has been years in the making. The name IGNET, in honor of St. Ignatius, founder of the Society of Jesus, is particularly appropriate for the network in that this Jesuit institution's celebration of the 500th anniversary of the birth of the saint marks the beginning of an entirely new way of communicating and resource sharing on the campus. Interest in the project incubated among various constituencies for a decade; however, it was not until January 1986 that serious planning got underway and January 1989 that a simultaneous groundswell of support and government funding came together to make the project a reality.

Early Planning

The earliest serious planning began during the spring of 1986 with a survey that sought input from the university community on the perceived value of a comprehensive telecommunications network for the campus. To avoid reinventing the wheel, the Integrated Information Systems Planning Committee contacted the CAUSE national office for names of schools involved in such surveys. CAUSE advised contacting Harvard University, which generously provided us with copies of their survey document. Modified to meet the university's specific requirements, the survey was distributed to faculty, administration, and students. The rate of return was about 50%, and the results were predictable. Most respondents could not fully appreciate the functionality and value of a network and, though generally satisfied with then current levels of telecommunications services, were not elated. Given

*Contributors to this chapter include: Editor, Margaret E. Craft, Assistant Director for Special Services, Library; "Overview" and "Voice Services" sections were written by Jerome P. DeSanto, Assistant Provost for Information Technology; "Data Services" was written by Ronald J. Skutnick, Assistant Director, Technical Services, University Computing Systems, and Charles E. Chulvick, Director, University Computing Services; "Video Services" was written by Larry J. Hickemell, Head, Media Services, Media Resources Center.

the university's other needs, the idea of a communications network was relegated to a back burner.

Substantive discussions with IBM in 1989 led to the formation of a task force to work on an Applications Transfer Study (ATS). Its purpose was to evaluate the current state of information technology resources on campus, assess current and projected needs of the campus community, and develop a series of recommendations aimed at planning the university's information technology needs into the future. These recommendations could then be incorporated into the strategic plan of the university. The final report underscored definitively the need for a comprehensive telecommunications network. The ATS report was presented to top-level administrators including the President and the Provost, and the seeds were planted.

Almost immediately following the report, a Network Planning Committee (NPC) was formed to develop a long-term telecommunications plan for the university. The group was composed of representatives from almost every constituency on campus. Armed with the results of the 1986 survey and bolstered by the emphasis on networking in the ATS study, the group had an agenda. Additional impetus came in the allocation of almost $200,000 in funds from a federal grant to establish a Technology Center at the university.

A major portion of the funding was earmarked for data projects discussed in detail below. The remainder, $50,000, was used to hire a consulting firm to assist the Network Planning Committee (NPC) in the development of a master plan. Despite some objection, the committee decided it was essential to develop a network blueprint under the guidance of Robbins Communications (now JPW Information Systems) prior to expending funds on network implementation. In retrospect, a more advantageous or timely decision could not have been made.

The Robbins Study

The value of the Robbins study lay not in recommended design standards, its assessment of prevailing attitudes or requirements on campus, or even in itemized cost estimates, although those were helpful. The study forced the NPC to look seriously and in depth at the campus in an organized and methodological way. Ken Reilly and Tom Goznell conducted the study for Robbins. While the approach, analysis, and intermediate recommendations were less than perfect, the process was educational and enlightening, clarified some puzzling issues, and confirmed NPC positions on other issues. Everything related to our design and future service offerings was critically examined.

The final report was presented to the Network Planning Committee in November 1990. Generally well received, it recommended that:

1. The university should establish a standard network architecture based on Ethernet.
2. A fiber-based backbone should be installed with future migration to FDDI possible.
3. A single vendor for Ethernet wire concentrators should be selected. (The original equipment used on campus was from Synoptics)
4. A hub-star wiring topology should be used in the backbone.
5. A composite fiber cable consisting of both single- and multimode fiber should be installed.
6. New station wiring with two separately sheathed 4-pair cables conforming to new 10Base-T standards should be used.
7. The private branch exchange (PBX) versus Centrex issue should be fully studied and a long term plan developed.
8. A voice mail/processing system should be installed as part of the overall campus plan.

The grand total cost estimated in the report was $2.2 million. This included a fiber-based interbuilding video system with no provision for station video cabling. After further analysis, the Network Working Group decided to delete the fiber-based video portion of the project and to substitute, instead, the lower cost, proven standard of broadband coaxial cable linking buildings and RG-6 coaxial cable for station purposes. Head-end and amplifier electronics for the broadband system were also considerably cheaper than their fiber counterparts. Therefore, the video plan was revised to include a total systems approach for less cost than the suggested limited fiber approach. Single-mode fiber remained in the backbone for future fiber-based video application.

Funding for the Project

The ink on the final Robbins report was barely dry when we learned the university's McDade Technology Center had received a second federal grant. Within days, $2 million was allocated for the campus network project, moving the project directly from drawing board to implementation.

Administrative expectations are that from the $2 million all that was outlined in the Robbins report will be accomplished. In all reality, the financial sections of the Robbins report merely provide the framework within which to operate. Before further work began on the development of a Request for Bid document, budget allocations were established (see Table 1). Institutional budgets will vary, obviously, depending on the scope of individual projects, numbers, and geographic distribution of the buildings to be networked, the state of an underground conduit system, for example.

Table 1: IGNET Budget

CATEGORY	TOTAL BUDGET	% OF TOTAL
Cabling	$800,000	40.00%
Conduit Installation	$250,000	12.50%
Electrical/Drop ceilings	$75,000	3.75%
Data Electronics	$200,000	10.00%
Closet Electronics and Racks	$100,000	5.00%
Ethernet Adapters Software	$150,000	7.50%
Video Electronics	$100,000	5.00%
Network Management Systems and Tools	$ 100,000	5.00%
Project Management and Consulting	$ 100,000	5.00%
Misc. Adm. and Contingency	$125,000	6.25%
Total	$2,000,000	100.00%

The Request for Bids

The final Robbins report was an excellent starting point for the creation of a bid document, but much work remained to fully complete the bid specifications (specs). After consultation with the various committees and a formal review process, the Network Working Group decided to hire Dr. Buddy Bruner of George Kaludis Associates, a higher education consulting firm, to assist in preparing the bid document. The issue of the level of detail to be included in the bid specifications required several days of mental wrestling. After much discussion, we determined it would be in our best interests to include as much detail as possible. Only in this way could we be assured that we would receive accurate pricing and acceptable alternatives. The downside of that decision was the amount of work involved in gathering and assembling all the necessary information. Once gathered, the information went to

Dr. Bruner for assembly into the document. Four months and many revisions later, the document was sent to the University Print Shop for final printing.

The Working Group decided to take a somewhat unique approach to providing a Request for Bid (RFB). In addition to preparing the standard written document, a videotape was produced to provide bidders with a visual overview and walk-through of the campus. The video included various buildings in the spec, Main Distribution Frame (MDF) and Intermediate Distribution Frame (IDF) closet locations, typical classroom, office, and conference room layouts, and beautiful aerial views of the campus. The aerial views were made possible by contracting with the local ABC affiliate, WNEP-TV, to shoot video from their news helicopter, SKYCAM 16. Though viewed by some as a luxury, the results were more than satisfying. Portions of the video footage have since been incorporated into university promotional materials, further justifying the $2,000 expenditure and signifying cooperation among the various units of the University.

Potential bidders were identified over the several months the RFB was in preparation. The list included over 50 vendors who had expressed interest in the project and several other firms recommended by our consultant. The solicitation letter sent in early July 1991 resulted in about 25 potential bidders purchasing the bid package for $75 (we learned that charging for a bid package is common). The $75 price did not even come close to covering out-of-pocket costs for developing the RFB, especially considering the amount of time expended by our personnel.

The next step in the process was a two-day pre-bid conference and campus tour held in late July. A physically draining briefing and tour were attended by over 50 representatives from 20 companies. Numerous questions, some requiring extensive research, resulted. These were answered in writing and forwarded to all attendees. Periodic contacts from serious bidders became commonplace between the pre-bid conference and the final bid due date. No bidder was provided with information that might give him an unfair advantage.

The due date of the final bid was extended ten days by request of many of the most serious bidders. Most of the nine final bids were delivered on that final due date, along with a required bid bond or cashier's check to guarantee the bid price. A few of these got lost in transit. To this day we are looking for one bidder's check which was last tracked to the University Catering Service. Another vendor sent two $20,000 checks from two different corporate locations!

The first phase of bid evaluation resulted in the elimination of five of nine bids for noncompliance with bid specifications. We sought a single-vendor solution, and several bidders provided only partial solutions. The remaining four responses were ranked in descending cost order. The top three bids based on cost (varying by less than $200,000) were selected for closer analysis. The process lasted another 30 days and included a page-by-page review of the responses (each several hundred pages long), reference checks, an on-campus electronics test and evaluation in one case, and a series of negotiated price reductions based on modifications to our original bid specifications. As may be suspected, all bids were over budget, and the Working Group was forced to make adjustments, scaling back a "Cadillac" approach to a functional, more affordable "Chevrolet."

Bell of Pennsylvania offered the university the best overall package and was awarded the contract. Unfortunately, the bid process was contested by the second place vendor who articulated his objections through a formal protest. The protest was reviewed in full by a university-assembled review board and found to be without merit. The third-place vendor submitted an informal letter of protest to express his disappointment. The conclusion was that the current economic climate made for a heated, competitive process and protests could result. Caution should be exercised during the bid process. Do not commit or imply a commitment to any vendor or product before the bid is awarded. Sign no memos, acknowledgements, or letters of intent that can be misconstrued or misinterpreted at a later date. Finally, do not trust any vendor's verbal exchanges. Get everything in writing; it takes more time and effort, but it is worth it.

Telecommunications Management System

The Angeles Group Telecommunications Management System (TMS) was chosen as the cable management system after a thorough search, which included attendance at the September 1991 ACUTA conference in Denver. The system was chosen for its impressive overall package including cable management to be used during network construction, the work order management component, and statistics. The CAD module providing for an AutoCAD interface is a benefit. The intent is to feed resulting construction as-built AutoCAD drawings into the TMS system. The Student Billing and Accounts Receivable portions of this package and that of other systems examined have some distance to travel toward perfection, but will be adequate to start. Substantial enhancements will be needed in the future.

Network Services Planning

As network engineering design and construction issues were being comprehensively considered, we also acknowledged that planning for network services was critical. Obviously, services could not be provided without the network infrastructure in place. Once the conduits, cabling, and electronics were in place, new services would be expected. The Network Planning

Committee was too large and unfocused as a group to deal with service issues. In addition, it was lacking in representation from the Student Affairs area. Since most new services would directly impact students, Student Affairs involvement and leadership was a must. A Network Services Committee chaired by the Vice President for Student Affairs was the result. Membership on the committee now includes students and personnel from Student Affairs as well as representatives from the voice, data, and video areas. This group has overseen development of the plans for services to be offered initially by IGNET and will be instrumental in charting the direction of future services. Student participation has been invaluable from its end-user point of view.

Organization Structure

The administrative and organizational structure of the Information Technology division is also in evolution. The advent of the campus network has resulted in a greater definition of areas on responsibility. Coincidental to the commencement of the network project, a new upper level position, that of Assistant Provost for Information Technology, was established. The Assistant Provost functions as the Chief Information Officer (CIO) of the university and is responsible for administrative and academic computing, IGNET, and the effective integration of information technology throughout the entire campus. Network responsibility includes control and management of telephone services previously under the charge of the Vice President for Administrative Services (Physical Plant). A new unit, Network Services, has been established to implement the campus network and to begin providing network services. Relationships between Network Services, University Computing Systems (responsible for all computing), the Media Resources Center (a division of the Library responsible for video services), the Library, and other departments providing network or technology-related services are evolving as Information Technology carves out a strategic place in the university.

VOICE SERVICES

Arguably, the most exciting services to be provided through the network project are in the voice area. A cash flow analysis prepared by our consultants at George Kaludis Associates proved that the Bell of Pennsylvania Centrex telephone system used by the university for the past decade was the most cost-effective vehicle for providing voice services on campus. The study's conclusions were based on numerous financial and logistical factors, with the overriding factor focusing on costs associated with local calling. The university's current Centrex contract contains a grandfathering provision guaranteeing free local calling for anyone on the university's system. This privilege would disappear if the university were to move from Centrex toward a PBX and would result in a substantial increase in telephone charges for the university community. Therefore, current Centrex service will be extended to resident students beginning in February 1992. Because of the nature of Centrex, the university will also be able to extend the service to students living in private housing in surrounding neighborhoods in Scranton.

Student telephone service on campus will be a new experience for all and a dramatic improvement in communication. Telephone services will be part of the network package provided to all university-owned residences. Student telephone service will be as follows: one telephone per student room (over 90% of on-campus student rooms are doubles). Students will furnish their own telephone instruments, and each resident student will be charged for basic services including dial-tone and voice-mail with the fee incorporated into basic room charges.

Coupled with regular dial-tone service will be a package of services consisting of unlimited local calling and Centrex features such as call waiting, call forwarding, distinctive ringing, four-digit on-campus dialing, and other benefits available usually only as extra cost options with regular residential service. A new long distance arrangement with a major carrier for the entire campus is being finalized, driving down long distance costs for faculty and staff and providing students opting for university long distance service with discounts over regular residential or calling card rates. The current university AT&T provided Pro-WATS plan will be replaced by a special campus plan based on T-1 circuits. For the present (December 1991) we have decided to start with one T-1 line and have the option of adding an additional T-1 line in about six months as we make full service operational in all student residences. There is concern about running out of channels on the T-1s during particularly busy periods. The intent is to provide overflow long distance service using more costly traditional circuits rather than delaying any calls during particularly busy periods.

Ron Galik, Director of Telecommunications at Keene State College (New Hampshire), wrote a very useful report. His report *Keene State College and the Telephone Operator Consumer Services Improvement Act of 1990* explains the impact of the Consumer Services Act on colleges and traces the steps followed in selecting a long distance vendor. The rating matrix grading each major vendor on services and specific features was most useful, especially for the listing of services one should inquire about before making a vendor selection. Securing a copy of this 1990 report is highly recommended.

Voice mail is a most desirable component in campus voice service for the university community. Storage and retrieval of individual voice messages is appealing to students, and voice processing applications for the university are intriguing as well. Our present Central Office-based telephone operation lacks personnel, resources, and space; consequently, we are exploring CO-based voice solutions. Such a solution may be costly in the long term, but easy implementation without substantial capital investment for a premises-based solution is attractive in the short term. The ability to partition mailboxes makes financial sense in examining the CO-based solutions that generally have certain costs associated with individual mailboxes. Voice mail works best in an environment where each user has an individual telephone line. Student residences present a straightforward, easily implemented environment for voice mail, but in the university's environment with numerous departments sharing lines in key and nonkey environments, voice mail engineering is complicated. A customized approach to installation of voice mail and voice mail processing systems in university departments is essential to its success.

The university seriously considered using a student billing service to collect student long distance bills, but decided it would be more advantageous financially to handle the task in house. There are increased risks in assuming this task. To establish a credit limit and provide a measure of security, all students seeking the university's long distance service will be required to sign a contract and provide a $100 security deposit. Appropriate university sanctions on students who fail to pay long distance bills are being considered. For additional security, each student will be provided with a confidential Forced Authorization Code (FAC) which must be entered before placing a long distance call. Arrangements for making the student's FAC code and voice-mailbox code identical are being discussed.

Because heavily used pay telephones in corridors are the primary means of student communication, the university's 150 pay telephones are a significant source of revenue. About $50,000 per year is realized in commissions. A projected 60% decrease is projected with the advent of student telephone services. Lost revenue is a consideration in a cash flow analysis or feasibility study of student telephone services. No doubt a re-deployment or reduction of pay telephones on campus will take place.

DATA SERVICES

Historically, the University of Scranton has maintained three separate computer systems and cable plants specific to each system over the past ten years. Administrative and academic systems were located in the Computer Center at St. Thomas Hall, with limited access to terminals and printers. A GEAC computer system housed in the library is used for library administrative services and online catalog services. Services provided on the library computer system were available only from within the library building, the Media Resources Center (Gallery Building), and by modem.

Multiconductor copper cable provided asynchronous communication supporting a handful of nearby buildings with terminals attached to a DEC

VAX 11/780 used for academic computing. An IBM 4300 system was used for administrative computing, leading to the creation of an extensive network of coaxial cable within St. Thomas Hall. Remote buildings were provided IBM 4300 access via local distance leased lines supporting remote IBM 3270 control units. Coaxial cable also found its way into many of those remote buildings.

In regard to data communication protocols, the university's academic VAX system supported terminals and printers via asynchronous ports only. A small Ethernet was later established in the computer room to support terminals and printers via LAT services on DECserver 100 terminal servers. Communication on the administrative IBM 4300 system was provided by IBM's binary synchronous communication protocol (non-SNA). Remote buildings were limited to data communication speeds of 9600 baud or less depending on location and available options. Communication services were augmented by the use of modems over standard telephone lines at both 1200 and 2400 baud transmission rates.

Numerous microcomputer laboratories for student use are located throughout the campus. Most are configured as local area networks (LANs) to facilitate maintenance and support. With the exception of a few PCs equipped with modems, no host (IBM/VAX/GEAC) connectivity was provided. As the number of terminals and printers grew, a nightmare of entangled cable plants with no clear standard in place was created. Ethernet's growing popularity and its role in our academic computing environment convinced us that this was a clear path to follow. This path led eventually to some of the initial design concepts included in Phase One of our campus networking project.

Objectives

The overall objective of the project was to plan and install a high-speed campus network to connect current computing resources and to allow for the connection of new technology into the twenty-first century. Moreover, it was equally important to encourage the use of the network within the university for communication, and efficient dissemination of information and to achieve some economic benefits while encouraging the acquisition of suitable computing resources and providing adequate training and support for network users.

To meet these objectives, the planning and implementation strategy not only took into account the requirements of certain users but also tried to anticipate future demands. The need to integrate our current resources as well as those of separate user communities remains a major short-term goal.

It was also of primary concern to recognize that the design and installation of a data network not be tailored exclusively for the needs of the computer programmer or high technology application user. The network is viewed as a mechanism for accessing and disseminating information (e.g., office automation and campus information services) by nontechnical personnel. This objective goes beyond the cabling infrastructure to address the need for adequate provision of terminals, computers, and workstations and the development of network services to insure access for students, faculty, and staff.

Standards

Topology. The overall design topology selected for the implementation of data communication is a physical star (see Figure 1). The primary campus hub (center of star) is located in St. Thomas Hall due to the location of the Computing Center and its natural location near the center of campus. Four outlying buildings are connected to the primary campus hub at St. Thomas Hall and serve as secondary campus hubs providing data communication to surrounding buildings. All cables that provide communication between hubs are enclosed in an underground conduit system. The overall network topology provides an extremely flexible system design that facilitates unrepeated traffic from the primary campus hub through the secondary campus hubs to designated building main distribution facilities.

Cabling. As the use of twisted pair copper cable matured and the 10BaseT Ethernet standard emerged, the university quickly adopted this standard for its intrabuilding cable plant. After much study and investigation, it was decided that four pair level 4 unshielded twisted pair copper be used for all data communications on campus. This decision provides topology options, including Ethernet and token-ring. Four pair level 2 unshielded twisted pair copper cable is the choice in support of voice communications on campus. Each cable is to be sheathed separately to provide greater options for both data and voice communications as these technologies advance.

Both twisted pair cables and a separate coaxial cable to support video distribution within buildings are to be terminated in a single common wall outlet. The Network Engineering Group decided to utilize the AT&T 258A cable pair sequence specification in regard to copper termination for data. Wall outlets are configured with an eight-conductor RJ-45 modular jack to support data connections. The network wall outlets selected for use on our network are MOD-TAP Universal System Outlets. Main distribution facilities in each building will be outfitted with matching 258A cabled modular patch panels to complete the termination of copper supporting data communications. This configuration will provide us with eight conductors of copper terminated straight through to support 10BaseT and other asynchronous equipment.

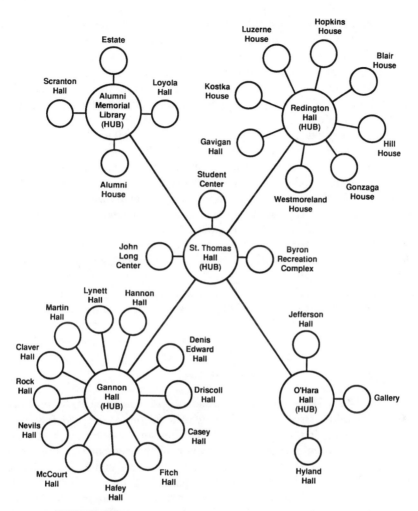

Figure 1. *IGNET Topology.*

A six-conductor RJ-11 modular jack is used to terminate twisted pair cable in support of voice communication. Standard 66 block termination gear is utilized to complete the voice cable termination at the main distribution facilities in each building. The USOC cable pair sequence is implemented to support voice communication on campus. This configuration also provided us flexibility in support of numerous telephone set configurations on campus. If needed, voice copper could be reconfigured to support two separate phone lines in a single wall outlet to expand services without pulling additional copper.

Fiber-optic cable was the obvious choice for interbuilding cable. A relatively small campus environment allows use of multimode fiber-optic cable to support current and future data communications. Dark single-mode fiber-optic cable is to be installed to support future video and/or high-speed data applications. Much study and research led us to specify the use of Siecor fiber-optic cable and components on campus based on performance characteristics and reliability.

Our multimode fiber-optic cable specifications call for a 62.5 micron fiber size enclosed in a loose tube filled with a buffer compound (gel) to protect the interior from moisture due to its use in various underground facilities. Single-mode fiber-optic cable specs call for an 8.3 micron fiber size similarly enclosed. Both single- and multimode fiber-optic cable tubes are to be contained in a single composite cable. ST compatible connectors are specified for all fiber terminations for their low optical loss, low cost, and ease of use.

In regard to fiber strand counts, final decisions called for twelve multimode and six single-mode fibers to be installed between each communication hub and its surrounding buildings serviced by that hub. Hub to hub fiber counts called for installation of 18 multimode and 6 single-mode fibers. The fiber counts for the backbone and other runs were developed to allow implementation of any logical system topology and provide moderate system growth capacity without excessive cost. These counts were the result of several studies conducted by JWP Information Systems, Siecor Corporation engineering services, and GKA Associates.

Protocols. The selection of a standard data communications protocol was a very serious issue at the University of Scranton. At the time, few standards were tightly in place, but several were emerging. Our goal was to select a standard for open system interconnection in the computer industry and achieve the highest degree of interoperability. Choices considered included DECnet, TCP/IP, OSI, and Fiber Distributed Data Interface (FDDI). Although DECnet has a large user base, it was considered proprietary. TCP/IP also has a large user base and is quickly emerging as a promising standard. OSI is considered in its infancy with proven implementation in the distant future. FDDI, owing to its high speeds and bandwidth, is not required at the desktop level but will probably play a future role in the campus backbone.

Since the University of Scranton had endorsed the use of Ethernet on campus and also had a large investment in Digital Equipment Corporation's VAX processors running VMS, the use of the DECnet protocol was a natural. The IBM communication protocol in use at the time on the 4300 system was their binary synchronous communication (BSC) protocol which will stay in place over the existing coax network. Our use of Novell Netware for local area networks also dictated our support of the IPX protocol. An influx of

UNIX-based workstations on campus introduced us to the TCP/IP protocol suite. With all these environments considered, the university sought a common data communications protocol that would provide remote log-in, electronic mail, and file transfer.

Observing the growth of the Internet and studying protocols used at other colleges, the university quickly became very interested in the TCP/IP protocol suite. The success of the TCP/IP technology and the Internet among computer science researchers led the University of Scranton to adopt the protocol suite as its standard data communication protocol. At the time, an implementation of the TCP/IP protocol seemed to be available for every computing platform and operating system that we supported. This certainly was not true of any one of the communication protocols used on campus at that time. Although the TCP/IP protocol suite was viewed to be in a process of evolution, it certainly appeared to provide the common ground we sought to bring together our diverse computer resources.

Electronics. Following strong recommendations by JWP Information Systems during our network study, the university sought to select a standard vendor to provide intelligent wiring centers. A very extensive process of vendor presentations and technical analysis resulted. The vendors considered, among others, included Synoptics, Cabletron, and David Systems Incorporated. The university also desired to implement IP routers in strategic locations to isolate network traffic and provide an added layer of security considering a mixed population of students and administrators. The vendors considered included Wellfleet, Cisco Systems, and Proteon.

Evaluation criteria used in the selection process included price, performance, reliability, features, network management, diagnostic capabilities, and maintenance. As an organization grows and more users need to be networked, the intelligent wiring center obviously needs to have the flexibility to grow with the organization. Of specific interest to the university was vendor compliance to standards including Ethernet, token-ring, FDDI, and Simple Network Management Protocol (SNMP) network management. Other evaluation issues dealt with types of copper and fiber connectors available on various equipment, single and multiple backplane support, asynchronous support, hot swap capabilities, and installation options.

Since the entire evaluation process is too lengthy to be included here, a summary of our conclusions follows. Our choice for a standard intelligent wiring center vendor on campus was David Systems Incorporated. This selection will implement the ExpressNet and ExpressBus product line of concentrators and hubs throughout the campus. All concentrators and hubs will be configured with RJ-45 data jacks and SNMP network management support. FOIRL modules and MAUs (medium attachment units) will provide direct connectivity to the fiber-optic cable plant. The ExpressView network management software was also selected to provide single-point management via a graphical user interface.

David Systems products were selected primarily because of price, performance, and robust features. The university determined that David Systems as a vendor offered a full range of network components, allowing us to implement, manage, and maintain our network with a comfortable level of ease. Cisco Systems IP routers were selected for implementation into the overall network design, also because of price, performance, features, and installed base of equipment throughout educational environments.

Asynchronous Support. In order to provide support for a large number of RS-232 asynchronous devices such as terminals, personal computers, and peripheral devices, we decided to implement TCP/IP terminal servers in each building. Terminal servers streamline multiple-host access by making it possible to log in to every computer resource on the network from one terminal. Terminal servers have also been implemented to frontend hosts that cannot otherwise be directly connected to the network, either because they do not support TCP/IP or because they lack an Ethernet interface. A vendor's terminal server offering for standard use on our network has not been selected. We are currently utilizing terminal servers from Datability and TRW and plan to further investigate offerings from 3-Com Corporation.

Standard Naming Services. In order to build the campus Internet and provide ease in the identification of computer resources and future e-mail services, University Computing Systems decided to implement the Domain Name System standard. After registration with the Network Information Center (NIC) for Internet access with the top-level domain uofs.edu, unique abbreviated subordinate domain names were further assigned to each department. At the machine level, each department within the university selected a name category and used that category to name individual machines. For example, our academic VAX 6320 located within University Computing Systems is jaguar.ucs.uofs.edu. While each computing resource on the network has a unique IP address associated with it, a name is much easier to remember than an address. To provide IP address resolution services on the network, local Domain Name Servers (one primary and one secondary) were implemented on separate computer resources available on the network. These name server functions are critical to most network services, including remote log in, file transfer, and future electronic mail services.

Implementation

Early Stage. In order to get our feet wet with all this new technology, NIC decided to build a prototype, the St. Thomas Test Network. At the time, use of unshielded twisted pair cable and the 10BaseT Ethernet specification were not available as a standard. The test was comprised of the installation of an Ethernet thick wire backbone cable throughout the entire first floor of St. Thomas Hall and the first and second floor of the Harper McGinnis Wing, an addition to St. Thomas Hall. Several thin wire Ethernet segments were then installed within the Computer Science, Physics, and Computing Systems departments. All thin wire segments were connected to the thick wire backbone via Cabletron multiport repeaters.

The first connection to this network was the VAX 6320 academic system allowing the movement of DECserver terminal servers out of the computer room and into equipment closets supporting two terminal labs via DECnet and Local Area Transport (LAT) protocols. Experimentation with TCP/IP began with the installation of the Wollongong WIN/TCP software package on the VMS-based VAX 6320, providing remote log in (Telnet) and file transfer (FTP) services on that specific computing platform.

In order to provide client TCP/IP services to personal computers within the Computer Center and the Computer Science department, 3-Com Ethernet adapters in all machines were installed first and connected to the thin wire segments. The public domain version of NCSA Telnet and FTP to provide TCP/IP client applications for the DOS-based personal computers connected to the test network were tested. A formal evaluation of TCP/IP software offerings for both DOS and Apple computing platforms began later. In the meantime, the NCSA implementations provided successful services to the VAX 6320 via the TCP/IP communication protocol.

Connections to several pieces of equipment within the Physics Department, which included DOS-based personal computers and a Sun MicroSystems workstation, were added. NCSA Telnet was also used to provide TCP/IP applications to those machines. Since the Physics Sun workstation was running UNIX, it inherently provided client and server TCP/IP applications to users of that system. The final connection to the test network was a DEC MicroVAX II processor running VMS. This system offered only DECnet services on the test network and was used predominantly by Computer Science via a small cluster of locally attached DEC terminals.

During construction of a three-story addition to St. Thomas Hall to house the university's Technology Center, Small Business Development Center, Computer Science, and the Physics/Electrical Engineering Department, the test network was expanded. With structured cabling systems emerging, UCS decided to wire the entire addition with two four-pair shielded twisted pair cables for voice and data along with coaxial cable to support video transmission. With the 10BaseT Ethernet standard still not in place, UCS chose to implement data services via Synoptics 1000 LattisNet wiring centers. Each of the three floors in the addition was configured with an IDF terminating all cables to each floor. The IDFs were connected to the St. Thomas test network via an extension of the thick wire Ethernet backbone. Desktop connections were also implemented via Ethernet adapters and the public domain NCSA Telnet TCP/IP package.

PREPnet. In order to extend data services on the St. Thomas Test Network and provide access to the Internet, the university became a charter member of the PREPnet consortium. This involved the connection of a 56KB data circuit from the local Bell of Pennsylvania switching office (PREPnet hub site) to our data center in St. Thomas Hall. Applications were processed to register the university with the Internet and obtain a block of IP address space. Connection to the network was accomplished via the installation of a Proteon router connected to the thick wire Ethernet backbone. Since our academic VAX system and many personal computers on the test network already had TCP/IP implementations, services to PREPnet and the Internet were quickly available. This proved to be an invaluable addition of data services to our test network users. Users within Computing Systems (formerly the Computer Center), Computer Science, the Technology Center, and Physics quickly began to explore and exploit the wealth of services available via the Internet. This later proved to be an excellent learning opportunity for information support staff within Computing Systems in providing end-user support of both TCP/IP-based networking and Internet services.

Standard TCP/IP Implementations. Because of numerous technical difficulties and support problems, our VMS-based Wollongong TCP/IP package was later replaced with TGV MultiNet and the TGV NFS Server for VMS. This replacement was based on recommendations from other educational institutions sharing information via a BITNET listserver special interest group. The TGV implementation of MultiNet was found to be much more stable and robust in its offerings of TCP/IP services for VMS. A decision to convert our administrative computing efforts from an IBM 4300 environment to a DEC based VMS 6510 system required another installation of TGV MultiNet to provide TCP/IP services for administrators.

Since we had decided to implement data services to our new administrative system via the TCP/IP protocol suite, an extensive evaluation of TCP/IP implementations for DOS and Apple personal computing platforms began. This process was necessary because of the problems with numerous versions of NCSA Telnet on campus and requirements to provide VT220 terminal emulation support. We also desired to offer NFS client support to all desktop computing platforms on campus. The packages we evaluated for DOS platforms included NCSA Telnet, the University of Maryland's MD-DOS/IP package, Sun MicroSystems PC-NFS, and FTP Software's PC/TCP Plus. FTP Software's PC/TCP Plus was selected as the standard TCP/IP offering for DOS-based computing platforms. We also implemented the public domain Clarkson University packet drivers to provide support for multiple protocol stacks such as Novell NetWare's IPX and TCP/IP. PC/TCP Plus was site licensed and made available to network users via Computing Systems Information Support Services staff within Computing Systems who offered standard installation, documentation, training and support services.

For Apple computing platforms, we also began offering TCP/IP client services via the public domain NCSA Telnet package. Desiring to maintain VT220 and NFS client support, we further evaluated Intercon Systems' TCP Connect II, and Apple's MacTCP. Evaluation results led us to select Intercon Systems' TCP Connect II as the standard TCP/IP offering for Apple-based computing platforms.

Phase One. Since our test network within St. Thomas Hall proved successful and numerous standards had been implemented, we began to expand network data services to several nearby buildings. JWP Information Services was contracted to expand our fiber-optic and broadband video backbone and implement 10BaseT Ethernet connectivity in one building. Nearby buildings included in the phase were Alumni House, Gallery, the Estate, Loyola Hall, and the Alumni Memorial Library, which will later be renovated to house the university's data center after the new library is completed. The accompanying campus map presents a picture of the entire campus.

In order to extend the campus network backbone, installation of several underground conduit sections to provide hub-to-hub and hub-to-building cable paths became necessary. Excavation efforts for one of these particular runs involved a street crossing filled with various public utility services. Inclement weather and a barrage of underground surprises quickly taught us that this was no small undertaking. At a depth of more than six feet, our conduit system passed below the street crossing to make way for the installation of our cable backbone. Fiber-optic data services were first implemented between our primary campus hub at St. Thomas Hall and the Estate building which houses administrative offices, including the Provost's office and the Graduate School.

Since the Estate was originally constructed as a single-family mansion in 1870, it required extensive renovation, including installation of 12-pair unshielded twisted pair copper to every telephone wall outlet. This copper was tested for compliance to the 10BaseT Ethernet specification by JWP Information Services and found to be acceptable for use. JWP then re-terminated all copper pairs to provide network wall outlets with both voice and data jacks. All copper data pairs were then terminated in a central equipment location (MDF) on patch panels providing connection to a David Systems intelligent wiring center. Until the fiber-optic cable installation was complete, the only connections supported in the building were those used to implement a local area network running Novell NetWare in the Institutional Research Office.

After JWP Information Services completed the installation, termination, and testing of our fiber-optic cable backbone, the Estate became the first building serviced via TCP/IP protocols over fiber and marked the beginning of IGNET. The broadband video backbone cable installed during Phase One was left unterminated for future implementation. As a result of the connectivity demands of BANNER, our new VAX-based administrative system, installation of new intrabuilding cabling in the Procurement Office of Claver Hall, Scranton Hall, and Alumni House was completed next. These installations followed our newly selected standards including level 4 copper for data, level 2 copper for voice, and RG-6 coaxial cable for video. New MDF facilities were constructed in these buildings to terminate all cables and to install all electronics to support 10BaseT Ethernet, asynchronous terminals, and fiber connectivity to our network backbone.

Since the fiber-optic cable backbone did not extend to Scranton and Claver halls, connectivity was accomplished via a serial line interface protocol (SLIP) running over leased data circuits to those buildings. A Novell NetWare LAN within the School of Management located at O'Hara Hall was provided TCP/IP connectivity to the campus network over existing copper also via the SLIP protocol. PCs were configured with Ethernet adapters and public domain software to support IP routing and SLIP functions as a low-cost temporary solution for connectivity before the campus backbone was complete.

Completion of Phase One involved the installation of new intrabuilding cabling in a major section of St. Thomas Hall, the connection of several Sun MicroSystems workstation labs, and network access to our campus library system, a GEAC computer system that provides an online catalog and other library administrative services. Since implementation of the TCP/IP protocol suite was not available for that system, several asynchronous terminal ports were front-ended with a TCP/IP terminal server. This terminal server was configured with a single IP address and rotary access to asynchronous ports to allow network users to access the online catalog via Telnet services under TCP/IP.

Phase Two. Phase Two of our campus networking project involves the expansion of the fiber-optic and broadband video backbone to 29 additional buildings on campus. Three additional secondary campus hubs will be established in O'Hara Hall, Gannon Hall, and Redington Hall to service surrounding student residences and administrative buildings. All buildings included in this phase will be equipped with structured cabling systems conforming to our set standards and intelligent wiring centers housed in centralized MDF facilities. IP routers from Cisco Systems will divide the campus up into five logical subnets.

Since this phase is in its early stages, work to complete the underground conduit system on campus to provide necessary cable paths began over the summer months. One section of conduit between St. Thomas Hall and O'Hara Hall was leased from Bell of Pennsylvania because of extensive excavation efforts and funding necessary to complete the backbone. MDF and IDF locations within all buildings included in Phase Two have been finalized, and a separate project has been completed to provide surge suppression-equipped power to each of these facilities. Intrabuilding cable and the remainder of the fiber-optic backbone are expected to be complete by spring of 1992.

Services

The investment in network infrastructure is essential but to fully capitalize on such investment, there must be a comprehensive offering of data services to encourage and instruct users of the network.

Network services are predominantly geared toward communication. The network also provides users access to resources otherwise not individually available. For example, it is not feasible to assume that every department within the university will invest in a high quality postscript printer, but it is quite practical for the university to invest in one printer and allow all departments its use over the network.

Not all the following services are fully described, and not all will be available from day one. It is paramount, however, that each be made available as quickly as possible and that users be provided with proper training and support. IGNET will

1. Provide a network interface with new and existing mail facilities. A cohesive electronic mailing agent provides the university with the ability to communicate to all users and allows access to information contained in the current agents such as schedules by any user with proper authorization.
2. Provide electronic information services to all users. Current computer services available only to select users would be expanded to the general university population, removing the obstacles of locality and availability from the current situation.

3. Provide a mechanism for uploading and downloading files to and from any network machine transparently. The transfer of files is imperative in information sharing.
4. Provide appropriate access to all computing resources. A user's connection to the network would give access to all necessary computing resources of the network at the appropriate time.
5. Provide a repository of textual and graphical information such as university policy documents on a full-text database. This service objective allows documents such as the university catalog to be available electronically and also provides access to collections of periodicals and books in full-text format.
6. Provide access to outside computing resources and services. Outside resources include supercomputers, informational databases, electronic discussion groups, and electronic mail exchange.
7. Provide access for remote users.
8. Provide access and sharing of high-cost resources such as output devices. Expensive and rarely used equipment can be shared and not duplicated at departmental levels, a financial benefit to the university.
9. Provide for transparent user interface that is not machine dependent. Ideally a network is accessed from a user interface that is consistent from machine to machine. This type of interface allows a user to change equipment without being forced to learn a new set of control commands. The more transparent the operations of the network are to the user, the greater the likelihood the network will be used.
10. Provide for graphics and image file transfers. Traditionally, graphics and image files have been too substantial to be easily transferred. The network, through the standards adopted, should allow for movement of files without degradation of normal operations.

Network Management

Management solutions for today's networks must encompass and address factors including size, multivendor makeup, diverse applications, dynamic nature, and unpredictable use. In order to assure network reliability and provide appropriate performance, the university desired to implement standards-based network management and provide technicians with the appropriate network management tools necessary to install, repair, and implement any changes. We also desired to implement a highly organized cable plant and a cable management system to ease network management and reduce operating costs. The standard we selected to implement centralized network management is the Simple Network Management Protocol (SNMP). All electronic networking components are required to be SNMP-compliant (contain SNMP servers) for use on the network.

Since the university standardized on the use of SNMP-compliant David Systems Inc. concentrators and hubs, we chose ExpressView software to implement centralized network management. This software provides support utilities and efficiency tools via a graphical user interface (GUI) based on Microsoft Windows 3.0. Major features include network mapping, alarms, alarm and event logs, printed reports, variable polling, access security, MIB I and MIB II support. Devices to be managed by ExpressView include concentrators, hubs, terminal servers, routers, bridges, and hosts. Configuration, performance, traffic analysis, fault analysis and resolution, and security will be monitored and reported.

In addition to the David Systems ExpressView, our technicians also utilize network management tools, including twisted pair cable testers, cable locators, labeling devices, and cable termination equipment. To aid in more in-depth network analysis, we have also acquired a Spider Systems network analyzer and plan to install remote network probes offered by Spider Systems in all logical subnets on the network. These remote probes will allow us to gather statistics and sample packets centrally to aid in problem resolution in various subnets created by our implementation of IP routers.

Problems

Although we have invested a great deal of time establishing standards and implementing policies and procedures in regard to our networking efforts on campus, there are still areas of concern which need further investigation and planning.

One issue of great concern is that TCP/IP does not support a printing protocol. Because of this deficiency, we have experimented with alternatives to accomplish distributed printing over the network. These alternatives include connecting printers to TCP/IP terminal servers and implementing DOS-based LPD (language processing and debugging) print servers with printers connected to those servers. We have had success with both alternatives, but no clear standard or direction has yet been established.

Nor have we selected a standard TCP/IP terminal server vendor at this time. The lack of a standard has forced us to support several different vendors' terminal servers, each with its own set of local commands and help facilities. From an end-user perspective, it is very difficult to provide adequate support since commands and functions differ, depending on which terminal server is providing the connection for the end user.

Our current standard local area network operating system, Novell Net-Ware, utilizes the IPX protocol, which cannot pass through an IP router. While help is on the way with the release of NetWare 3.1 and its support for TCP/IP encapsulation, as yet we cannot directly communicate with all Novell servers on campus via a central management location.

The process of investigation will continue, and additional problems and issues will surface as the network grows and matures.

VIDEO SERVICES

The Media Resources Center of the University of Scranton began as an Audio/Visual Department in a small office/storeroom in St. Thomas Hall. Film-strip, 16mm and slide projectors, and record players were distributed to faculty members for classroom use. Later, the department was incorporated into the Library administrative structure and housed in the Library basement. In 1982 the Media Resources Center moved across campus into its present location, Gallery Building. In 1989 the Center was expanded to incorporate a television studio and campus radio station facility (Media Broadcast Productions) housed over a block away in Jefferson Hall. The Media Services unit of the Center houses a collection of videotapes, films, filmstrips, slides and audio recordings of over 6,000 tiles and includes a 20-station viewing and listening area for video, slides, and filmstrips and audio materials, repair facilities, and office space for six full-time-equivalent staff members and twelve student work-study employees. Equipment is stored in closets in classroom and other buildings around campus. In addition to providing classroom media support through equipment and collection distribution, Media Services also provides satellite downlink capabilities for teleconferencing or off-satellite taping on both C and Ku bands, videotaping of classroom and campus activities such as lectures and class presentations, 35mm slide production (copy work and computer imaging), lamination, thermal transparency production, and video and audio duplicating services. Media Broadcast Productions provides support to university and studio video production projects and supports the laboratory facilities of the Communication Department for television and radio production courses. Media Broadcast Production also supports a carrier current campus radio station. It recently received an FM construction permit from the FCC to begin broadcasting sometime in 1992.

The Media Resources Center began to look for more efficient means of delivering services to the campus community as early as 1986. Movement of delicate electronic equipment is time and labor intensive and hard on that equipment. Use of equipment is limited to the number of available pieces in the building. The concept of a campus-wide video network developed as a most viable method of delivering services and increasing the number of clients served.

Network Planning and Development

Recognition of the Importance of Video Technology. The several studies mentioned above included a video component. In each, views toward video from the academic side ranged from unnecessary to a strong sentiment that the ability to broadcast instructional material was vital to the learning process and that the university was at a competitive disadvantage to colleges and universities with an installed video network. Student responses to the survey conducted by the Telecommunications Subcommittee of the Integrated Information Systems Planning Committee indicated that access to outside or off-campus broadcasts in student housing was somewhat important (31.2%) to very important (42.2%). Recognizing that video would be an important part of the university's educational program, once the decision was made to develop an integrated campus network, video was included.

Because of the differences of opinion demonstrated in the surveys, the video portion of the network was separated into two areas: instruction and entertainment. Instructional use of the video network will include transmission of educational media holdings, satellite teleconferences, and foreign language programming to classrooms and conference areas. Entertainment programming provided to the head-end either by a link to the local cable company or by satellite reception will be distributed primarily to student residences.

System Scope and Design. Areas in 14 administrative and classroom buildings have been identified for video service. In most cases, standard office areas will not be provided with video outlets. Classrooms and conference areas will be provided with one video outlet. Several larger classrooms in strategic locations and certain conference areas will have an additional outlet to serve as a sub-band feed location to the head-end for program origination. Users of the educational system will have remote control capability of the videocassette units at the head-end through an inexpensive control device operating over touch-tone telephones and standard telephone lines. Although reception equipment is in short supply, long-range plans call for each classroom to be equipped with at least one 27 inch receiver and, in the case of large classrooms/conference areas, video projection equipment by 1997.

Programming in these areas will be provided on 21 channels through the use of videocassette players, 16mm and slide-to-video transfer units, and satellite feeds from two TVRO dishes located on St. Thomas Hall (Foreign Languages) and Gallery Building (teleconferencing). A sub-band modulator will provide the satellite receiver feed from St. Thomas Hall to the head-end. To be included in the programming mix is an informational bulletin board listing special events and announcements, with the campus radio station operating as background audio. The Bulletin Board will also function as the closed class listing for registration purposes.

Twenty-one student residences have been identified for service to individual student rooms. In the past, cable television service has been provided to the lounge areas by a local cable vendor. As of November 1991, no vendor had been chosen, but it is expected that between 20 and 29 broadcast channels will be distributed over the network. Premium television services will not be available on the network, but will be available in the lounge areas through a separate agreement with the local cable service provider.

Head-end facilities for the network include agile modulators for the educational channels, sub-band modulators and agile processors for the satellite feed and remote camera feeds, time base correctors for the remote camera feeds to switching/special effects generators, agile processors for off-air and/or cable entertainment channels, an antenna system for off-air local programming, character generator for titling and bulletin board operation, an FM tuner for radio signal reception, standard NTSC and multistandard VHS units, U-Matic VCPs, 16mm and slide-to-video transfer units, and a 32-channel computer-controlled routing switcher.

The video portion of the network will be run over a coaxial cable trunk system, a proven and less expensive technology. However, six strands of single-mode fiber will be laid to provide for future expansion. Special attention was paid to outlining specifications that will permit future use of the cabling and electronics for data transmission as a redundant feed in the event that the fiber trunk experiences a break or failure.

The interbuilding cabling specifications call for 75 ohm broadband, copper-clad aluminum center conductor with expanded polyethylene dielectric and solid aluminum sheath, 0.16 inch nominal conductor center; 1.055 inch nominal outer diameter/shield; 14.9-115.1 pF/ft capacitance; 73-77 ohm impedance; 0.86 ohms/1000 foot DC resistance (inner conductor); and 1.22 ohms/1000 foot loop resistance. The interbuilding aerial cabling specifications are identical to the underground cabling, with the addition of a 0.250 inch galvanized steel messenger. Station cabling specification is RG-6/U coax-18 AWG-PVC jacket equivalent to Belden 1189A, with plenum jacket provided where required by building code.

Specifications for trunk electronics are 5-550Mhz frequency range; 18Db or less insertion loss; 14Db gain; 20Db port to port isolation; 60dBmV output level; and 75 ohms impedance. Coupler specifications include no more than 12Db tap value; 1.5Db insertion loss; 30Db isolation; 18Db return loss; and 5-550Mhz bandwidth.

FUTURE APPLICATIONS

Future applications currently under study for inclusion in the network include Level 1 interactive video capability, on-campus video conferencing, distance learning, and on-campus origination of teleconferencing. The addition of any or all of these applications to the network is dependent on future budget availability and a university-wide commitment to video technology.

Campus Networking at Seton Hall University: Moving Quickly After a Late Start

Nancy Enright
Director of the Computer Assisted Instruction Center
Seton Hall University

Tom Burtnett
Director of Academic Computing
Seton Hall University

INTRODUCTION

Prior to 1987 we at Seton Hall University in South Orange, New Jersey, had very little to do with networks. In fact, general computer use on our campus was behind that of many other comparable institutions. We had several classrooms of Apples and personal computers (PCs) in various locations, as well as a lab in the Chemistry Department using UNIX software. However, none of these labs were networked, either as local area networks (LANs) or to each other. Through an IBM mainframe, some students and faculty were able to use BITNET, an intercampus network, and MUSIC, our mainframe IBM operating system, allowing for e-mail and other applications. Although students in some computer courses used BITNET and MUSIC, the majority of the population did not.

Despite our slow start, networking at Seton Hall has developed from a single department's venture with a Mac lab in 1987 to our present efforts: laying the groundwork for a campus-wide network. We also plan to connect the original Mac lab with the many DOS-based LANs that have developed on campus and, eventually, to link our campus network with nationwide and international electronic mail systems, such as the Internet.

THE BEGINNING

Our venture into networking began with the Department of Communication. In 1985, with a New Jersey Department of Higher Education (NJDHE) Computers in Curricula Grant, the Communications Department set up an MS-DOS lab with eight stations for graphics and three-dimensional animation, for classes and open sessions. Utilizing Lumina Software and Studio Works Programs, the lab services advertising and art classes, as well as some introductory courses. A large (30 inch, Mitsubishi) monitor allows the instructor to project graphics or animation from his screen for all students to view. This lab was not a network, but it paved the way for the first true network at Seton Hall when, in 1987, the Communications Department, through another NJDHE Computers in Curricula Grant, established a Mac lab of 17 computers, connected by Appleshare and used for desktop publishing. WordPerfect, the campus-wide selection, is the word processor for this lab. Three laser printers, plus a Linotype 300 digital typesetter, service the Mac lab.

Several of the PCs in the Communication Department's MS-DOS lab have been linked to the Mac's Appleworks network. Eventually, all eight PCs can be linked up and share printers and files. This networking permits some creative combinations of text and imagery. For example, the student resume shown in Figure 1 was typed in the Mac desktop publishing lab, but the image was created in the MS-DOS graphics lab using Lumina Software. It was then transferred to the Mac network and effectively joined with the text of the resume. Images taken with a still video camera can be digitized and retrieved by computers in the MS-DOS lab, allowing for some interesting effects. This network is used for some practical purposes on campus; for example, *The Setonian,* the campus newspaper, and Seton Hall's summer catalog are produced in the Mac lab by the Communications Department in conjunction with Advertising, Art, and Design students.

During this period, the DOS-based and Apple classrooms were being used for a variety of courses. In 1988 several English and other classes were being conducted in these computer classrooms on a regular basis, and plans were being made to incorporate computer-assisted instruction into a larger segment of courses.

NETWORK DEVELOPMENT AND ACCESS

In 1989 we began DOS-based local area networking with the receiving of two NJDHE grants, one for the English Department and the other for the School of Business. The first to be established was the English Department's LAN (called the Computer-Assisted Instruction Center), housed in the Library and consisting of 33 IBM PS 25s, networked through Novell NetWare to a 386 file server. On this network students have access to WordPerfect v. 5.1, Writer's Helper (a prewriting stimulus and revising software), Mavis Beacon Typing Tutorial, and a CD-ROM menu. The CD-ROM menu runs through the server from a "jukebox" or CD-ROM player that can hold up to 14 disks. Available through CD-ROM are several periodical indexes (at present only one or two work properly, but by purchasing a more powerful server we hope to alleviate some of these difficulties) and Word Cruncher

REACHING
FOR
THE
STARS

Danielle J. O'Neil

OBJECTIVE: A position in advertising drawing upon my educational and work experience while offering an opportunity for growth and development.

EDUCATION: SETON HALL UNIVERSITY South Orange, New Jersey
College of Arts and Sciences
Bachelor of Arts Degree, December 1990
Major: Advertising Art   GPA: 3.7

HONORS: Dean's List: all semesters.
Military Science Academic Achievement Award: Fall 1988, Spring 1989.
Alpha Gamma Delta Founder- Highest GPA: Fall 1988.
Alpha Gamma Delta Junior- Highest GPA: Fall 1988, Spring 1989.

SKILLS: Proficient knowledge of IBM and MACINTOSH computer software: American Page Planner, Time Arts' Lumena, Pansophic's Studioworks, Aldus Pagemaker, Word Perfect, Microsoft Word, Letrastudio, Adobe Streamline, Adobe Illustrator and AppleScan. Familiar with various word processing programs, Aldus Freehand, Smart Art and QuarkXpress. Ability to set up an electronic design system. Operation of Agfa-Gevaert Repromaster 3500 Photostat machine.

EXPERIENCE: Seton Hall University - Office of Public Relations, Spring 1990 and Fall 1990 to present
Internship Position - **DESIGNER**
Design through production of brochures, folders, flyers, invitations, ads and programs on a MAC using Wordperfect, Pagemaker and various draw and paint programs. Effectively use clip art for projects.

Seton Hall University, June 1990
FREELANCE ARTIST
Vectorized University Seal and Crest using AppleScan, Adobe Streamline and Adobe Illustrator.

Seton Hall University **SUMMER CATALOG**- 1990 issue, October 1989 to January 1990
Worked with a team of 7 students and 2 faculty members to create, design, typeset and produce entire catalog. Prepared comp of cover for presentation and printer reference.

South Orange **PROFILES**- December 1989 issue, October 1989 to December 1989
Designed cover for community newspaper. Interacted with clients to create ads, which were produced on Aldus Pagemaker. Took ads from concept through completion.

Lohmeyer Simpson Communications, Inc., February 1989 to June 1989
Cooperative Education - **PHOTOSTAT TECHNICIAN**
Operated the photostat machine and prepared INT's and Color Keys. Established and organized an efficient filing and storage system. Produced mechanicals, comps and dummies.

Big M Inc. - The Mandee Shop, March 1985 to September 1988
SALESPERSON
Designed all in-store displays. Created interior and exterior decor. Advised customers on the latest fashion trends.

ACTIVITIES: Seton Hall University Cheerleader, 1986-1987; SHU Crew; and Welcome Back Crew.
Founder Zeta Tau Chapter of Alpha Gamma Delta Fraternity (international).
Zeta Chi Rho Sorority (local).
Phi Beta Lambda Future Business Leaders, 1986.
Seton Hall University Images: Festival of the Visual Arts, 1990.
Floor Representative for Hall Council, 1988-1989.
Reserve Officer's Training Corps.

INTERESTS: Skiing, swimming, dancing, painting, exercising, music and fashion.

REFERENCES: Available upon request.

520 Laurita Street Linden, NJ 07036   (201)862-2811

Figure 1. Student resume.

text retrieval software with its accompanying library of texts (*The Riverside Shakespeare*, two versions of the Bible, the works of several famous American authors, the Constitution Papers, and Famous Speeches). We have recently ordered, but not yet installed, the CD-ROM database of poetry from 600 to 1900 A.D. by Chadwyk Healey (purchased for this LAN by the library through NEH funding). All of this CD-ROM material will be accessible to any workstation on the network. Four Hewlett-Packard LaserJet Printers service the CAI Center, and any one of these printers also can be accessed from any workstation.

The CAI Center is used for English classes; some meetings are held on a regular basis, and others are for one or more special "orientation" or "workshop" sessions conducted by a tutor working with the instructor. For classes LANSchool software allows an instructor to take control of students' screens for a demonstration or exercise and then release them so that students can work on their own. When not being used for classes, the CAI Center is available to any student during open hours when it is staffed by a "tutor," a student worker skilled in computer use and competent to help with English problems. Tutors must have at least a B in English and the recommendation of an English professor to work in the English Department's LAN. Next year we hope to expand the CAI Center by adding another 30 computers and, probably, two more printers. We also hope to expand our computer-assisted instruction to include more literature classes.

Meanwhile, as the English Department was developing its LAN, the School of Business opened up its first LAN, consisting of 20 PCs linked to a 386 server. Like the CAI Center, this LAN offers WordPerfect 5.1, but also includes LOTUS for spreadsheets and other applications. The options are listed on a menu like that of the English CAI Center, created through WordPerfect Office software. Students also follow the same logging in procedure as that used in the English LAN, by typing log in guest for open sessions or a particular class or individual code, if appropriate. (We have tried to keep the basic features of the LANs similar so that students can move easily from one to the other and so that it will be easier eventually to network all the LANs together.) After the first 20 stations were successfully functioning, another 20 stations were added to the LAN, in a different location in the School of Business but linked to the same file server. Two laser printers serve each room of 20 workstations. Both of these labs (two sections of one LAN) are used for classes and for open hours.

After these two LANs were in operation, we began developing several small networks in other locations across campus. Counseling Services set up the first IBM PC LAN in an administrative area. This network allows staff to share WordPerfect documents, printers, e-mail. Housing and Residence next set up a LAN of eight stations, allowing workers to access data about students' residence halls, fees, and the like. Twelve PCs were networked in Computer Services, which supports computer operations on campus, to allow testing and mainframe connection for Computer Services staff. Career Services then set up a LAN with eleven used PCs donated by Prudential plus six others, three of them located in a student work area; this LAN is serviced by several printers (two laser, two dot matrix). Two software packages (COM-

LINK, which helps students arrive at a major or a career goal, and KINEXIS, for developing resumes) were installed on this network and have since then been made available on all campus networks for more convenient student use.

In the academic area, LANs continued to be developed. The School of Nursing established a LAN consisting of 28 computers, 14 of which are public, the rest being used by office staff or faculty. This LAN, using a menu system similar to those of the other academic LANs, offers WordPerfect 5.1, as well as three special menus with software for nursing. One laser printer and one dot matrix printer serve the public workstations; seven other various printers are located in offices. Classes are only occasionally held in the Nursing LAN, but it is open every weekday for walk-in students. Most nursing classes require the use of PCs.

The most recent and largest LAN on campus is housed in the Academic Computing area. This LAN consists of 96 IBM PCs, linked with Novell NetWare. The menu, once again, closely resembles those of the English, Business, and Nursing LANs and offers WordPerfect 5.1, Lotus, Dbase, Turbo Pascal, Derive (a mathematics program), Turbo C, and Basic. This network is serviced by six Laserjet IIID printers for student use plus two Laserjet II printers for staff. The LAN is used for classes, such as Computer Fundamentals, and is also available for open hours, when it is staffed by student workers. This LAN is directly connected to the university mainframe to allow up to all of the 96 workstations to log into the main frame.

FUTURE PLANS

The Library plans to network its various databases, such as the card catalog, now on GEAC software (a UNIX system), to each other and to the English Department's CAI Center. This library network would also include a large number of CD-ROM periodical indexes, which would expand those already offered by the CAI Center. In fact, the library is financing the expansion of the CD-ROM player in the CAI Center to hold 21 disks as well as the purchase of a new, more powerful server.

Since all of the IBM LANs used by students have been intentionally set up using basically the same menu system and log in protocols, our next step of linking these LANs together and to the mainframe should be made simpler. Cables have been laid between President's Hall, which houses the mainframe; Bayley Hall, an administrative building; the Library, where the English Department's CAI Center is housed; and Academic Computing's LAN in Corrigan Hall. In the future, we hope to link this campus network to the School of Business, the School of Nursing, and the School of Education (see Figure 2).

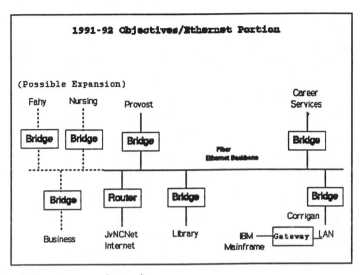

Figure 2. Campus network overview.

Through this campus-wide network, it will be able to be possible to transfer files from LAN to LAN and data shared between them. Furthermore, software formerly accessible only on one LAN (such as Writer's Helper, now available only in the English Department's CAI Center) will be able to be accessed at any workstation in any LAN on the network. For example, the library's card catalog could be perused by a student in the Business School, across campus, and then that student's paper could be sent to a tutor in the CAI Center for proofreading via e-mail. Plans call for all university computers to have access to the Internet, so students and faculty will also be able to communicate with other institutions more readily than they have been able to do via Bitnet. For the academic year 1991-92, at least a few LANs and the mainframe should be connected to the Internet.

Although Seton Hall University cannot claim to have been historically in the vanguard of computer technology on college campuses, we have certainly moved quickly in the area of campus networking. Ironically, our slow beginnings in computerization have, in many ways, served us well in the area of networking, for when we began to make large investments of time and money in the area of computer technology, the age of networking was upon us. Seton Hall, therefore, was able to establish all our newest computer classrooms as LANs, and faculty and students alike are learning to use computers and networks at the same time. This serendipitous situation puts us in a favorable position for making strides into the future in the area of campus networks.

The Creation of AngelNet: A Case Study of Network Evolution

Laurence R. Alvarez
Associate Provost
The University of the South

John L. Bordley
Director of Academic Computing
The University of the South

INTRODUCTION

The University of the South, commonly known as Sewanee, is a rural, residential, highly selective, traditional liberal arts college with 1,080 undergraduates and 70 students in its School of Theology. Located in Tennessee and owned by the Episcopal Church, it was founded in 1858. The university publishes the *Sewanee Review*, the oldest continuously published literary quarterly in America; it has had more Rhodes Scholars than any institution of comparable size; and the number of graduate recipients of National Collegiate Athletic Association (NCAA) postgraduate fellowships ranks it twenty-sixth in the nation among all 3,500 NCAA schools and third among Division III schools. Computing at Sewanee dates from 1963 when the university used a National Science Foundation (NSF) grant to purchase an IBM 1620. It was not until 1973 that the university purchased an administrative computer, a Hewlett-Packard 2000, which served both academic and administrative purposes. In 1985 the university owned few microcomputers; the only network consisted of RS-232 connections to a data switch; and the university performed both academic and administrative computing on an H-P 3000 model 48 which was heavily overloaded.

THE MACINTOSH PROJECT

In the fall of 1985 the Director of Academic Computing, the Faculty Consultant for Computing, the Director of Data Processing, and the Coordinator of Program Planning and Budgeting, all of whom were faculty, three of whom were tenured, suggested to the Provost and Dean of the College that the University should think seriously about how to support students and faculty in the coming microcomputer revolution. With the encouragement of the Dean and the Provost, this group began weekly meetings to explore the need in Academic Computing for support for microcomputer activity. The University owned two IBM personal computers (PCs) and seven H-P 150s; students and faculty members were beginning to use microcomputers in their work; there was little support on campus for them; and microcomputers were not used in the classroom except in Computer Science.

The Microcomputer Committee, as the group was known, decided that enabling faculty to incorporate the use of microcomputers into the classroom was an important goal for the college, but to make it happen the university needed to make a major effort to support the faculty. Because of the relative isolation of Sewanee, and because of the small staff in Academic Computing, the committee decided that the university should decide on a particular hardware and software configuration which it would support. It also decided that the most productive way to learn how to use a microcomputer is to have, as near as possible, one computer to one student. Thus, the committee recommended to the Dean and Provost that the university should (1) select a microcomputer and a collection of software which the university would support; (2) create a microcomputer laboratory of about 15 of those machines; (3) beginning with the entering students in the Fall of 1986 encourage students to purchase one of the chosen microcomputers (it was presumed that the university would enter the resale business); (4) provide interest free loans to any faculty member for the purchase of a microcomputer; (5) provide, on a semipermanent loan, microcomputers to any faculty members who wanted to incorporate the use of microcomputers in their classes; (6) provide a part-time clerk for Academic Computing; and (7) train the two technical support staff members to maintain the hardware. The Dean and the Provost supported the proposal, and the faculty, which had been informed regularly about the progress of the Committee, raised no objections to the proposal.

The committee invited hardware vendors to provide their microcomputers and their recommended software for word processing, spreadsheets, and either BASIC or Pascal for evaluation during the Christmas break of 1985. The vendors who responded were Apple, Data General, IBM, Tandy, Zenith, and two local vendors. The committee had a strong bias toward hardware and software that was easy to use and easy to maintain. This bias was based on the knowledge that support staff for the project would be limited and on the strongly held opinion that the primary intent of the program was to have a microcomputer that would be an aid to learning, not an object of study itself.

The choice of the Apple Macintosh was unanimous. It satisfied the bias of the committee, there was ample software available, Apple seemed to know how to deal with educational institutions, and it also offered to equip the microcomputer laboratory. The University was able to negotiate favorable contracts with Apple for the hardware and with Microsoft Corporation for Microsoft Word and Microsoft Excel which were to be bundled with every Macintosh purchased. The purchase price to a student and faculty member for a Macintosh with Microsoft Word, Microsoft Excel, MacPaint, and MacPascal, all of which were bundled with the hardware, was at least $500 less that the best price in stores. The reasoning behind bundling the software was threefold: it put into the hands of the students the primary tools they needed to use the Macintosh; it allowed the university to obtain the best pricing from Microsoft; and it provided a partial answer to the question of unauthorized copying of software. The present software package includes only Microsoft Word and Microsoft Excel.

NETWORK PLANNING

Except for being able to connect to the University's Hewlett-Packard minicomputer through an existing data switch, there was little thought given to creating a network. However, with a Macintosh comes AppleTalk which induces the creation of small networks that allow sharing of printers. Soon after Sewanee began its emphasis on Macintoshes, Apple provided file-sharing ability through AppleShare, so the AppleTalk networks gained larger utility, and in August of 1988 a six-foot Ethernet called AngelNet was established to connect four AppleTalk zones in four buildings so that approximately 50 administrators and 30 faculty members would have access from their offices to both academic and administrative file servers.

In the fall of 1987 the Provost created a special committee to report on the needs of the university for a campus-wide network. The committee's report included the statement: "The Committee recommends that plans be made for establishing a network on campus which will allow access from faculty and staff offices and from student rooms to the library catalog, mainframe computers on campus, file servers, and printers. The access should be easy to obtain and the system should be easy to use. The model the Committee used was the telephone system. Access to it is ubiquitous and friendly; the access to the network should be just as ubiquitous and friendly." With this recommendation as its guide and with an aging, overloaded telephone system that provided no service to the residence halls, the university began to plan for the installation of a new telecommunications system and the physical connections among buildings that would allow for the creation of such a data network. Those plans included wiring offices and residential hall rooms with voice and data jacks with 8 sets of twisted pair wiring; in addition, 12 fibers were run from each of 36 buildings to a newly created computing and telecommunications equipment room.

In September 1989 the library was deeply involved with Computing Services in planning an online catalog system; the university was planning the new telecommunications system and cable plant; the creation of the network which reached all offices and residence hall rooms was high on the agenda; there were organizational questions about computing; there was a new President; and there was no crisis in the computing areas. These all suggested that the time was right for consultants to evaluate the computing endeavor at the university, with special attention to the network plans, the library system, and the organization of computing services. The EDUCOM Consulting Group provided a team of two consultants to report on computing at Sewanee. Based on recommendations from the consultants, the university reorganized computing so that both academic computing and administrative computing report to the Associate Provost; the plans to extend AngelNet to all buildings on campus as a part of the installation of the telecommunications project were confirmed; and the planning for the creation of an online library system that would be housed with the other administrative minicomputers and which would be accessible over the network was continued. In a sense the university asked the consultants for a sanity check on its plans for computing, and the results were positive. The data wiring and the fiber connections were completed in the summer of 1990 as a part of a $3 million project that created the computing and telecommunications building and installed a new telephone system for the whole campus. The incremental cost for the data wiring including fiber was about $472,000, which was not great when compared with the total wiring cost of $1.5 million.

In January 1990 the Library completed plans for its new online catalog system; the university ordered a Hewlett-Packard 3000/922 with the VTLS software; and it was time for another sanity check. Representatives from VTLS, Hewlett-Packard, and Apple Computer were invited to spend the day in discussions about how those vendors would help the university create the computing environment that was desired, that is, using the same network which allowed access to printers and file servers to access the library system and administrative Hewlett-Packard minicomputers. The library computer was to be installed in the equipment room which was being created for the telecommunications equipment and to which the central computer and file server were to be moved. Once again the university was judged sane, and the library system was installed in September 1990.

So, in the fall of 1990 ten AppleTalk zones were connected via Fast-Paths to the Ethernet. The network allowed all Macintosh users to access both the Academic Computing file server and the administrative file server, and users were sharing files through the use of those file servers. The university was depending on being able to connect to both of the Hewlett-Packard machines over the AppleTalk to Ethernet network, and in November 1990 software on the Hewlett-Packard machines was installed which allowed Macintosh users with Business Session terminal emulation software from Tymlabs to make such connections. The university purchased the KeyServer software in December 1990, planning to use it to control the use of 50 copies of Business Session. Now any Macintosh on the network with a keyed version of Business Session can use it to access either Hewlett-Packard machine, and the key server software prevents more than 50 concurrent users. Tymlabs readily agreed to the use of the KeyServer software to protect their product. The next challenge the university attacked was connecting all residence hall rooms to the network. That work was accomplished during the summer of 1991, so students now may obtain PhoneNet connectors from Academic Computing and connect their Macintosh in their rooms to the network. They also obtain from Academic Computing keyed versions of software that may be shared over the network. Thus, students with Macintoshes in their rooms may access the file servers, use the library online catalog, use various applications including Mathematica, SPSS (statistical package for the social sciences) , Systat, Pascal, and C, and they have access to SNN, the Sewanee News Network (Sewanee's version of PNN, Princeton News Network, software licensed from Princeton at no charge). The cost of the hardware used to connect the residence halls to the network was $90,000. There are now 21 AppleTalk zones on AngelNet, with 300 university-owned Macintoshes connected to it. The University sells approximately 100 Macintoshes per year to students, and one can see that they are creative about their use by looking at the shared file services they have created on the network.

Sewanee's plans for the near future are to establish an Internet node on campus to allow use of external computing power for some faculty and to provide mail services for faculty. Faculty, staff, and students will be able to reach the Internet mail services and local mail services using the Macintosh-based mail system, Eudora. Eudora will reach all members of the campus and provide a uniform interface for both external and internal mail, whereas HP Mail, installed on the Hewlett-Packard administrative computer in 1986, serves only the administration (not because it cannot serve faculty, but because the interface is not one that a typical faculty member wants to spend time learning how to use). The Physics and Chemistry departments have a proposal for the university to install a UNIX number cruncher for use in research and classes, and that proposal, if funded, will place another resource on the network. Sewanee is continuing to develop SNN to make it a more valuable public information system. The important consideration for all these enhancements to computing and services is that they will all be available to any Macintosh on the network, and all students, faculty and office staff are part of that network. Without the presence of AngelNet each of them would be considerably less valuable.

Distributed Computing at Sonoma State University: A Case Study

Mark Resmer
Director of Computing, Media and Telecommunications Services
Sonoma State University

In characterizing the computing environment that is currently in place at Sonoma State University (SSU), it is hard to do better than to quote a catchphrase that was popularized some time ago by a major computer vendor: "The Network is the System." Over the past three years, SSU has developed its networking capabilities to the point where every computer system on campus is fully functional within the TCP/IP Internet and AppleTalk network environments. In addition, the university has played a very active part in the development of advanced network systems throughout the state of California, through its support of the development of CSUnet over the past three years. CSUnet is a network that links all 20 California State University (CSU) campuses, as well as a number of K-12 schools and community colleges throughout the state.

At present, campus computing resources consist of upwards of 700 institutionally owned networked Macintosh computers and approximately 150 MS-DOS systems, which constitute a de facto campus standard for desktop systems, coupled with a Digital Equipment Corporation (DEC) VAX 6360 system and a number of smaller UNIX-based systems. A relatively small number of "grandfathered" terminals still remain on campus, but these are rapidly being phased out.

On the software front, SSU has a site license for all current ORACLE products across all platforms—thus ensuring that all campus systems have the ability to access all campus databases. Similar licenses are in place for major communications tools, such as Quickmail, Stanford University's Mac-IP, and Alisa Systems' MaxNotes, and statistical packages such as SPSS (statistical package for the social sciences) . In addition, the university has been increasingly relying on a network-based software-licensing technology called KeyServer to manage the licensing of individual copies of software for campus use.

These network, hardware, and software systems together constitute the university's information technology infrastructure. Having designed and implemented the major part of this infrastructure, the Office of Computing, Media and Telecommunications Services (CMTS) is now primarily concerned with using the infrastructure as the basis for distributed applications development. Our eventual goal is to create a completely unified information systems environment, in which all campus data and information technology resources are accessible within a common framework, using tools that are integrated into a common desktop environment. Along the way, we expect to give individuals and departments across campus much more control and ownership of their data and computing resources, and to greatly improve the quality of computing tools available to students, faculty, and staff. An additional strategic aim is to ensure that data are not needlessly duplicated in various systems, so that data owned by various offices can be easily integrated by users who need to access them.

NETWORKING STRATEGY

When planning the creation of a campus-wide data network in 1988, CMTS had the good fortune to be working in an environment where there was virtually no networking in existence. As a result, we were able to create a coherent and consistent networking environment, without needing to integrate existing incompatible LAN installations. The result is a highly standardized set of network configurations and services, which offers users the same view of the information universe, wherever they are located on the campus, or indeed, even if they are accessing the network from another campus or from home.

Network Design

Our network design philosophy was based on the premise that during the initial phase of networking the campus, it was more important to ensure that every possible location had access to the network than it was to provide the highest possible transmission speed for those locations. For this reason, during the initial phase of network development, the great majority of workstations were connected using LocalTalk (Farallon PhoneNet) cabling. All the LocalTalk segments were connected to a campus-wide Ethernet backbone, consisting of standard (thick wire or 10base5) coaxial cable, together with fiber-optic runs linking widely separated areas of the campus. All the time-sharing systems (initially an old CYBER 830 and a Prime 9755, together with the current VAX and UNIX systems) and a select group of heavily used workstations were connected directly to the backbone, using a mixture of thick and thin wire (10base2) technology.

Notwithstanding this low-cost approach to network implementation, the original design foresaw a time when the limited capacity of the LocalTalk connections would need to be substantially enhanced to keep up with increasing demands for network bandwidth. We have now moved to the second phase of network implementation, with the gradual replacement of LocalTalk connections with Ethernet over unshielded twisted pair wiring (10baseT). Having designed the cable plant in such a way that it would support either standard, the conversion process consists simply of installing a 10baseT hub alongside an existing Farallon Star Controller, reconnecting a given station cable to the new equipment, and adding a suitable card.

Similarly, the original network design anticipated that the capacity of the Ethernet backbone would also be exceeded when 10baseT became the norm for workstation connectivity. We envision two approaches to ensuring that backbone capacity remains adequate: initially, we are splitting the backbone into increasingly small segments, separated by routers and bridges that limit unnecessary traffic from propagating across the entire network. In the long term, we anticipate that the existing backbone will be entirely replaced by a Fiber Distributed Data Interface (FDDI) fiber-optic ring, which will utilize the existing fiber, together with such additional strands as may be required to replace the existing coaxial backbone cable.

In almost every instance, our plans call for the reuse of hardware liberated by these upgrades. For example, it is very likely that as LocalTalk is replaced by 10baseT in faculty and staff offices, the associated hardware will be reused to provide network connectivity in other areas, such as student dormitory rooms. Thin wire Ethernet hardware rendered obsolete by our move to 10baseT and FDDI will likewise be reused in student workstation labs or other highly concentrated workstation clusters where this technology is an appropriate answer to networking needs. By taking this "hand-me-down" approach to network planning, we have been able to achieve a great deal of network connectivity within a short period of time, at relatively low cost, without risking being left with a great deal of obsolete hardware and cabling as the technology develops.

Software/Protocols

We decided to support TCP/IP as the nonproprietary universal standard throughout the network, which all network devices would be able to use, and to complement this protocol suite with a range of vendor-specific protocols that the network transmits transparently across the campus. At present these protocols are AppleTalk, DECnet, and Novell IPX. Given the preponderance of Macintosh systems on campus, it is hardly surprising that AppleTalk has become the most heavily used protocol, for Macintosh and DOS systems alike. While TCP/IP offers unsurpassed connectivity and ease of management, AppleTalk has proven to be extremely popular with end users because it is so transparent in operation, provides transparent support for network printing, and allows network navigation and resource discovery with little or no knowledge of the network's characteristics.

Security

Having made the decision to create a single unified network that links all points on the campus, without any distinction between academic and administrative users, security is naturally a paramount concern. We have addressed this issue in two ways. All labs and other locations where students have access to the network are separated from the campus backbone with Shiva Fastpaths, which provide "stay in zone" security at the AppleTalk level, and thus prevent unauthorized access to administrative file servers, printers, and so on. At the same time, as the backbone becomes increasingly segmented, bridges and routers prevent local traffic from propagating outside its immediate segment. This strategy reduces the probability that a student or other unauthorized user might intercept and decode confidential packets on the backbone. In addition, all sensitive information is typically stored on time-sharing systems within a relational database, thus adding two levels of password protection to the network access limitations. No electronic security system is foolproof, but it has been our experience that the security provided by this arrangement is considerably greater than that offered by common physical safeguards on traditional paper-based storage media, file cabinets, offices, and storage areas.

Wide Area Networking

The campus network described above is an integral part of a statewide network known as the CSUnet. This network originated as an X.25-based system that linked mainframes and PADs at each of the 20 CSU campuses. Over the past three years, it has grown to become an advanced multiprotocol network, which has multiple links into the Internet, through the BARRnet and CERFnet regional networks. The current wide-area network implementation uses Cisco routers and Stratacom frame-relay multiplexors, which connect all the campuses over T1 circuits. Unlike other regional networks and the Internet, CSUnet supports multiple protocols over the wide area network, including all those used on the Sonoma campus. This multiple protocol capability, coupled with the considerable performance advantages offered by frame-relay technology, as compared with traditional circuit-switched T1 networks, has created a network capability that blurs the distinction between campuses. From the Sonoma campus, it is just as simple, and almost without any perceptible performance penalty, to select and use a printer or file server located 400 miles away in Long Beach, as it is to select one in the same building or in another building on campus. In a multicampus system such as the CSU, the ability to blur campus boundaries in this way presents an opportunity for the development of many challenging new applications of information technology, ranging from campus-based systemwide specialty centers supporting individual academic disciplines to intercampus electronic document delivery for administrative purposes.

Implementation/Funding Strategy

At the time that initial consideration was being given to networking the campus, the university was in the midst of replacing the existing Centrex campus telephone system with a new digital switch. While the switch selected, the Ericsson MD110, has digital data capabilities, we felt that the limitations of a PBX-based approach to data transmission were too great for the university to consider the switch as a data-switching device. Instead, we took advantage of the telecommunications system procurement to install a comprehensive twisted pair wiring system throughout the campus, including the dormitories, with sufficient extra capacity between the building Intermediate Distribution Frames (IDFs) and each telephone jack to accommodate almost any combination of voice, asynchronous data, LocalTalk, or 10baseT.

The existence of this modern wiring system has been critical to the success of the remainder of the networking project. The laws of physics seem to change on a regular basis when it comes to the amount of data that it is possible to cram down a quality unshielded twisted pair (UTP) telephone line. The capacity of the wiring system has already grown from hundreds of thousands of bits per second to 10 million bits per second with the advent of the 10baseT standard. Without resorting to such expensive options as fiber to the desktop, we expect that within the next five years we will be routing hundred million bit per second FDDI to the desktop using this existing wiring—truly an astonishing performance improvement over the lifetime of a cable system. Not least of the advantages of using UTP as the primary distribution medium for the campus network was the minimal incremental cost of adding extra pairs to the telephone wiring when this was undertaken. For all intents and purposes, what could have been the most expensive part of the networking project came along as a free option with the campus telephone system.

Once the distribution wiring was in place, the campus undertook a building-by-building network building operation. Among the activities undertaken within this part of the network implementation was connection of building IDF closets to the campus backbone, installation of repeaters, bridges, routers, and so on, in the IDF closets, and connection of all UTP distribution wiring to the workstations and routers. Associated with the hardware installation has been a comprehensive software installation procedure for each workstation, which ensures that all campus computers have a standard repertory of network software installed on them, for example, MacTCP, MacIP, and Quickmail. Finally, for every workstation connected to the network there has been an extensive recordkeeping process to ensure that the network database remains current at all times. Depending on the size of each building and the complexity of the installation required, each of these building installations typically took between a week and several months to complete. The entire process took approximately three years from the time the first network port was connected to the completion of the last building in the summer of 1991.

The entire network has been funded centrally as part of the campus telecommunications budget. No charge is made for provision of LocalTalk connectivity to departments (other than auxiliaries such as the Bookstore and other nonstate-funded entities) and to individuals on the campus. In the case of DOS systems that require additional hardware within the computer for network connectivity, purchase of the required cards is the responsibility of the machines' owners. Similarly, for 10baseT connectivity, the university provides the live network outlet at the wall at no cost to the user, but the required 10baseT cards for the workstations are the responsibility of the individual departments. Similarly, the standard network software packages mentioned above are provided free to all users, whereas any specialized commercial software for network access is the responsibility of the end users.

Leaving aside the costs of UTP and backbone cable installation, which are difficult to break out from the total cost of the PBX installation, the entire network has cost approximately $120,000 in hardware and software to implement. Network design, configuration, and installation has been a full-time job for two staff members over the past three years—a systems software specialist and a telecommunications technician. At peak times, an additional systems software specialist has been involved in the work on a part-time basis. In addition, two systems software specialists are engaged on an ongoing basis in software and systems support of networked resources.

Organizational Implications

One of the most important factors in ensuring the success of the campus networking project has been the very tight organizational integration of all aspects of information technology on the campus. A single department, CMTS, is responsible for academic computing, administrative computing, voice telecommunications, data networking, electronic video distribution system, classroom audio-visual support, and video production throughout the university. Apart from the obvious advantage of eliminating turf battles over which piece of wire belongs to whom, this structural integration has offered SSU a great deal of flexibility in funding projects that span multiple areas, and has ensured that the needs of all the various constituencies were considered when the infrastructure was being developed.

Now that the network is substantially complete, another aspect of the integration between the different areas of information technology is coming to the forefront. Many of the networked information systems and applications that are now under development span more than one of the traditional areas of specialization within the organization. Thus, for example, faculty may use advising tools to assist their students by consulting the "administrative" student records system. Administrators are finding new uses for "academic" electronic information maintained within the campus library. Students are using electronic mail and conferencing to communicate with their instructors, as well as for social interaction and participation in off-campus discussions of current affairs. Many of these applications are still new to their users and require the computing support organization to provide extensive training and support. An integrated organization allows and indeed demands that every member of its staff be actively engaged in such support. We have no "user services" unit within the CMTS organization—every staff member is a part-time user-services person, regardless of the other tasks they perform.

CLIENT/SERVER APPLICATIONS

Since most individuals on campus now have access to a networked Macintosh or DOS system, SSU has made a strong commitment to developing client/server systems to support the major functions of the university. The advantage of this approach over more traditional systems, which rely on terminals and mainframes, is that software which runs on the desktop workstations is typically much faster and better than that available on mainframes. In addition, making desktop machines do most of the work allows us to provide much more computing power to everyone without having to invest in huge and costly new mainframes.

The university is implementing client/server solutions based on a combination of locally developed applications and commercial products. These applications typically operate in a relational database environment, with VAX systems being used as database servers and Macintosh systems being used as clients. The TCP/IP protocol is currently used for all our client/server applications.

Our intention is to create clients for all the common functions presently performed through VT100 screen interfaces in the VAX-based systems, and to develop new functions that can only reasonably be provided within a client context, such as executive information systems and integration with standard desktop productivity tools (spreadsheets, e-mail, word processors, etc.). This approach promises to limit the amount of development time required, as compared to an implementation strategy based on in-house development of complete systems. At the same time, from an end-user perspective, the systems will appear to be entirely new and radically different from the terminal-based systems that presently form the core of most MIS applications. The resultant systems typically consist of vendor-developed database structures, client software developed at Sonoma, and terminal-based maintenance screens and/or batch utilities provided by the vendor for performing less common functions. Over the lifetime of the individual applications, functionality will typically move from existing terminal screens to newly developed clients.

A number of client/server systems are already in production use at the campus. The following two examples are intended to provide a flavor of the appearance and functionality offered by the applications.

Admissions System

The application screen below is the initial window into the SSU Admissions System, developed by Frank Tansey, Office of Admissions and Records. This client software is the front end of a distributed system. All information is validated within the HyperCard stack. Only when all information is validated will the program allow applicant information to be added to the relational database on the server. The card includes extensive help, and all validations indicate acceptable coding. The screen in Figure 1 shows a combination input, lookup, and update screen.

The screen shown in Figure 2 shows another component of the Admissions System. It is one of several screens used to admit students to the univer-

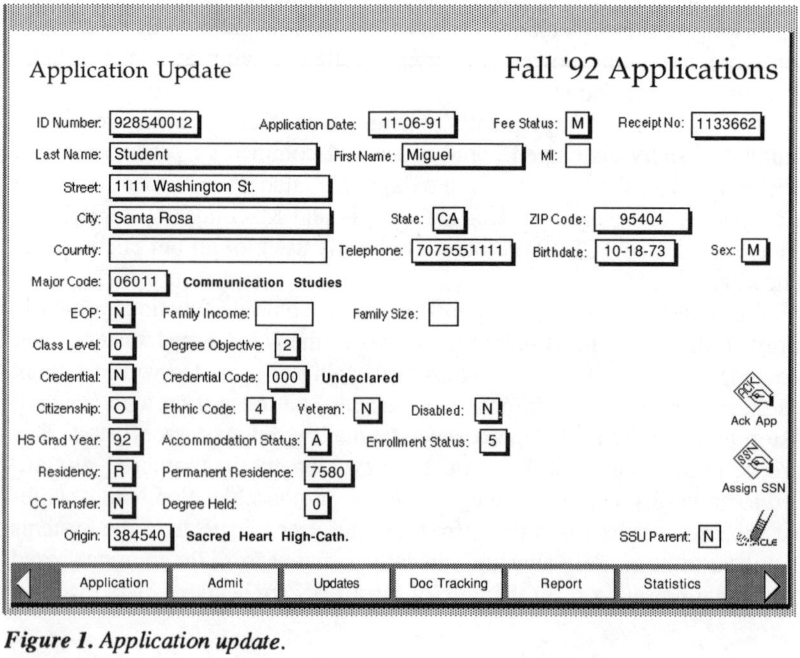

Figure 1. Application update.

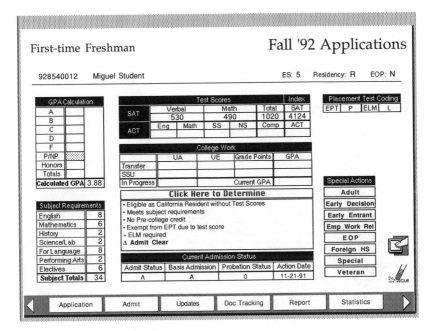

Figure 2. Freshman admission.

sity. Information is entered, and an admissions decision is made at the click of a button. The basis of the decision is displayed so that staff can try out "what if" scenarios by changing information and clicking on the "Click Here to Determine" button. Because there are so many decision crossroads on the way to an admission determination, this package is actually an expert system built using HyperCard. All these functions take place on the Macintosh, and only when a final decision is reached is the VAX database updated.

Purchasing System

This application is a comprehensive procurement system that runs over a relational database on the VAX. The system is presently a hybrid one—part of it is a traditional terminal-based application, and part is a client/server application. The two parts work together, so, for example, the VT100 terminal screens are used to enter and update requisition information, while the client/server portion is used to look up vendors and requisitions, and to approve requisitions electronically. As an example, the electronic requisition lookup/approval screen is shown in Figure 3.

Any field or combination of fields can be used to generate ad hoc queries against the database without any knowledge of the database structure, or of structured query language (SQL). The Macintosh application performs all

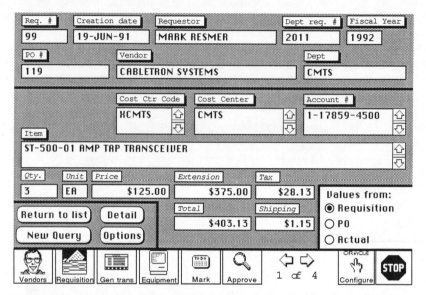

Figure 3. Lookup/approval screen.

data verification, generates SQL code on the fly (transparently to the user of the software), passes the SQL to the VAX for processing, and then formats the data returned from the VAX. Electronic verification is used to simulate signatures, thus allowing requisitions to be entered and approved without having to be printed. Potentially, the first time a requisition ever appears on paper is when it is issued as a hardcopy purchase order. Over a period of time, we expect that the remainder of the system will be rewritten as a client/server application.

ELECTRONIC COMMUNICATIONS

Among the most significant direct benefits of virtually universal network access is that electronic communication becomes a viable alternative to more traditional tools like the telephone system and interoffice memoranda.

Electronic Mail

SSU has made a commitment to providing every member of the university community—faculty, staff, and students—with access to electronic mail. A key strategic decision made early in the development of the campus e-mail system was to provide every individual on campus with an Internet address, whether or not they had access to the network, or indeed a computer. We accomplished this by building a campus mail database and mail-forwarding system, which not only routes mail between the various mail systems on campus, but also maintains the entire campus telephone directory as a database. For any mail recipient without a valid electronic destination for a message, the system automatically prints the message in a format suitable for folding, stapling, and mailing through the on-campus unstamped mail. All information about on-campus routing is taken directly from the current telephone directory, so that the sender of a message does not need to know anything more than the recipient's Internet address (conveniently listed next to each name in the campus telephone directory) nor even whether or not the recipient has a computer, for example:

Resmer, Mark (Emily)	2889/2347
Salazar Library-1502	
Director, CMTS	QuickMail
1449 Magnolia Avenue,	
Rohnert Park 94928	
(707) 792-0553	
Mark.Resmer@sonoma.edu	

The significance of this decision is that even at a time when the e-mail system was in its infancy, and only a relatively small number of people had network access, those individuals could use it to communicate with everyone. Any communications system is only as useful as the number of people with whom it offers connectivity, so this ability to immediately use e-mail to communicate with the rest of the world, both on and off campus, was one the most instrumental factors in changing the prevailing communications style of the campus from paper to electronic format.

This wholesale adoption of e-mail was also aided by our decision to deploy CE Software's Quickmail as the mail system seen by most users of both Macintosh and DOS systems. The simplicity and power of the software was immediately apparent to everyone from senior administrators to faculty, and to this day, there are individuals on campus for whom Quickmail is "the network". Except in the case of mail messages that stay entirely within the Quickmail environment, all other mail routing is handled using standard UNIX mail software, Simple Mail Transfer Protocol (SMTP), and Internet addressing. The mail router is a dedicated UNIX MicroVAX system that performs all address translation functions, holds the e-mail database, and provides a full name lookup service for off-campus users. This e-mail router is tightly integrated with the campus telephone directory database; thus, there is basically a single point of maintenance for all address, phone, and e-mail information for all individuals on campus, even though the technical implementation actually involves a number of batch processes to ensure synchronization with other systems that use the same information.

Telephone Directory System

In the past, the campus telephone directory was published once a year as a hardcopy document, produced using a word processor, and updated annually. Given the length of time it takes to print and distribute a document of this size, and the rate at which people move around on campus, the document was substantially out of date from the day it was published. In 1990, CMTS transferred all telephone directory data into an SQL database on the VAX, and developed a Macintosh client that can access these data. As updates are made to the database, everyone on campus immediately gets access to the correct information. The software is very simple to use—the user simply enters the name or any other attribute of the person or people they are looking for (such as their title or department), and the software presents a screen as shown in Figure 4.

As well as allowing users to obtain current information about anyone on campus, the software allows them to extract specific portions of the directory into fully formatted text files or spreadsheets, so that they can easily

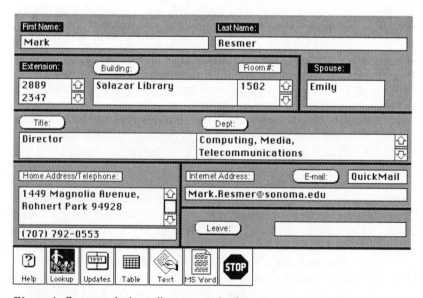

Figure 4. Campus telephone directory on database.

create customized directories for specific areas, or create mailing lists for mail-merge applications.

Networked Fax Service

As part of the campus e-mail implementation SSU has installed a pair of fax systems used, respectively, for incoming and outgoing transmissions. Outgoing faxes can be sent directly as either fully formatted Macintosh documents from any application or as simple e-mail messages from any computer on campus. The system uses a Quickmail gateway machine to provide the required functionality, coupled with a direct connection into the university telephone billing system so that the cost of the phone call associated with each fax transmission is automatically billed back to the correct individual or department. Incoming faxes are received by a central high-speed plain-paper machine with Group 4 capabilities and immediately delivered to recipients. As with hardcopy e-mail delivery, the intent of this arrangement is to ensure that all individuals on campus have access to common communications tools.

The result has been that, for all intents and purposes, everyone on campus has direct access to a high-quality fax machine, without any of the costs associated with mass deployment of fax machines. More importantly, this service is presented in a way that is intimately related to existing communications tools, such as the e-mail system, thus blurring the distinction between different communications tools and making their use more intuitive. As an example, it is a simple matter to set up an e-mail group that consists of an administrator on campus who can receive Quickmail on a Macintosh, a student who prefers to receive mail on a UNIX workstation, a groundskeeper who does not have access to a computer, and hence receives his or her mail in hardcopy form, a faculty member at another campus who can be reached through the Internet, and an individual at a company who has a fax machine but no other form of electronic communication capability. A single message can be sent to the group and automatically delivered by the e-mail system using whichever technology is appropriate. The distinctions are transparent to the sender of the message. Once the addresses are in an address book or the campus mail directory, the technique used for sending all these kinds of messages is identical, and the addresses can be mixed and matched at will.

Computer Conferencing

Another aspect of electronic communications is represented by computer conferencing. SSU is one of the founding members of BESTNET (Binational English-Spanish Teaching Network) — a consortium of institutions of higher education in the United States and Mexico whose purpose is to facilitate the application of information technology and electronic communications tools for teaching, learning, scholarship, community service, and research. In particular, Bestnet is implementing and studying applications of distributed network conferencing, mail, videotext, and related technologies in the areas of instruction, interinstitutional cooperation, research, and administration. The project is currently being funded by Digital Equipment Corporation through a research grant. SSU is one of the primary research partners in this endeavor. The university has a license for MaxNotes, a Macintosh client that accesses the VAX as a Notes server, and is using this software as the primary means for accessing VAX Notes—one of the primary tools being used within the Bestnet project.

LIBRARY ACCESS

Current trends in the development of both libraries and information technology support organizations indicate that a much closer relationship between these areas is likely to become the norm in the 1990s than was typically the case in the 1980s. The university has made a notable effort to reflect and respond to these trends.

Information support organizations are facing a period of rapid change in their missions and in the technologies that are used to provide access to information. On one hand, libraries are no longer merely repositories of books and periodicals, but rather information centers that provide patrons with access to a wide range of nontraditional computer and video-based materials in addition to books. On the other hand, computer centers are serving primarily as facilitators of client access to information, rather than merely as sources of computing power. The library of the future will not be tied to print media. Rather, the Library will serve as a gateway to many products and services that are not located within the library building. These nonprint and electronic gateway products demand the closest partnership between library, computing, and telecommunications operations.

In many ways, electronic access to library information and campus networking mutually justify each other. Without a well-developed data network and associated infrastructure throughout the campus, whatever strides a library might make toward developing nonprint information resources will be of limited value, because patron access to the information will necessarily be limited. Conversely, in the absence of the kinds of information that a library can make available over a data network, it is arguable whether the considerable costs of universal networking can be justified in terms of their benefit to the core academic programs of the institution.

Internet Library Access Software (LIBS)

A very tangible outcome of the partnership between CMTS and the SSU Library has been the development of a network navigation software package for library patrons. Until now, one of the major obstacles to effective use of the Internet by nontechnical individuals, as exemplified by typical library patrons, has been the difficulty of learning about exactly what resources are available at any given remote institution. In many ways, the Internet is somewhat like a library without a catalog—it contains thousands of extremely valuable sources of information, but finding them all is almost impossible. Even when armed with the required information for connecting to a remote system, however, patrons tend to be wary of technical details, such as the differences between Telnet and tn3270, or the syntax of nonstandard Telnet port specifications.

The LIBS software package was developed at SSU in an attempt to address this problem. It is an interactive front-end system that contains a database of the connection parameters for hundreds of On-line Public Access Catalogs (OPACs) throughout the United States and in a number of other countries. The software also contains information about each service, so that patrons can decide whether it may be useful to them before actually initiating a connection. Once a patron has read the description of a service, the menu-driven software handles all the technical parameters for the connection and provides information regarding what a patron needs to do once he or she connects to the remote system in order to use it.

The software is in the public domain and may be downloaded at no cost by anonymous FTP from sonoma.edu. The file is called libs.com and is stored in the /pub directory on the server. A demonstration account is available on another of the SSU VAX systems, so that prospective users of the package can evaluate it before installing it on their local systems. To use the demonstration account, Telnet to vax.sonoma.edu, and log-in as LIBS, no password is required. At the time of writing, the software can be run on almost any VAX/VMS system connected to the Internet. A UNIX-based version is presently under development.

NETWORK-BASED UTILITIES

While the development of distributed systems promises to change the shape of campus information systems for the better in a great many ways, there is no question that from a management viewpoint, some of the relatively simple solutions that mainframe environments made possible are now a thing of the past, and distributed systems, if not carefully managed, do indeed pose some real danger of anarchy. Ubiquitous networking is probably one of the best defenses against such anarchy, and a number of tools have been developed which re-engineer, within a network paradigm, the classic operations that used to be an integral part of mainframe environments. In a well-designed network-based computing environment, it is thus possible to have the best of both worlds: the management benefits of time sharing, together with the freedom offered by distributed systems. Three of the most interesting examples of this kind of rethinking of traditional functions that are presently in use at SSU are network-based software licensing, network-based backups, and network dialup.

Network-Based Software Licensing

In the world of time-sharing computers, tracking and control of software licenses was a relatively simple task. Once a piece of software was installed on a time-sharing system, it immediately became available to all the users of the system. The question of software piracy was in many ways a moot one. Tracking software utilization was similarly generally a simple matter—indeed many operating systems provided extensive accounting packages to perform such functions. With the advent of microcomputers, not only has software distribution and license tracking become a nightmare, but also there is virtually no way of measuring software utilization—a major shortcoming when one considers the costs of software, when multiplied by the number of microcomputers on a typical campus.

One of the less intuitively obvious applications that ubiquitous networking makes possible is network-based software licensing. SSU has implemented an innovative program called KeyServer™ from Sassafras Inc. to perform this function. The KeyServer is a dedicated Macintosh that performs two distinct functions. It can modify any Macintosh application so that the application can only run if it receives authorization to do so from the KeyServer; and it can respond to requests for license keys from client programs it has modified.

In essence, we distribute only the modified versions of applications that have been processed through KeyServer. The applications can be freely copied onto any machine—that is, they do not need to reside on a file server, or on the KeyServer itself. Whenever one of these modified applications is started, it requests a license key from the KeyServer machine. The KeyServer maintains a list of all authorized software packages, the number of licenses for each that are owned by the university, and the number of licenses that are currently checked out.. If a license is available, the KeyServer gives out a key, and the application starts normally. If no more licenses are available, or if someone tries to run a KeyServed application on a nonnetworked computer, the application will refuse to run.

The functionality provided by this package allows us to limit the number of simultaneous users of any Macintosh software package and provides an extremely effective barrier against software piracy. In practical terms, the KeyServed software is completely useless without authorization from the KeyServer—thus rendering software theft pointless. Second, KeyServing software offers us a great deal of flexibility in making software available in multiple labs at different times without having to physically install or de-install the software. Finally, KeyServer provides a built-in tracking mechanism that ensures that we can purchase additional copies of software that is heavily used, rather than purchasing software licenses based on anecdotal evidence.

This combination of features solves most of the major problems associated with microcomputer software support in a university setting, and it has represented a major step forward for the campus in ensuring that such software can be made available and tracked in an effective manner. Despite ceaseless efforts to discourage software piracy by students and faculty, no policy or procedure can ensure that such piracy never takes place. Software protection schemes have proven unreliable and have interfered with software functionality. KeyServer has provided us with a solution that is both secure and functional. The major overhead associated with establishing KeyServed software has been negotiation of specialized license agreements with those vendors who do not currently permit concurrent-use licensing, but this effort has been more than repaid by the functional benefits of such licensing.

Network-Based Backups

In the "good old days" of mainframe-based computing, the Computer Center typically looked after backing up all the data on the computers on a nightly basis. As computing moved from time-sharing systems to microcomputers, backup became the responsibility of individual users, and often this meant that backups simply did not get performed on any kind of regular basis. The result was that when microcomputer disks failed, a lot of valuable data was often lost.

In an effort to prevent this from happening, we have used the network to support an automated campus-wide backup system for all the Macintosh systems. The software used is Retrospect Remote, with a central backup server that uses a 2 gigabyte 8-mm tape drive as the backup medium. The Retrospect client software is purchased centrally and is provided at no cost to end users. Other than leaving their systems on at night, users do not have to take any special steps to ensure that their systems are backed up on a regular basis. Server administration is handled by CMTS in the same way as any other regular backup procedure. The entire cost of the campus-wide backup system, including software and hardware, has been under $10,000—a small investment to ensure the safety of approximately 12 gigabytes of data distributed around the campus on individual microcomputers.

Network Dialup

Another way in which microcomputer-based computing environments typically differ from traditional terminal/host systems is that the latter typically provide remote access through a modem pool of some kind, thus enabling individuals to perform similar tasks, regardless of their physical location. The combination of two relatively new technologies, namely, high-speed V.32/ V.42bis modems, and Macintosh System 7.0, has presented us with an opportunity to create an even more functional version of the traditional dial-in modem pool in the form of remote network dialup access. SSU operates a pool of Shiva NetModems that are available for dialup access to the network. With the appropriate client software on a home computer, and System 7.0 on a networked system on campus, all users can connect to the campus network from anywhere in the country and operate as if they were physically present at their desk. The remote disks on an individual Macintosh can be mounted just as if they were on the local machine, and all network services, including printing, file-serving, Quickmail, and TCP/IP (Telnet, FTP, etc.) are available in exactly the same form as on directly connected Macintosh systems.

FUTURE DIRECTIONS

To quote another vendor: "The best way of predicting the future is to invent it." At this point, the distributed computing environment at SSU is representative of how much can be achieved with readily available tools when they are integrated within a comprehensive overall vision of an information technology architecture. Even though this environment is, by any standards, state-of-the-art, we are actively planning for future developments in the field of networked computing and expect to invent at least some of the future in the process. It is likely that forthcoming developments in the field of network applications will focus on the following areas.

Virtual Labs

As microcomputers continue to get cheaper and more powerful, and at the same time are increasingly used in almost all academic disciplines, it is at least arguable that traditional computer labs as we know them are rapidly becoming an anachronism. If most students are using computers as an integral part of several courses at any given time, it is not realistic in terms of either cost or space requirements for the university to build enough labs to satisfy student demand. Instead, there is a growing trend toward relying on student purchases of microcomputers to meet such demand.

While educational equity considerations suggest that there will always be a place for some labs for those students who cannot afford any other kind of computing access, even for those students who have the resources to purchase their own systems, doing so may not presently be a satisfactory option. In order for student-purchased computers to adequately replicate the functionality available in labs, it is essential that they have the same level of access to network services as do the lab systems. While networking dormitories and providing dialup network access for off-campus users is a good first step in this direction, there are many other ramifications of distributing student access in this way, which need to be recognized and dealt with if such "virtual labs" are to become a worthwhile part of the campus computing environment. Among these issues are questions of software access (network licensing through KeyServer offers some real possibilities in this regard) and support. (Timbuktu, a software package that allows remote users to see and control a network Macintosh, is a viable option for providing remote consultation when a student runs into problems while using their computer outside a lab environment.) While these problems are not yet fully solved, or even completely defined, it seems extremely probable that a single campus-wide virtual lab will be the eventual configuration for day-to-day student computing, consisting of multiple traditional labs and individual student workstations, all with seamless access to a common set of software, peripherals, and information resources. This virtual lab would be supplemented with specialized facilities that exceed the capabilities of the generic environment (e.g., GIS or Multimedia facilities).

Voice/Video/Data Integration

The development of a statewide high-capacity data network has opened the door to a range of innovative applications in which digitized images and/ or sound are transmitted as data over the existing network. We are actively investigating the use of compressed video as a means of remotely delivering instructional programming to off-campus centers. In an era of diminishing resources, we are also considering course-sharing between campuses. On the voice telecommunications front, traditionally voice facilities have been used for data transmission, whether through the use of modems, or as has been the case at SSU, through utilization of campus UTP wiring for data. At this point, the technologies of voice and data transmission have approached each other to such a degree that it is feasible to start considering a reversal of the traditional process. For this reason, the CSU is about to embark on a pilot project that will carry voice telephony over the state data network. Doing so not only avoids long distance telephone charges for intercampus calls, but potentially integrates multiple PBX system into a single voice telephone network, so that enhanced calling features, such as automated forwarding, caller identification, callback for busy lines, and other similar options, become available between campuses, as well as within each campus.

Electronic Document Storage/Retrieval (MARS)

Any educational institution, and especially one that operates within the twin bureaucracies of a large multicampus university system, and a state government system inevitably generate a great deal of paper in the course of doing business. Much of this paper is distributed in multiple copies, and then stored archivally, thus wasting supplies, space, and staff time in its handling. SSU has embarked on a project to store much of this paper documentation in a scanned image format on a MARS WORM optical jukebox system that acts as an image server for the campus and provides access to the documents from any networked Macintosh. At present, all historical paper transcripts dating back to the foundation of the university have been scanned into the system. In addition, various policy documents, the University Catalog, and other significant documents are being stored within the system. We plan to extend the system to include other significant documents, such as Materials Safety Data Sheets (MSDS), for all hazardous materials on the campus, campus publications, and many other types of existing paper-based information.

In each of the instances described above, the beginnings of the project are already in place, or under development on the campus. Therefore, it is reasonably safe to predict that these developments will actually bear fruit in the near future. Looking further ahead is considerably more difficult, but whatever the latter part of the decade may hold, it is a virtual certainty that networking and distributed computing systems will be at its core.

The CREATE Project: Stevens Institute of Technology

Joseph J. Moeller, Jr.
Vice President for Information System
Stevens Institute of Technology

ABSTRACT

A fundamental goal of Stevens Institute of Technology is to prepare all students for successful careers in a rapidly advancing technological world. More than a decade ago Stevens concluded that capable and effective graduates would need to be "computer fluent," and the institute embarked on a plan to guarantee that every Stevens undergraduate student achieved the attributes associated with computer fluency by the time of graduation. Since then, Stevens has been implementing a comprehensive, college-wide approach to the integration of computers in curricula. The educational goal of this program is to develop in each student the high level of computer fluency necessary to benefit learning and to assume a leadership role in the utilization of computers and communications technology in all aspects of professional life.

Stevens spearheaded new approaches to the incorporation of information technologies in the teaching/learning enterprise. This campus-wide initiative is embodied in a multimillion dollar plan for academic computing and networking, the CREATE Project (Computing in Research and Education for an Advanced Technology Environment). The strategic use of computers both to enrich the learning process and to enhance the professional preparation of students is fully consistent with the institute's educational goal of providing the highest quality programs, which are grounded in fundamentals, yet which incorporate significant innovation. Stevens has implemented a leading edge institution-wide network linking computing resources in all academic, administrative, and residence buildings. This seamless mosaic of knowledge stations is utilized by students, faculty, and staff to call on the full distributed processing, information retrieval, and communications facilities, within and outside Stevens, from dormitory rooms, offices, laboratories, and homes.

INTRODUCTION

The mission of Stevens Institute of Technology is to sustain a community of individuals who are dedicated to the achievement of excellence and who share a vision related to engineering, management, and applied and pure science. This includes a dedication to renewing and transmitting established knowledge and understanding; the creation of new knowledge; respect for the wisdom and ethics derived from the humanities; and the development of personal and institutional professional leadership. Stevens aims to impart to each of its graduates, whether from undergraduate, graduate, or continuing education programs, significant new capabilities for successful careers in the worlds of industry, commerce, government service, and academia.

For the past 15 years the Stevens community has been actively establishing a distributed computing and communications environment that is changing the ways in which we learn, teach, conduct research and communicate. The CREATE Project—Computing in Research and Education for an Advanced Technology Environment—focuses on the strategic use of computing and networking to engender creative and productive efforts by all members of the Stevens community. As with our curricular approaches, the CREATE Project is both comprehensive and unified in its implementation.

Stevens has focused on three essential issues. First, our students must be prepared to accept the computer and related technologies as partners in the educational process and in professional practice. Second, our faculty members must be presented with incentives to experiment with information technologies and to reexamine their pedagogical approaches. Finally, our institution must provide the technological and organizational infrastructure necessary to support a creative and effective teaching/learning environment.

THE CREATE PROJECT

The CREATE Project is an institute-wide initiative designed to serve all students, faculty, and staff. Secondary audiences include special programs involving precollege students and teachers, corporate clients and government personnel, as well as those from other higher education institutions. The primary educational goals of this effort are:

1. To establish an enhanced teaching/learning atmosphere through the integration of computers, communications, and information technologies in each of the undergraduate curricula.
2. To impact the professional preparation of students such that they can assume leadership roles in industries and businesses in which the use of computers, communication systems, and related technologies is becoming increasingly pervasive.

Within this environment Stevens has developed a seamless, and essentially transparent, web of computer stations that is utilized by students and faculty to call on the full distributed processing, information retrieval, and communication facilities of the institute.

More than a decade ago the faculty concluded that capable and effective professionals would need to be "computer fluent." Fluency, as Stevens defines it, is manifest through the following attributes:

1. A willingness and propensity to use the computer as an educational aid and tool for professional practice.
2. The ability to engage in dialogue with the computer and to utilize related technologies in a comfortable manner.
3. A knowledge of the capabilities and limitations of available computational facilities.
4. The ability to develop and use computer programs written in a high-level language and to apply them in solving significant problems.
5. A specific knowledge of and experience with numerical methods; modeling, simulation, and design; problem formulation for efficient computer-based solutions; available software packages and their applications; and computer-based instrumentation, data acquisition, and processing.

Stevens was the first college in the country to require undergraduates to own a personal computer. Currently, each Stevens undergraduate owns or leases a sophisticated personal computer system (an AT-compatible computer running the MS-DOS operating system), and hundreds of additional personal computer systems are in the hands of faculty and administrators and in public access laboratories on campus. With the personal desktop computer as a focal point, faculty members at Stevens have identified or produced courseware and computer applications in every academic discipline offered at the institute. These materials range from computer-assisted instruction and tutorial modules and simulations for core courses to professional-quality analysis and design programs for engineering practice in upper level electives.

Yet even with a capable personal computer on each desktop there are limitations in both computational power and information resources. This led, in the mid- to late 1980s, to the creation of a wide variety of departmental computing laboratories for instructional and research activities. These laboratories contain personal computers (PCs), workstations, and minicomputers that serve specific disciplinary courses such as computer-aided design, simulation and modeling, computer graphics, languages and operating systems, and automated manufacturing systems. Commercial, public domain, and in-house software applications are featured in these departmental facilities.

The latest phase of information technology development at Stevens has focused on resources for college-wide access. We have significantly expanded the central systems in our computer center. A cluster of computational servers, a series of file/database servers, a computer conferencing server, an information server, and a communications server have all been installed, hosting a wide variety of systems, utilities, and applications software. In addition, the most important component of this recent phase is the establishment of a state-of-the-art, campus-wide Ethernet and fiber-optic network infrastructure that supports fully distributed, multivendor computing and communications.

The incorporation of computing and information technologies has the potential to fundamentally affect the nature of the teaching and learning process as we know it today.

Through the CREATE Project, a number of curricular objectives have been addressed, including:

- The incorporation of interactive learning involving computer-based instruction and tutorials.
- The development of learning activities involving simulation and graphics.
- The establishment of computer-aided design activities.
- The use of complex modeling involving databases and analytic techniques.
- The use of computers for experimentation.
- The development of student programming skills involving writing, using, and debugging software.
- The incorporation of student-developed applications and utilities in each student's personal library of software tools.

The distributed information technology environment created at Stevens provides the data and communications paths to support these curricular objectives through a series of educational initiatives. The network appears transparent to the user, so that it becomes a natural extension of the user's workstation and learning setting.

Education in a networked environment at Stevens is carried out through a wide spectrum of educational activities, such as

1. Distributed computing applications for design and simulation involving interprocess communications and online databases.
2. Online electronic classroom extension and support services.
3. Online data collection and laboratory interactions.
4. Online discussion, seminars, and conferences.
5. Online self-paced instruction.
6. Online educational development tools.

7. Online access to alternative computing environments.
8. Online access to library resources.

EXTERNAL SUPPORT

The technological infrastructure at Stevens would have been very difficult to implement without active participation by vendors in the form of hardware and software donations and allowances, as well as contributions of technical expertise. We have established strong partnerships with Digital Equipment Corporation and AT&T on a campus-wide basis. In addition, companies such as Sun Microsystems, Apple Computer, and Ardent Computer have worked closely with several departments to meet discipline-specific computing and networking needs. On the software side, educational agreements with Microsoft, Borland International, and Boston Business Computing, among others, have permitted a comprehensive distribution of software products to the entire campus population.

As previously mentioned, a large number of courses have been identified for the incorporation of computing activities. Many of these require dedicated time for planning and software development, funded through grants from more than two dozen corporations, foundations, and government agencies in support of the CREATE Project. The state of New Jersey has aggressively pursued the introduction of computing and networking activities in higher education by establishing several competitive grant programs for public and private colleges; Stevens has been the beneficiary of this support through a series of awards for both single-course and campus-wide projects.

HUMAN AND TECHNOLOGICAL RESOURCES

The organizational structure at Stevens has changed substantially to accommodate the increasing emphasis on computing and information technologies. Initial efforts were nurtured with then existing structures, such as the Educational Development Office and the Undergraduate Curriculum Committee. Technical support for the assessment of personal computers and the design of the network was provided through the Computer Center. It soon became apparent that modified or new entities were required. We initially established two ad hoc faculty-administration committees, on computer planning and computer operations, that reported directly to the chief academic officer.

As new opportunities evolved, so did the organization responsible for computing and networking. A vice president for information systems now provides a point of coordination and planning for all academic and administrative computing, communications, and information-related initiatives and support. The directors of computing and communications resources, the computer service center, management information systems, and the library report within this group. In addition, a 13-member Committee on Academic Computing, which has succeeded the two ad hoc committees and is composed primarily of faculty, is chaired by the Vice President. This committee meets on a regular basis to consider strategic directions for CREATE and for the personal computer program. It is responsible for providing guidelines and recommendations for the continuing development of academic computing initiatives and is concerned with instructional computing activities, research computing, computer planning and operations, assessment activities, and information dissemination.

The computing and communications resources staff is responsible for all major computing systems based in our computer center, for distributed computing including time sharing, local area networking, and external data communications as well as for user services. The computer service center has evolved from an initial focus solely on personal computer logistics, distribution, and maintenance to a full-service operation attending to personal computers, peripherals, terminals, workstations, and data communications equipment throughout the campus. The library, our largest information system on campus, has recently installed an automated system for its operations. Through this system, and through additional student-developed software and interfaces, all members of our community can have direct access through the network to an electronic catalog, a suite of information services, and a variety of database servers providing both abstract and full-text search capabilities.

BENEFITS

A hallmark of our approach to a computer-intensive campus has been the focus on curriculum development. This approach has been possible largely because of significant support (in the form of summer compensation, academic-year release time, programming assistants, and professional staff consultants) for faculty-led development initiatives. It has enabled faculty to target course topics and concepts that can be more effectively presented and understood through computer-based activity. With the availability of higher quality application and utilities software from commercial and other external sources, development projects have increasingly incorporated the use of such products in courses.

Many of the software development projects have been oriented to personal computer applications that students can execute on their own systems. These range from tutorials on engineering mechanics to simulations of biology laboratory experiments. Other projects have targeted workstation platforms in departmental laboratories for activities based on computer-aided design and modeling. The following are examples of several projects currently being implemented:

- Incorporation and use of integrated software (e.g., spreadsheet/graphics/report writer) in the engineering experimentation laboratory. These software tools are supplemented by computer-based data acquisition and control of experimental apparatus.
- Simulation of procedures that a student would use to breed fruit flies for genetic analysis in introductory biology courses. Initially, the program is used by students to assist with the experimental design to correlate types of genetics associated with fly traits. For the advanced student, this SITfly program facilitates gene-mapping experiments.
- Introduction of computer-based tools and visualization resources in freshman calculus courses to facilitate an understanding of course concepts and to enhance problem-solving skills and mathematical experiments.
- Network-based access to and distribution of course materials for the personalized system of instruction (PSI) courses in physics. The electronic format of these materials will enhance individual, self-paced progress in course activities.
- Synthesis and development of a two-dimensional mesh generator for finite element analysis, to be used by students in several mechanical and civil engineering courses. This generator includes an expert system and several knowledge bases. It is part of a pilot project in the development of a Mechanical Systems Modeling Center.
- Creation of a full-text search and analysis facility to enhance study of the writings of Galileo and correlation of themes influencing his work.

More sophisticated development efforts incorporate multiple distributed systems in network-based applications. For example, a three-year grant from the U.S. Department of Education's Fund for the Improvement of Post-Secondary Education (FIPSE) supported an interdisciplinary team of faculty and programmers to integrate network-based simulations of real, complex systems (e.g., chemical reactors) in a multicomputer (PC, workstation, mainframe, and off-campus supercomputer) setting. Students working at their desktop computers transparently utilize the processing and data management resources of all these systems to solve engineering and scientific problems presented by the instructor. As a result, they gain greater insight and a more fundamental understanding of the dimensions and interdependencies involved in such problems.

Efforts to assess the effect of computer integration and computing resources on the educational process have been ongoing at Stevens since the personal computer requirement was established in 1982. This information has been used to guide curriculum and faculty development efforts. Evaluation projects are conducted to determine if the educational goals and the computer fluency attributes are being achieved.

Evidence of success and benefits to date includes:

- A recent survey of faculty indicated that computing and networking activities/projects are incorporated in over 75 courses across the undergraduate curricula.
- Approximately 60 faculty members, out of a total full-time faculty of 120, have been awarded in-house courseware/curriculum development grants during the past eight years, to integrate information technologies in teaching/learning.
- Undergraduate students report an average use of about 15 hours per week with their personal computer and networked resources.
- A recent cohort of cooperative education students on work assignments reported that they utilized computing extensively and that employers considered them to be well prepared regarding use of information technologies—in fact, they were often called on to lead projects involving computing and software development.
- In 1991 many faculty members attended a Computing in Curriculum Symposium, hosted by the Committee on Academic Computing, to learn about and discuss their colleagues' use of computers in coursework.
- External competitive grants, awarded to faculty to address integration of information technologies in undergraduate education, have been received from the U.S. Department of Education, the National Science Foundation, the New Jersey Department of Higher Education, and many corporations and private foundations.
- An extensive evaluation effort (including customized test instruments, surveys, and interview techniques) to assess the impact of the FIPSE-funded interdisciplinary project entitled Integrative Thinking: Education in a Networked Environment has been conducted. General findings show that even brief encounters with computing technology yield measurable improvement in students' confidence and self-rated proficiency in computing. The use of information technologies made clear concepts that were difficult to grasp from more conventional presentations. The added dimension of realism through the simulation environment was a motivating factor for students.

Another benefit of this project was the model established for cross-departmental collaboration involving several academic disciplines and the computer center. This led to more effective sharing of technical resources, expertise, and existing software technology.

- A distinguished Advisory Panel on Computers and Learning, composed of educational leaders of international distinction, worked with Stevens faculty and administration to guide our assessment of the CREATE Project. At one of its concluding meetings, this group voiced the opinion that it is "hard to imagine any other effort which could involve the energies of the entire Stevens community."
- A survey of the first Stevens graduates to have participated in the Personal Computer Plan, conducted a year following graduation, confirmed the feeling that they profited from the experience. They overwhelmingly endorsed the concept of a student computer ownership requirement and contributed valuable suggestions regarding improved integration of computing in the curriculum.

CONCLUSION

The three most critical factors that have contributed to successful implementation of the CREATE Project are:

1. Strong and active faculty involvement in the planning and decision-making aspects of the project. Through the Committee on Academic Computing, the Software Development Support Group, the PC Selection Committee, the Network Planning Committee, the Computers in Education Development Grant program, and commitment to course and curriculum enhancements, faculty contributions have been the key element for success in integrating technology effectively within the teaching/learning enterprise.
2. Planning. A strategic plan integrating both the pedagogical and technical requirements for such an endeavor is essential. The CREATE Project plan is a comprehensive document linking course/curriculum development with the technological resources needed to accomplish the educational goals in both the short and long term.
3. The CREATE Project, and the consequent funding and resource requirements, would be virtually impossible without

the commitment at the highest levels of the administration. At Stevens, the President and Board of Trustees recognized the potential benefits and, therefore, dedicated the appropriate resources to support the project.

Since its inception, our approach to establishing an environment rich in information technologies has involved a significant amount of experimentation—with new ideas, new technologies, and new instructional activities. We have been fortunate to benefit from these efforts through positive effects on teaching, learning, research, and scholarship. Yet, there are many challenges and opportunities ahead.

We are convinced that using computing and information systems strategically through the CREATE Project can enhance our abilities to work effectively and efficiently, while also sharpening the professional preparation of students and the scholarly endeavors of faculty.

The St. John's Networks: A Tale of Two Campuses

Robert Lejeune
Director of Academic Computing Services
St. John's University

In this account I will focus on the evolution of the Academic Computing networks on the two St. John's University campuses over the past three and a half years. By looking at these networks through developmental and comparative lenses, I hope to highlight the influence of changing circumstances as well as the impact of different campus environments on the emergent networks.

The major difference between the two campuses is the size of student population. The main campus of St. John's University is located in Jamaica, Queens. It has an FTE (full-time equivalent) of approximately 14,000. The smaller campus is on Staten Island, located some twenty-two miles away. It has an FTE of approximately 2,300. There are also demographic and cultural variations that contribute to the unique character of each campus. Out of these differences there has emerged two distinct modes of organizing the campus networks.

As part of a major effort to upgrade academic computing facilities, I was hired in April 1988 as Coordinator of the Faculty Support Center for Computing. In that role I was to create a curriculum and an organization to provide computer support to faculty in the pursuit of their research and teaching endeavors. When I arrived on the scene there was a broad outline of St. John's commitment to upgrading computer facilities, but the concrete development can best be seen as an evolutionary process emerging out of the interaction of needs, human and financial resources, and changing technology.

THE JAMAICA CAMPUS: THE ACADEMIC COMPUTING NETWORK'S "EARLY DAYS"

Our story begins at the Jamaica campus in the summer of 1988 when Academic Computing and Administrative Computing were still under the same umbrella. At that time the Honeywell mainframe running under the Multics operating system was the hub around which academic computing at St. John's was organized. Summer, a time when most academics rest and refresh,

183

is usually the busiest time for academic computing professionals: new labs, new classrooms, new equipment, new software. But this was a relatively leisurely summer dedicated to installing the first local area network (LAN) which was to connect 50 IBM PS/2s model 50Z in three new microclassrooms.

These computerized classrooms would offer a unique opportunity for educational innovations. The professor would enter information on his or her computer. It would be projected on a large screen at the front of the room by means of an Electrohome projector. The students could then replicate at their computers what the instructor had just demonstrated. The summer of 1988 was a turning point in the teaching of computer science and other subjects at St. John's. The old way of learning programming and computer applications with chalk and blackboard, notebook, and pen had been replaced by a much more effective method.

Designing a LAN was also a turning point for the Academic Computing group at St. John's. Because of the strong IBM presence and the conversion from a Honeywell to an IBM 4381 mainframe, it was decided to implement the token-ring topology. At that time my only input was to voice strong objections to IBM's recommendation of IBM's networking software (PC LAN) and to push for Novell NetWare. (I was then Coordinator of the Faculty Support Center for Computing, an observer of this emerging network, rather than a participant at its creation.) The matter was settled when Novell Corporation granted us a free copy of NetWare 286.

The two people assigned to the task of setting up this first network had never installed a LAN before. The cabling, IBM TypeI, was completed in the early part of the summer. Installing Novell NetWare 286 v 2.01 and the applications was done in August, before the new semester started. With little training, some guidance from vendors, much reading, some trial and error, and a huge amount of enthusiasm, the fall of 1988 semester opened with a fully functional network. Some three dozen applications and programming languages were running off a PS/2 model 80 with a 311 megabyte hard drive and (initially) only 2 megabytes of RAM. They were each being accessed from the Novell menu, sometimes by as many as 50 students each at their own computers pressing the enter key almost at the same instant as they all launched an application.

The three classrooms, separated from each other by folding doors, could be opened to form either one or two larger classrooms, depending on need. Two of the rooms were equipped with Electrohome projectors connected to the instructors' computers in the front of the room. In addition, two other presentation classrooms with only a computer for the instructor connected to an Electrohome projector were also created that summer. In these classrooms the instructor could demonstrate software or programming techniques which the students would try out later in the micro-labs.

Both the micro-classrooms and the presentation classrooms were huge successes in the academic year 1988-89. Remarkably, the network, running on an IBM PS/2 model 80 never went down for even a second in that first year. The persons responsible take great pride in the care they took in setting up that first network. And well they should. But in retrospect it is clear that, in addition to excellent workmanship, sturdy equipment, and beginner's luck, the first network benefited from a leisurely schedule. It was created in an orderly manner, with plenty of time for cabling, software installation, and testing. This does not mean that everything was done perfectly or that we did not experience many minor difficulties, from the projector failure to memory problems—both persistent challenges to this day. All in all, despite the usual bugs, the micro-classroom was a success technically as well as pedagogically.

That first year was an absolutely essential time of learning prior to our subsequent growth. It was also a time, and it continues to be, when the system was improved incrementally, almost every week as the Academic Computing network group experimented and learned. For example, in that first year, the file server was upgraded to 4 and to 6 megabytes of RAM. Repeatedly, the user interface was made more friendly. Eventually—in part to improve memory management—we changed from the built-in Novell Menu System interface to the more powerful Saber Menu System interface. But the desire to keep within a tight budget on the part of a budget administrator who had minimal understanding of the new technology also led to skimping on essential "behind the scene" equipment. Some items that should have been purchased that first year were not. This proved to have been false economy. Only later, for instance, did we learn from punitive experience that it is absolutely essential to have an uninterruptible power supply (UPS) attached to each file server.

Meanwhile, as the microcomputer group became proficient in network support, the "old" equipment in two micro-labs (mostly IBM PCs and Lear Siegler ADM5 dumb terminals previously connected to a Honeywell mainframe) were replaced with PS/2s model 50Z installed with 3270 emulation cards. For the 1988-89 academic year, the university's microcomputer facilities were running on two tracks: a network in the micro-classroom and stand-alone PS/2s in the micro-labs and presentation classrooms. The administration and upgrading of software were becoming formidable tasks as faculty began to request an increasing number of applications and services.

In the spring of 1989, Academic Computing was split off from Administrative Computing. The Academic Computing group came under the direct supervision of the Executive Vice President, who was to take an active role in the growth and enhancement of Academic Computing in his last two years before retirement. This split removed Academic Computing from the control of individuals who had very limited understanding of the potentials of micro-computers and LAN technology. In June 1989, I was appointed Director of Academic Computing Services. I assumed the position on July 1. By then plans had already been made, and work was well underway, to expand and increase the number of micro-labs from two to four and to network all Academic Computing facilities. It was also decided to bridge the micro-labs to each other and to the micro-classrooms. In effect, one seamless microcomputer network was being created where just a year before there had been some stand-alone PCs and dumb terminals connected to the mainframe.

Whereas the summer of 1988 had been relatively relaxed, if not uneventful, the summer of 1989, both before and after I assumed responsibility, was a mad race to put together a network consisting of four micro-labs in four separate buildings separated by as much as 1,200 feet. The Academic Computing network staff on the Jamaica campus had grown to six full-time persons, and a dozen or so part-time student workers. Three labs totaling 120 workstations were being redone from scratch: carpeting, painting, wiring, furniture, and of course setting up of the hardware and software. A fourth lab of 50 workstations simply needed to be networked. In addition, 20 standalone Mac IICX and the application software were ordered and installed that summer. The task fell on a young crew, none of whom had ever had experience in such an undertaking. All cables were run by electricians, but the demanding task of soldering the ends of the coaxial cable for the mainframe and the ends of the type I cable for the token-ring Network was to be ours. Once again we were spared the expense of Novell NetWare. We received five additional free copies through the educational grants program.

There was much to do and even more to keep track of: furniture, hardware and software to order, receive, and allocate was just the beginning. NetWare had to be installed four separate times for each micro-lab, followed by the applications. A fifth server was also installed for the use of the staff, as a backup for any of the other file servers and, most importantly, as a test network where we could try out new procedures and software. Equipment arrived late, and the soldering had to be done at the last minute, largely by enthusiastic but inexperienced student workers. They saved the university much money, and a fabulous esprit de corp was built up over those last few weeks before the fall 1989 semester was to begin, but the cost in badly soldered joints—and consequent downtime—plagued us for many months thereafter. When the semester started, three of the four labs were functional. A fourth, the last one put up in the utmost rush, was a problem. The server would power down unpredictably. After several days and nights of frustration, I called in a consultant, who, if nothing else, had appropriate testing equipment. Several days later the network was up. On the basis of our consultant's recommendations, I was able to justify the purchase of some UPSs (uninterruptible power supply), a tape backup, and other needed equipment. We were also reminded of the importance of thorough documentation: keeping a log and scrupulously labeling cables. These were procedures that, in small but significant ways, had been neglected by the troops in the trenches in the mad rush to open the lab on time. There had been several contributing factors to the troubles we experienced, not the least of which were electrical problems that resulted in power fluctuations. But, most of all, it is clear that the need to meet unrealistic and externally imposed deadlines and budget (without essential equipments such as a cable tester, UPSs and a tape backup system) had led to too many compromises. Networks should be planned and installed in an orderly work environment and with the appropriate tools. The contrast between the installation of the first network and these subsequent networks once again indicates that in such a complex technical environment haste (and inadequate financing) makes waste.

All the micro-labs were now ready for the new semester and all Academic Computing facilities were tied together as one network. Until September 20, 1989, the system was a huge success. On that date we were hit by our first virus: Jerusalem B. Since we were now bridged, the virus spread in a matter of hours to the four labs and the micro-classrooms. The whole system, except for the Faculty Support Center which had not yet been networked, had to be shut down at this peak time. Fortunately, in those "early days" all of the software on the network could be run from a 60 megabyte local hard disk, and the essential applications could fit on a 30 megabyte disk. Through no great foresight on our part—it was the only way we could buy PS/2s from IBM—all computers in the micro-labs and the micro-classrooms were equipped with at least a 30 megabyte hard disk. Most had 60. We were back in operation within 48 hours. After doing a low level format of every machine to make sure that the virus was not lurking on any of the local hard disks, we installed fresh software on one machine and backed it up on floppies. We then restored it to all micro-classroom and micro-lab computers. Eight computers in each micro-lab were attached to a Buffalo Box connected to a laser printer, in order to continue to provide printing services without a network. For the rest of the semester it was back to the standalone "stone age" from which we had just evolved.

The virus attack of 1989 was a blessing in disguise. It gave us the breathing room we had not had during the summer. It justified the initial shutdown of the network and allowed us to take the necessary time to create a secure system. A security committee was formed, and in the next few weeks we all learned a great deal about viruses and virus detection software. We purchased Scan from McAffee Associates for the IBM network and Symantec Antivirus from Symantec Corporation for the Macs. A checkpoint was set up in each lab where all student disks were checked for viruses before being used in the micro-lab computers. Many other procedures were instituted to protect the system from future infections. In addition to restricting access to the file server drive, we also denied all student access to the local hard drives. The vast majority of students could easily maintain all of their semester's data on a 1.2 megabyte high-density micro-diskette. A few students in advanced courses were given access to directories in the micro-classroom server, but essentially the network became a closed system. By the time we resumed as a fully bridged network in the spring of 1990, we had set up a very secure network, the way it might have been done had we had more time, the funds, and the foresight that previous summer. Since then we have intercepted many viruses, but none has ever infected our system again. Probably the most important lesson learned from the virus infection was the need to have, in an academic environment, fortuitously or not, a secure and fault-tolerant system.

CONTRAST BETWEEN THE JAMAICA AND THE STATEN ISLAND CAMPUSES

During the fall of 1989 attention had also turned to networking the Academic Computing facilities on the Staten Island campus. This smaller campus did not as yet have a micro-classroom or presentation classroom. Both teaching and lab usage occurred in the micro-lab consisting of 20 IBM PS/2s model 50Z and a few XTs. A new staff of two had just been hired in October: one full-time manager with Novell experience and his assistant. They, working with a small crew of part-time student workers, were to be responsible for the one micro-lab, all microcomputer support on the campus, as well as the future expansion of Academic Computing facilities. That fall, plans were made to network the lab during the winter break. Further expansion and development was planned.

The organization of Academic Computing Services was very different at the two campuses. Because of its smaller size, the Staten Island campus was more informal, less bureaucratic. The previous manager and only full-time computer person on the campus had passed away that summer. He was from a mainframe environment and knew very little about microcomputers. The micro-lab on Staten Island had essentially been run by student workers, particularly on weekends and in the evening. In addition to its smaller size, the Staten Island campus had an active "hacker" subculture whose members "hung out" at the micro-labs, whether or not they were being paid. By contrast, the students on the Jamaica campus were for the most part less knowledgeable in the use of computers when they were hired as micro-lab workers. Only a handful had any programming skills. (Computer science majors and other students with computer skills tend to find more lucrative employment off campus.) It would have been impossible to keep the labs open on the Jamaica campus on weekends and at night without at least one full-time network administrator. Of necessity, the micro-lab on Staten Island was (and is) maintained much of the time by student workers.

At both campuses, student utilization of computer facilities fluctuates over the course of the semester, with peak use occurring two weeks before midterms and finals. At these times the labs are used to capacity, and there is frequently an overflow of students who have to be placed on waiting lists. At other times, more in the "early days" than now, the labs are relatively empty. It is a challenge to keep student workers productively occupied during slow periods so that they will be available during peak periods. But because of campus differences, the management style required on the two campuses is also different. At the Jamaica campus, student workers who use the labs need training in application software and the basics of the computer language interfaces. Slow periods are used for training and preventive maintenance of equipment. On Staten Island, the student workers can be assigned programming projects, software installation, and troubleshooting; the main managerial objectives during slow periods are to keep student workers busy with challenging tasks, coordinate their activities, as well as prepare them to be responsive to the needs of faculty and students.

While the Jamaica campus adapted to its much improved facilities, the Staten Island campus moved forward. In the fall of 1989 semester, the cabling for the Staten Island micro-lab was completed, and a test network consisting of one IBM PS/2 model 80 running Novell NetWare 286 v 2.15 and one workstation was set up. During the winter break, the Staten Island micro-lab was fully networked and ready for the spring semester. At that time, the Staten Island micro-lab was essentially a smaller mirror image of any one of the labs on the Jamaica campus. For the future, the manager of the Staten Island Academic facilities had the autonomy to configure the system as he saw fit to meet the particular local needs.

In the summer of 1990 Academic Computing facilities at St. John's continued to grow. While the Jamaica campus added two new presentation classrooms, the Staten Island campus added a full micro-classroom with 25 IBM PS/2s model 55SX and a presentation classroom. The Staten Island micro-lab's seating capacity was also increased from 20 to 30 by the addition of ten IBM PS/2s model 55SX.

Staten Island facilities, being smaller in size and more flexible, seemed ideal for trying out new technology. It was less risky and less expensive to experiment with a 25-node network than with one of 240. Microcomputer software vendors do not always deliver what they promise. Experience makes one cautious. I decided we ought to test out Novell 386 in the soon to be created Staten Island micro-classroom. The need for a network operating system that would support more than 100 users on the Jamaica campus network was becoming evident. Novell 386, which had just come out, would meet future as well as present needs. The Staten Island classroom, with 25 PS/2s model 55SX and Novell NetWare 386, was up and running without a hitch by the fall of 1990. Also implemented on Staten Island was a new Faculty Support Center for Computing with six workstations attached to the micro-lab network and a presentation classroom computer attached to the micro-classroom network.

A TIME OF CONSOLIDATION

We had met the primary objective of setting up the required facilities under fairly tight schedules. By the spring of 1990, with a significant experiential base and some breathing space before us, we could take some time and look at ways to improve the system in the light of identified needs, and to try to find ways to make it as cost effective as possible. But the time for reflection was very brief indeed. We had changed from a "primitive" standalone system to a networked system in less than three years. As the services had improved, the demand for new services had also increased: new software, upgrades of old software, and most of all, a growing amount of micro-lab utilization. In the fall of 1990 semester, a total of 5,831 students had used the micro-labs, compared to 5,342 in the fall of 1989 semester. This was only a 9 percent increase, but, over that same time period the amount of usage, measured in terms of number of sessions at the computer, increased from 31,395 to 47,753—a growth of 52 percent. (There had also been a dramatic growth in the number of software packages installed and supported—from under 40 in 1988 to more than 85 currently.)

Upon analysis three points stood out:

1. Fault-tolerance was paramount. We could not afford to have the micro-classroom down for even a day. This would disrupt a half dozen or more classes. In the micro-labs a small number of computers was serving a large population of users. During peak periods, a micro-lab being down for more than a few hours might lead to long waiting lines.
2. A way had to be found to economize on human resources. The staff was limited by budgetary and other constraints, yet the need for services increased at more than 10 percent per semester. Maintaining five separate networks, which needed to be updated on a weekly basis, was very labor intensive.
3. We needed a way of metering software usage for the combined Academic Computing facilities in order to reduce software cost and conform to license requirements. With five sep-

arate networks, metering was not possible unless each micro-lab was dedicated to a subset of the total software library. Even if this type of software fragmentation had been practical, it would still have been necessary to duplicate most of the software used in the micro-labs networks on the micro-classroom network. In fact this was not possible; students and faculty had to access most software packages from all locations on campus.

Several innovations in software and hardware technology led to the decision to upgrade the Jamaica campus in ways that would meet these objectives. On the hardware side the development of high-performance servers ("superservers") suggested the possibility that all microcomputer software for the 240 Academic Computing PS/2s that were networked on the Jamaica campus could be stored on one file server. This would only be desirable if, on the software side, the network operating system could support that many nodes and if effective metering software was available. The first condition was met when NetWare 386 was released, and the second, with the release of Sitelock software from Brightwork Development. The plan was to attach the superserver to one central ring or backbone and hang each of the micro-labs, the micro-classroom, and our Academic Computing staff network off this backbone. Each of the subsidiary or local rings would be bridged to the backbone through each of the local PS/2 model 80 servers.

In the spring of 1991, I obtained approval for the funds to upgrade all the Academic Computing networks to NetWare 386 and to purchase a PS/2 model 95 to be our "superserver." (We were no longer getting a free ride from Novell.) Justification for the new system was based on projected software savings that would pay for the upgrade within two to three years, but there were three additional reasons for upgrading the system.

1. We anticipated significant labor savings from having all software installed in one central location. It would reduce the effort and time required to add, delete, and upgrade applications.
2. The superserver was a cost-effective way of increasing the fault-tolerance of the system. Should the superserver go down, the local servers (PS/2s model 80) in each of the micro-labs or micro-classroom network could kick in as file servers, with no visible interruption of service. When not used as file servers, each of these machines would act as bridges to the backbone ring and as print servers.
3. An integrated LAN with a superserver on the backbone would permit us to install a gateway from the mainframe to the LAN.

By doing this we could reduce our hardware costs, eliminating some controllers on the mainframe and all 3270 emulation cards in each of the PS/2s. A combination of NetWare for SAA installed on the superserver and NetWare 3270 LAN workstation for DOS v 2.0 would allow us to support 64 host sessions with one 3174 cluster controller.

In the summer, we began the conversion to the system outlined above with no major hitch. Novell 386 was certainly easier to install than its predecessor. So far, we have supported nearly 250 workstations at peak load without experiencing any difficulties. The PS/2 95 has performed admirably as a superserver. As I write in the last days of November 1991, we have had nearly one semester's experience with this system. We are beginning to see some of the anticipated software savings. Similarly the time savings gained by having to make software additions and changes in one location rather than six has been a lifesaver as the number of users and software packages increases.

It is in the area of fault-tolerance that we have probably gained the most. Although our superserver has not failed us yet, it is certain that it will one day. We routinely back it up and restore to each of the local servers, for that eventuality.

Fault-tolerance was also of concern on Staten Island. But different circumstances led to a different solution. In the summer of 1991, a cable was run between the micro-lab and the micro-classroom, which are located in different buildings. In the fall of 1991 the manager of the Staten Island campus was able to install both micro-lab and micro-classroom software off one of the two PS/2 model 80 file servers. This had the effect of freeing the second server to become a backup to the first. Weekly backups and testing of the system guarantee that a server failure will create only minor disruption in a system that is used to capacity much of the time. The implementation of Sitelock for software metering on the Staten Island campus has also reduced software costs on that campus.

As we continue to upgrade our facilities in stages, from 286 to 386SX or 386DX, we also plan to speed up the network by upgrading the token-ring cards from 4 to 16 megabits per second. By using a topology in which each ring is attached to a backbone ring, we will be able to upgrade the CPU at each node, one ring at a time, and increase the speed of the network in stages. Thus far, we have just upgraded the backbone and Academic Computing staff rings to 16 million instructions per second (mips). The classroom ring is next, followed by each of the micro-labs. (In the token-ring topology the transmission speed on a ring is limited by the speed of the slowest card on the ring.)

As we look to the immediate future, the major improvements relate primarily to host-to-LAN connectivity and upgrading of equipment to support

Windows and (perhaps) OS/2. These two projects are well on their way to completion. Our gateway to the IBM 4381 should be operational by the beginning of the spring 1992 semester. By the fall 1992 semester, all the micro-classroom computers and a significant proportion of the micro-labs will be upgraded to 386SX and 386DX machines.

For the more distant future, we are working on various pilot projects intended to enhance the services provided on the networks. For example, we have set up and experimented with remote access and the use of CD-ROMs on the LAN. CD-ROM access has been set up on an experimental basis on the Staten Island network. A remote access server has been operational for nearly a year on the Jamaica network. (Unfortunately, the technology is not sufficiently developed to serve large numbers of students and thereby relieve some of the utilization pressures on the micro-labs.) The list of additional projects is endless—from linking the Macs to the network and host, to connecting to Internet.

Many innovations in the years ahead will have to be organizational and procedural. They will need to address the problem of continuing growth of services under conditions of limited resources. One typical example can stand for many: two additional presentation classrooms are scheduled for the spring semester 1992. Their additions, as well as the secular trend in computer use, will inevitably add to micro-lab utilization. Each semester we will be called on to provide more services to faculty and students, but the size of our staff is frozen owing to financial constraints. Most of the procedures we will be using to increase productivity in the years ahead are likely to involve the use of office automation—from bar codes to electronic mail and scheduling. In the university, well into the next century, the major challenge will be to use human resources more creatively. Departments of Academic Computing have many of the tools necessary to lead the way.

The Development of a Local Area Network at Trinity University

Robert V. Blystone
Professor of Biology
Trinity University, San Antonio, Texas

Lawrence H. Gindler
Assistant Director for User Services and Networking
Trinity University, San Antonio, Texas

The establishment of a unified campus local area computer network requires financial resources, human resources, and a common goal. As obvious as these three ingredients may seem, they are difficult to align. At Trinity University the development of a common goal for the campus local area network (LAN) has been the most difficult element to put into place. Human resources usually follow when a goal has been articulated. And with a goal and human resources coupled, appropriate arguments can be raised to obtain the financial resources. This report is directed to our experience at Trinity University in aligning these three elements for the purpose of establishing a unified campus local area computer network.

INTRODUCTION

In terms of defining the goal of the unified campus LAN, the Trinity faculty and administration have much to do. A starting point is the development of a definition, for the term *local area network* conveys different meanings. To some, LAN merely means terminal service to a mainframe computer. To others, the term implies a series of intelligent workstations with peer-to-peer connections. These extreme views of a LAN must be resolved when establishing a campus network. Initially, Trinity faculty and staff perceived the LAN only in the general terms of connectivity. The stated purpose for the connectivity, however, varied greatly depending on who was asked. Even now other than connectivity, the goal for the campus LAN is still subject to debate and mere connectivity does not adequately define the objective of a LAN.

The human resource element of the LAN development equation at Trinity has three constituencies: administration, faculty, and students. The administration participation in a LAN is usually a loop closed to faculty and students. The sensitive nature of institutional finance and student records sequester much of the administrative use on a unified campus-wide LAN. Faculty view a LAN from three general perspectives: the first, facilitating courses taught by individual faculty; second, e-mail access to both on- and off- campus colleagues and to students; and third, support for professional research. Students have the least defined role and voice in a campus LAN. Although outnumbering combined administration and faculty computer users by a margin of greater than 5 to 1, students assume a passive nature in LAN design and implementation. LAN utilization for students usually means access to common, course-oriented software from servers maintained by departments or by larger restricted access domains. Too frequently each constituency sees a unified campus LAN from the basis of special interests. At our campus, therefore, the human resource element is fragmented in terms of what each perceives to be the objective of the campus LAN.

The financial component of the Trinity LAN equation is surprisingly the element of least resistance. Trinity's experience with LANs follows the usual evolutionary course. We began 20 years ago with clusters of "dumb" terminals hardwired to the campus mainframe. As microcomputer technology improved, special function satellite LANs based on personal computers (PCs) appeared. We now face the proposition of merging satellite LANs and the mainframe LAN into a comprehensive campus-wide LAN. This last stage of LAN development is encouraged by the availability of financial resources. Installation of an extensive NOTIS-based, online library database system is almost complete. The administration has budgeted for a new campus telephone system. Our faculty has been successful in gaining extramural funding for computing. The proper disposition of financial resources requires the clarity of a defined goal with the backing of the human resource element.

As can be seen by the information above, LAN development at Trinity is most dependent on defining and ranking the universe of applications that a LAN would support. This defining and ranking has proven to be a substantial problem. As you will read, our work on the problem has led to some specific recommendations.

THE COMPUTING LANDSCAPE AT TRINITY

The university's institutional mission statement begins by stating: "Trinity University is an independent, nonsectarian, coeducational university, in the tradition of the liberal arts and sciences." To this end our institution resembles many small, private, liberal arts colleges. Our 2,300 selectively admitted undergraduate students are joined by 200 graduate students (in three graduate programs) on a primarily residential campus near the center of a multi-cultural city of 1.1 million people. Although a pleasant city in which to live, San Antonio is geographically isolated from major technological centers. Trinity's access to major computer networks is by way of the Texas Higher Education Regional Network via the University of Texas Health Science Center at San Antonio. The gateway to the NSF backbone is through Rice University in Houston, Texas.

The user profile and physical environment is quite varied. Of 231 tenure-track faculty, 107 have accounts on the campus mainframe. Only five of these faculty use the mainframe for something other than e-mail. Over 600 students have accounts on the mainframe. The university maintains just under 600 microcomputers on its service inventory, with 40% being Apple manufactured. The institution currently inventories 330 printers. This PC-based equipment is nearly evenly divided between teaching and administrative uses. The majority of the computers are distributed among 16 major teaching buildings. The student residential areas have very limited access to university computer equipment and networks other than by modem over standard telephone lines.

Several elements combine to give our institution a distinctive networking environment. Although a small campus, the Trinity mainframe is an IBM 4381, model Q13. The Science departments are important to the overall curriculum but not dominating. There are no graduate programs in the sciences. The campus has a large library with over 700,000 volumes. The endowment of nearly $300 million allows the university to make choices. However, like all educational institutions, Trinity is finding it difficult to cope with the costs of technology.

All academic departmental offices have at least one personal computer; however, few of these machines are networked to each other, especially in the humanities and fine arts. Three departments (health care, philosophy, and classical studies) have inclusive departmental LANs consisting of every faculty member, the departmental office, a file server, and a printer server. Six departments (geology, chemistry, engineering science, computer sciences, physics, and math) are now on an emerging unified LAN. Some faculty members in this six-department cluster are not on the network. One additional department (communications) has a LAN that excludes several faculty. Several small multiple machine LANs exist, generally within one faculty member's lab (such as Biology) or between several contiguous faculty (psychology). The six Science department LAN has become the nucleus of the mainframe independent, unified campus LAN known as the "backbone." Eight high-density microcomputer clusters of ten or more machines are available for student use. Four are university-operated (two Apple-based and two PC-based) and four departmentally operated (communication, math, biology, and physics). Administrative computer networking needs are primarily mainframe dependent. There are, however, five small satellite administration LANs in operation: security, personnel, physical plant, continuing education, and financial aid.

COMPUTER POLICIES AT TRINITY

The requirements for a bachelor's degree at Trinity University include a statement about computer skills: "students must be able to use computers to organize, analyze, and communicate information." This statement was initiated by the faculty and agreed to by the administration and the governing board of trustees. The statement's intent was that a student be computer literate to the point where he/she could effectively use a computer in professional life. The literal meaning has become that a student can perform usual software manipulation involving word processing and spreadsheet functions and that the student has some basic understanding of how the computer and programming works. Many students satisfy this skill requirement with a proper one-year high school course or by completing one of five different introductory computer courses at Trinity.

This recognition of the need for computer skills as a component of the general curriculum is highly important. It signifies that the university is willing to commit resources to implement the meeting of the curriculum requirement. In addition, the faculty recognizes that computer use can serve as a tool to further the ideas of a liberal arts and sciences education.

As important as computer use is to the curriculum, potential incongruities are apparent. No hard data exist as to how many faculty have computers in their campus office or daily work area. No hard data exist as to how many faculty personally own computers. It is generally accepted that more than half of the faculty use a computer daily. Furthermore, it is estimated that about a quarter of the faculty use the computer for a function other than word processing. Reciprocally, it is estimated that about a quarter of the faculty could not meet the students' curriculum requirement for computer skills. Related estimates are that about half the faculty have had no formal computer training. Two of five top administrative personnel (the President and four Vice Presidents) maintain computers in their personal offices. One maintains a personal account on the mainframe. Only one administrator has day-to-day experience with networking. These administrators' activities are structured in such a way that computer use information, including networking, generally comes to them from intermediaries.

Many faculty consider the administration's view of computing as a cost to be contained rather than an opportunity to be seized. Conversely, the Administration finds the faculty often inarticulate as to their computing needs. Adding to this tension concerning computing, new faculty frequently receive microcomputers as a condition of employment. During the interviewing process, these candidates can effectively argue for a computer based on an ongoing experience and/or research dependence. Established faculty, who often developed their principal academic skills without a reliance on computing, often have too little computing experience to justify a computer properly. Some institutions solve the problem of dichotomous faculty computing experience by placing a computer in every faculty office. Trinity chose not to take this approach to faculty access to computer resources.

About half the Trinity faculty buy their own microcomputers. These machines are typically Intel 286- or Motorola 68000-based. These computers are more likely to be kept at home rather than the campus office. Surprisingly, many faculty who purchased their own computers balk at buying modems for their machines. The majority of faculty with microcomputers in their campus offices received access to such equipment as conditions of employment and/or from various types of grants.

Two major groups examine computer use on campus. The Administrative Users Group (AUG) is quite effective but is largely unknown to the faculty. The AUG meets regularly and is overseen by the Registrar. All components of the administration are represented on the AUG. This group determines resource allocation concerning the mainframe. The second group is known as the Computer Activities Committee (CAC) and has a 13 person structure: 6 faculty, 4 administration, and 3 students. The CAC advises the administration primarily as to the general academic needs for computing on campus. The CAC does not have the same resource allocation authority as does the AUG. The CAC is involved in setting university academic computer lab policy. The principal function of the CAC for the last three years has been advocacy of a campus-wide LAN.

An additional policy is worthy of mention. As a computer loses its utility to one person, it can be passed on to another. However, the donor department receives no credit for the computer as it leaves its inventory. This action has resulted in the hoarding of old equipment. Hoarding has been solved with a new computer service policy. All university computer service is now performed in-house, with each machine charged a mandatory, set monthly service fee. Many departments returned seldom-used CPUs to avoid paying the service fee, and machines changed hands rapidly.

THE LIBRARY ANALOGY

The relationship between computer resources and library resources bears special mention and comparison. Support for the library consumes 8% of the educational budget of our university. On college campuses the library represents the single most identifiable academic resource other than faculty.

Information and services associated with the library are considered indispensable to the academic program. In the minds of most, the library is the center if not the heart, of the college. Some would argue that computer resources should be given similar budgetary and esteem status. By contrasting library to computation as resources, LAN development issues can be sharpened.

Library resources are centralized into one self-contained facility at our institution. Similarly, the campus mainframe, its peripherals, and operating staff are centralized in one building which is shared with only one other occupant, the Computer Science Department. There are no divisional or departmental libraries. In contrast, several departmentally maintained computer facilities exist. Thus, the library is centralized whereas computational facilities have a focus with numerous satellites.

The physical currency of resource exchange of the library is a book, and for computation it is a PC. The distribution of the currency poses a contrasting problem. Faculty have unlimited, semester-long checkout privileges of standard library materials. This practice in principle means that a faculty member could easily sequester several thousand dollars worth, of library resources in his or her office. There is no comparable university lending program for computer resources. Thirty library books on the shelves of a faculty member are lost among the other printed matter, whereas a new 386 with a VGA monitor attracts attention. The brace of books and the PC cost about the same.

The library operates as a discrete budgetary unit under the control of the Office of the Vice President for Academic Affairs. The Director of the Library serves on the Vice President's Deans' Council. All library resources are purchased through the library budget. Academic departments rarely buy books or similar library materials from their academic budgets. The Computing Center also operates under a budget managed by the Vice President for Academic Affairs. However, the Office of Fiscal Affairs can make significant demands on that budget to support administrative computing needs. This action complicates administration of the Computing Center's budget. Another management difference is reflected in that the Director of the Computing Center is not a member of the Academic Deans' Council. Furthermore, academic departments are expected to provide departmental funds for computer equipment operated within the department. Budgeting procedures for library resources and computational resources can vary a great deal, although the Office of Academic Affairs maintains all budget authority.

The library maintains a staff of eight whose major function is to provide bibliographic instruction and help. Such instruction is designed to broaden access to the extensive library holdings. These librarians are also afforded tenure-track faculty positions. In contrast, the Computing Center maintains a staff of two academic computer specialists in nonfaculty positions. These individuals serve to facilitate computer efforts in both university-maintained facilities and departmental units. Continuing this personnel comparison, the library has staff who function to "network" into other academic library collections. This library networking provides for both cataloging needs and patron requests. Reference librarians are given continuing network training in order to help faculty and students with online information gathering. However, the Computing Center is not staffed to provide formal training in Bitnet, Internet, FTP, and TCP/IP protocols. Finallly, the library has a number of resources designed to help a patron navigate the bibliographic collection. Far fewer materials are available for easing computer patrons into the software collection.

Faculty perception of the library is also different from computer resources. Every faculty member takes ownership of the library. Every faculty member considers himself or herself an able user of library resources. Faculty see other faculty in the library. And remember, the library maintains a staff of eight people to teach and facilitate the use of the library as a resource. Faculty find it more difficult to take ownership of computer resources. Faculty rarely visit the mainframe, a place where administrators are more commonly found. The administration is the chief client of the mainframe, whereas the faculty and students are the chief clients of the library. Yet, faculty raise funds to purchase computer equipment, but play a lesser role in library acquisition, especially fund raising.

The library analogy has been designed to contrast the resource perspective of both library and computational assets. There is convergence in the real world. The library at Trinity is rapidly computerizing. The paper catalog has been replaced by a digital one. Some faculty for the first time (and with a wink, some administrators) are having to use a computer keyboard to access the library database in order to find a favorite book. Library patron use of the mainframe now rivals administration use. (The library database is operated from the campus mainframe.) Some departments are requesting that the library cancel certain hardcopy library reference material in favor of online access to the same materials. In many ways the library mimics the grocery checkout lane; instead of asking "plastic or paper" they say "digital or hardcopy."

TOWARDS A CAMPUS LAN

The automation of the Trinity Library during 1991 has been the single most important event urging the completion of a unified campus LAN. Faculty members in large numbers are appreciating what database searches can mean to them professionally. The NOTIS system allows online Boolean searches of the library holdings. Faculty are also appreciating the advantage of remote spontaneous library searches by means of modem. Many now realize that through networking they can access significant library databases at distant research universities at nominal expense. Faculty also realize just how fast undergraduate students are taking advantage of the new computerized Trinity library database. The importance of an automated library database to faculty involvement in computing beyond word processing cannot be stated strongly enough.

A second critical element leading to LAN development has been the need for a new campus telephone system. New fiber-optic cable was laid in the ground during the summer of 1991. Cabling was done in such a way as to allow LAN development as well as standard telephone communications. As faculty realized that the addition of routers could quickly complete needed LAN links over the new fiber-optic, such boxes began to appear, although the faculty involved consider the progress too slow. Significant faculty agitation now exists for the completion of the campus backbone because of the availability of fiber-optic cable and the promise offered by library automation.

A third event supporting LAN development is now underway. A Degree Audit Report System (DARS) is in early stages of development. DARS will allow faculty advisors to remotely access student academic data. It is conceivable that a faculty advisor could call up student records from his or her office. The administration finds this prospect attractive because more decision making about individual student curriculum and course taking could be done in the faculty advisor's office. Very few faculty are currently aware of DARS developments; nor have faculty been consulted in terms of being possible end users of the system.

A fourth and surprising turn of events supporting LAN development occurred in the fall of 1991. The university installed three electronic classrooms during the summer. Two of the classrooms contain a full complement of computer-controllable AV presentation systems: one room designed for Macintosh, the other for a DOS-based CPU. The Mac-based classroom was immediately utilized by engineering, math, physics, chemistry, and biology instructors. The CPU hard drive was rapidly devoured with applications for the various classes and faculty quickly discovered that ten-minute classroom transition times were insufficient for installing needed lecture materials for that day. They began to realize that a campus LAN, including the electronic classroom, would allow lecture data access from the instructor's office or lab computer. Both hard drive space and installation time problems could be solved by this LAN approach.

A fifth development based on faculty ability to obtain funding for computer equipment is rapidly being realized. Equipment such as color printers, computerized media producers, visualization workstations, and extensive software packages are appearing in faculty labs and offices. "Sneaker net" just won't do anymore. Peer-to-peer connectivity is the only efficient way to access the value of this equipment by a wider audience of faculty.

These five developments (library automation, telephone system, student records, electronic classrooms, and faculty-obtained equipment) are excellent points for providing focus to the general LAN concept of connectivity. Each development listed above substantiates LAN use for much more than mere e-mail. Other developments related to connectivity are also possible. Students could access lab computers 24 hours a day from remote points. Network document sharing with multiple editing sites could speed documents such as this one along its way. Campus-wide file service would make current release software more efficiently available. These and other applications all represent vital and valid uses of a unified campus LAN.

The uses listed appear to many to be both futuristic and idealistic. It is all too easy to ask, "Do we really need all this connectivity on campus, especially a small campus, and especially given the costs?" Will LAN connectivity really afford a gain in the educational environment? This is a very reasonable question. The answer requires a well-stated plan for a LAN that fits the specific environment for which it is intended.

COMMON MISCONCEPTIONS AND MUNDANE RESPONSES

The articulation of a clear LAN goal requires addressing some common misconceptions and avoiding certain mundane responses. Under the misconceptions category, the following are common:

- *Where will the LAN be?* Some expect that the LAN will have a major identifiable physical point such as the mainframe. These individuals do not yet understand that every computer is an equal on the system. The LAN is everywhere yet nowhere at the same time. This is a difficult concept for some.
- *LAN access to the library will reduce the number of people in the library.* This reasoning argues that people won't go to the library since they can get the information from their office. Because the library data can be more readily obtained, an increase in library patronage is highly likely and thus, the supposition incorrect.
- *LANs are useful only to large research universities.* Such statements at small institutions are borne of ignorance of the productivity made possible by networks such as Bitnet and Internet. Through networking both on campus and between campuses, a larger community of scholarship is possible.

Mundane responses for LAN justification are just as harmful as the misconceptions. Some examples are:

- *We need a LAN to be competitive.* This is the academic version of "keeping up with the Joneses." LAN justification must make sense for the campus. Administrators rightly should bristle when competitiveness is the only reason given for a LAN.
- *It really doesn't cost that much; just a couple of routers.* Such a view really expresses only a specific outlook to a LAN. Every router will be accompanied by a number of $200 Ethernet cards. A general long-range plan must be drawn which identifies the "just a few more" requests. Administrators receive a dozen "just $5,000 more" pleas every week. A LAN plan must avoid fragmented requests. Administrators must see the whole pie and not just the pieces if they are to make logical funding decisions.

SPECIFIC RECOMMENDATIONS

These typical misconceptions and mundane responses reveal that a considerable education program is necessary. Of course, to say that an education program on a college campus will solve all the problems has the ring of an oxymoron. To reach the objective of developing a supportable comprehensive plan for a LAN, the following steps must be considered.

1. Campus users groups should be established. At Trinity there were no computer user groups during initial stages of LAN planning. A users group focuses word-of-mouth information and facilitates its transfer. The technology associated with networking can best be disseminated by people who are themselves networked. Users groups should include students who often have more time to explore technology.
2. A program for software education must be established. Most computer users do not fully understand the features of the word processing program they use daily. Self-help audio and videotapes could provide continuous training opportunities. Campus-produced AV materials could address specific needs such as how to use Internet or Bitnet. Hypercard stacks could be developed to perform this function. Each peer on the LAN must be able to participate, and that requires specific hardware and software knowledge.
3. A specific LAN committee or subcommittee should be established as either an independent committee or part of an existing committee. The committee members must become familiar with the physical layout of the LAN, a sort of "Lay of LAN"

policy. By walking the service corridors, looking into closets, and inspecting labs, the entity known as the LAN can be better visualized. By having faculty and administrators working together on this physical layout, many questions can be resolved. Whole departments should also be given the tour, possibly on videotape. Users and potential users of a LAN become far more knowledgeable if they see how it works.

An important distinction must be made here. A statement can be made: "You don't have to visit the telephone switching station in order to use the telephone." The software options available over a LAN are far more numerous than the procedures necessary for a long distance credit card call. Frequently, the end user also assumes maintenance duties for a part of the LAN. Therefore, familiarity with the physical LAN can be important.

The committee should be charged in such a way that it knows its recommendations will be acted upon. Knowing that its actions will have "bite," the committee's progress should have more determination and speed. Parenthetically, the most likely faculty members of the committee have already been working in computer consulting roles off campus. Administrators sometimes overlook the fact that they have faculty with considerable extramural experience in such matters.

And finally, it is imperative that the LAN committee work with all potential users of the system.

4. Training in computer-based teaching technology is a must for faculty. This technology will be increasingly LAN-oriented. The first volley at Trinity has already been fired with the on-line library database and the electronic classrooms.

The concept of a Socratic classroom, a room with chairs and possibly a blackboard, is idyllic. Socrates didn't teach with smallpox vaccine, antibiotics, and antihistamine in his blood. Socrates didn't have a telephone, printed books, and a PC in his office. Socrates didn't have a photocopy machine and a fax machine in his departmental office at Greek U. The classroom must go beyond having an overhead transparency machine. LAN connectivity is the next logical step to organizing and controlling computer-operated AV equipment.

Introduction of technology in the classroom is a very difficult step to take. It costs money, money not needed for a classroom with only a blackboard. Faculty have to assume responsibility for integrating the technology into the educational process in meaningful ways. That means faculty time, time not needed for a classroom with only a blackboard. It may be trite to say, but LANs and associated technology are a Pandora's box. The major advantage afforded by this computer-based teaching technology is to provide a mechanism by which the volumes of information that must be brought to our students can be managed. Introductory college textbooks today present four times the volume of information they did 30 years ago.

5. Budgeting for a LAN should become a line item in budgets as is the case for telephone equipment on our campus. Trinity has been trying to coordinate expenditures for computer equipment, computer maintenance, and software. It has not been easy. However, developing a LAN plan does provide a means of connecting all the budgetary elements involved in supporting campus computer technology.

As people study the problems associated with establishing a campus-wide, unified LAN, most begin to realize that the objective is peer-to-peer connectivity. Those faculty who seldom, if ever, use a computer, can find little immediate use for a LAN. Those faculty who use the computer as a typewriter have a difficult time finding the utility of a LAN. Those faculty with computer skills and computer dependence fully recognize the productivity gains associated with a functional LAN. Since the common bond between all professors is teaching, then efforts to unite faculty behind a common objective should focus on what needs to be done in terms of teaching. Library automation and electronic classrooms are but the first common teaching applications involving computers which must be networked. Thus, for total faculty involvement in LAN planning, one should focus on the impact of LANs in teaching and advising.

And to complete this idea, there are faculty, like people in general, who are tool users and some who are not. A LAN is a tool, a pervasive tool, a compelling tool, an expensive tool. Tools require knowledge to use and practice in use to be skilled. LAN planning must keep these thoughts in mind.

As has been stated, at Trinity our most difficult problem has been to establish the goal for a unified campus local area network. The five recommendations above have been borne out of our experience. In many ways we are trapped in a paradox: we need a campus network in order to create a campus network.

Using AppleTalk to Create a Low-Cost Campus-Wide Network: A Case Study

Noel C. Hunter
User Support Consultant for the Computer Center
Wake Forest University

When first confronted with the voluminous information available about campus networking strategies, and with the high prices and complex specifications of the various networking devices, one might conclude that campus networking is always preceded by extensive centralized planning and an outlay of a considerable amount of money. For many institutions, the investment required to create a state-of-the art network may seem to be impractical or even impossible. Fortunately, there are ways to create a flexible and reliable campus-wide AppleTalk network at a very low cost, using existing building wiring and computer equipment. Furthermore, advanced network services such as electronic mail, file sharing, and terminal emulation are available for AppleTalk networks at little or no expense. This case study will describe in detail how we have created such a network to link student labs and organizations at Wake Forest University. It will begin with a discussion of an inexpensive AppleTalk wiring topology and routing scheme, followed by a discussion of network services. In keeping with the spirit of a "case study," this chapter will emphasize Wake Forest's own experiences in each area and the reasoning behind each decision made.

APPLETALK WIRING SCHEMES

In the early days of Apple networking, LocalTalk and AppleTalk were one and the same. Soon after Macintoshes and LaserWriters were available, Wake Forest set up four Macintosh labs consisting of 15 single floppy Macs, two ImageWriter printers, and one LaserWriter printer. In the first stages of networking, these Macs were daisy-chained together to connect them to local printers and to MacServe file servers, using Apple's LocalTalk cables. Although the printers have long since been replaced and MacServe has given way to AppleShare, the original LocalTalk cabling is still in place, a testament to the durability of the original medium for AppleTalk.

The LocalTalk cabling has served well, but it has one serious limitation: it cannot span distances great enough to connect buildings. In order to overcome this limitation, we began using Farallon PhoneNet connectors. To achieve the greatest possible cable length, it is necessary to replace all Local-Talk components with PhoneNet; however, we were able to interconnect our LocalTalk labs simply by installing a PhoneNet to LocalTalk adapter for each lab (see Figure 1). Depending on the exact topology of the network, one can achieve distances of up to 4,000 feet with such an arrangement, more than enough to connect buildings on a small campus. The greatest advantage of PhoneNet is that it uses "pair two" of a standard twisted pair telephone jack (RJ-11), which is unused in virtually every telephone jack on our campus. Using PhoneNet to LocalTalk adapter, we created a connection between the telephone jack in each lab and a panel of telephone jacks in the Computer Center.

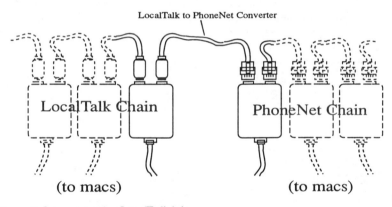

Figure 1. Interconnecting LocalTalk labs.

Within the Computer Center, we used AppleTalk Internet Router software on our existing Macintosh AppleShare File Servers to route traffic between the labs. We chose a software router because of its portability, flexibility, and low cost. Software routing allows us continually to upgrade our router capacity by upgrading our server Macintoshes, and if a router goes down, we can quickly and simply replace it with another Mac. At the time of our decision, hardware routers were more expensive, offered no better performance, and were more difficult to upgrade and replace quickly. We preferred AppleTalk Internet Router to Infosphere's Liaison, which offers dial-in access as well as routing, only because of our experience with MacServe, which Infosphere abandoned. Since that time, Farallon has acquired Liaison and now presents a reasonable alternative to AppleTalk Internet Router.

Rather than purchase a prewired patch panel for the Computer Center connections, we enlisted the aid of our telecommunications staff to construct a small patch panel specifically designed to meet our needs. In order to connect the remote labs into a PhoneNet-only Internet, we connected one incoming jack from each lab to the modem port of a routing Mac, and then connected all of the routing Macs' printer ports together to form a PhoneNet backbone (AppleTalk Internet Router uses both the modem and printer ports as AppleTalk ports). To simplify connection of the backbone side, we jumpered "pair two" of several of the data jacks together, creating a "passive star patch panel." This arrangement can be expanded to four or more ports, as long as the cable lengths remain short. The resulting Internet required one Mac running AppleTalk Internet Router software for each remote lab, and easily could be expanded to include other remote networks by adding additional routing Macs to the backbone. Because the AppleTalk Internet Router software can run in the background on an AppleShare File Server, we were able to arrange the servers so that each lab could access a directly attached file server without passing traffic onto the backbone (see Figure 2). This setup results in much quicker file server performance when using a PhoneNet backbone.

For a year, the above network ran reliably. The most common source of trouble was a disruption of the wiring within a lab—usually caused by the

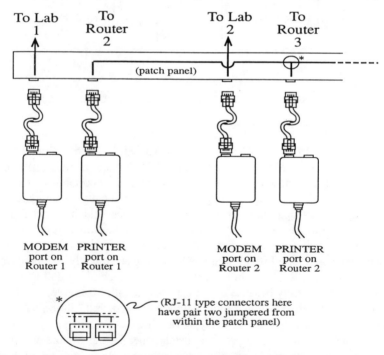

Figure 2. The servers are arranged so that each lab can access a directly attached file server.

careless moving of equipment. (LocalTalk connectors tend to work loose when equipment is moved; PhoneNet connectors are less likely to come loose.) Having demonstrated the reliability of the network, we decided it was time to add the Benson University Center building, which houses student organizations. Benson presented us with a new challenge: to connect a large number of widely dispersed offices. Fortunately, the building had been pre-wired with RJ-45 type data jacks in every room, and we were able to install a single Farallon PhoneNet Star Controller in a wiring closet to serve the entire building. The Star Controller was connected to the existing network with the addition of another Mac router, using a single twisted pair cable running between one port on the Star Controller and the patch panel in the Computer Center. The remaining eleven ports were available for workstations. We found that each port on the Star Controller could connect as many as four separate data jacks (a four-branch passive star), allowing us a total of 44 connections within Benson. We created the passive stars by simply jumpering pair two of each jack on the telephone punchdown block. The Star Controller network has proven more reliable than the LocalTalk daisy-chain networks, because the PhoneNet connectors are less easy to disconnect, and because the Star Controller isolates any problem to a single port (affecting at most four workstations). Eventually, we hope to replace all the LocalTalk connectors with PhoneNet.

As our network traffic increased, we eventually decided to replace the backbone side of our network with a twisted pair Ethernet network. With ethernet cards in each router, we now have two open LocalTalk ports available on each Mac, allowing us to serve twice as many remote labs. Our experience has been that the Ethernet backbone greatly improves performance during times of peak load, but makes little difference during moderate and low load times. In other words, the Ethernet backbone has increased our maximum network capacity, but not our "top speed." This is because the end node on our network is still running at LocalTalk speed.

APPLETALK NETWORK SERVICES

The campus-wide student lab network provides four basic services: (1) printer sharing; (2) file sharing; (3) terminal emulation; and (4) electronic mail. Each of these services extends to all the Macs, as well as to the campus TCP/IP network and the Internet world, and is available to all students. The basic client and server software for all these services is free to the university, and the only hardware required to make the connection between the PhoneNet network and the TCP/IP backbone is a single GatorBox.

Printer sharing for Macintoshes has always been included with the operating system and LaserWriter printers, as has the AppleShare client software needed to access AppleShare File Servers. With the recent release of System 7, free file server software is now available for every Mac with at least 2MB of RAM. System 7 file sharing is used for less demanding services, such as file sharing among a few individuals. For the heavily used lab servers, we have installed AppleShare File Server software (which is not free). Version 3.0 supports up to 300 simultaneous clients, has software licensing and copy protection, and can create log-in messages or send messages to individual clients.

The most challenging file-sharing task was creating a link between our student Macs and the UNIX academic minicomputer (a Hewlett-Packard 9000/852). The challenge was to allow up to for 4,000 academic users to store Macintosh files in their UNIX home directories. While it was necessary to accommodate 4,000 users over the course of their studies at Wake Forest, it was only necessary simultaneously to serve a small number, at most 50, at any given time. We considered three possible methods of connection: (1) using Network File System (NFS) client software on the Macs, (2) using third-party AppleShare file server software for UNIX, and (3) using a hardware device to bridge AppleShare and NFS. NFS client software was ruled out because of the expense and administrative overhead of installing NFS client software on all our student Macs. AppleShare for UNIX was ruled out after our research and evaluation showed that none of the products available for our UNIX machine could adequately handle our configuration. PacerShare ran well on our machine but could not allow users to automatically connect to their home directories. (We would have had to configure 4,000 separate volumes or scroll through 4,000 folders when saving.) Other software would do what we wanted but would not run on HP-UX.

Having eliminated all other options, we were forced to try a GatorBox, which we had often heard described as unreliable. Fortunately, the GatorBox did exactly what we wanted it to, and it has performed flawlessly. The Gator-Box serves as a bridge between AppleShare and NFS, allowing us to run the native file-sharing software on both the Macs and UNIX systems. There are several unique advantages to the GatorBox. The GatorShare software is flexible enough to accommodate a variety of UNIX configurations, including BSD and System V. It can read user information from standard password files, a yp server, or a pcnfs server, or from a user-specified password file. Since HP-UX uses a system of secure password files, we created our own special password file for GatorShare to read. The flexible configuration of GatorShare made this setup possible—no other product we could find would have allowed such specific customization to fit our needs. Another useful feature of GatorShare is its automatic translation between Macintosh and UNIX end-of-line sequences, making it easy to edit text-only UNIX files with standard Macintosh word processors. Two additional advantages of the GatorBox are that one GatorBox can be set up to access multiple UNIX hosts and that UNIX-to-AppleTalk printing is bundled with GatorShare.

Terminal emulation for student Macs is provided by NCSA Telnet, public domain software available from the National Center for Supercomputing Applications at the University of Illinois at Urbana-Champaign. Telnet connects LocalTalk Macs to the academic minicomputer (and any other Internet host) through the GatorBox. The GatorBox has both LocalTalk and Ethernet ports, and performs the translation, or encapsulation, between AppleTalk and TCP/IP. Telnet provides full terminal emulation, Tektronics graphics emulation, and FTP (file transfer protocol) to all the student Macs. Before the GatorBox, a Shiva EtherGate provided AppleTalk-to-TCP/IP encapsulation. Although the EtherGate performed reasonably well, the GatorBox functions more reliably in our network environment. We also evaluated a Shiva FastPath, but found that its relative cost and complexity made it inappropriate for our situation.

Electronic mail for the student Macs is provided by Eudora, public domain software from the University of Illinois at Urbana-Champaign. Eudora is a surprisingly full-featured mail interface that allows Macintosh users to read their mail stored on a POPMAIL server (in Wake Forest's case, our UNIX host). The server software, called "Popper, is available for UNIX systems from the University of California, Berkeley." Additional Mac mail interfaces, as well as client software for the PC, are also available from Berkeley. The POPMAIL system has united UNIX, Mac, and PC mail, allowing every student to send and receive electronic mail, using the same POPMAIL mailbox, from UNIX, Macintosh, or PC. Senders no longer need to know how the recipient will receive mail; all mail can be directed to the primary UNIX host.

The most costly element of our low-cost AppleTalk network is the integration of MS-DOS PC's , which have needed additional hardware. PC's are integrated into our Mac Labs with the use of Farallon's PhoneNet Talk PC cards. Where Ethernet cabling is available, PC's access AppleTalk services via PhoneNet Talk software and 3-Com Ethernet cards. The relatively low cost of PC Ethernet cards now leads us to prefer Ethernet for PCs whenever possible. Farallon has now resolved earlier problems with AppleShare PC (renaming it PhoneNet Talk PC), making it easy to print from MS-DOS PCs to AppleTalk printers, and allowing PC users to access their UNIX home directories via AppleShare and the GatorBox. While the per unit cost of adding PCs to the network is much greater than that of Macs, it is nevertheless comparable to that of adding PCs to similar non-AppleTalk networks.

CONCLUSIONS

For those who wish to provide basic networking services to a large number of users, rather than advanced services to a small number of users, or those whose budgets prohibit large-scale installations of fiber, Ethernet hubs, and the like, a twisted pair AppleTalk network similar to that of Wake Forest's student labs might be the answer. We have created a flexible and reliable network spanning seven campus buildings, using AppleTalk over existing twisted pair wiring, and the Macintosh's built-in networking hardware. AppleTalk Internet Router and AppleShare File Server software has allowed us to smoothly upgrade our network server performance simply by upgrading the server Macintoshes, and to migrate from LocalTalk to Ethernet simply by adding network cards to the servers. Free networking services provided by System 7 and public domain software are available to all Mac users, and the combination of a GatorBox and inexpensive PhoneNet Talk PC (or Ethernet) cards has allowed us to expand our services to include Internet access and PC client services at a cost comparable to that of other PC networking platforms.

Finally, we have benefited from what we have learned about twisted-pair AppleTalk as we have planned for expansion of the campus fiber backbone. As this backbone has expanded to include many of the university's dorms and classroom buildings, we have found that twisted pair AppleTalk networks make an efficient last link from network hubs to end nodes. For those who are providing advanced networking services, twisted pair Apple-Talk networks can be used to make the difficult last step into dorm rooms and offices.

ACKNOWLEDGMENT

The illustrations for this chapter were prepared by Christian B. Hall.

Computing at Wesleyan University

Douglas Bigelow
Director of Academic Computing
Wesleyan University

OVERVIEW

Wesleyan University is a selective liberal arts institution in Middletown, Connecticut, serving a student population of approximately 3,000 and a faculty population of 250. Although primarily an undergraduate institution, Wesleyan has a few small but respected doctoral and master's degree programs. Founded in 1831 as a men's Methodist college, it is now a coeducational, nonsecular institution that maintains high academic standards.

Computing technology has been used in Wesleyan course work for more than 25 years, in the departments of Economics, Government, Astronomy, Chemistry, Physics, Psychology, Mathematics, and others. Technology has traditionally served scholarship rather than being an object of study in itself—there are no departments of Computer Science or Electrical Engineering, although there is a computer science concentration within the Mathematics Department.

Early users had IBM 1620, IBM 1130, Digital DECsystem-10, and later, DECSYSTEM-20 time-sharing services available. In the 1980s, VAX VMS systems started taking over the time-sharing load, and many users turned to personal computers. By mid-decade, many personal computers (PCs) were connected to local area networks (LANs).

The larger computers on campus started being interconnected in 1984, when a backbone Ethernet network and a link to BITNET made comprehensive electronic mail services a reality. Wesleyan joined the Internet in 1987, and by the early 1990s most users considered network access on campus to be a fundamental part of computing services.

Wesleyan's computing and network growth has had the following characteristics:

- We were early users of LANs, BITNET, and Internet among small schools.
- Our network growth has been more tactical than strategic: we have a strategic plan, but much growth has been opportunistic.

Without large-scale funding for network development, we often piggyback network installations on renovation projects.

• We use low-cost public domain software whenever possible, to keep costs down and stretch development dollars further.

Despite (and in part because of) these constraints, Wesleyan has been successful in developing a campus network that is well integrated, extensive, and useful to many different constituencies.

ORGANIZATIONAL STRUCTURE AND PLANNING

Wesleyan has unified computing support, with academic and administrative computing served by a combined staff. The Director of University Computing reports to the Provost and provides direction and long-range planning for central and distributed computing activities. The Director of Academic Computing manages the central facilities, the programming, consulting, and operations staff, and the campus network. The Director of Administrative Systems manages the applications programming staff, data entry and administrative operations. The computing facilities are shared, and systems and support staff members serve end users from all disciplines and constituencies.

Strategic planning is done by the three directors with the advice and assistance of two key groups, which are the academic computer advisory committee and the administrative computer advisory committee. These groups are appointed annually by the President or Provost and represent a cross-section of faculty and staff who are interested in or involved with computing.

For shorter range planning assistance and the allocation of yearly capital computing budget funds, we turn to the divisional deans and to the Treasurer's office. The Director of University Computing assembles and prioritizes computing equipment requests from all departments, and the deans allocate the available dollars for the three academic divisions. The Treasurer does the same for administrative departments.

NETWORK COMPONENTS

Wesleyan chose the TCP/IP protocol suite for the campus network backbone in 1984. Although DECnet was an alternative and there was a preponderance of digital equipment on campus, we wanted a vendor-independent protocol. TCP/IP was mostly unknown outside of the ARPAnet world at that time, and the effort of getting started was substantial without ARPA colleagues to help. However, we gained early expertise, useful now that IP has become a true national standard.

Our early (and continuing) goal was to have electronic mail programs on all major networked machines compatible with each other and with BIT-NET mail. This required much custom software development to achieve, but Wesleyan end users had been using electronic mail since 1978—supporting and expanding its use remains one of our highest priorities.

Topology and Technology

Figure 1 shows an overview of Wesleyan's current network, which is mainly Ethernet running over various media: fiber, thick and thin coax, and twisted pair. About 12 buildings are connected by fiber, and several more are connected by "temporary" AppleTalk links.

Central Backbone

Wesleyan uses a "distributed backbone" strategy and differentiates between a backbone for major time-sharing machines and one that interconnects only subnetworks.

We have a Class B IP network number assigned and use an 8-bit subnet mask to provide up to 255 internal networks with up to 255 hosts each. Sub-

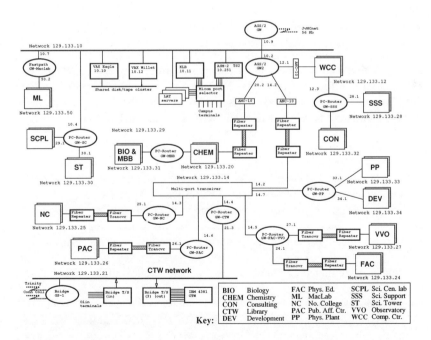

Figure 1. Wesleyan networks.

net 10 contains our main time-sharing hosts and the terminal servers that communicate with those hosts. We have a mixture of servers, some using Digital's Local Area Transport (LAT) protocols rather than Telnet. However, the LAT servers cannot connect to the many TCP-only hosts and will eventually be replaced with Telnet servers.

Subnet 14 is a communications subnet, contained within a small room near the geographic center of the campus steam tunnel system. Most of the fiber links originate here, where a multiport repeater interconnects several IP gateways. Network interfaces on the gateways connect to fiber-optic transceivers, which in turn communicate via fiber to remote repeaters in end-user departments.

Most subnets have IP gateways filtering communications with other campus areas. Although individual networks use a variety of protocols, (AppleTalk, Novell IPX, DECnet, etc.), only IP traffic passes the gateway. The primary Computing Center gateway is an exception; a Cisco AGS router connects four key subnets and handles several protocols. We may soon add IPX to IP as a campus-wide routed protocol, since Novell NetWare is continually gaining in importance for both administrative and academic use.

Future backbone expansion will include Fiber Distributed Data Interface (FDDI) when traffic growth warrants the increased speed. The current star-shaped fiber backbone is designed to turn into an FDDI ring when needed, with enough fiber capacity to run dual Ethernet and FDDI during the transition.

We have a wide mixture of cable types in place: thick Ethernet for our main machine rooms and building backbones, fiber between buildings, thin Ethernet within floors wired before 1991, and twisted pair Ethernet in current installations. Shielded twisted pair is used in Science departments with high-voltage equipment nearby; unshielded twisted pair is used elsewhere.

Time-Sharing Hosts

Wesleyan's general time sharing is provided on a Digital VAXcluster, with an academic 8550 and an administrative 6410 sharing a common set of disks and tapes. Most users have an account on this cluster, which serves as the primary mail conduit for the university. Although individually named, the two machines also share the generic node names of WESLEYAN.EDU on Internet and WESLEYAN on BITNET. Since we use the common convention of assigning user names to be a person's first initial and last name, reaching someone on campus is fairly easy. For example, I can be reached as dbigelow@wesleyan.edu from Internet or dbigelow@wesleyan from BITNET; either address will in turn forward to my "real" address of dbigelow@sandpiper.wesleyan.edu. Most users who read mail on other machines also maintain central aliases for convenience.

The VAXcluster also handles Wesleyan's network news feed, providing more than 500 Usenet news groups daily as well as access to all Internet and BITNET mailing lists of interest.

External WANs

Wesleyan's Internet connection is provided through JvNCNet, an NSFnet regional network headquartered at Princeton University. Our connection is via a 56KB leased line, which at present provides adequate capacity.

Our BITNET connection also uses Internet, having been converted from a 9600 baud leased line to an RSCS/IP connection using VMNET protocols. This makes a BITNET connection very inexpensive, and we plan to continue providing BITNET services to our users and to continue providing an upstream link to other sites.

Library Consortium

The CTW Library Consortium was implemented to share a combined library catalog system among Connecticut College, Trinity College, and Wesleyan. The Consortium operates an IBM 4381 system running NOTIS library software, and a combined catalog allows users to browse through the holdings of all three schools. The system is housed at Wesleyan but is accessible to the other institutions through a private 56KB leased-line network.

Access to the system is through Telnet terminal servers on all three campuses, as well as from any campus hosts running TCP/IP. An IP gateway to Trinity and Connecticut College provides the main traffic path for the system, but the system can also be configured to allow access from anywhere on the Internet. This system was designed before any of the three schools had joined the Internet, but we anticipated that widespread connectivity through TCP/IP would become quite useful.

The IBM 4381 is not network-aware, but it is served by several 7171 asynchronous communications controllers that in turn are connected to Telnet terminal servers. This is commonly called the "milking-machine" mode, because the servers and communications controllers are attached by many serial cables. The servers work in reverse, accepting incoming connections from the network and attaching the connections to local IBM ports.

Networked Micros

Many of the desktop computers on campus have Ethernet network cards that allow them to participate in local Novell networks as well as in the wider IP network. In addition to public labs, several administrative and academic departments use NetWare servers to share software and printers, and to simplify file transfers between MS-DOS personal computers (PCs) and Macintoshes.

The public labs are designed for low maintenance whenever possible—almost all PCs have boot PROMs on the network cards enabling them to boot from the network without a local disk. This reduces virus spreading and eases software maintenance. The Macintosh computers are more labor-intensive because boot PROMs are not available, requiring us to sell individual boot diskettes.

MS-DOS machines (mostly generic PC/AT clones) dominate on the networks at present, but the trend is starting to lean toward Macintosh. Ethernet cards for Macintoshes, initially much more expensive than PC cards, have become affordable. Faculty purchasing desktop machines on a limited budget no longer need to base the choice of hardware on the cost of network connectivity.

Because the PCs were acquired from many different funding sources, there is little consistency in the amount of money available for initial and ongoing software support. Accordingly, we try to standardize on software affordable to all users, and we purchase network or site licenses whenever possible. We take software licensing seriously and attempt to enforce compliance on campus machines. Public domain software is heavily used, particularly NCSA Telnet, which provides basic network service to PCs and Macintoshes alike.

UNIX Workstations

Powerful UNIX workstations have been appearing on Wesleyan desktops at the rate of five or more per year. Most are in Science departments and are used for high-speed computing or graphical visualization research, but the combination of RISC hardware speed and UNIX software power makes the workstations popular with many types of users.

Workstations introduced the NFS (Network File System) protocol as a file service alternative, and we have many central and remote disk drives cross-mounted between systems. PC and Macintosh systems may also participate in NFS by purchasing the appropriate software, and this can be an alternative to NetWare in some circumstances.

Users and Their Applications

Much of the network is invisible to end users, simply being the conduit by which mail and news arrives. Others have integrated network use into their daily computing in some of the following ways:

- Several researchers access remote database services through Telnet rather than via modem, giving them high-speed access plus the ability to cut and paste the contents of screen windows between different connections.
- Experimenters doing real-time data collection on laboratory PCs collect megabytes of data, and then use FTP to transfer the data to high-speed UNIX systems for detailed analysis.
- Administrative users log into central systems and extract information from large databases, and then transfer the data via FTP for local analysis using PC tools.
- Researchers in the Chemistry, Biology, and Molecular Biology and Biochemistry departments use the Internet to obtain machine time at various supercomputer centers.
- Scientific workstations share disks via NFS, allowing them to combine resources for data analysis and display.
- A history professor uses three UNIX workstations to run the Great American History Machine for class instruction and research. This program, acquired from another university, combines census data with a powerful query language to draw U.S. or other national maps with statistical data highlighted. The master system is networked in a faculty office and serves two diskless workstations in a remote public lab.
- Computing center staff members use network news and mailing lists to stay current with software and hardware developments, and use anonymous FTP to collect software from public domain repositories around the world.

Funding

Most of Wesleyan's computer funding comes from internal sources, since relatively few faculty have significant grant income that is available for computing. We minimize charging for network services since it would be mostly paper shuffling and internal transfers. While we follow the basic philosophy that backbone links are an institutional expense, connections within a building are a departmental expense. When a new building is connected via fiber, central funding is usually allocated for the fiber, labor, site preparation, electronics, and building backbone.

Departmental funds are then allocated for Ethernet concentrators, wiring from offices, and PC network cards. This places funding and access decisions in the most appropriate hands, those of departmental chairmen or directors.

MANAGING THE NETWORK

Network Installation and Maintenance

Wesleyan's networks grow quickly, almost outstripping the support staff's ability to maintain them with production quality. It is a constant temptation to skimp on the recordkeeping and mapping for the job just completed in order to start on the next. If we yield to this temptation, we encounter difficulties a few weeks or months later when attempting to trace a problem with a poorly documented line.

New end-user connections are documented in a general database that contains information about all types of data connections. Online maps are maintained for the various buildings, although post-installation changes or additions are not always reliably recorded.

Basic automated status reporting is provided by a monitoring program that periodically checks the status of key network links. When a component's status changes, networking personnel receive electronic mail indicating that a gateway or terminal server (for instance) has gone down. The program uses a simple ICMP Echo technique to check status, rather than more sophisticated Simple Network Management Protocol (SNMP) queries, but it serves our needs at present.

A program that will combine detailed network mapping with sophisticated status monitoring is at the top of our wish list. Such programs exist but are either quite expensive or lack some of the features we desire.

Network Administration

Backbone equipment, concentrators, and lines are maintained and administered by the central networking staff, who maintain control over protocols transmitted over the backbone. Furthermore, we troubleshoot problems to the desktop level, and we assist with installation and training where needed.

For local area networks, we maintain the hardware and software on the servers, but distribute daily operations and administration to the end users whenever possible. Server software changes or upgrades are handled by the networking staff, but local server managers generally install new user accounts, administer disk quotas, and do backups.

Network Software Development

We work with standard software whenever possible, but we have frequently needed to develop custom solutions in order to save money otherwise spent on commercial software. In addition, our use of public domain software has been very cost-effective, although at the cost of additional development labor.

The public domain PCROUTE program, an IP router package developed by Vance Morrison at Northwestern University, has been a key success. Morrison's program gives basic IP routing functionality and good performance using dedicated DOS PCs, and has enabled us to develop a highly subnetted network when we could not have afforded the widespread use of commercial routers.

Similarly, the NCSA Telnet package from the National Center for Supercomputing Applications at the University of Illinois has saved us hundreds of dollars for every networked PC or Macintosh.

Enabling the simultaneous use of Novell NetWare (an IEEE 802.3 protocol) and IP (an Ethernet V.2 protocol) on our PCs required the use of packet drivers from the Clarkson University collection, which allows totally different protocols to share an Ethernet card.

These solutions all require the willingness to spend time finding the information, obtaining and testing the software, and making the pieces fit. They also require experience with networking protocols, but that can be learned on the job—if you have access to a national network.

Security

Network security requires careful planning, because an Ethernet network is inherently vulnerable to passive eavesdropping. Almost any networked PC or Macintosh in a public lab can be turned into a basic network analyzer that can capture packets and extract user name and password information.

Our best safeguard is breaking up the network into many small pieces, each separated from the others by gateways. Public labs are always segregated from private office machines, and no desktop systems share subnets with the main time-sharing hosts. This compartmentalization cuts down on network traffic as well as enhancing security, but more is needed. There are protocols like Kerberos which provide encryption for key authentication information sent over a network, and we expect to start implementing such techniques within the next two years.

THE NEXT STEPS

Comprehensive Wiring

Wesleyan's greatest networking need is a well-designed wiring plant. Except for recent renovations, there is little data-grade wiring in place and each new project requires new cabling. There is rarely money available to do an entire building at once, so wiring installers will frequently make repeated trips to a building within the course of a year. Naturally, a piecemeal approach to wiring drives up the overall labor costs.

The opportunity to install comprehensive data wiring will likely come with the installation of a new telephone system. The existing system is short on capacity and features, and a new electronic switch will require replacing the existing quad wire with high-quality twisted pair. When this takes place, new data wiring will also be installed. Our goal is to support an Ethernet, AppleTalk, or terminal connection at every desktop.

Dormitory rooms lack connections at present, and a new telephone system will probably bring both telephone and data service to the students. (The economics of telephone service resale are being weighed.) When this occurs, there will be a whole new set of challenges and a great deal more equipment to maintain. We expect AppleTalk protocols to be in high demand, and we will be working on ways to support local dormitory clusters and printer sharing.

CONCLUSIONS

Central computing services at Wesleyan are focusing more on communications and distributed computing than on mainframe support, but this does not mean that time sharing is obsolete. We view a distributed system as a sort of "virtual mainframe," requiring the same types of support: access to common software, file system backup, printing management, electronic mail and more. Distributed computing can mean isolated computing if poorly implemented. Done correctly, networking brings a wealth of resources to the desktop.

The next few years should see our networks expanding to include almost all the campus—but they should also be less visible to the end users. Our goal is to have computer communications become as reliable as electricity and as easily available.

Case Study on the Birmingham CWIS

Michele Shoebridge
Systems Librarian
Birmingham University, UK

INTRODUCTION

Like a number of other higher education institutions in the United Kingdom, the origins of the University of Birmingham's present campus-wide information service (CWIS) lie with the Academic Computing Service (ACS), which began making computer-related information available to both campus and off-campus users on a regular basis in 1986. This initiative relied (and still does) on the financial support of ACS and the enthusiasm of ACS staff. Recently, the university has invested a large sum of money installing the infrastructure for a High Speed Campus Network (HSCN), and this has led to the reevaluation of the objectives of a true campus-wide information service.

This case study will relate the configuration of the present Birmingham CWIS, currently called ACSIS (Academic Computing Service Information Server) and outline future developments planned for the delivery of networked information for the University of Birmingham.

ACSIS

The software for ACSIS was written in-house by a member of the ACS staff. It was originally written as a prototype in the Bourne Shell for a Torch XXX. Despite running fairly slowly the service was taken up, but by 1990 response time was becoming a significant factor in preventing it from being accessed more heavily and it was ported to an IBM RS-6000. The system was run on the new machine using the Korn shell, and improvements were made which took advantage of the built-in integer arithmetic and character handling of the Korn shell. Once again these changes were undertaken with ACS funding and staff time.

The system has an Ethernet card and an X.25 board that allows terminal access via X.29, Pinkbook, and Telnet, although Telnet is only available locally. The ACSIS is available to external users on the JANET network as UK.AC.BHAM.INFO. Accesses average 400 per week.

GENERAL FEATURES

The ACSIS was designed to provide a number of basic features:

- Ease of use for novice users
- Consistency of commands
- Express routes through the data tree
- Flagging menus for later return
- Usability from any type of terminal
- Search facility
- Comment box
- Ability to send messages to system manager
- E-mail facility to retrieve part or whole or documents

Data Structure

The system is hierarchical and menu-driven. Users have the ability to navigate menu by menu or from menu to top menu. There is some element of cross-menuing.

Type of Information Included

- Text files
- Lists of e-mail addresses, telephone numbers

Methods of Searching

- Displaying pages that contain a character string
- Selecting all lines containing a given character
- Using the index which is displayed as a text file

HELP Facilities

- A standard Help file is available throughout the tree.
- There is no case-sensitive Help.

Administrative Functions

- Files can be updated using automated scheduling software (e.g., CRON on UNIX) which takes the file from the host machine using bluebook file transfer and slots it into the data tree at the appropriate point by the system manager from an FTP file. This can also be done from a file on a floppy disk or from paper (although the latter is not encouraged).

- Detailed usage statistics are available. They are stored in text files and can be accessed via a menu by the system administrator or privileged users.

PARALLEL DEVELOPMENTS TO THE ACSIS SERVICE

The university had a campus network based on X.25 and Gandalf switches running at approximately 1,000 bytes per second. In 1989 the first phase of the HSCN was implemented. A cross-campus fibre optic was installed using the Fiber Distributed Data Interface (FDDI) transmission method operating at 100 megabits per second. An extensive local area network using thin wire Ethernet (10base2) was installed in the Engineering Faculty. The second phase of the project, begun in 1991, extended the Ethernet wiring (using unshielded twisted pair, 10baseT) into other departments; for example, the Library received over 40 connections. Many more staff now had the opportunity to connect to services on campus and the outside world. There was some concern that both new and existing network users were not aware of the potential of connection to the new network and the services it could offer.

NATIONAL DEVELOPMENTS

A number of universities and polytechnics were developing sophisticated CWISs containing large amounts of data, and they were proving very popular. Some local authorities were also introducing videotext systems, for example, Berkshire Viewdata. Locally, Birmingham City Council launched a pilot project called Keypoint which made information terminals available at strategic access points around the city.

National bodies were also turning their attention to networked information services. The University of Reading updated "A Review of Information Servers on JANET." The Inter-University Information Committee (IUIC) and Standing Conference of National and University Libraries (SCONUL) Joint Information Services Working Party produced "A Report on Computer-Based Information Services in Universities " (1990) which made certain recommendations about CWIS. As a result of this report, the IUIC set up a subgroup to look specifically at CWIS. Called the Information Services Working Group (INFSWG), this group meets regularly and has undertaken electronic surveys to establish the current state of affairs regarding CWIS and to compile a set of guidelines for CWIS development. The surveys resulted in two useful documents: "Summary of the Results of IUIC-INFSWG CWIS Development Survey" and "Report on the IUIC-INFSWG Survey on Core Information Sets." Both were compiled by Colin Work at Southampton University.

The university's Information Technology Committee took note of all these developments and in November 1991 set up a Working Party to look into the subject.

THE WORKING PARTY ON CAMPUS
INFORMATION SERVICES

The group was set up with a wide brief: to draw together information circulated to staff and students in electronic or printed form into a coordinated electronic information service that would also give access to remote services. They were charged with developing a cost program for providing the necessary hardware and software, along with a suitable training/familiarization program. All recommendations[1] had to be put before the IT Committee in early 1992, and then submitted to the university's Strategy, Planning and Resources Committee (SPRC) for appropriate funding.

The group consisted of representatives from the major information providers on campus.

- Library
- ACS
- Administrative Computing (ADPU)
- Guild of Students
- Public Affairs
- Computer Users Advisory Group (CUAG)
- Research Support and Industrial Liaison
- Planning Office

The full group met three times. It became clear that the Library and ACS would play the largest role in fostering the development of a full-blown CWIS because of their existing commitment to providing information in electronic form. ACS was already running ACSIS, and the Library provided the online catalog, networked databases on CD-ROM, online search service, and so on.

The group identified three main tasks: the evolution of a data tree; the need for a technical specification; and the importance of the user interface. ACS and Library staff spent some time evaluating existing CWIS software by looking in some detail at five UK and North American CWISs: Birmingham's ACSIS, York, Bristol, Oxford and Princeton. This exercise was twofold: it aimed to identify possible first-generation software that could be purchased/obtained for use at Birmingham, and it gave the group some ideas about the what type of data should be made available and the style of user interface required.

THE DATA TREE

A comprehensive data tree was drawn up, although it was recognized that not all the data required to complete the tree would be available at once, and that the tree should be flexible enough to allow extra categories to be slotted in. Hierarchical menus form an important element in the tree, since they are seen as an aid to novice users. It was also recognized that an express route through the tree would be desirable for the more expert user.

Categories of information in the tree are as follows:

Introductory Information
  1.1 History
  1.2 Mission and policy statements
  1.3 Press releases
  1.4 Court, Council and Committee Structure
  1.5 Academic organization: faculties, schools, departments
  1.6 Administrative organization, academic services, and customer
      service plans
  1.7 University statistics
  1.8 Telephone directory
  1.9 E-mail Directory

Teaching and Research
  2.1 Course directory
  2.2 Examination timetables
  2.3 Seminars, conferences, lectures, and meetings
  2.4 Publications and research database
  2.5 Research funding and news
  2.6 Birmingham Research & Development Ltd.
  2.7 Institute for Advanced Research in the Humanities

Faculty and School Information
  3.1 Arts
  3.2 Commerce and Social Science
  3.3 Education and Continuing Studies
  3.4 Engineering
  3.5 Law
  3.6 Medicine and Dentistry
  3.7 Science

Information Technology (IT)
  4.1 IT providers
  4.2 IT skills training
  4.3 Campus user groups
  4.4 Hardware and software purchase
  4.5 Guide to local facilities
  4.6 Guide to remote facilities
  4.7 Public clusters

Academic Computing Service Based on existing ACSIS:

University Library
6.1 Library news
6.2 Opening hours
6.3 Regulations
6.4 Charges
6.5 Catalog and information module
6.6 Accessions list
6.7 CD-ROM network
6.8 Courses and user education
6.9 Booking board

Other Support Facilities
7.1 Careers service
7.2 Staff Development Unit
7.3 Staff vacancies
7.4 Television services
7.5 Language laboratories
7.6 Print Unit
7.7 Centre for Computer Based Learning
7.8 IBM Information Centre
7.9 Safety Unit

University Social, Recreational, and Cultural Facilities
8.1 Guild of Students
8.2 Staff House
8.3 Banks and shops
8.4 Catering
8.5 Sport and Recreation
8.6 Clubs and Societies
8.7 Accommodation
8.8 Exhibitions and music
8.9 Health, welfare, unions, and chaplaincy

City of Birmingham and Its Region
9.1 Travel information
9.2 Cinemas and theatres
9.3 Music
9.4 Restaurants
9.5 Libraries, museums, and galleries
9.6 Bookshops
9.7 Institutions of higher education

9.8 Sport
9.9 Religion

External Services
  10.1 Guide to remote services
  10.2 JANET Bulletin boards
  10.3 CHEST databases
  10.4 Library catalogs (OPACs via JANET and Internet
  10.5 Other campus-wide information services
  10.6 X500 directory

Technical Specifications

The group recommended that the hardware platform should be a UNIX server, capable of supporting at least 20 terminals and routing calls to both internal and external services. Initially, the internal services would be limited to the Library's OPAC and CD-ROM network, along with the X.500 Directory service (when implemented on campus) and later the Centre for Computer Based Learning and ADPU. Externally it was suggested that services on JANET like remote OPACS and Bulletin Boards should be accessible, but later these should be extended to Internet services, USENET, for example.

Protocols

Birmingham has been following the developments regarding CWIS and Z.39.50 and would hope to implement these protocols at some stage.

Data Collection

Responsibility for editing and transfer of information will reside with the various departments supplying data. Automated scheduling software will be used and some guidelines laid down on layout, and so forth, although it may not always be possible for these to be adhered to. It is not envisaged that significant amounts of information will be gathered and keyboarded centrally.

Staffing Implications

Significantly, most CWISs have emerged through the enthusiasm of a particular staff member. Birmingham has identified this as a potential problem and recommended the appointment of a half-time post to provide central coordination. One element of this post will be the "evangelical role" of converting people to the importance of a CWIS for information dissemination; the other will be to manage the information flow.

Requirements for a User Interface

Mandatory requirements include
- Running 0800-2200 hours
- Access from terminals, PCs and UNIX workstations
- No login password required
- Support novice and expert users
- Predictable screen handling
- Clear context sensitive help screens
- Menu-driven but with flexible navigation of the data tree
- Search and find facility within documents
- Currency and quality of information
- Use of plain English
- Authorship of information be displayed

Desirable features include
- Continuous running
- Straightforward log-in from all entry points
- Consistent command language
- Expert routes for expert users (there was much interest in the USENET style of service)
- Sophisticated screen style (colour, graphic,s etc.)
- Search and find between documents
- E-mail interface for retrieving documents
- Print option
- User comment

INVOLVEMENT OF BLCMP LIBRARY SERVICES

The University of Birmingham was a founding member of BLCMP Library Services, one of the major library vendors in the United Kingdom. BLCMP were interested in the CWIS project from an early stage, having been made aware of the need to disseminate community information by their public library sites. Early efforts had resulted in the community information module being written as part of their BLS Library system.

This only met a few CWIS requirements, however, and since a number of their other sites were also interested in CWIS, it presented itself as a viable commercial proposition for BLCMP and non-BLCMP libraries. The idea of writing a UNIX-based product at a time when BLCMP were redesigning their BLS product to operate under UNIX using a relational database fitted in well with their time scale.

After a series of meetings between BLCMP, Data General (current suppliers of their hardware) on one side and Library and ACS staff on the other, to discuss practical aspects of the software, followed by meetings between policymakers, a joint project was set up to specify system requirements and time scale. BLCMP could draw on the expertise of Library and ACS staff , while the university would receive benefits from taking the BLCMP software, for example, assured support and documentation; standards compliance; proven information; systems expertise; and the prospect of involvement in the city and region.

FINANCE AND IMPLEMENTATION

The CWIS will be available to all campus users connected to the Gandalf X.25 and HSCN. This should include student accommodation in the next few years. In addition, extra dedicated terminals will be placed in public areas, for example, Staff House, the Sports Centre and Guild of Students.

The hardware for the project will be resourced from central university funds. Staff costs will be supported by the Library and ACS in the first instance, although this may not continue in the long term.

The system, whether running existing CWIS software or software supplied by BLCMP, will be publicly available in the 1992-93 academic session. It is envisaged that a considerable amount of promotional work will have to be done to encourage information providers to actually submit data. Once the delivery of information begins, an editorial group will be set up to oversee the quality of the information included in the CWIS.

FUTURE DEVELOPMENTS

The software will be implemented in phases, with the first phase aimed at encouraging novice users to access the CWIS. Most of the data will be mounted centrally, with some limited access to nationally networked services. Subsequent revisions of the software will be designed to give access to a much larger range of services both on JANET and on the Internet, for example, bulletin boards, USENET. It is hoped that eventually more sophisticated users will be able to design their own interface.

ACKNOWLEDGMENTS

I would like to acknowledge the assistance of Roy Pearce, Academic Computing Service, and Dr. Clive Field, University Library, in preparing this chapter.

NOTE

1. Working Party on Campus Information Services. Second progress report, January 1991. Third Progress report, January 1992.

Bristol Info Server

Ann French
Head of Information Group
University of Bristol, UK

Paul Smee
Senior Systems Programmer Computing Service
University of Bristol, UK

At the beginning of August 1991, the Computing Service of the University of Bristol, England made available to the higher education and research community in the United Kingdom the software, tools, and documentation designed to provide and support the Bristol Info Server. The Bristol Info Server was described as "a general-purpose, UNIX-based information resource, which provides a means of collecting and presenting details relating to an organization such as a university." More importantly, the Bristol Info Server was designed to be very easy to use for the benefit of those who do not use computers regularly, without being frustrating for "experts."

What follows is a description of how we came to write this software, some of the problems we had in designing it, how it is being used now, and our plans for the future.

THE MULTICS INFO SYSTEM

Prior to September 1988, the University of Bristol ran a Honeywell Multics system as its main computer resource. Among its wealth of features, Multics had a command interpreter called exec_com, similar to UNIX shell scripts, which could be used to write simple applications quickly. In 1985, exec_com was used to create the Multics Info System. This was a very simple system with a sequence of menus giving access to the university telephone directory, lists of software on various platforms, information about Computing Service courses, and the network addresses of computers at other UK academic sites. Of these choices, the Info System was most used for looking up network addresses. The Multics Info System was reasonably well used and was popular with its users, who in general appreciated its simplicity. When Multics was replaced by an IBM VM/CMS system in 1988, many mourned its passing, and requests were made to replace the Info System with a similar facility.

There were many things wrong with the Multics Info System from a design point of view:

- It was implemented on a general-purpose computer that was used for undergraduate coursework and computationally intensive applications. This meant that the response was very variable, dependent on the current workload.
- The control program and the menu text were integrated, which made it difficult to update any of the menus and a major task to add any new menus.
- There were no facilities for formatting the text being displayed or even for checking that it was in a reasonable format for being displayed.

At that time we had no computer management system (CMS) experience (a situation that has not changed much since—it's not an easy transition from Multics to IBM, even for those with early ICL experience). However, we did have a committed group of UNIX devotees and a growing number of UNIX hosts on site. We decided that any new information processor should be UNIX-based and that preferably it should have its own UNIX system to avoid problems of variable loading. We wanted to overcome the design limitations of the Multics system. Our main aim, however, was to make the user interface as straightforward as possible. An early specification said that the interface should

- Work on any terminal
- Be accessible without having to log in
- Be as intuitive, helpful, and forgiving as possible
- Be fast and simple to get into and out of

Early plans (March 1989) were for a combined information server, documentation server, and bulletin board with an online course-booking system thrown in. We thought that we could add status-reporting on local hosts, online courses, and expert systems in the future. At this stage we still expected that some suitable software would be available off the shelf.

THE BEGINNING OF THE PROJECT

The project to provide the current Info Server started with a paper with the what now seems like overambitious plans mentioned above. At the time, we also had a need for a mail server that would receive mail for everyone at Bristol University and redistribute it to the systems that people used most of the time. This would also allow us to have mail names related to people's real names rather than using their (obscure) registered user names, which was the alternative in those pre- X.500 days.

A further requirement was for an easy-to-use mail interface for people who did not use multiuser hosts for anything other than electronic mail. These three facets were combined, and a noncomputational server (NCS) project was set up.

Our director mailed inquiries to directors at other sites, asking if anyone had already developed software that met our needs. Many responses indicated that we were not alone in our desire to set up an information server. Some sites were already developing software, but none of the specifications sounded like what we were looking for. A few sites suggested production systems that we could try out. One or two of these would have been suitable for us—except that they were running on Digital Equipment Corporation (DEC) VMS systems. We had even less VMS expertise than CMS locally, and anyway the cost of DEC systems ruled out these options. In the end we decided that we would have to write the software ourselves. A systems programmer, Paul Smee, who was interested in the project, started to code—though it was made clear that this project was a low-priority task.

A prototype Info Server was written and tested using a Gould PN system. The original version could be used from any terminal at all, including completely dumb terminals that could do no screen handling. This had been an initial requirement since at that time there were many such terminals in everyday use around the university. However, the situation was changing rapidly, and by the time the ur-prototype Info Server was on trial most of the dumb terminals had died. More and more people, particularly Computing Service staff who were testing the server, were using IBM-compatible personal computers (PCs) for terminal access to multiuser hosts. The terminal emulator programs most commonly used emulated VT100 terminals with full-screen handling capabilities.

As a result, Paul Smee started work on a new version that would incorporate much better screen handling, using the UNIX "curses" facility. One of the features to be included was the ability to choose commands and menu items by moving the cursor using the cursor keys, then pressing the PC Enter key. This version was ready in November 1989.

We eventually submitted a request for funds for a production NCS system in January 1990. The funds used were from the Computer Board grant to the University. (The Computer Board, now called the Information Systems Committee, is a UK government quango that funds computing in universities.) The request was approved with no opposition and we ordered a Sun SPARCserver 4/330 Entry-level Office Server with 24MB of memory and a 600MB disk in the middle of January. In February the Computing Service moved into a new purpose-built building, and the new system was installed in the new Machine Room in March. The Sun is still used for all its original purposes, although we are now thinking of upgrading the filestore and of moving the mail server component to a separate system.

DEVELOPMENT OF THE USER INTERFACE

During the design stage of the software, there were many internal discussions about what the interface should look like, and we tried out several ideas before settling on our current design. The next section describes some of the discussions that took place.

ORGANIZATION OF THE INFORMATION

This aspect of the design affects the information providers rather than users of the service. However, since we anticipated that much, if not most, of the information would be provided and maintained by people outside the Computing Service, who might have little computing experience, we wanted to ensure that adding and changing menus and information would be as easy as possible.

We initially thought that we might use a database or text retrieval package to store the information in an organized fashion. It soon became clear that it would require more time than we had available to write a system using this method. Furthermore, there are very real difficulties in designing an interface to such a package which is both secure trivial to use. It is important to remember that most of our target audience is not highly computer-literate and that the system is open for use by anyone who can connect to it across the network with no registration. So, instead of designing the system around a database, we opted to use flat files, relying on UNIX's hierarchical filestore to organize the information.

The Info Server has two basic types of files: menu files and information files. Menu files consist of lines specifying the type of file the menu line points to (another menu file or an information file), a number and text to be displayed for the menu item, and the path of the file. A later enhancement allows you to specify the name of a program that will create an information file when the menu item is chosen instead of the path of an information file. Menus are created in real time when they are selected by a user. This approach means that files can be updated at any time without affecting people using the system and the most up to date information is immediately available. Another benefit is that the system can check the current file permissions and display the lines for only those menu items for which the user has read permission. We use this facility both for testing new items and for making information private to a particular group.

If the menu item points to an information file, the date when the file was last modified is displayed beside the item. We have often been asked to display the most recent date that any file further down the menu path was modified against all menu items. Since the menus are created every time they are displayed, working through the menu structure to find this out for the top level menus would slow the system down unacceptably. Up to nine menu items can be displayed at one time; menu items are selected by typing the number of the item. All menus therefore fit on a single screen. There has been much discussion about whether we should change this format to allow menus to be longer than one screen. This would complicate the software quite a lot, but the main reason for rejecting it was to force information providers to structure their information. We think that it is easier to negotiate your way around information that has been organized into a hierarchical structure than to page through very long menus.

At the same time, we recognize that sometimes this approach forces an artificial structure on lists of similar items (such as papers for a meeting, newsletters). This has not been a problem for us yet, but it may well become one in the future, and so we are trying to think of a mechanism of presenting longer lists. There is room for ten menu items on the screen. We were reluctant to use 0 to select a normal menu item (would it come first or last?— neither is particularly intuitive), but it could be used to display more items on a list.

Information files can be of any length. Each line is indented by four spaces at the left. For ease of reading we recommend that lines should be no longer than 72 characters long. Lines longer than 76 characters are truncated. The maximum number of lines that can be displayed on a screen depends on the terminal type being used but is it 17 lines for a typical 25-line display. The software avoids splitting paragraphs over two screens. (Paragraphs are separated by blank lines.) Information providers are responsible for ensuring that the text is in a suitable format, and we provide very few tools to help them get this right. This is the weakest area of the Info Server. It has always been our intention to create utilities for preparing and installing information files. So far we have managed very few, and as a result, we find that only relatively sophisticated computer users are prepared to take full responsibility for maintaining information.

Information files can be divided up in several different ways which affect how you can select parts of the file when reading it. The parts that can be selected are lines, paragraphs, and sections (which can be several paragraphs long). If the information file is divided in this way you can, when using the Info Server, create a temporary extract of the file by selecting all the parts containing a specified text string. Thus, for example, you can extract all the entries on a particular topic from a list of courses.

LAYOUT OF THE SCREEN

The screen has a title at the top, the menu or screen of information in the middle, and commands at the bottom. The main menu screen at the university of Bristol currently looks like the following:

```
University of Bristol Info Server 2.02          Main-menu

    1. Directories and telephone lists
    2. Equipment lists and prices
    3. Courses, seminars, and events
    4. What and where in the university
    5. Documents and publications
    6. University minutes and papers
    7. News and headlines
*          *          *          *          *
Help        Main-menu    Suggestion   Redisplay
Content     Quit
Command?
```

Originally there were an additional two lines in the command area. These were removed recently to allow two more lines of information on the screen. We thought this might make the screen too crowded but, as far as we can tell, very few people even noticed the difference! Only the commands that can be used at the time are displayed. A typical screen of information can be seen on the following page.

One early debate centered on how to indicate that there was more information in the file. We tried several different methods—putting plus signs and arrows (actually "∧" at the top or "v" at the bottom) in the margin, and lines saying "<more>" where appropriate. All these indications just looked messy, and in the end we opted to rely on the messages "Press Enter for next page" when there was more information following, and "At end of information" when the last screen-full had been displayed. The page number is given in the heading, so it is easy to see when you are at the beginning of the information.

The heading information also gives an estimate of how far through the file you are (66% in the example above). Many people suggested that the page number should be followed by the total number of pages in the document. This would be a significant overhead because of the Info Server's capability of displaying different numbers of lines per screen depending on the

---

Why networking   M5211
                                        Page 1   (66%)
   Networking is a very simple concept. It is a linking process to allow
computer users of all sorts to communicate and to share facilities. Unfortunately, it is an area that is full of jargon, initials, and acronyms. Some of this
jargon will be mentioned in the following sections, but you don't need to
learn or remember it in order to use the university network. If you want to
"look under the bonnet" and understand some of what's going on, then you
can't avoid some jargon. A glossary is provided on the menu.
   Information processing is a major function of the university. Information
is passed to and fro between staff, students, books, papers and screens. It is
processed at every stage. It is often time consuming, frustrating, and sometimes expensive to locate the information you require in the mountain available. Networking can help you to do this, speeding up the access and investigation, and leaving more time for you to process the information.
*   *   *   *   *

Help   Find   Prev-menu   Main-menu   Suggestion   Redisplay
Up   Goto   Down   Transfer   Quit
Command?
Press Enter for next page

---

terminal type. The number of pages would have to be calculated for every file
each time it was displayed.

COMMANDS

The complete list of commands currently is:

Help	Find	Prev-menu	Up	Goto	Suggestion	Redisplay
Contents	Extract	Main-menu	Down	Whole	Transfer	Quit

The command set originally proposed was very different:

Help	Find	Last-menu	Next	Page	Comment	Redisplay
Index	Goto	Main-menu	Back	Top	Send	Quit

   In fact, although the names have changed considerably, the functions
provided by the two command sets are much the same. To summarize the
changes:

Contents	Replaced Index (which we could not work out how to implement)
Down	Originally Next
Extract	Originally part of Find
Find	Specification changed (see below)
Goto	Originally went to a menu; now goes to a page, or top or bottom of an information file
Help	Unchanged
Main-menu	Unchanged
Prev-menu	Originally Last-menu
Quit	Unchanged
Redisplay	Unchanged
Suggestion	Originally Comment
Transfer	Originally Send
Up	Originally Back
Whole	Available after using Extract to redisplay all the document

In the first iteration of the software, you could type in any number of letters of a command name before pressing the Return or Enter key to send the command. If the command required an argument, you could type it before pressing Return or wait to be prompted for it. This approach split the staff who were testing the software basically into microcomputer and mainframe camps. Those who worked mainly on PCs were irritated by the need to press Return after every command; the others found it difficult not to press it when using packages that did not require it. The non-Returners won the argument, largely because the electronic mail package we were just starting to use (Elm) did not use Return to end commands and we wanted to retain some consistency between the packages.

In the resulting new style of operation, a command is executed as soon as its initial letter is typed. This, of course, requires that each command begin with a different letter. In fact, Comment was changed to Suggestion in order to free the letter C for the Contents command.

At the same time, Paul Smee added the facility to use arrow keys to highlight command names or menu items, so that people with limited keyboard skills could select commands and move around the menus without having to search for the appropriate keys. The implementation of this feature marked the final abandonment of any support for dumb terminals. The decision to abandon the original design goal that the system should work on any terminal was not an easy one. However, the gains in presentation and operation from assuming a minimally intelligent screen were too great to forego.

The main discussions of the command set revolved around the command for selecting text. The original design had the one Find command. In plain documents, Find found the next occurrence of the specified text string. In documents divided into parts (lines, paragraphs, or sections) Find selected all the parts containing the text string and displayed the selection as a new document. This caused a surprising amount of confusion (well, I was surprised at the time; looking back, it is not surprising at all). We solved it by ditching the Find command and introducing two new commands, Locate and Select, which separated the two functions; Locate located the next occurrence of a string in any document, Select selected parts of a divided document. This cleared up the confusion but brought cries of outrage from people who could not come to terms with the names we had chosen. Finally, we renamed Locate as Find and Select as Extract, and everyone seemed happy. Later, we added the Whole command to make it easy to get back to the whole file after using Extract.

The command set has remained stable for some time, partly because there is no room on the command lines for any more commands. A current plan is to extend the number of commands for the benefit of "expert" users by introducing a + command that would display a list of the less frequently used and more difficult-to-use commands. These would include the Transfer command, used to transfer files to your personal filestore, and possibly a command to display files without any control characters so that they could be printed on a printer attached to the terminal or PC being used as a terminal.

IN PRODUCTION

The production version of the Info Server was released for general use in October 1990. The release was very low key: we just kept mentioning it more and more in courses, documents and newsletter articles. The Info Server is available from any terminal that can be connected to the JANET network. It can also be accessed from any of the local UNIX hosts run by the Computing Service. All access is interactive. We considered adding FTP and e-mail access but rejected it on the grounds that this was not how we wanted the system to be used. It is essentially a local facility holding information of interest to members of this university, and we still want to keep it as simple as possible. We started logging usage fully in June 1991. Weekly logs show the number of sessions and how often each command has been used. Table 1 shows the growth in use, based on using sample weeks from each month from June to December 1991.

The number of information files available increased from 19 in October 1990 to 125 in December 1991. The files include the university telephone list and lists of subscriber trunk dialing (STD) codes, electronic mail addresses of

Table 1.

	June	Jul	Aug	Sept	Oct	Nov	Dec
No. of sessions	303	395	466	914	875	991	1002
Average session length	N/A	4m57	6m12	5m33	5m41	4m37	4m25
No. of file accesses	480	790	1304	1753	2057	2522	2221
No. of files accessed	49	71	66	67	103	106	101
Command usage							
Down (pressing Return)	2806	4104	8907	10737	15424	15586	12619
Find	673	609	905	1977	1492	1874	1574
Extract	91	201	205	261	278	331	242
Transfer	8	11	45	79	54	35	50
Contents	2	48	73	54	73	85	55

staff and postgraduates, network addresses, equipment prices, swap and shop advertisements, information about courses held by various departments, drama, music, and film listings, other information about several departments and student societies, a micro bulletin, local documentation about networking, Senate papers, and a news section. In addition, the Computing Service makes use of the restricted access facilities to store some internal information, such as an extended price list. We also store PostScript versions of all our documents on the Info Server so that members of the staff can print copies of documents that are out of stock. It was decided not to make these generally available because of the potential for abuse in allowing anonymous users to print files. Similar considerations explain the choice of file transfer rather than e-mail as the mechanism underlying the Transfer command.

The news section contains a menu of the nine most popular items in the past week. This may be a self-perpetuating list—it certainly does not change much from week to week. The top item is almost always the fortune cookie program. Fortune cookie was introduced to test the feature of running a program to create an information file for display and rapidly became very popular. Although it is still there as a test, some people, both within the Computing Service and in other parts of the university, regard such applications as inappropriate and a waste of time and resources. The rest of us think that anything which makes the Info Server more attractive and pleasant to use is a good thing.

The Suggestion command generates a healthy number of corrections to information and suggestions for improvements. There are slightly fewer blank messages, presumably from people typing "s" and then failing to read the instructions about what to do next. We have had only 15 obscene messages since the beginning of the service, well outnumbered by the complimentary ones.

THE FUTURE

So far we have not been at a loss for ideas and suggestions as to what could be put on the Info Server. Information such as local train and coach timetables, what's-on details, and weather forecasts can transform a CWIS into an everyday resource, and we would like to provide such information someday.

However, the problems of running a CWIS are well known. They mostly boil down to lack of staff resources to gather, format, install, and maintain information. We are not particularly fussy about what information is included. We will take anything that looks useful, providing it is not too much trouble to get it into a suitable format. We actively pursue some information as well, so far with limited success. However, there does appear to be an increasingly positive attitude in many areas of the university towards online information as people become aware of the potential for savings in printing costs as well as the benefits of having up-to-date information available to everyone. One positive development in this direction is the increased interest shown by the administrative departments, who have recently started to make Senate papers available on the Info Server. The obvious solution to the problem is to spread the load of information maintenance as widely as possible, and we have tried all along to do this. I mentioned earlier that a major weakness of our system is that we do not have many utilities to help people with preparing and installing information files. Although the process is not difficult, it involves many fiddly details that are hard to remember if it is something you do only every few weeks or months. Lacking anyone with both the technical knowledge and time needed to develop the tools, we decided that we should make the software available to other higher education institutions in the United Kingdom in the hope that other sites would be better placed for development. The response to our offer has been encouraging, and we are hopeful that other people using the software will develop enhancements to the software.

Hull University Information Service

Bridget Towler
Systems Librarian
Hull University, UK

INTRODUCTION

Hull University is a medium-sized university (approximately 6000 students) situated on a single campus on the outskirts of the city of Hull in the county of North Humberside (formerly the East Riding of Yorkshire). The university's Brynmor Jones Library has been in the forefront of library automation provision for the past decade, and in 1980 it was the first library in the United Kingdom to install a GEAC library system. The GEAC is connected to the campus X25 network which supports about 1,100 personal machines on campus, of which about 800 are fully networked.

The Hull University Information Service is possibly one of the earliest examples of a campus-wide information service. It has been in existence since the early 1980s, running initially on a GEAC 8000 and then being transferred to a GEAC 9000 in 1988.[1] Although the system started out purely as an Online Public Catalogue with additional options for accessing Departmental Stores and Careers information, it has gradually grown over the years until it now encompasses many of the features identified in the Report on Core Information Sets drawn up by the UK IUIC Information Systems Working Party.[2] The Library, University and Local Information Bulletin Board (Option 8 on the main Information Service Menu) is in fact the only part of the system that was actually designed as a campus-wide information service (see Figure 1).

This chapter describes the Hull Information Service in general, with particular emphasis on the Library, University and Local Information Bulletin Board.

THE HULL INFORMATION SERVICE

The Hull Information Service is based on a suite of programs written in ZOPL, GEAC's proprietary programming language and now running on a GEAC 9000 with the following hardware configuration:

```
┌─────────────────────────────────────────────────────────────────┐
│                 HULL UNIVERSITY—INFORMATION SERVICE               │
│                 ------------------------------------              │
│           WELCOME TO THE BRYNMOR JONES LIBRARY GEAC 9000          │
│                                                                   │
│                    This network service gives access to the       │
│                 Library Catalogue and to other information systems.│
│                                                                   │
│              Terminal/network faults: Call Computer Centre, ext 5685│
│                 Other queries: Call GEAC Computer Room, ext 6203   │
│                                                                   │
│        1. Look for a Library Book ( or T for Title, S for Subject, etc.)│
│        2. Look at record of own Loans and Reservations.            │
│        3. Look at Bibliographies and other catalogues.             │
│        4. Look at Careers Vacancy Bulletin.                        │
│        5. Look at Stores catalogues.                               │
│        6. GEMS - GEAC Electronic Message System (BJL).             │
│        7. Connect to other Academic Library Catalogues.            │
│        8. Library, University & Local Information Bulletin Board.   │
│                                                                   │
│        E. END SESSION AT ANY STAGE AND RETURN TO THE NETWORK       │
│        Enter here:                                                 │
└─────────────────────────────────────────────────────────────────┘
```

Figure 1. Campus-wide information service.

3 full function processors
2.2 Gbyte disc storage
12MB memory
68 ports
4 X25 ports

The above hardware also supports standard GEAC Circulation and Acquisitions modules. It must be emphasized at this point that the software for the Hull Information Service has not been written by GEAC personnel but by members of the Information Services group of the university's Computer Centre. An important feature of the local software is that it does not use the ANSI X3.28 protocol (for polled, block-mode asynchronous terminals) which is standard for all GEACs' own software. There were two main reasons behind this decision. First was the financial consideration: it enabled cheap, off-the-shelf terminals to be used in the Brynmor Jones Library itself where a number of BBC (British Broacasting System) micros were already available. After special programmable read-only memory (PROM) had been written (again, by an earlier member of the Information Services team) and produced by the Electronic Engineering department to provide the appropriate Cipher emulation, the BBCs were connected to the GEAC at a cost of about $150 per terminal. Second, since the standard for data transmission is simple ASCII, the only control character used being linefeed/ carriage return, all the display-only versions of the programs could be run on any dumb terminal accessing the GEAC from anywhere on the campus (where a significant number of

Dacol, Cipher, and other assorted ancient terminals still existed) or from within the JANET network or via dialup modem. The software for the display programs therefore uses neither clear screen nor cursor addressing techniques.

In the early days, the GEAC 8000 was connected to the campus X25 network via four reverse pad lines. Since 1990 the GEAC 9000 has been connected to a CAMTEC PAD by 1 X25 line which is connected in turn by a 64K baud link to the university central switch, a SEEL Telepac. All users accessing the GEAC whether on campus, via the JANET network or via dialup modem, are routed through this central switch where the simple command "CALL GEAC" connects them directly to the Information Service. The system does not ask for log-on IDs or passwords, nor are users required to identify the type of terminal they are using. Although the system is currently configured to allow up to 30 concurrent accesses, the average number of concurrent accesses from the network is about 12.

At Hull many of the facilities identified as standard CWIS features are separate programs within the parent program NETWPQ. This allows greater flexibility of access for those programs that have corresponding data input programs as, for example, the Archives; Estuarine and Coastal Law; South East Asia and East Yorkshire Bibliographies; and the HULTIS (Humberside Libraries Technical Information Service) periodicals database. Data input for all the above databases is limited to the Library Clerical Office where staff carry out most of the data input in the library or to individual members of library staff who are responsible for the different databases. For example, the Archives system is currently restricted to the Archivist's Office only, whereas data input to both the Estuarine and Coastal Law and South East Asia databases is enabled both on terminals in the Clerical Office and in the appropriate Librarian's Office. Other programs in the Information Service merely extract data from the main library catalogue database and display the information in a different format. This is the case with Recent Accessions, which is accessible from Option 3: Bibliographies and Other Catalogues (see Figure 2) and Reading Lists and University of Hull Theses which are accessible from Option 1: Library Catalogue (see Figure 3).

Access to other Academic Library Catalogues is available from Option 7 on the main menu of the Information Service and is provided by a locally written front end to GEACs X25 software (see Figure 4). This provides basic information regarding the instructions needed to access the remote system, including log-on ID and password, terminal type, and the appropriate commands for exiting from the remote system. Initially, all library catalogues available on the JANET network were included on the menu, but unfortunately several have had be removed either because the remote system demands a specific terminal type, usually VT 100, or because once connected to them, it

```
┌─────────────────────────────────────────────────────────┐
│              BIBLIOGRAPHIES AND OTHER CATALOGUES          │
│                                                           │
│   1. HULTIS Databases.                                    │
│   2. East Yorkshire Bibliography.                         │
│   3. Estuarine Law Bibliography.                          │
│   4. Southeast Asia Bibliography.                         │
│   5. Recent Accessions.                                   │
│   6. Archives.                                            │
│   7. Commonwealth Literature Database.                    │
│   8. Bishop Grosseteste Library.                          │
│   X. to eXit.                                             │
│                                                           │
│   Enter here:                                             │
│                                                           │
└─────────────────────────────────────────────────────────┘
```

Figure 2. Option 3: Bibliographies and Other Catalogues.

```
┌─────────────────────────────────────────────────────────┐
│                Brynmor Jones Library Catalogue            │
│           """"""""""""""""""""""""""""""""""""""""        │
│                                                           │
│   Q   Quick author/title search    U   University of Hull These │
│   T   Title search                 P   Periodicals search │
│   A   Author search                L   Lecturers' reading lists │
│   K   Keyword in Title search      R   Record/Poetry Library │
│   C   Classmark search                                    │
│   N   Keyword in Author search     H   Help               │
│   S   Subject search               X   Return to main menu│
│                                                           │
│   How do you wish to search? :                            │
│                                                           │
└─────────────────────────────────────────────────────────┘
```

Figure 3. Option 1: Library Catalogue.

is impossible to get out. One of the penalties of being in the forefront of the development of information systems is that when replacing the original BBC terminals four years ago, we decided to buy Wyse 50 terminals which do not support VT100 emulation. Unfortunately, within a year of this decision, VT100 emerged as the industry standard. Financial constraints now prevent us from replacing our 30 existing terminals with VT100 terminals but obviously any terminals bought in the future will be VT100 compatible. Although access to other academic libraries was included mainly for the benefit of users within our own library, analysis of usage of the Information Service has shown that many people on the campus connect to the GEAC from the uni-

The following Academic Library Catalogues can be accessed
from this terminal. Simply enter the site you wish to call.

1.ABERDEEN	2.BANGOR	3.BATH	4.BELFAST
5.BIRMINGHAM	6.BRISTOL	7.BRUNEL	8.CAMBRIDGE
9.CARDIFF	10.EAST-ANGLIA	11.EDINBURGH	12.EXETER
13.GLASGOW	14.LANCASTER	15.LEEDS POLY	16.LEICESTER
17.LONDON-CITY-POL	18.LONDON(LIBERTAS	19.LONDON LSE	20. LONDON KINGS
21.LONDON IMPERIAL	22.LONDON Q.MARY	23.LOUGHBOROUGH	24. NEWCAST-LE
25.NOTTINGHAM	26.SALFORD	27.SHEFFIELD	28. SOUTHAMPTON
29.ST ANDREWS	30.STAFFS. POLY	31.STRATHCLYDE	32.SUSSEX
33.SWANSEA	34.UCL	35.WARWICK	

Figure 4. Option 7: Access to other Academic Library Catalogues.

versity network simply in order to access the Other Academic Libraries menu rather than calling the external libraries directly from the network. This also happens occasionally with users from other parts of the United Kingdom who access the Hull Information System via the JANET network and then use the Academic Libraries menu to connect to another library system.

Several stores' databases for some of the large Science departments within the university have been available on the Information Service for many years and the read-only information that is displayed in Option 5 is simply a byproduct of the accounting and stock control systems written by the programming team for the departments concerned. Although the material included in the Chemistry, Electronics and Life Sciences databases is obviously very specific to the departments concerned and is therefore used mainly by the staff and students of those departments, a significant number of administrative and clerical staff throughout the university use the Stationery Stores database for checking the availability of supplies on campus.

The Careers Vacancy Bulletin which is available from Option 4 is again a byproduct of a program written for the University Careers Office which, in 1986, required a system for matching students job requirements with vacancies reported to the Careers Office by companies looking for graduate recruits. As with the Stores systems above, all the data are input directly by careers office staff who have password-protected access to the system via the university network. Although the Bulletin was again designed specifically for Hull University students, any user accessing the Information Service via the JANET network may make use of the facilities.

A major dataset still to be added to the Information Service is the Hull University Research Database. This is currently being compiled by the External Relations Office in the university and will consist of details of all ongoing research in the university. Once collated, the data will be entered on a personal computer (PC) using dBase III, and when the work is complete, only relevant, that is, nonconfidential, parts of the database will be extracted and mounted on the GEAC Information Service for public use.

Another standard CWIS facility that Hull does not currently provide is an Internal Telephone Directory. The long-standing debate about whether, when, and who should mount this information has now been overtaken by events with the arrival on campus of a dedicated mailserver, enabling the university to take part in the X500 Directory project. A transparent gateway from the Information Service to the X500 server will therefore, it is hoped, be available within the next 12 months.

INFORMATION BULLETIN BOARD

The Library, University, and Local Information Bulletin Board was first designed in 1988 and was intended initially as a replacement for the Information Monitor that had been available in the Brynmor Jones Library for some years. The previous system had consisted of screens of information regarding library opening hours and other library facilities that were displayed in rotation on one monitor situated on the ground floor of the library. The information was entered onto a BBC microcomputer and, in addition to being displayed on the standalone monitor in the library, was also transmitted to the networked version of the Information Service running on the GEAC 8000 but was not available on the public terminals within the library.

As the plans for a new information bulletin board system was of potential interest to several areas of the university, a specification for the new system was presented to the university's Information Strategy Committee, which is made up of senior members of the university, including the Librarian and the Director of the Computer Centre, and whose remit is to coordinate information services throughout the university. Although the committee approved the specification, the decision that the new system should be mounted on the GEAC was made only with reluctance. However, at that point (1988) no other departments had the hardware or staffing resources to provide such a system, and so it was agreed that the GEAC should be used until a more suitable machine became available. It is gratifying to know that three years later the Information Bulletin Board has been so successful that the Director of the Computer Centre has agreed that the GEAC system should remain the principal vehicle for the Bulletin Board and that responsibility for the system should remain with the library.

The Bulletin Board is a simple hierarchy of menus, submenus, and information pages, and the user may move up and down between the various levels of this tree structure. The current system is the second version of the original system.

Originally, making the tree structure the basis of the system seemed to be the simplest and most natural design. Each "page" of information had several pointers attached, one pointing up to its parent menu and others pointing down to its children (if any) and the program moved from one level of the tree to another by following the pointers.

This system posed two great disadvantages, however. First, the only way to move about the tree was to follow the pointers between pages. Users could not skip sideways, but had to go up the tree and then down again. For example, if they had been looking at a list of library regulations and wanted to look at train timetables, they had to go up to the main menu and then move down again, one step at a time. This was especially irritating for experienced or regular users, who might know exactly what they wanted and where it was, but still had to wade through several layers of menuing to get there. There were no shortcuts. The second disadvantage was that inexperienced users were easily confused by several layers of menus, for INFO could not tell them whereabouts in the system they were. Although we had tried to limit ourselves initially to two levels (i.e., the only menus were the main menu and its submenus), this meant that there were more pages at the same level and there was obviously a practical limit to the number of screens that the user would want to page through before getting to the information he or she wanted.

Therefore, after some months of testing the system and looking at other bulletin boards available in the United Kingdom such as HUMBUL and BUBL, we decided to rewrite INFO completely. In the current version, when users enter the Bulletin Board by selecting Option 8, they are shown the top-level menu (Menu M). This menu lists a number of broad subject areas that help the user find the subject of most interest or relevance to them.

Users then move to any part of the Bulletin Board by typing in the alphanumeric code of the section they wish to see (e.g., A2D). This section may contain another menu, or it may contain one or more screens (or "pages") of information. At the top right-hand corner they are told which section they have onscreen, and at the top left-hand corner they are told the total number of pages in the current section and which page is currently on display. Users can press the <ENTER> key to view the next page of information, or move to a specific page by keying in the page number. They can also return to the previous menu level by typing R (for Return), or go directly to the main menu by typing M.

The great advantage of this approach is that, if users are familiar with the codes for various sections, they can skip around the system quite quickly, whereas novice users can follow the menu structure. Any valid code can be entered from anywhere in the system, and the user will move directly to the appropriate section. In addition, the codes used should, in theory, make the current position obvious.

The current version of INFO is based on a pseudo "menu-structure." It still looks like a tree structure to the user (i.e., they are still moving up and down a hierarchy), but internally it is nothing of the kind. All the pointers between pages have been abolished. The system is based on two database files, **INFO and **CODE. **INFO holds all the screen pages (19 fields of 80 characters), and **CODE holds all the section codes as well as the "page numbers" for **INFO. **CODE is sorted in order of code.

When a user types in a code, the program searches through **CODE until a match is found. It then reads in the "page numbers" for **INFO and displays those pages. From the programming point of view, the great advantage of this design is its simplicity; it is very easy to implement, and the programmer could go on to add features that would make inputting and updating easier for the clerical staff. Although the system is based on index searching, very little processing power is used. At the moment there are 350 pages of information but only 130 separate codes, so binary-chop searching though **CODE is still very fast.

There are some current limitations to the system. For example, we have only allowed four levels of menuing, for it was felt that any more would overcomplicate the system (see Figure 5). Also, at the moment the system will

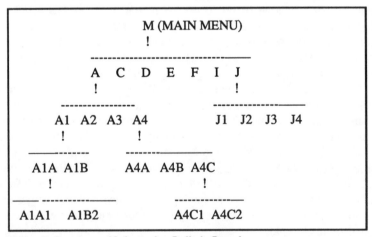

Figure 5. Structure of Information Bulletin Board.

only allow approximately 2,000 different codes. This is not because the size of the files is limited, but because this is the number of available codes currently programmed into the system. For example, A0 and A1 to A9 are permissible, but no allowances have been made for A10, that is, for more than two-digit numeric codes. Finally, only 30 pages of information are allowed for each code. We do not anticipate, however, that either of these system limits will cause problems, at least not for the next couple of years! In any case, both limits could be changed if necessary.

Daily maintenance of the system is carried out by a batch file that removes pages marked for deletion and re-indexes the **CODE file. The batch takes less than five minutes to run.

The specification for the Bulletin Board states that "The success of the system will depend on the ease of inputting and updating of information." Although the GEAC 9000 has a sophisticated editor for programming use, its facilities cannot easily be made available for applications programs. Therefore, inputting to the unstructured 19x80 screen caused some problems in the early days for clerical staff who were used to more sophisticated word processing features such as line wrap, and move and copy commands. However, as the software was gradually enhanced and particularly as a program was written to enable text or ASCII files to be downloaded from a PC, inputting has become much easier. The system is particularly flexible in that additional screens, that is, pages can be added at any time either at the same level as an existing screen or as a submenu. The software also enables screens of information to be copied from one page to another or to be copied to "hidden" screens. This is useful in instances where information needs to be temporarily deleted until it is required again later in the year or at the same time the following year. The command NEW CODE also allows code numbers to be changed, thus enabling an entire section to be moved to another slot on the hierarchical menu. Another useful feature is that when screens are added or updated, they may be flagged with a Date for Deletion. Once the specified date is reached, the screen is automatically deleted during the UPINFO batch that is run at the beginning at each day.

The software that downloads text or ASCII files from a PC has simplified greatly the maintenance of information on the Bulletin Board and will be particularly useful as an increasing number of nonlibrary information providers start using the system. As long as the information is formatted in 20 lines of 80 characters with **** denoting end of page and is output to a standard text file, data can be prepared by a variety of individuals across the campus. Floppy disks are then sent to the library clerical office which is responsible for downloading the data and adding them to the relevant pages of the Bulletin Board. The program I.MOVE allows the clerical staff to view the data first and then to insert the information at the relevant page by simply typing in the code number. If the page code does not already exist, it is added automatically. However, if pages do already exist at the specified code number, new pages are appended at the end of the existing pages.

The implementation schedule identified in the original specification for the Bulletin Board has in the main been followed successfully (see Figure 6). A staggered implementation was planned starting with library information (based on the information available in the printed leaflets produced by the

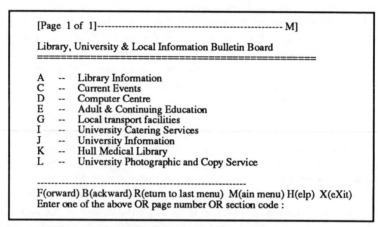

```
[Page 1 of 1]--------------------------------------------------- M]

Library, University & Local Information Bulletin Board
=================================================

A   --   Library Information
C   --   Current Events
D   --   Computer Centre
E   --   Adult & Continuing Education
G   --   Local transport facilities
I   --   University Catering Services
J   --   University Information
K   --   Hull Medical Library
L   --   University Photographic and Copy Service

-------------------------------------------------------------
F(orward) B(ackward) R(eturn to last menu) M(ain menu) H(elp) X(eXit)
Enter one of the above OR page number OR section code :
```

Figure 6. Library Information Bulletin Board.

Brynmor Jones Library), gradually extending to other departmental information in the university, and then finally to local community information. Although all library information is now available on the Bulletin Board (see Figure 7), including most recently the full text of the Brynmor Jones Library

```
[Page 1 of 1--------------------------------------- A]

Library Information
~~~~~~~~~~~~~~~~~~~
A1  --   Library hours
A2  --   Staff
A3  --   Regulations
A4  --   Services
A5  --   Library news
A6  --   BJL News (Full-text newsletter)
A7  --   Archives and Manuscripts
A8  --   Friends of the Brynmor Jones Library

-------------------------------------------------------------
F(orward) B(ackward) R(eturn to last menu) M(ain menu) H(elp) X(eXit)
Enter one of the above OR page number OR section code :
```

Figure 7. Library Information Bulletin Board.

Newsletter, other departments in the university have proved reluctant to provide information for the system. Now, however as campus-wide information service is becoming more widespread across the United Kingdom and indeed appears to be the "flavour of the month" in computer services as well as in library services, this information appears to be becoming more readily available. Local community information has so far been limited to cultural events in Hull, York and Leeds, train services between Hull and London, and local bus services to the university.

The Bulletin Board was originally created by existing library and computer centre staff and has since been maintained by the library with no additional staffing or hardware resources. Since the initial test period when data were entered either by the Systems Librarian, who drew up the original specification, or the programmer who wrote the software, responsibility for the day-to-day supervision of the Bulletin Board has been passed to an Assistant Librarian who spends approximately 4 hours a week monitoring the currency of existing data and contacting new information providers. Data input is carried out by members of the library clerical office who spend approximately three hours per week on the system. This addition to their workload has been offset largely by the reduction in data input in other areas, for example, downloading of cataloguing records.

The main problem with maintaining a Bulletin Board is obviously currency of information. Although this problem was anticipated, it has still proved more difficult than expected to keep the information completely up-to-date. Recent discussions have led to the reduction in the amount of information on the Bulletin Board, which needs to be constantly updated.

Mounting the Bulletin Board on the GEAC 9000 has not been without its problems. As mentioned above, the lack of word processing facilities on the GEAC has increased the staff time required for inputting data. More importantly, because of the different communications protocols used by standard GEAC software and our local software, neither the Bulletin Board, nor for that matter any of the Information Service available to the users in or outside the library, can be accessed by library staff on their GEAC Circulation, Acquisitions, or cataloguing terminals. Our decision not to use control characters obviously denies us the benefit of reverse video techniques for highlighting command lines or other important information and hypertext interfaces that are now becoming readily available, for many systems cannot be used by GEAC's proprietary operating system. Finally, owing to the proprietary nature of the GEAC, it is unlikely that the information system as it stands now will be easily ported to another machine when the 9000 reaches the end of its life in three to four years time, although the data can, of course, be transported to other systems.

Statistics of use of the entire Information System indicate a pleasing number of accesses of most of the features on our campus-wide information service (see Figure 8) with the number of accesses of the Information Bulletin Board increasing gradually within the first two years. Analysis of X25 accesses, that is, users accessing the GEAC from outside the library, also indi-

Number of LOAN enquiries	:	6499	Number of EXTERNAL LIBRARY enquiries	:	1192
Number of CAREER VACANCY enquiries	:	777	Number of EDUCATION CENTRE enquiries	:	13
Number of STORES enquiries	:	286	Number of RECORD DATABASE enquiries	:	996
Number of INFORMATION enquiries	:	839	Number of READING LIST enquiries	:	1447
Number of GEMS enquiries	:	8484	Number of RECENT ACCESSION enquiries	:	186
Number of HULTIS enquiries	:	99	Number of ESTUARINE & COASTAL LAW	:	57
Number of YOBI enquiries	:	74	Number of PERIODICAL enquiries	:	15869
Number of THESIS enquiries	:	502	Number of SOUTH EAST ASIAN enquiries	:	155
Number of ARCHIVE enquiries	:	25			
User Reservations - in Library	:	200			
User Reservations - over Network	:	23			

Figure 8. Information Service Statistics, 1992.

cate a significant number of users from outside Hull. Furthermore, from anecdotal evidence we know that a user has accessed the Hull Information Service from as far away as Florida to check the Archives database, and a librarian in Hungary connected to the system via EARN and JANET to check the train times from Hull to London prior to her visit to this university in the summer of 1991. Such concrete examples of usage provide very satisfactory responses to the skeptics who say, "Does anyone ever look at your system" or "What's the point of it?"

ACKNOWLEDGMENTS

The following have contributed information to this chapter: Bob Lane, Head of Information Services group; and Bronwen Reid who joined the Information Services programming team in 1988. The Information Bulletin Board was one of the first projects she worked on for the library.

NOTES

1. Bridget Towler, "An Extended Public Enquiry System at the University of Hull," *VINE*, no.78 (May 1990): 25-30.
2. Colin Work, Report on Core Information Set for CWIS Survey, prepared for the Information Services Working Group of the IUIC.

Kentel—An Early CWIS at the University of Kent at Canterbury

Jane Millyard
Head of Information Computing
University of Kent at Canterbury, UK

ABSTRACT

In 1987 the University of Kent at Canterbury (UKC) first considered the introduction of an electronic information system running on its campus network. The following year the author became involved as the secretary of the Editorial Committee for the system.

This case study sets out the aims of the originators of this early system, followed by a brief description of the software chosen and its implementation at Kent. The problems experienced are then discussed and related to future plans to move to a new system early in 1992.

The views expressed in this study are those of the author and not necessarily those of the University of Kent.

BACKGROUND

The University of Kent at Canterbury was one of a group of seven new universities founded in the United Kingdom in the 1960s to accommodate the postwar baby boom. It occupies a hill-top campus overlooking the cathedral city of Canterbury, with buildings widely spaced across the slopes and in the surrounding woodland.

Academic life is based on four interdisciplinary colleges, four science laboratories, the library, the Computing Laboratory, and one or two specialist departmental buildings. It remains today a small university, with about 5,000 undergraduate students and 1,100 postgraduates. The four faculties are Humanities, Social Sciences, Natural Sciences (Physics, Chemistry, and Biology), and Information Technology (Computer Science, Electronic Engineering and Mathematics). In spite of the fact that computing courses have been available to students within the faculties of the Humanities and Social Sciences since the early days, there was, three or four years ago, a large body of non-computer literate students and, more especially, academic staff.

The 30% or so of those on campus who were registered members of the Computing Service in the late 1980s were no strangers to electronic information services, however. Kent was one of the first UK universities to plan its services around a local area network—at that time Cambridge Ring-based (X 29 terminal protocol), with a few local Ethernets. A terminal base of 8-900 VDUs supported a dual VMS and UNIX servic, and extensive use was made of electronic mail and of UNIX news, supplemented by local newsgroups. An unsupported broadcast teletext information service (BBC CEEFAX and ITV ORACLE) was also available. The University Library had recently introduced an online catalogue, accessible from all networked terminals on campus, but a somewhat inward-looking central administration was only then beginning to think of the future provision of online management information. The use of microcomputers in offices was not standardized, with a variety of personal computers (PCs), Ataris, Macintoshes, and so on, running different word-processors.

This, then, was the state of computing at Kent in 1987 at the point when the founding Director of the Computing Laboratory, Brian Spratt and the innovative university Information Officer, the late Roland Hurst, decided that the time was right for the introduction of a campus-wide information system. Encouraged by members of their staff who had attended a course on the subject at the University of Leeds, they proposed the introduction of a view-data service at Kent. This would provide a means of displaying a database of text and graphics to terminals across the campus network in a form more or less compatible with British Telecom's Prestel or the French PTT (Public Telephone and Telecommunications) Minitel service. The standard was somewhat dated but thought to be the best solution affordable at the time.

There were only a handful of other universities ahead of them; some had already tried to set up a CWIS and failed because of lack of staff resources. All had experienced the problem of recruiting editors and maintaining the information. Rather than spending time undertaking a survey of possible electronic information requirements at Kent, in November 1987 they put forward an imaginative proposal to the university, requesting authority to purchase the software and set up an editorial committee.

AIMS

The service envisaged was to be based on a commercial package running under UNIX with a minimum of effort on the part of Computing Service staff. This viewdata system was designed for nonspecialists and would open up electronic information services to the whole campus (and beyond). It was made clear that the success of the enterprise would depend on recruiting staff (and possibly students) throughout the campus to prepare and enter information onto the database. However, the use of a commercial product was felt to imply that "entering the information would be a relatively straightforward task and should at most only require a short course and the necessary documentation." Every effort would be made to avoid keying information more than once, although reformatting might be necessary.

Management of the service would be in the hands of an "Electronic Information Committee" headed by a senior member of the academic staff and should be seen to be independent of the Computing Laboratory. The brief of this committee in the longer term would extend to oversight of all electronic news and bulletin board services on Computing Service systems.

Compatibility with other viewdata systems would enable the export and import of data to and from other public networks, including an educational network for schools and (with some conversion) the French Teletel service. Information on current student vacancies and short courses offered to the general public were suggested as suitable pages to be made available to people accessing the CWIS over external networks. The possibility of charging for the display of certain categories of data was not ruled out.

The range of information to be offered on the initial service was classified into two stages. The first stage covered those parts of the university which were said at the time to be "keenly interested" and prepared to make an active contribution. This information was to be supplied through Roland Hurst and his Information Office.

- Diary of events
- Bus/train timetables
- College menus
- Details of scholarships, fellowships, and such
- Registry notices
- Digest of recent news, press releases, and such
- Rules and regulations
- Wants/sales advertisements
- Course information (publicity material)
- Appointments to UKC
- Job advertisements
- Campus guide
- Faculty/laboratory/academic information
- Telephone directory
- Exam and teaching timetables

The second stage would involve the recruitment of editors throughout the campus and might include

- Computing Laboratory—user information (e.g., News/alerts/ newsletter)
- Student Information—holidays, societies, union meetings
- Faculties—course information, faculty notices, laboratory information
- Appointments Board
- Supplies Office (possibility of ordering supplies)
- Advertisements from local shops/suppliers of equipment
- School of Continuing Education

Brian Spratt believed that little central funding would be forthcoming for the purchase of the software package. A contribution of about £4,000 from the Computing Laboratory would be added to about £7,000 made available from a recent grant to the University Library to automate its services.

No attempt was made to identify funding for the specialist terminals - perhaps akin to public telephone booths—he suggested should be sited in circulation areas throughout the campus.

CHOICE OF SOFTWARE

The range of suitable software packages, already surveyed by Computing Laboratory staff before Brian Spratt made his proposal in 1987, was severely limited. The intention was to purchase software that might run for five or six years until such time when more choice was available. UNIX had already been identified as the preferred operating system of the future for the Kent Computing Service, so a UNIX package offered by Brainstorm Computer Solutions in the United Kingdom emerged as the only serious option. The software was being run successfully by British Telecom in their telephone exchanges and was Prestel compatible. Although the full commercial cost of the package was greatly in excess of the budget, Brainstorm was prepared to supply it for about £10,000 in the hope of breaking into the academic market. The company would port the package to UNIX BSD, on a High Level Hardware Orion mini, and offered unspecified ongoing support.

The simplicity of the Brainstorm package for novice users and the attractiveness of its display on a terminal capable of exploiting its colour and graphical facilities were the obvious points in its favour. The system was menu driven, with data arranged in pages, broken down into individual frames of 40 characters on 24 lines (see Figure 1). It also supported hardcopy output to a suitable printer. Groups of pages could be allocated to individual editors (password protected) by the super editor, who would also be responsible for building up a master index for keyword access. Page links across the

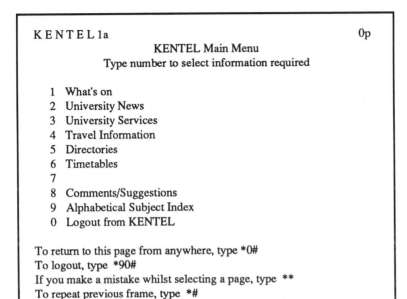

Figure 1. The main menu of Kentel.

database were supported enabling a page of information to be accessed from different menus, either from those under the control of the subeditor "owner" of the page or right across the database.

An editing subsystem and a range of utilities were supplied for editors, enabling them to create, view, edit, reroute, and delete information. An access count for each page was included (see Figure 2).

Another advantage of the package was that it provided for termcap entries, so data could be displayed automatically in either Prestel or character terminal mode. Data could, therefore, be displayed without colour or graphics on the full terminal base, albeit in a less attractive format. The BBC microcomputers in common use on the campus at this time could be set up with suitable viewdata emulator as graphics terminals and, with the addition of colour monitors, would be capable of exploiting most of the facilities of the Brainstorm package. To realize its full potential, however, a special viewdata terminal was required. In a freestanding vandal-proof cabinet with space for a thermal printer, these terminals cost about £2,000 each.

IMPLEMENTATION

The purchase of the Brainstorm package was approved, and work to set up the Kentel Service, as it came to be known, began in the first half of 1988.

```
┌─────────────────────────────────────────────────────────────┐
│  Viewdata Editor                                         910b │
│                   Viewdata Editing System                     │
│                                                               │
│   Editor option?  A  <for amend>                              │
│   Page No. 150          Frame a                               │
│   User Group 0          User access Y                         │
│   Frame type I          Frame price 0p                        │
│                                                               │
│   Routing  F  <for free>                                      │
│   0  2041       5  1505                                        │
│   1  1501       6  15061                                       │
│   2  1502       7  1507                                        │
│   3  1503       8  1508                                        │
│   4  1504       9  1509                                        │
│   Access count 12912                                          │
│   Frame owner 610   Edit 150                                  │
│      Type CTRL-V for help                                     │
│                                                               │
│   Amend this frame?                                           │
└─────────────────────────────────────────────────────────────┘
```

Figure 2. Example of the editing system page for one of the main menus.

Brainstorm mounted the software and installed an additional facility to enable files to be read into the package from the UNIX filestore. Ian Dallas, the Computing Laboratory's system manager for Kentel, wrote some UNIX tools based on the nroff/troff text processing suite to break UNIX files into the Kentel page format and insert "Type # for more . . . . ." at the foot of each frame with follow-on text.

A small editorial committee was set up in July of that year, and planning began for the launch of a pilot service to take place early in 1989. Although a master taxonomy of pages representing all possible interests on campus was devised, it was agreed that the initial service would include information provided by the following:

- The Information Office
- The Colleges
- The Library
- The Computing Laboratory
- The Careers Office
- Mathematics Department

A "Suggestions Box" would be included and a master index was to be maintained by Ian Dallas.

Training and documentation for editors were prepared and carried out and there was frequent encouragement to provide a minimum number of pages issued during the latter part of 1988 .

A large public access terminal was ordered for a college foyer, and dedicated colour terminals were planned for the Library and the Computing Laboratory. No separate technical group was set up to chase the installation of equipment, provision of network access and suitable hardware, and terminal emulation for the editors (for which no funding existed), therefore, the editorial committee spent a large portion of its time on this activity.

Various hardware and software problems were overcome at the end of 1988 and the beginning of 1989, and the Kentel Service was launched at the university in March 1989. At first, the pilot service was a success—the early editors were enthusiastic and invested a great deal of time in providing information on the system. Users, particularly in the college with the large terminal, tried it out and made constructive and (mostly) favourable comments. The suggestion box contained many requests for expansion of the service, particularly in the area of general campus information and social and travel details in and around Canterbury.

The Careers Office section was particularly successful. The local editor was able to sell pages to prospective employers who advertised their vacancies and thereby raises a small income for the project.[1]

THE PROBLEMS

Very early on, however, the project had run into difficulties. These difficulties stemmed from two major causes: a lack of central resource and support and the design of the software package.

One of the prime supporters of Kentel was Roland Hurst, the University Information Officer. His position in the project was a key one, with the bulk of the central information to be put on the system through his office. Late in 1988, staffing problems in the Information Office coincided with a (continuing) need for the university to tighten its belt financially. Although he had hoped to persuade his masters that he had the capacity to continue with the project, he was not permitted to do so and, therefore, reluctantly withdrew his offer of editorial input. In fairness to the central administration, they were not condemning Kentel out of hand. In principle, they regarded it as potentially useful, but a luxury at a time when they were encouraging economy of resources. There had been no campus survey of demand for such a service, no audit of resource taken, and they could see no real evidence of need. Furthermore, the problems of transferring data between various word processors in use centrally and the Kentel system were not easily overcome, and there appeared to be a requirement for data to be rekeyed. In spring 1989

Hurst resigned from the university and the new Information Officer, though supportive, was not in a position to make any commitment to the project.

There was, then, a considerable gap in the central information to be provided on Kentel. Attempts were made to remedy the situation, but they were not entirely successful. Ian Dallas, the systems manager who was committed to the success of the project, invested a great deal of his own time in keying or transferring central information to Kentel. The small income generated by the sale of pages was used to employ a part-time keyboarder, who entered data supplied to her by the Information Office and the Students' Union. What was lacking, however, was a central editor who could spend time gathering information from all sections of the university, advising information providers on the format of their entries and solving the problems of data transfer to Kentel.

The need for this central editor might not have been so great had the recruitment of local editors been successful. Here the project ran into its second problem, largely as a result of the software chosen. Nearly three years after the launch of the pilot service, the number of local editors has not increased. In spite of publicizing the service and great efforts on the part of the chairman of the Editorial Committee to draw others in, departments have not considered the benefits match the resource cost of training a member of staff in what is seen as a complicated editing system. Some potential editors withdrew after taking the short training course; the colour and graphical facilities of Kentel seemed too complicated to those used only to a word processor. Others experienced difficulties in obtaining network connections and a terminal suitable for colour viewdata emulation.[2]

The advantages of compatibility with other external networks, which might have justified the choice of the Brainstorm software, were not exploited, for no links were established either into or out of Kentel. The system's incompatibility with other information systems on campus (i.e., its 40-character, 24-line frame) meant that integration with the Library catalogue or UNIX news, for example, was impossible. The computer literate dismissed it as unworthy of their attention and continued to use the local UNIX newsgroups for disseminating general information that should have had a place on Kentel.

Faced with these difficulties, the existing editors began to lose their early enthusiasm, especially in the face of criticism of the very limited range of information available. Data left on the system after its relevance had passed further prejudiced its critics. In an attempt to increase awareness of the service and encourage more participation, the Editorial Committee was expanded to represent interests throughout the campus. This did not work either.

Very little central funding was available for public terminals that might have made an impact on the community, and when the funding did come, it came too late.

Support of the software was also a problem. Brainstorm assisted with a few early difficulties but then requested high maintenance fees for ongoing support after providing two or three fixes. Their hopes of establishing the package in the academic market had not been fulfilled. The Computing Laboratory realized that the cost of, for example, porting the package to a new version of the operating system would be prohibitive. At the same time, the operation of the package itself began to give cause for concern. The time had come for a change.

THE FUTURE

Early in 1991, a decision was taken to move away from the Prestel-compatible viewdata system to a CWIS written in-house by the University of York. This had been running successfully for some time under VMS. During the remainder of the year, Ian Dallas worked on porting the system to UNIX with a view to relaunching "Kentel Mark II" early in 1992. This coincides with the central administration's increasing interest in disseminating information electronically and an awareness of the need for an integrated IT strategy for the whole campus.

The new Kentel will address some, but not all, of the problems experienced with the earlier CWIS. The format of the (monochrome) display will be acceptable over the whole terminal base. Data, which will carry its author's name, will originate from directories of UNIX files, maintained by means of the UNIX vi editor. A facility to include a "stop" date on a file will remove out-of-date information from the system and make it of current interest. Compatibility with other UNIX systems will allow access through Kentel to the Library catalogue, and beyond to external information services for those authorized to use them. External users will be able to access Kentel via the UK Joint Academic Network (JANET).

The move to a UNIX-based system will, no doubt, ease the problem of recruiting editors in some areas and perhaps encourage the UNIX community to contribute to Kentel, particularly if some integration with UNIX news is attempted. It is wishful thinking, however, to expect the large body of microcomputer users on campus to be enthusiastic about learning the UNIX vi editor. Until such time as Kentel can easily accept input from WordPerfect (now widely used on campus) and from Microsoft Word (used by the Information Office), it will not succeed. A less attractive alternative is for someone to be made responsible centrally for the transfer of information between the various systems.

This information must be seen to be important. To be adopted by staff and students, Kentel must provide information in an acceptable format that they cannot easily acquire by any other means. Preferably, this information must be more useful and readily available than anything they have received previously in any other form.

CONCLUSIONS

There are three principal lessons to be learned from the experiences at Kent. First, find out what people want from an electronic information system (and, if possible, look ahead to give them a little more). Survey the market and draw up a clear plan of the resource implications of providing such a CWIS.

Second, obtain support throughout the campus at the highest levels before launching the project, particularly from the principal information providers. It will not succeed without it. Plan how it is to be managed; it is a mistake to assume that the management of data and the system has to be done by the same people.

Third, provide a system that is easy to use and to maintain, and that is integrated with all other information systems on campus. This system must be seen to offer a distinct advantage to its users over conventional information provision. If a member of the university can obtain the information more easily by asking someone to send a copy of a paper or by picking up a telephone, the project is doomed to failure!

ACKNOWLEDGMENTS

I would like to thank the following for their help in this case study: Ian Dallas, who has been responsible for the technical implementation of Kentel at UKC, and uncomplainingly bears the brunt of my criticism of the system! Steve Binns, the former Head of Software in the Computing Laboratory; Peter Brown and Gordon Makinson, the past and present Chairmen of the Editorial Committee, respectively; Brian Spratt and David Millyard, the Director of the Computing Laboratory and the University Academic Secretary, respectively, both now retired.

NOTES

1. This income dwindled to almost nothing by 1991, as a result of the United Kingdom's economic recession.
2. One UK university met this problem by offering its editors a hardware "package," as an incentive to participate in its CWIS.

Lehigh's Second-Generation Campus-Wide Information System

Timothy J. Foley
Associate Director of Computing and Consulting Services
Lehigh University

Kevin R. Weiner
System's Programming Manager
Lehigh University

INTRODUCTION

Over the past five years, Lehigh University has implemented a campus-wide information system that has become an integral part of the campus environment. Over 300 departments, clubs, committees, classes, and support organizations provide information services on our system. The number of individual users of the system has grown to over 7,000, or about 95% of the university community. While the success of this system is evident, the use of the services has grown far beyond what had been originally anticipated. Software designs that had been appropriate on a smaller scale no longer provide the necessary performance and level of control. Demands for new services and enhanced functions have pressed the existing hardware and software to their limits. To address these problems, Lehigh has implemented a new system on IBM RISC 6000 computers using the relational database ORACLE and Lehigh developed interfaces.

THE ELECTRONIC CAMPUS

By its nature, a university is composed of individuals and groups that have many diverse interests and needs. A continuing goal has been to employ modern information and communications technologies to help the university community more effectively understand and deal with the complex educational, research, administrative, and social infrastructures that exist. Lehigh's commitment to this endeavor has resulted in the successful implementation of an electronic support system that has become integral to the campus way of life.

It is ironic that not until we had begun to implement new electronic services on a campus-wide scale did we fully realize the scope of the problem—

more specifically, the great number of previously unrealized opportunities we had been missing. Electronic mail, for example, has become a chief method of communication on campus—in excess of 1 million messages per year are delivered. Ninety-five percent of the campus community now participates in the use of electronic mail and associated information services.

Special interest groups of all kinds maintain communication among members through the use of electronic bulletin boards and conferences. These include classes, departments, clubs, committees, and various support organizations. Information resources such as schedules, software libraries, numerous databases, and online services, all combine with the communications facility to form an extensive support network spanning literally hundreds of topical areas.

CAMPUS OVERVIEW

Lehigh University is a private, coeducational university located in Bethlehem, Pennsylvania. Lehigh has a total enrollment of approximately 6,500 students. It offers baccalaureate, master's, and doctoral programs through the College of Arts and Science, the College of Business and Economics, the College of Engineering and Applied Science, the Graduate School, and the graduate-level College of Education. Research opportunities are provided through both externally and university sponsored research projects, as well as in ten institutes, fifteen research centers, and three academic centers on campus.

Present and Future Computing Environment

Lehigh's Computing Center houses several mainframe computers. These include a CDC CYBER 180/850 and a DEC VAX 8530, both used for academic and research purposes, an IBM 4381-11 used for administrative processing, and an IBM 4381-14 used for communication and information services. The IBM 4381-14 has been dubbed the Network Server, and functions as the campus-wide information system. In addition, the Computing Center manages approximately 350 public workstations (mostly IBM-compatible microcomputers) in 23 sites on campus. Departmental equipment on campus includes the Library's GEAC 8000 online catalog system, and various machines for CAD/CAM work in Industrial, Mechanical, and Civil Engineering. Most engineering labs also employ numerous high-performance workstations.

The majority of faculty, professional staff, and support staff have IBM-compatible microcomputers on their desks, with a growing number acquiring higher performance UNIX-based workstations. In addition, approximately 2,000 students own their own microcomputers.

Over the next two years, the Computing Center is planning to replace its CDC CYBER Model 850, VAX 8530, and IBM 4381-14 with IBM RS-6000s running AIX. The campus-wide information system is currently running on an IBM RS-6000 Model 950 in beta test mode and will be available to the entire campus by May 1992. Along with these transitions, approximately 200 RS-6000 workstations will be installed in public sites.

Network Environment

An InteCom IBX S/80 digital phone system provides simultaneous voice and data capabilities to every usable room on campus. Currently, there are approximately 4,600 active data connections—each of which allows asynchronous communication up to 19.2Kbps. Also supported is point-to-point synchronous communication up to 56Kbps, and simulated Ethernet capabilities. A pool of thirty-two 2400 baud modems provide off-campus asynchronous communication capability.

High-speed connectivity is provided via a growing backbone network based on fiber optics and IP routers. This network presently connects major research and computing centers in 13 buildings. Using a T1 link, the backbone, in turn, connects to the national Internet via Pennsylvania's PREPnet. Numerous local area networks (mostly Ethernet) are in operation in labs, public computing sites, and offices. Several of these are now connected to the backbone, and the goal is eventually to connect them all.

PROJECT HISTORY

As stated in an unpublished report drafted in March 1986[1] by Lehigh University, the primary objective of Lehigh's campus-wide information system (CWIS) was to provide machine-to-machine data capabilities and people-to-people information services to the entire campus. The major implementation strategies were to: (1) provide faculty and students sufficient access to microcomputer workstations; (2) provide data connections throughout the entire campus; (3) augment this hardware with the implementation of a centralized CWIS; and (4) develop easy-to-use interfaces to the campus-wide network services.

Sufficient access to microcomputer workstations came about when Lehigh entered into an agreement with Zenith Data Systems to obtain 600 microcomputers. Four hundred of these computers were distributed to faculty members. The remaining 200 were placed at public sites, which included the campus libraries. At the same time, Lehigh established a microcomputer store to provide the university community with substantial discounts on microcomputer hardware and software.

Data connectivity throughout the campus was accomplished with the installation of a digital PBX, the Intecom IBX/S80. After determining that none of the computer vendors contacted had a complete solution to Lehigh's needs, Lehigh entered into a developmental project with IBM. As part of this project, IBM provided Lehigh with an IBM 4381 Model 13 to perform the functions of the CWIS; the machine ran the MUSIC operating system and was upgraded to a Model 14 in 1990.

The developmental design strategy was to create menu-driven interfaces using microcomputers as workstations to provide a consistent environment for accessing the information system. It should be noted that this platform proved very efficient for designing and implementing this system but is now being replaced with an IBM RS-6000 running AIX to improve performance and follow the overall goals of Lehigh's current five-year plan for computing.

The developmental project with IBM involved the creation of two interfaces. The CWIS interface, LUNA (Lehigh University Network Applications), provided the communications hub functions, and the microcomputer interface, NetDial, provided automated connections to a variety of supported campus computers (including the CWIS). NetDial has since been replaced by the ACCESS program which provides menu-driven access from both UNIX workstations and microcomputers and works over serial lines as well as over the campus backbone network using TCP/IP.

THE CAMPUS-WIDE INFORMATION SYSTEM INTERFACE

Current applications on the CWIS include

- Electronic mail
- Document preparation
- Bulletin boards and conferencing
- Calendaring and scheduling
- Access to national networks
- Online software libraries
- High-quality printing
- Online forms processing

The CWIS interface was designed to meet the requirement of providing a centralized communication facility for the common transfer of information between people. The interface was developed using various MUSIC operating system utilities that permitted the rapid prototyping of applications. Initial applications were developed in an interpretive language and then converted to compiled languages to provide better performance.

Since it was expected that a large proportion of the user base would be novice computer users, a menu-driven interface was chosen. The interface is a series of hierarchical menus; the menu that the user first sees upon accessing the CWIS is referred to as the LUNA main menu and is shown in Figure 1. The number of items on most menus is kept to a minimum, based on the rule of seven plus or minus two. [2] Consistency of keyboard definitions, navigation, and screen presentation was stressed throughout the design stage. [3]

```
---------------- Lehigh University Network Application --------------
New Mail Waiting!
                          ===============        Date:  01/13/92
User: tjf0                =    MAIN   =          Time:  15:26:43
                          ===============        Users: 24
Enter Selection ===>

   INFO      Information and Services
   MAIL      Electronic Mail Functions
   FILE      File Operations
   DOWNLOAD  Download host file to PC
   UPLOAD    Upload PC file to host
   UTILITY   General Utilities
   INDEX     Full Topic List
   PROBLEM   Problems or Comments
   LOGOUT    Logout


=======================================================================
F1=Help   F5=Schedule     F9=View accessed topics    F10=Updates
          Shift/F2=Logout
```

Figure 1. Main LUNA menu.

Keyboard definitions were based on the use of MS-DOS micros as workstations. Screen navigation is accomplished by selecting the desired menu option; furthermore, the F3 function key is used to exit the current menu or application, and the F1 function key is used to obtain help text for the menu or application being run. A list of the most important function keys is displayed in a region at the bottom of the screen, and the command input line is placed at the top of the screen to ensure consistent screen presentation. One of the major design requirements was that the screens contain all the information needed to navigate through the system so that no commands would have to be memorized.[4] Another major design feature is the capability to move to any menu by typing in the topic name. For example, a person can get to the Sale topic by typing Sale from any menu. A new feature is an updates facility that allows users to check a personalized list of topics that have changed since they were last accessed.

The major options on the CWIS main menu are described below:

- Information and Services provides such features as bulletin boards, conferencing, searchable text files, forms, and survey facilities. Users can post messages under different topics as long as they are given permission by the conference moderator assigned by the Information and Services system administrator. Conference moderators have complete access to their conferences or bulletin boards and maintain all the files. A public bulletin area is provided to allow any user to post messages; it also provides access to a large library of public domain microcomputer software. Using forms, people can make requests for various services (e.g., an interlibrary loan or a seminar registration). The survey facilities allow users to create and administer electronic surveys to specified groups.

- Mail provides access to Lehigh's in-house mail system which allows sending both on-campus and off-campus messages. Other useful features include the creation of mail folders, the automatic forwarding of messages, and the creation of nicknames for individuals and groups.
- File Operations allows users to edit, list, print, copy, rename, encrypt and share files. Its Scan option allows users to specify operations for a number of files at once.
- Download and Upload provide an easy method for transferring files between the CWIS and the local workstation.
- Utilities allows users to change passwords, schedule meetings, set up default system options, and perform other miscellaneous functions.

The Information and Services section grew from a simple news-posting mechanism into a massive subsystem. This facility, called INFO, is now the major service offering on the system next to electronic mail. It is also the model for the user interface and basic functionality of the replacement system now under development. One interesting problem that occurred as a result of the popularity of the system was the large number of requests to be placed on the main Information and Services menu. The initial departments on the main menu were the Library, the Research Office, and the Computing Center. The Computing Center removed itself, but left the Library and the Research Office on the menu (see Figure 2). Since these two groups were pioneers in promoting the usage of the system, it was felt that they should remain on the main INFO menu. For example, the Research Office initially offered free coffee mugs when people responded to their announcements.

Growth and Usage of the System

The CWIS was made available to the campus community of over 7,000 potential users on January 14, 1987. Individual users can open accounts on

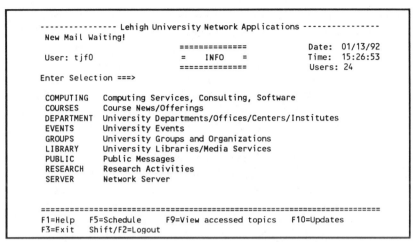

Figure 2. Information and Services menu.

the system online from anywhere on campus using information on their university ID cards. As of September 1991, the number of users who have voluntarily opened accounts on the system has exceeded 7,000—in other words, most of the campus community (see Figure 3). Of those, approximately 82% are active in a given one-month period. Weekday log-ins average about 5,000, with maximum loads to 180 simultaneous users.

Electronic mail and Information and Services have been the most frequently used functions on the CWIS. Over 300 topics now exist in Informa-

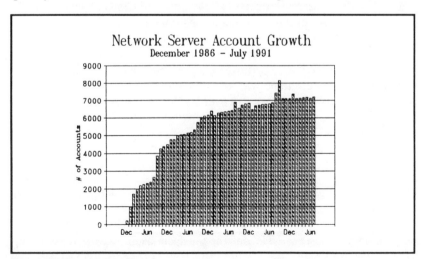

Figure 3. Account growth.

tion and Services. The key to its rapid growth has been the Distributed Services model, which places responsibilities for maintaining and updating the information in the hands of the information provider. For example:

- The Library maintains online forms for interlibrary loans, access to their online catalog, access to other databases residing locally and at other locations around the country, Media Center request forms, and bibliographic search and reference question areas.
- The Computing Center maintains electronic libraries of public domain and site-licensed software, online forms for seminar registration and file reloads, copies of the Center's newsletter and technical bulletins, assignment due dates, the university's five-year plan for computing, and the Center's computing and information policy.
- The Registrar's Office maintains searchable text files consisting of course offerings, catalog information, and final exam schedules. A roster application is also available which allows faculty to obtain electronic addresses for students in their classes.
- The Human Resources Department maintains a listing of all currently available jobs, along with a conference for discussing topics relating to Human Resource problems.
- The Computing Center also maintains other public areas such as sale, general, rides, and lost and found.
- The Research Program Development Office maintains a bulletin board of research funding opportunities.

Figure 4 shows some of the most popular topics on the CWIS and how many times they were accessed over a typical one-month period. As can be seen, the most popular topic was items for sale on campus, but many other items such as inter-library loan had over 100 requests processed electronically per week. Over 60% of our 2,000 seminar registrations are also processed online.

User Satisfaction

User Satisfaction with the CWIS was measured using an online survey which consisted of 7 questions about the user's background, 4 questions about the user's attitude towards computers, and 35 system attributes questions designed to measure user satisfaction. The satisfaction attributes were then combined to create a single, normalized satisfaction score per individual based on work done by Bailey and Pearson.[5]

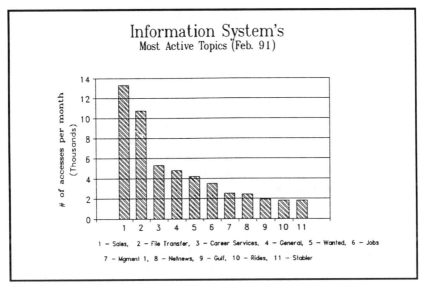

Figure 4. Most popular topics.

The overall satisfaction with the information system was excellent. Figure 5 shows that only 6.4% of the users responding to the online survey were dissatisfied with the system, while 77% were satisfied with the system.[6]

When satisfaction attributes were examined on an individual basis, it was found that users were generally satisfied with the menu-driven interface of the CWIS. The attribute that was most in need of improvement was re-

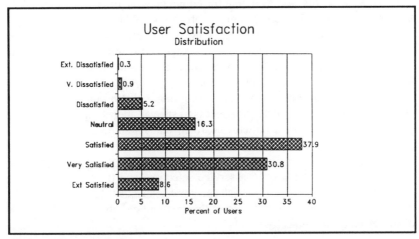

Figure 5. User satisfaction.

sponse time, which will hopefully improve with the new CWIS implementation running under AIX on IBM RS-6000s.

SYSTEM OVERVIEW

The overall function and design goals for Lehigh's information and communications support system is to provide a uniform mechanism for identifying and accessing all available services. Part of the reason for the initial success of the system was its simplicity—that it was tried at all was actually the key factor. While new complexity is being introduced in a controlled fashion (in the form of more automation and more efficient access methods), much of the original simplicity remains.

General

The CWIS interface provides a single, logical point of entry into the system, with each service being defined as an item in a hierarchically organized structure. Each service is uniquely named to provide access directly, as well as through menu navigation. Moreover, since there are inherent difficulties in designing large, meaningful menu structures, access via keyword search is also available.

There are currently seven basic service or topic types defined. The simplest, and most often found, is the flat text file—useful for providing general reference material. These are used for lists, schedules, and other documents that are easily searched sequentially.

Next is the "library"—an arbitrary collection of files of any type, categorized by keywords, and available for online viewing or downloading. A library of public domain microcomputer software would be an example.

Another popular service type is the online request form. A skeleton form is built using a high-level design package and is linked to a specific recipient. When it is filled in by the user, the collected information is transmitted to the service provider for processing.

Two important service types are electronic bulletin boards and conferences. Although both provide easy access to special interest message bases, a conference differs from a bulletin board in that its subject areas are more structured and better suited to interactive discussion.

A very general service type is the "application," which permits any program to be run in response to a service selection, and therefore provides a means of extending the basic service categories. An example of this would be the online survey program that allows the creation, distribution, and analysis of survey data electronically.

Finally, a topic can itself be a menu, pointing to other topics. Menus can be defined either by the system administrator or by section administrators.

Distributed Services

One of the chief factors permitting successful operation of this type of information service is the distribution of administrative duties. The overall structure and operational guidelines are determined by a central system administrator, but each of the hundreds of individual topic areas is the responsibility of the appropriate department or group. Information posted on the system for general access is monitored by the person responsible for the specific information.

Beyond this, physical distribution of resources can provide certain benefits. Since many services simply provide access to databases, nonlocal file residence is an option. Provisions are made in the individual service descriptions to designate alternative hosts and data directories. Part of the Computing Center's ongoing investigation is to identify an optimal method (or methods) for supporting this kind of distributed file structure. One advantage of this approach is that high-use, specialized databases may reside on local, departmental machines where unimpeded access is required. Due to central coordination of access, however, the information is still available to the rest of the campus without specific knowledge of its location.

A step beyond distributed file bases is the implementation of distributed applications, such that when a service is selected, execution of the requested application is initiated on a designated host. This, of course, should be entirely transparent to the user. This is also the subject of current investigations.

Both of these forms of physical distribution have the advantage of allowing easier and less disruptive incremental hardware upgrades. In addition, they can permit processing power to be more easily targeted to specific applications. These are both very important since system response time and continuity of service have been shown to be crucial factors in user acceptance.[7]

One additional aspect of distributed support is the decoupling of the user interface from the actual application. The current development effort is emphasizing functional separation as a design goal so that the main user interface can reside, for example, on a workstation and still provide the same services now available via direct interactive access to the information system host. This is yet another way to achieve more uniform response times and efficient hardware utilization.

The overall goal is to gradually migrate from a single system supporting all available services, to a more diffuse "system." Data and processing power would be distributed to the most appropriate locations, but with coordinated, central service descriptions, allowing full accessibility and a single-image perception to remain.

Developing and Implementing the Second-Generation CWIS

As mentioned earlier, portability was one of our primary concerns in developing a new information system. Toward that end, a decision was made to proceed assuming three basic requirements:

1. The basic operating system platform would be some variant of UNIX. Every attempt would be made to utilize facilities common to major variants, unless a particular feature proved overwhelmingly advantageous in terms of reduced development cost.
2. All program development would be in ANSI standard C. Critical code would be tested on various platforms to check conformance.
3. A readily available database management system supporting the relational data model would be employed. That system should be supported across the widest possible range of hardware platforms. Distributed database support employing common networking protocols should be built in. Locally developed code should attempt to minimize the dependence on a specific package through a generic programming interface.

With these requirements in mind, prototype development was begun in two basic areas: electronic mail and the basic organizational mechanism for the information system.

Electronic Mail

In late 1988 specifications were developed for the user interface and functionality of a new mail system. There were three main goals: to keep it as similar as possible to what users are accustomed to; to add significant new functions based on our experiences to date; and to maintain a high level of portability in the major components to assure easy migration.

The first portability aspect to be addressed was the presentation interface. An initial assumption was that traditional character-oriented terminal facilities would remain the norm on campus for the next several years. A form design package was implemented which generates C code for inclusion in the actual application, and a portable runtime library was written with a minimal system-dependent interface specification. One goal is to extend this facility to support window-based environments, with X11 as the most likely initial protocol. At present, this facility has been successfully ported between MS-DOS, UNIX, and a block mode 3270-based environment.

The prototype mail system, completed in late 1989, was implemented on a Novell LAN with MS-DOS microcomputers. The next step was to move the package to the current information system running on the IBM 4381 under MUSIC. Once the ultimate migration to the new UNIX platform is accomplished, the mail facility will appear essentially unchanged to the user.

Base Information System

The heart of the information system is its organizational mechanism. The current design employs a relational database management system to support this organizational activity. While the types of control information stored are relatively simple, many thousands of pieces exist to describe the system states, structure, and user profiles—thus the need for the more sophisticated capabilities of a database manager.

Presently, the development platform consists of an IBM RS-6000 running AIX, plus the ORACLE database management system. The basic screen interface code is the same portable code developed for mail. Implementation of the basic management mechanisms have been completed, along with general functions such as bulletin boards, conferences, libraries, and other end-user features. The new system is currently being beta tested by volunteers from the university community and should replace the current CWIS completely by May 1992.

MANAGEMENT ISSUES

With the increased acceptance of the CWIS, many management issues that existed on a small scale in the past were magnified and took on greater significance. The following management issues need to be considered when embarking on implementing a CWIS: censorship, security, training, and special requests.

Censorship

With access to outside information systems, the implementors need to examine their role as censors of information based on resource utilization and also possible legal liabilities. At Lehigh, the Computing Center had to make a decision on the nature and content of the material it wanted to make available on its information system and also develop a policy statement to inform users of their rights and responsibilities. It was decided that in general, all material placed on our CWIS would follow the guidelines of our Information Policy which was approved by a committee composed of faculty, students, and staff.[8]

Security

Security risks are increased with the addition of many novice users who need to be educated about security measures such as password selection and protection. Increased efforts are needed to educate users about security precautions. One of the biggest problems occurred when a "hacker" planted a program in a public site to collect users' passwords. The program mimicked the standard access program while recording the person's user ID and password in a hidden file on a hard drive at the public site. After a period of two weeks, he had collected about 100 user IDs and passwords. He then sent messages to various groups and people on campus warning them of system security breaches, and he sent obscene messages to other individuals. Incidents such as these occur, and steps need to be taken immediately to inform users of the security threat to the system. Users also need to be informed of the various state and federal laws that make actions such as these criminal.

Training

Computer training is a major activity that will probably increase upon the successful implementation of a CWIS. At Lehigh, the Computing Center planned a two-phased training approach, with faculty receiving hands-on training in using their microcomputers and then hands-on training in using the CWIS and campus network. The Computing Center felt that training needs for use of the CWIS would be substantial in the first year of implementation and then decrease.

As can be seen in Figure 6, seminar attendance jumped 110% in 1985-86. The growth in training was not caused solely by training on using the CWIS which amounted to a small percentage of our seminars. It is estimated that less than 20% of the users receive training directly on using the CWIS, with the majority of users learning how to use the systems from peers (faculty, students, or staff). It appeared that once users started using the CWIS, they became aware of other possible uses of computing which caused our overall seminar attendance to grow. Figure 6 shows the growth in seminar attendance since the implementation of the CWIS.[9]

Special Requests

Special requests will grow with the popularity of the system. The Computing Center had to develop a policy to deal with the continual requests for mass mailings and system messages. Placement on the main CWIS screen is

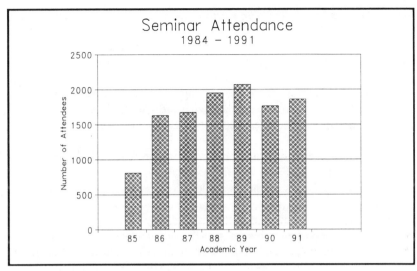

Figure 6. Seminar attendance.

also a major topic that has been avoided in general by not having any departments on the main screen, but occasional requests are still received for reor-
ganization of this screen. It should be noted that occasionally the Computing
Center policy does get modified based on who has made the request for a system bulletin or mass mailing. When this does occur, the Computing Center
informs the user community of the sender of the message, so that comments
regarding "junk mail" can be directed to the requestor and not to the Computing Center.

SUMMARY

The establishment of a campus-wide information system at Lehigh provides
an entire academic community of over 7,000 faculty, staff, and students with
easy access to communications facilities that are relatively easy to use and
operate. Institutions embarking on campus-wide network and communications projects should also be aware of the increased focus that is placed on
the computing services department. Once widespread acceptance and usage
of the system develop, users perceive the network and the information system
as a service to them rather than as an experiment.[10] The information facility
is thought of as a utility (e.g., a phone system). Users quickly forget the experimental nature of these developmental activities and expect the same reliability and consistency of operation that they are accustomed to with any other
utility.[11]

Key Design and Implementation Factors

Below is a list of some of the design and implementation factors that were critical to the initial success of the information system.

- The commitment and risk taking of key administrative personnel at the presidential and vice presidential level to provide computer resources and networking capability to the entire campus.
- The accessibility of microcomputer workstations to faculty and students.
- The project's emphasis on low-cost microcomputer workstations.
- The development of functional and easy-to-use software.
- The opportunity to work on a developmental project with IBM.
- The commitment of the Computing Center staff to support what at times appeared to be impossible requests for services in a relatively short period of time.
- The overall design of the Information and Services facility, which distributes the responsibility for maintaining campus-wide information to individuals, departments, and groups.
- The early users of the information system, such as the Research Program Development Office and Library, who were instrumental in its design. These early users helped to interest other users and create what is now a critical mass of users, necessary for the success of a campus-wide information system.

NOTES

1. W. R. Harris, R. Gruver, K. R. Weiner, and T. J. Foley, *Network Server Request for Proposals*, March 1986.
2. G. Miller, "The Magical Number Seven Plus or Minus Two: Some Limits on our Capacity," *Psychological Review* 63 (1956): 63.
3. M. L. Mushet, "Standardizing Online Systems Architecture," *Journal of Information Systems Management* V4 n2 (1987): 8-14.
4. T. J. Foley and M. A. Newman, "An Empirical Study of User Satisfaction with a Microcomputer-Based Campus-wide Information System," *Proc. of ACM SIGUCCS User Services Conference* 16 (1988): 91-100.
5. E. Bailey and S. W. Pearson, "Development of a Tool for Measuring and Analyzing Computer User Satisfaction," *Management Science* 29, no.5 (1983): 519-529.
6. Foley and Newman, "An Empirical Study of User Satisfaction"; T. J. Foley, "The Design, Implementation, and Evaluation of A Campus-wide Electronic Information System," (Doctoral Dissertation, Lehigh University, 1988), *Dissertation Abstracts International*, 1988.

7. Ibid.
8. T. J. Foley, "Developing a Campus Computing and Information Policy: Issues and Concerns," *CAUSE/EFFECT* 14, no.4 (Winter 1991): 25-29.
9. T. J. Foley, "Managing Campus-wide Information Systems," *ACM SIGUCCS* 17 (1989): 169-174.
10. K. C. Cohen, Project Athena Student Survey Findings, Massachusetts Institute of Technology, 1986.
11. Foley and Newman, "An Empirical Study of User Satisfaction," pp.91-100.

An Overview of CWIS Developments in the United Kingdom

Colin K. Work
Computing Services
University of Southampton, UK

INTRODUCTION

This chapter summarizes the state of campus-wide information system (CWIS) development in the United Kingdom. Rather than examine any particular system in detail it attempts to provide an overview of the current situation and identify common trends in CWIS implementations. Some key areas of particular concern are noted, along with a tentative outline of the direction of future developments. To properly understand the various issues involved, it is first necessary to provide the context in which the various CWIS projects are taking place.

BACKGROUND

In the United Kingdom, the computing services and facilities available to higher education and research institutes are supported largely through central funding. This has necessarily resulted in the formation of various bodies, some of which have the power to allocate resources for particular projects, while others perform a largely advisory and/or coordinating function. The ability to interwork with other institutions is recognized as an important method of maximizing resources, and this has long been supported by a centrally funded academic network (JANET).

The net result is a strong sense of community within academic computing, particularly with regard to information services. On the one hand, this has facilitated the provision of a range of national services intended for use by the community as a whole, while on the other hand it has encouraged developers of primarily local services to keep one eye on their potential for access by members of other institutions.

EARLY CWIS DEVELOPMENTS

Most institutions in the United Kingdom have had some form of online news service for some time, consisting in most cases of simple noninteractive text display of items relating to the central mainframe computing facilities.

More recently, however, the proliferation of workstations around the campus, the installation or upgrading of campus networks, and the observed popularity of various national information services have encouraged many institutions to provide more comprehensive online local services.

With few exceptions, the first generation of what may be described as CWIS systems were typically mainframe-based, being developed and maintained by the institution's computing service. While this first phase of CWIS development has resulted in some useful and effective services, almost without exception they are heavily oriented toward a computing service and fail to reflect the institution as a whole.

This was due to a number of factors. Firstly, the initial services were by and large developed by dedicated enthusiasts in the Computing Centre. It is probably not unfair to say that the main interest was in providing a viable information service vehicle rather than in studying the problems of information needs and provision.

Second, the problems associated with collecting information for the service, and then maintaining it, were poorly appreciated. With few exceptions, these tasks fell on an individual or small group—often the software development team. Hence, if the service proved in any way successful, those responsible for maintaining the system were soon overwhelmed with the task of keeping it current.

Finally, the degree of usefulness of such systems was limited by the proportion of users who could gain access. Even today few institutions are able to provide the majority of staff with easy access to network services. This meant that the CWIS could only be used as a secondary, alternative medium for information provision and that interest in, and input to, the service was largely limited to the few that did have access.

Fortunately, the situation is rapidly improving. Increased computer literacy, new or upgraded campus networks, and an ever-growing number of national and international resources available over the network have given more and more users both the facilities and desire to become networkers.

This has led to the current stage of development in the United Kingdom—and what might be considered second-generation CWISs.

THE CURRENT STATE OF CWIS DEVELOPMENT

As of October 1991, there were 22 CWISs known to be in full operation in the United Kingdom. Of these, the majority were first-generation services, and some can be described as a CWIS in the most general sense.

More important is the amount of effort being put into the development of new or enhanced services. In a recent survey, discussed in more detail below, 13 sites were willing to state that they were actively involved in developing a CWIS. It is estimated that another five to ten sites were working on systems but unwilling to publicly announce the fact. In addition, many institutions have expressed an interest in CWIS but are awaiting developments in software and guidelines.

In view of the current interest in CWIS, and the centralized organization of academic computing in the United Kingdom, it is not surprising that in the last year efforts have been made to encourage the cooperation and interchange of ideas among CWIS developers. To date, this has been done primarily through the Information Services Working Group of the Inter-University Information Committee (IUIC-INFSWG, hereafter referred to as INFSWG).

THE ROLE OF INFSWG

The Information Services Working Group was formed in late 1990 and consists of implementors and providers of information services over JANET. It evolved from an earlier, informal, grouping of interested parties and includes representatives from the major national information services, the Joint Network Team, as well as university and polytechnic computing services. Additional representation exists from the library sector; however, the group is based primarily in computing services.

Terms of reference for the Working Group primarily involve acting as a forum for discussion between service providers, providing an opportunity to both exchange ideas and prevent unnecessary duplication of effort. In addition, the group attempts to disseminate to the community as a whole information concerning available services and current developments.

SUPPORT FOR CWIS DEVELOPMENT
IN THE UNITEDKINGDOM

From its formation IUIC-INFSWG realized that CWIS would become one of the key information service areas in the immediate future. INFSWG therefore considered ways in which it could assist CWIS development. A number of areas were identified which could benefit from discussion and cooperation at a national level:

1. Promotion of information exchange. Difficulties encountered in implementing a CWIS will be shared by many institutions. By making the community as a whole aware of ongoing projects, the door is opened for cooperation. Furthermore, by dis-

seminating information about the various approaches to CWIS being used, future developers could be provided with a range of options.

2. Integration with other services. CWIS has been identified as one of a number of significant network resources either already in place or in development. An essential role has been identified in making CWIS developers aware of these services, how they might relate to CWIS, and any technical implications that might arise.

3. Monitoring developments both in the United Kingdom and elsewhere which might impact on, or be of use to, CWIS development, for instance, search and retrieve protocols.

4. Encouragement of local CWIS developments in a direction that would lead to a valuable community wide resource.

To date, the work of INFSWG has concentrated on information gathering, first to create a picture of current development work, and second, to gain a community-wide consensus of opinion on the role of CWIS.

SURVEY OF CURRENT AND PLANNED CWIS PROJECTS

One of the first actions of INFSWG was to conduct a survey designed to establish the state of current CWIS developments in the United Kingdom.

This survey was conducted during late spring of 1991 using electronic mail through a distribution list established the previous year specifically for the discussion of information services in the UK academic community.

Although the use of this particular vehicle limited the number of people who would receive the questionnaire, it was felt that it would reach those who were both active in the area and interested in cooperating in the exchange of information.

The survey asked developers to describe their CWIS, whether already in development or planned, with specific questions addressing the following areas:

1. Current status
2. Hardware/operating system
3. Software
4. Interface
5. Implementation/support of standards
6. Intended coverage
7. Intended audience

Thirteen responses were received. These described both completely new developments and, in a few cases, significant upgrades to systems already in place. This response is known to be an incomplete coverage of current activity, for subsequent private communication indicated that a number of sites were, for a variety of reasons, not willing to make their activities publicly known at that stage.

From the responses that were received, it was possible to construct a generalized picture of a "typical" CWIS development project.

Current Status

Of the 13 systems described, 4 were completely new systems actually in development, 4 were upgrades or enhancements to existing systems, and 5 were still in the initial planning stage.

Hardware/Operating System

Of the ten responses indicating that a decision had been made, all had opted for UNIX and mostly running on a machine dedicated for the CWIS.

Software

Software seemed to be a major problem area. Only five sites were able to report a definite plan. Of these, two were writing programs in-house, 1 was using a CWIS package developed at another institution, one was utilizing a commercial free text retrieval package and one was discussing the incorporation of a CWIS module as part of the automated library system with the system's supplier.

Most sites were actively looking for an existing software solution, for there is a general reluctance to write new software. This is one area where it was felt that some form of centralized evaluation process would be welcome, or if necessary, funding could be secured for software development at a community-wide level. Only one site stated that they were specifically looking for a client server solution.

Interface

Without exception, most sites planned to support access to information through a menu-driven interface. A number of sites also specified the inclusion of mechanisms with which the user could bypass the menus (for example, free text searching). Some sites indicated a desire to incorporate advanced window-based interface but saw this as a subsequent development.

In addition, most sites expected to support document delivery from the CWIS via electronic mail and/or file transfer.

Implementation/Support of Standards

Most responses indicated a general awareness of protocols and standards which may have an impact on CWIS development. Chief among these were CWISP, Z39.50 Search & Retrieve protocols, and X.500 directory service protocols. Although there was no clear understanding of how these protocols might be applied, there was a general concern that CWISs currently under development would be able to take advantage of developments in these areas. This is another area where guidance was sought from the community as a whole.

Intended Coverage

All plans involved providing a broad-based coverage of campus life, although few intended to handle information that could not be said to be in the public domain. Most replies indicated the intention of distributing the task of information provision and distribution throughout the institution.

This latter intention was put particularly strongly by those sites that were upgrading or replacing an existing system, citing the problems of centralized information processing as a major problem with the existing system.

Intended Audience

In general, it is planned to make the CWIS freely available to all members of the institution and permit remote access from other institutions over the JANET network. Only one site indicated that access would be restricted to registered users.

An important user group that was identified in the survey was visitors to the institution. CWIS was seen as an efficient way of providing visitors with essential information about the institution.

MOVES TOWARD DEVELOPING THE POTENTIAL OF CWIS

The number of concurrent developments, coupled with the generally high degree of interest in CWIS, has prompted INFSWG to look at the possibilities of encouraging developments in such a way as to contribute to a national resource.

Just as the academic community has routinely accessed each other's library catalogues over the network, it is felt that local CWIS systems should provide a standard reference source for the various resources, services and facilities available at a particular institution.

INFSWG formulated the concept of a minimal level of CWIS service, based on a collection of core information topics. The intended outcome was a community in which users anywhere in the community could reliably obtain information on a given set of topics from any institution belonging to the community.

Furthermore, INFSWG is concerned with the problems of integrating this potential CWIS resource with other available information resources in such a way that the user can move easily between the various services. These other resources include library catalogues, national information services (e.g., bulletin boards and community news services), and directory services.

A first step toward this was to refine the concept of CWIS and to attempt to establish developers' and users' expectations. To this end, a second survey was conducted during the summer and early fall of 1991.

Once again, the survey was conducted via electronic mail, although this time a number of distribution lists were used in order to target information providers and managers in both the library and computing communities.

Responses were received from 23 sites, representing approximately 25% of academic institutions connected to JANET. Of these responses, about 60% originated from the institution's computing service, and the remainder from the library. The response from the library community was much higher than expected, and this has had implications on future work on CWIS coordination, discussed in more detail below.

SUMMARY OF THE INFSWG CORE INFORMATION TOPICS SURVEY

1. What topics would you expect to find covered by a CWIS for your own institution?

From the responses received, to this question, it was possible to establish a "league table" of possible information elements for CWIS. (Topics are in no particular order within each group.)

Topics included in ten or more responses:
Diary of university events
E-mail and/or phone directory (name directory)
Computing service information
Library service information (excluding OPAC access)

Of these, e-mail/phone directory was the most common suggestion, but as more than one person pointed out, this might be better covered by X.500 directory services.

Topics included in five to nine responses:

University/polytechnic calendar	Community information
JANET and other info services	Student union and/or societies
Travel information	Research interests
Diary of cultural events	Course information
News and/or newsletter(s)	Diary of sporting events
Useful contacts	Institution rules and regulations

Other Topics Suggested. The following were included in at least one response:

Health service information	Bookshop
Resources available to community	Careers service information
Student records	Special interest group newsletters
Job vacancies	Accommodation information
Faculty/departmental information	Committee papers
Conference announcements	Annual reports
Research grants information	Public domain software information
University publications	Foreign student events
Wanted/for sale section	Catering information
Special interest groups	General help and advisory
Adult education	Media services
Religious information	Weather
Committee membership	

Suggestions that really had to do with functionality of the CWIS rather than topics in the sense of the above:

Access to X.500 services	Access to library catalogue
Access to other database services	Conference facility

2. What topics would you expect to find if you accessed a CWIS for another institution?

The responses to this question clearly indicated that the most important topics were (in no particular order):

E-mail/phone directory	Library information
University/polytechnic calendar	Travel information
Computing service information	Diary of events
Course information	

The name directory was the most favored item by a large margin, but as stated above, this might be better handled by an X.500 service. Other topics that were mentioned to a significant degree were:

Useful contacts   Jobs vacancies
Community information   Research interests
Other information services available

Most of the topics mentioned in response to the first question were also mentioned here by at least one respondent, but the above topics stood out from the rest.

3. Are there any topics concerning your institution which should be available on a national service (e.g. , NISS[1]) as well as or instead of the local CWIS?

With a few isolated exceptions, the answer to this question was "no" apart from pointer information and possibly brief general information about the institution. Concern was expressed about maintaining duplicated data.

The exception to the rule was job vacancies. A number of responses indicated that these should be held on a national database.

4. Are there any topics that you would like to see on your local CWIS, but that should NOT be accessible from other institutions?

This question generated some controversy. Many sites indicated that they would not put up any information UNLESS it could be made freely available. However, it may not be possible to implement some of the suggested topics without provision for restricting access; for example, student records. A few responses indicated unease about making ANY personal information generally available (which might rule out "useful contacts").

Arguments against adding security included the difficulty of implementation and the need to register users. In part this may in fact be a software problem. Some systems do allow sections of data to be protected while giving free access to other sections.

An important argument offered for having a restricted access facility is that it makes the system more saleable, particularly to administrative departments.

5. If you have an operational CWIS, please provide an indication of the most popular topics (quantify if possible).

From those sites that responded to this question, the most popular items appear to be (in no particular order):

E-mail/phone directory	General information about the institution
Travel information	OPAC access
Downloaded CEEFAX/ORACLE[2]	News
JANET addresses	"Fortune Cookie" database
Library/Computing services and hours	
Guide to Real Ale	

6. If you access CWISs at other institutions, which topics do you view most often?

The responses to this question suggested fairly low usage of other CWISs. Topics that were listed included

Name directory information	News
Library catalogue	Job vacancies
Computing service information	Library service information

This list does not correspond particularly well with the list of items that people thought they would like to access on other CWISs which may indicate that in general CWISs are not catering for the information requirements of outside users (which may be a valid position) or that the information is not available in a suitable form.

7. If you access any national information services, which topics do you view most often?

The NISS Bulletin Board is the most frequently mentioned service. Others include NPDSA,[3] JANET.NEWS,[4] BUBL[5] and Mailbase.[6] Only a few topics were specifically cited, the more predominant being

Software information	Computing services information
Job vacancies	Reports of meetings
Latest news	Conference Information

Network addresses were only mentioned once, despite responses elsewhere in the questionnaire which indicated that this was thought to be an important information resource on both local and remote CWIS systems.

8. Any comments on the attempt to produce a set of "core topics" for CWIS systems?

A number of issues were raised here including:

- General support for establishing a core information set for CWIS
- The need for a realistic definition of such a set so as to facilitate implementation
- The need to consider multiple systems to achieve the desired information service (e.g., Bulletin Boards, X.500 servers, e-mail, etc.)
- The need for significant effort in obtaining information and/or recruiting information providers
- Items to be included in the core set must be clearly defined, and given a name that then can be used consistently by all CWISs.
- General preference for distributed systems rather than centralized data
- The need for guidelines for CWIS developers
- the relationship of CWIS to other information services (e.g., X.500 Directory Services)
- The availability and relevance of standards and protocols (e.g., X.500, Z39.50, WAIS, etc.)

ACTIONS RESULTING FROM THE INFSWG SURVEYS

It was realized from the outset that the surveys summarized above were limited in scope and did not directly poll the mass of potential CWIS end users (i.e., the majority of staff and students), although it was hoped that those who did respond incorporated their own knowledge of what their users wanted.

Nonetheless, despite obvious limitations, it was felt that the "core topics" survey provided a basis from which INFSWG could formulate a preliminary set of core topics which would be set forward for further discussion and refinement.

PROPOSED LIST OF CORE CWIS TOPICS

The following topics are being put forward by INFSWG as recommended for inclusion in all CWIS systems in the United Kingdom which support remote access:

Diary of university events	Course information
News and/or institution's newsletter(s)	Travel information
Institution rules & regulations	University/polytechnic calendar
Network resources information	Diary of cultural events
E-mail and/or phone directory	Diary of sporting events
Computing service information	Library service information

The formulation of this list reflects careful consideration to the issue of sensitive information and an attempt to avoid topics that would lead to administrative complications in their implementation.

The topics are best understood as a guideline to the type of information that should be provided. They do not attempt to prescribe the actual content to be included under each of these headings. At a later stage it is hoped to be able to provide some additional guidelines on content and format.

Some institutions may choose to implement certain elements of the core topics as services independent of the CWIS. In these cases, it is recommended that linkages be established between the CWIS and these other services in order to present the user with an apparent single reference source insofar as is technically possible.

TASKS IDENTIFIED FOR FURTHER INVESTIGATION

Besides providing a basis for formulating the core topics, the surveys have highlighted a number of areas that need to be addressed in more detail. However, the first issue that needs to be considered is the suitability of the INFSWG group to carry out this work.

As indicated earlier, INFSWG is composed primarily of members from the computing community. Clearly, the responses received to the second survey indicate that there is a significant degree of interest in CWIS in the library world. Furthermore, as the issues of confidentiality and sensitive data become more significant, further progress will necessarily involve participation of the institutions' administrative departments. Finally, there will ultimately be a need to incorporate the views of the ultimate users of CWIS, regardless of their role in the institution.

For this reason, INFSWG believes that having initiated the community-wide discussion on CWIS, it is now time to create a more broadly representative body that would focus on CWIS exclusively and tackle the various issues that have been raised. It is hoped that it will be possible to make progress on this during 1992.

Of the more critical problems to be addressed, INFSWG has identified the following:

1. A definition and standard terminology for each of the topics would be required. It would be desirable to provide guidelines for a "minimum information set" for these topics (e.g., Travel Information should include directions on how to get to the institution).
2. An agreed method of implementing the core topics is required to facilitate user access over a range of systems. Various possi-

ble mechanisms are under consideration, in particular the use of client server models incorporating search and retrieve protocols.

3. A minimum level of service and functionality needs to be defined and implemented on all CWISs in order to promote and facilitate internetworking.

4. The need for guidelines for developers was clearly indicated in many of the survey responses. The most urgent of these can be categorized into the following areas:
   a. Software tools
   b. Models for the provision and maintenance of information
   c. The incorporation of standards and protocols

5. Cooperation and coordination of CWIS activities with related services, especially X.500 directory services. The X.500 question is particularly urgent given that:
   a. At least 50 sites in the United Kingdom are already actively involved in, or intend to provide directory services, and it is expected that such services will eventually be implemented community wide.
   b. The surveys indicate that the name directories are the single most important item expected to be made available through CWIS.

CONCLUSION

This chapter has attempted to show that there is currently a considerable amount of interest and activity in the United Kingdom regarding CWIS. This is further borne out by the ever-increasing appearance of the topic at conferences and workshops.

Of perhaps more significance, however, is the realization of the value of CWIS and its potential importance as a national resource. Although a number of problems are involved in trying to coordinate community-wide developments, timely steps have been taken to attempt to steer the current surge of interest in CWIS in a direction that, given proper support, should result in a fully integrated national information service.

The goal of such a service would be both to create a comprehensive local information resource for the staff and students of a particular institution and, provide these same members with the benefits of a networked "virtual campus" enabling easy access to the resources of the community as a whole.

Finally, those wishing to study and monitor CWIS developments in the United Kingdom should access the NISS Bulletin Board service. Information regarding current and future initiatives will be found here, as well as notifica-

tion of upcoming workshops and conferences, as well as the network addresses of available services.

The NISS Bulletin Board is available on the UK JANET network with
the address UK.AC.NISS. The service requires no special terminal characteristics and no userid or password are required.

NOTES

1. NISS (National Information on Software and Services) is a centrally funded online
   information service. It consists of the NISS Bulletin Board, which provides a bulletin board/news service pertaining to academic computing in the broadest sense,
   and NISSPAC (NISS Public Access Collections), a set of catalogues and directories of software and datasets available in or to the community. Launched in mid-
   1988, the NISS service has proved to be an extremely popular community resource. NISS is based at the universities of Bath and Southampton.
2. CEEFAX and ORACLE are both broadcast teletext news and information services
   generally available throughout the United Kingdom.
3. NPDSA (National Public Domain Software Archive) is based at Lancaster University and acts as a repository for public domain software and shareware.
4. JANET.NEWS is an online, interactive news service run by the Joint Network
   Team which also runs the JANET academic network. It concentrates primarily on
   network-related news and to a lesser extent on academic computing.
5. BUBL (Bulletin Board for Libraries) is a bulletin board primarily serving the academic library community based at the University of Glasgow.
6. Mailbase is an electronic mail distribution list service based at the University of
   Newcastle. It provides facilities for users throughout the community to set up and
   maintain discussion lists. E-mail and interactive search and retrieve facilities are
   provided.

The Development of a Microcomputer Network Laboratory at St. Cloud State University: Design, Funding, and Internetworking

Dennis Guster
Professor of Computer Science
St. Cloud State University

Thad Wakefield
Research Assistant, Department of Computer Science
St. Cloud State University

INTRODUCTION

St. Cloud State University (SCSU), like many universities, has struggled to provide computing power to its students. There have been several obstacles to realizing this goal. First, securing adequate funding for state-of-the-art equipment is always a difficult endeavor in an educational environment. Second, there is a diversity of need among the various departments that makes both short- and long-range planning difficult. Last, obtaining adequate personnel to install and manage computer systems is also complicated by a diversity of need and a constantly growing user base.

The impact of the personal computer (PC) revolution affected SCSU in much the same way that it influenced processing power in industry. PCs were widely embraced as a processing tool for individual use, and educational programs were developed to take advantage of this new platform. This resulted in two types of users within the university: PC users and mainframe users.

Rapid growth and diversity of use precipitated a large-scale environment of multiple nodes, and the provision of adequate access to the high-end processing power necessitated networking. The PC environment was much slower to embrace networking, and when networking did appear in the PC environment, it included only PCs. It has only been in the last couple of years that a distributed processing environment embracing a high degree of connectivity has been stressed.

Many departments have influenced this chain of events, but the available space here precludes describing each department's contribution. The development of SCSU's campus-wide information system, past, present, and future, will be described from the viewpoint of the Microcomputer Studies program within the Computer Science Department.

HISTORICAL BACKGROUND CAMPUS-WIDE

Prior to 1983, the computing facilities for academic computing at SCSU consisted of a PDP 11/60 and Data 100 terminals connected to a UNISYS mainframe at another campus in the State University System. In 1983, as a result of a State University Board decision to start developing on-campus computer facilities for its campuses, SCSU received a Digital Equipment Corporation (DEC) VAX 11/758. In early 1984 two DEC VAX 11/758s and a DEC VAX 11/780 were added to the network for the use of the newly created Department of Electrical Engineering. A DEC VAX 11/785 was added to the network in the fall of 1984 for the use of the Computer Science Department.

In 1985 the College of Business building became the first remote Ethernet segment added to the network. It was added to the network in 1985. A plan was developed in 1987 for prioritizing the expansion of Ethernet segments beyond the Engineering and Computing Center and the College of Business. At that time the goal was to add three buildings per year to the network, but the ubiquitous "budgetary constraints" have limited those expansion goals. In 1988-89 the College of Social Sciences was added to the network when its building was remodeled. The Math/Science building was connected to the network in 1991, and the Learning Resource Center will be added to the network in early 1992. Each building's Ethernet segment is connected to the computer room in the Engineering and Computer Science Center by fiber-optic cable.

The academic computer network at SCSU currently consists of six primary computers. A DEC VAX 8550 and a DEC VAX 11/780, which are running VMS, and a DEC 5000/200 running Ultrix, are designated as general-purpose computers. Most of the general academic computing is done on these computers. A DEC 5000/200 running Ultrix is designated for use by the Computer Science Department. The Electrical Engineering Department has a DEC MicroVAX 3400. An IBM AS/400 B60 is on loan from IBM under the University Partnership Program. The program expires in September 1992 but is renewable for two additional years. The network currently has approximately 12 gigabytes of disk storage available.

The network is managed by the Academic Computer Service. It is responsible for the day-to-day management of the system and handles the updating of the software and the administration of the users' accounts at the direction of the various departments. There are approximately 1,800 quarterly student accounts on the system, 60 permanent student accounts, and 150 permanent faculty accounts.

The funding for the system comes from grants, the individual departments' budgets, and the State University Board. Most of the hardware is funded by the State University Board, which is also responsible for the computer maintenance costs. Each department is responsible for purchasing its own software and the software's maintenance costs.

Most users access the network through approximately 310 terminals located throughout the campus. There are also twelve 2400 bits per second (bps) local phone lines available for access to the network. Both the Electrical Engineering Department and the Computer Science Department have SUN workstations connected to the SCSU network. The Manufacturing Engineering Department has a token-ring network connected to the AS/400. The Geography Department also has a token-ring network with IBM RS-6000 workstations connected to the system for their geographical information system program. The Chemistry, Biology, and Mass Communications departments have their AppleTalk networks connected to the network.

MICROCOMPUTER STUDIES DEVELOPMENT

The Microcomputer Studies (MCS) Department was created in 1981. With the increasing use of microcomputers and the increasing computing power of microcomputers, it was recognized that there were going to be very few careers that would not require microcomputer literacy. Since the Computer Science Department's courses used terminals to access minicomputers and mainframes, the students that would be working in a microcomputer environment needed courses that would give them the skills necessary to compete in the job market. The courses would also give students the opportunity to learn skills that could be integrated into their other course work to enhance their educational experience at SCSU.

MCS offers a 24-credit minor, a 36-credit minor, and an MCS User's Certificate Program. The minor programs begin with BASIC programming, continue through the applications programs, and finish with a sequence of microcomputer networking courses. Under the MCS User's Certificate Program, a user's certificate is put in a student's placement file to indicate a proficiency in using spreadsheet, database, word processing, and graphics applications.

The MCS program began with 20 Apple II+ computers and offered BASIC and assembly language programming. The MCS minor was completed with other classes from the Computer Science Department. In 1983 the department switched to the MS-DOS environment with the purchase of 70 IBM personal computers.

From the beginning, all hardware and software for the program have been funded with student user fees. The fee started at $10 per class; it is currently $40 per class and generates between $24,000 and $30,000 per quarter. All user fees are designated for equipment and software for the program.

In the late 1980s it became apparent that the networking of microcomputers with local area networks (LANs) was becoming an increasingly important aspect of computing. With the growth of local area networks and the emergence of the eclectic computer network, the need for network managers/ supervisors and network-literate users was rapidly increasing. The MCS networking program began with an ARCnet network consisting of an EPSON Equity III+ file server and two IBM personal computer workstations using the Novell 286 operating system. In the beginning, the program was at the bottom end of the equipment ladder. The network received the equipment that was not needed elsewhere. Because of the increasing importance of networking, the program has moved to the top of the ladder. The new equipment is now used by the networking lab; as they acquire new computers, the excess computers filter down to the other users in the other MCS programs.

The MCS computer lab currently consists of the original EPSON file server, a 386/25 file server, and 14 workstations. It also has a small UNIX network consisting of an EPSON Equity II+ and four terminals running SCO XENIX. The lab is used for research and development, programming projects for other network users on campus, and as a lab for the five networking classes offered by MCS. (See Figure 1.)

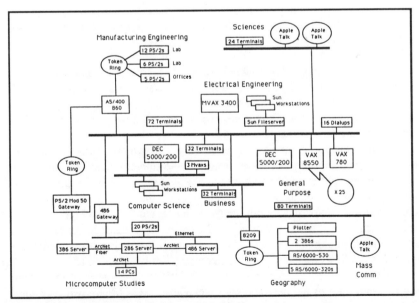

Figure 1. SCSU's Academic Computing Network.

The initial class in the networking series uses the lab to gain hands-on experience with MS-DOS, UNIX, and Novell NetWare. As the students progress through the series, they become more involved in the details of the network. In the second class in the series they work in small groups to design, install and manage a Novell network on 386 file servers. In subsequent classes they subdivide the network with routers and study internetworking by using gateways to other networks. The penultimate class uses statistical analysis to maximize network performance. Finally, in the last class of the series, the students design a network from scratch.

One of the problems facing businesses today is the linking of all their computing facilities into one intercommunicating network. By internetworking the existing lab with a variety of computer systems, the students will be exposed to problems they will encounter after graduation. One of the next major developments in the growth of the lab involves internetworking the lab with the campus' academic network, connecting to the AS-400, and adding the other MCS programs to the network.The ultimate goal is to have all the MCS classes connected to the network and, provide connectivity among all campus information systems. In meeting this goal, the MCS program has devised the following plan.

FUTURE CONNECTIVITY PLANS

The first step in the plan is to connect the 20 standalone PS/2s used by the MCS applications programs. The receipt of a Title III grant that has a networking component will provide a 486/33 file server for this connection. The PS/2s will be connected to the file server by an Ethernet LAN. This server will have Btrieve available for research and for the networking classes. The server will be used primarily by the MCS applications classes using Lotus 1-2-3 and dBase IV. Connecting the applications classes to the network will give the students networking experience, and the instructor will have more control over their computing environment.

Giving the professor more control may seem to be antithetical to the spirit of microcomputing. However, many of the students in these classes are from other disciplines and are taking the classes to earn the MCS User's Certificate. In many cases these are the only classes they will take in the MCS program. Their inexperience with microcomputers can lead to a high "frustration quotient." The network will allow the professor to tailor his or her interaction with the student to the individual student's needs. For all students the network will eliminate the use of "sneakerware" for exchanging files.

The MacIntosh computers used by the MCS graphics applications class will be connected to the network with NetWare for the MacIntosh. Because of the sharing of files, such as clip art files, these computers are currently connected to the academic computer network. The addition of these computers to the network will further the integration of the MCS programs into one system. The final link in the integration process will be the connection of the entry-level computer literacy lab to the network. This lab consists of 60 Epson Equity II+ computers. Both of these connections will be made with Ethernet LANs. (See Figure 1).

Ten 386 computers will be added to the lab to be used for special projects and student file servers. Small groups of students will design, install, and manage a NetWare 386 file server. Rather than designing hypothetical network environments on paper, students will actually create user profiles, group assignments, and file structures on their file server. IBM PCs on carts will allow them to create a network by connecting workstations to their file server. Another project will be the creation of UNIX networks using these 386 computers. Again the students will receive the benefit of hands-on experience versus hypothetical exercises.

All of the above networks will be using Novell network operating systems. The final link in the interconnectivity of the MCS networking lab will be the connection to the academic computer system. The main connection to the system will be through a 486/33 that will be running Mach 386 UNIX. This computer will act as a router between one of the Ethernet LANs and the campus system. A connection will also be established to the AS-400 using a PS/2 Model 50 as a gateway to a token-ring LAN which will be connected to the AS-400.

When all these plans are completed, all students taking MCS classes will be exposed to the microcomputer networking environment. Students will also have the opportunity to increase their networking skills to any level along the network user to network designer continuum. They can learn about ARCnet, Ethernet and token-ring LANs. They can study the interconnection of LANs; the interconnection of LANs to larger host/client systems; and the interconnection of LANs to wide area networks. Someday the "year of networking" will actually arrive, and this lab will allow the students to be ready to take advantage of it.

The University of York Information Server

D. L. Atkin
Systems Programmer
University of York, UK

ABSTRACT

This chapter describes the design, implementation, and experience of management of a campus-wide information server system. The information is structured hierarchically, and sections can be provided by different users or departments. The software is easy to use and has some novel features not found in similar packages. It was originally written for VAX/VMS but has recently been ported to UNIX.

INTRODUCTION

The Computing Service at the University of York provides general computing facilities to both staff and students of the university, based on a Digital Equipment VAXcluster that was installed in 1986, and more recently on Silicon Graphics UNIX systems.

There were two strands to the Information Server project, which was started in 1987. First, there was the need to provide users of the central computing services with information about hardware, software, maintenance schedules, and the like. This was the original objective of the project. However, it was soon realised that a large amount of information from many other sources needed to be housed centrally in order to make it easily available, and the scope of the project was widened to include this information.

OBJECTIVES

The Computing Service had in the past used various methods of keeping users informed about changes to the service and about the status of faults. These included a whiteboard, a recorded telephone message, a Notice of the Day that was displayed on log-in to the VAX system, a NEWS system implemented on the VAX, and the standard VMS HELP system.

The information to be disseminated consists of different types:

1. General information and reference material about services, hardware, software, courses, and so on.
2. News about new features, known problems, and scheduled downtime.
3. Status information when services are affected by a fault.

A list of requirements was drawn up: it was decided that a new system was needed with the following capabilities:

1. Hold general information in a structured way.
2. Hold messages of the day and distribute them to other computer systems.
3. Replace the existing NEWS system

Requirements for the dissemination of other university information were:

1. The system had to be easy to use by novices but not tedious for experts.
2. The privilege to update parts of the data had to be delegated to specified users.

EXISTING SYSTEMS

A survey was carried out on information existing systems and software. The standard Digital Equipment Corporation product VAX/VTX was investigated but was rejected because it was not considered very easy to use by complete novices; it was also tied very strongly to VAX/VMS. Other commercial and academic packages were also looked at, but none was found to be ideal, and it was decided to write the software from scratch. It was written in the C programming language for portability across different systems.

OVERVIEW OF THE DATABASE

The information is held in a hierarchical structure, as a number of TOPICS. Each TOPIC can occupy one or more PAGES, where a page corresponds to a screenful of information. The full name of a topic consists of several fields separated by full stops, for example, LIBRARY.OPENING_HOURS.

Rather than invent an entirely new database structure, the Information Server database was implemented as simple text files within a VMS (and later, UNIX) directory structure. This had the advantage that few support tools needed to be written. Each topic maps onto a directory of the same name. The system manager has flexibility in deciding where different parts of the data should reside. Each topic has a file associated with it, called PROFILE.DAT. This file contains several records that specify the topic attributes (see below), sometimes followed by the textual information corresponding to that topic. For example, the details of a text topic called LIBRARY.OPENING_HOURS would be held in the file INFO$SERVER:[MAIN.LIBRARY.OPEN-ING_HOURS]PROFILE.DAT. An index file is maintained containing details of all the topics, for use with the INDEX command. For performance reasons, the whole index is read in when the Information Server image is executed. The index contains enough information for any menu in the database to be displayed correctly; further disk accesses are necessary only when the user selects a text, pointer, or action topic.

TYPES OF TOPIC

Four distinct types of topic were implemented: Menu, Text, Pointer, and Action.

Menu Topics

These are effectively directories of lower level topics. When a menu topic is displayed, the user is invited to choose from a number of topics at the next level down in the tree. Most menu topics contain only one page, but multiple pages can also be accommodated. The user views each menu page in turn by pressing RETURN; this simply cycles round all the pages in the current menu topic. The user can choose a subtopic from the displayed menu by entering either its number or a unique abbreviation of its name. Page n of a multipage menu can be selected by entering #n.

Text Topics

A TEXT topic consists of one or more pages of text. The pages are normally displayed in sequence, but the user can select a particular page simply by entering its number. Each page contains a maximum of 15 lines. Page breaks can be controlled by the use of ASCII formfeed characters within the text.

Pointer Topics

These provide the facility to display text either from a specific file or from another (TEXT) topic. The former can be useful when the text is to be generated by another application program. Linking to a TEXT topic can be useful where information logically belongs in two different places, but it is preferable to keep just one copy. For example, a topic on Advisory Service opening hours might be useful in the two places:

1. CSERV.ADVISORY.HOURS
2. CSERV.OPENING_HOURS.ADVISORY

Action Topics

An ACTION topic gives the user the ability to perform some specific action, such as making a call to a remote computer system or searching a database. In the original VMS implementation, a DCL command procedure is invoked; the later UNIX version can invoke either a Shell script or an executable program. The COMMENT facility, which is available on the main menu of the York system and which allows users to leave comments on the Information Server, is implemented very simply using an Action topic.

TOPIC ATTRIBUTES

A number of attributes are associated with each topic. In the following list, items (1)-(6) are common to all types of topic:

1. *Name:* The topic name consists of between 2 and 20 letters, digits, hyphens, and underscores. Single letter names are not allowed because this would cause an ambiguity with the user commands, which each consists of a single letter.
2. *Short title:* This is a string of up to 48 characters which appears against the topic name on the menu page above. It gives a brief description of the topic.
3. *Priority:* The priority of a topic is an integer between 1 and 99, and determines the position at which the topic is displayed in the menu. Lower numbered topics are displayed first. Topics of equal priority are displayed in alphabetical order.
4. *Start and End date-times:* When a topic is created, the updater has to decide whether the information is of a permanent or temporary nature. If it is not permanent, the updater can specify the dates and times between which it should be displayed to users, in the form of a "start date-time" and an "end date-time." The VAX/VMS date-time format is used, for example: dd-mmm-yyyy hh:mm e.g. 23-Jan-1999 10:00

If a date-time specification is left blank, this signifies that there is no restriction. If both the start and end date-times of a topic are blank, the topic is permanent.

5. *Visibility:* While most topics become visible to users as soon as they have been created, there are times when it is useful to "hide" a topic from users, possibly because it is incomplete. Hidden topics are only displayed to updaters. The facility to hide a topic is useful when a complex topic or set of topics is being entered. If a menu topic is hidden, none of its subtopics are available to users. This facility can be used by an updater to hide a whole sub-tree, until he or she is certain that all the information is correct, before releasing it to the user community.

6. *Revision date-time:* This field records the date and time that the topic was last changed. When making minor changes, the updater can specify that this should not be changed, so that the topic is not automatically flagged as "recently updated."

7. *Author:* The Author field is intended to be the name of the person who provided the information (not necessarily the person who typed it in). It is only relevant to TEXT topics.

8. *Pointer specification:* This is a string that specifies from where the text of a POINTER topic is to come—either a VMS or UNIX file specification or another topic within the Information Server. If the string is starts with an "at" sign (@), the remainder is interpreted as a topic name.

Examples:

SYS$SYSTEM:SOFTWARE_LIST.TXT
@CSERV.ADVISORY.HOURS

9. *Action command:* This is a VMS or UNIX command to be executed when an ACTION topic is selected by a user. For example, an action page to display the network status on a VMS system might do a SHOW NETWORK command.

USER INTERFACE

A good deal of effort was spent in designing the screen layouts and user interface. Figures 1 and 2 show the Main Menu and Computing Service menu topics. On each screen, the top line (which is shown in reverse video on an ANSI terminal) displays the full name of the topic. The data, whether a menu or

```
┌──────────────────────────────────────────────────────────────┐
│                U N I V E R S I T Y OF Y O R K                  │
│              Computing Service Information Server               │
│                                                                │
│        Information is available on the following topics:       │
│                                                                │
│          1. INTRO       Introduction to the Information Server  │
│        + 2. CSERV       Computing Service information           │
│        + 3. TELEDIR     University telephone directory          │
│        + 4. LIBRARY     University Library information          │
│        + 5. DEPTS       Information from academic departments   │
│        + 6. UNIV        Other University information            │
│        + 7. SU          Information from the Students' Union    │
│        + 8. EXTERNAL    Access to external information systems  │
│          9. COMMENTS    Leave comments                          │
│                                                                │
│                                                                │
│        + = Menu topic                                          │
│   ─────────────────────────────────────────────────────────   │
│   Enter a topic name or number, or one of the options below, and│
│   press RETURN                                                 │
│                                                                │
│   H - Help       I - Index       Q - Quit                     │
│   Choice:                                                      │
│                                                                │
└──────────────────────────────────────────────────────────────┘
```

Figure 1. Main menu.

simple text, come in the middle of the screen, and then the user options are displayed concisely below. Again the exact display depends on the terminal type —graphics line-drawing characters are used on an ANSI terminal, but the non-ANSI user has to make do with a line of dashes.

The items in a menu topic can be "flagged" in some circumstances, in order to display more information about the topics. The following characters are used:

+ means that this topic is itself a menu.
* means that this topic has been updated within the last week.

The system at York is configured so that users can log in under an anonymous account from any terminal connected to the campus network, or they can access the Information Server while logged into the VAX system

CSERV   Page 1 of 2

Information is available on the following topics:

+ 1.	NEWS	Computing Service news
+ 2.	NOTICES	Important notices displayed when you login
+ 3.	VAX	The VAXcluster
+ 4.	WORD	The Word Processing System
+ 5.	MICROS	Microcomputers
+ 6.	NETWORK	The Campus Network
+ 7.	PRINTERS	Hard copy output from printers and plotters
+ 8.	TERMINALS	Availability of Computing Service terminals
+ 9.	NETINFO	National & international network information
+10.	TEACHING	Courses, seminars etc.
+11.	DOCUMENTATION	Documentation
+12.	RECEPTION	Reception Service

+ = Menu topic

Enter a topic name or number, or one of the options below, and RETURN
H - Help   U - Up to menu   I - Index   M - Main menu   Q - Quit
#page
Choice (RETURN for next menu page):

Figure 2. Computing Service menu.

under their own individual account. Some facilities, such as sending pages to a printer, are not available to anonymous users.

USER COMMANDS

Commands available to the user at any point consist of a single letter and include:

1. *HELP command:* The "H" command provides a help screen, which is context-sensitive, in that different help screens are displayed for each type of topic. The four screens are for MENU, TEXT, POINTER, and ACTION topics.
2. *MAIN MENU command:* The "M" command returns to the main or top-level menu topic.
3. *UP command:* The "U" command returns the user to the menu immediately "above" the current topic.
4. *PRINT command:* The "P" command is used to enter the current text topic in a queue for printing. This is only available to authorised (i.e., logged-in) users.
5. *INDEX command:* The "I" command allows the user to (a) browse through the whole list of topics, (b) look for recently updated topics, or (c) search for a text string contained in either a topic name or the short title.
6. *QUIT command:* The "Q" command exits from the Information Server.

UPDATING THE DATABASE

In order to update the information held in the database, a user with appropriate privileges can enter the information server in UPDATE mode. This is achieved by the VMS command:

$ INFO/UPDATE

or by the UNIX command:

% info -u

In update mode, extra information is displayed about each topic, and several commands are available in addition to those available to normal users. An additional flag character is displayed on menu topics:

& Means that a topic will not be displayed to ordinary users

An example of the screen layout in update mode is shown in Figure 3. Updaters can allow other users access to any topics under their control, for example, the Students' Union can delegate the task of updating information from a given society to officers of that society.

The commands that perform update operations are:

```
┌─────────────────────────────────────────────────────────────────┐
│                                                                   │
│   LIBRARY                                          Page 1 of 1    │
│   Menu/50/Visible/Valid—University Library information            │
│                                                                   │
│   Information is available on the following topics:               │
│                                                                   │
│       1. (20)ACCESS      How to access the Library computer       │
│       2. (30)CALL        Make a call to the Library computer      │
│     & 3. (40)LOG         How to record Library catalogue searches │
│   * + 4. (50)EXTERNAL    Access to external library systems       │
│       5. (70)HOURS       Library opening hours                    │
│       6. (80)STAFF       Staff list                               │
│       7. (85)BULLETIN    Library Bulletin Board                   │
│                                                                   │
│                                                                   │
│                                                                   │
│   Start:       End:        Updated: 10-JUN-1989  16:33            │
│   * = Recently updated     + = Menu topic       & = Invalid topic │
│   ─────────────────────────────────────────────────────────────  │
│   A - Add   C - Change      D - Delete  T - Transfer              │
│   H - Help  U - Up to menu  I - Index      M - Main menu  Q - Quit│
│   Choice:                                                         │
│                                                                   │
└─────────────────────────────────────────────────────────────────┘
```

Figure 3. *Update mode.*

   a. *ADD command:* The "A" command is used to create a new topic. The updater is prompted for the name and type of the topic, the short title, and the other attributes listed above. Textual data are entered by means of a text editor, which in the case of VMS is the standard editor, "EDT". UNIX users can choose their favourite editor, but the default is "vi".
   b. *DELETE command:* The "D" command allows a topic to be deleted. The updater is prompted with "Are you sure?" Menu topics cannot be deleted until all the subtopics have also been deleted.
   c. *CHANGE command:* The "C" command allows the updater to alter the name, short title, or any other attribute. The Revision date-time is updated unless the updater explicitly elects to leave it unaltered.
   d. *TRANSFER command:* The "T" command allows a topic to be moved to a different place in the information tree. In the case of a MENU topic, all its subtopics are also moved.

HARDWARE CONFIGURATION

The Information Server runs at York on a VAXstation 3100, but it will run on any VAX/VMS system. The UNIX version has not yet been widely tested, but it has been compiled for various systems based on both BSD and System V.

NOTICES AND NEWS

There are two areas where Computing Service information is treated in a special way. Notices of the day for each computer system administered by the Computing Service are held under the menu topic CSERV.NOTICES. Examples are:

> CSERV.NOTICES.VAXCLUSTER(The central VAXcluster)
> CSERV.NOTICES.WORD (A word processing system)

News items are held in another menu, CSERV.NEWS.

Notices of the day are generated automatically for each computer system and transferred to it across the campus network. The file generated for a particular system consists of the notices for that system, followed by news items that are less than one week old.

On ANSI-compatible terminals, line drawing characters are used to make the display look neater, and notices that have a high priority are displayed in reverse video.

USAGE STATISTICS

All user-mode accesses to text, pointer, and action topics are logged, and a procedure is available to updaters to provide statistics on topic usage. This output consists of a list of topics and usage counts, one per line, sorted in descending order of popularity (see Figure 4).

The VAXcluster will not be available from Thurs 12:00 to 17:00 while one of the processors is replaced.

See NEWS EASTER - Easter Holiday informationl
See NEWS GRAPHICS - Exciting new graphics package available

Figure 4. Sample notice.

USAGE EXPERIENCE

Much of the local information currently in the database comes from the Computing Service itself. Most of the additions to the VMS HELP system, such as details of printers, have been removed and placed instead in the Information Server. Some academic departments, notably Archaeology, use the Information Server to hold details of courses, assessments, reading lists, and other information needed by their students. Some other departments have expressed interest in providing information but have not been able to invest the time required.

University-wide information includes the internal telephone directory (which can be searched by means of an ACTION topic), concerts, and catering information. The University Library has provided ACTION topics for accessing many other library systems over different networks. This has proved popular with users unfamiliar with computer networks.

The Students' Union also provides some information, and several student societies update their own sections.

FUTURE ENHANCEMENTS

Several enhancements are under consideration:

1. *ANSI function key support:* Some users have requested Support for the arrow keys on an ANSI terminal for topic selection, and the Next/Previous screen keys for navigating around a multipage topic keys.
2. *X-windows support:* As windows terminals and workstations become more popular, support for the X protocol will be desirable.

CONCLUSIONS

The York Information Server has proved very successful for the provision of both Computing Service and other university information, and most of the original aims have been achieved.

The amount of time taken to administer the information and to help updaters in other departments in structuring their information was somewhat underestimated, as was the amount of "marketing" effort needed to persuade potential information providers of the benefits.

The Information Server is still gaining momentum at York and is expected to grow considerably over the next few years.

ACKNOWLEDGMENT

The port of the Information Server software to UNIX was carried out by the University of Kent at Canterbury.

Library Automation Network: Connectivity in a Multicampus Environment

Jean F. Coppola
University Microcomputing Support
Analyst of Academic Computing
Pace University

Robert Yannacone
Manager of Computing Operations and Network
Administration for Academic Computing
Pace University

ABSTRACT

We present our experiences with automating library functions at Pace University. The functions include an online public access catalog, circulation, acquisition, generating reports and statistics. Pace University is a medium- to large-size business and liberal arts institution that is comprised of three major campuses (large city, suburban, and rural) plus several small sites. Pace has four libraries, including a law library. Many options were considered while keeping in mind selection criteria such as user friendliness, functions/ applications, system sophistication, expansion capabilities support, and expense. In addition, planned and unforeseen problems were managed and are described in the following case study.

INTRODUCTION

This chapter presents our experiences with automating a library in a multi-campus academic environment. We describe our approach, options, and reasoning from the beginning of the project, through its realization. However, even at this stage, we are still learning something everyday. Our recent experiences are with library automation systems in the areas of hardware, software, physical plant limitations, funding, multilocations, backups, vendor, and internal support.

BACKGROUND

The Need for Computerization

Many libraries are already, or are in the process of, computerizing their systems. Several years ago, Pace University, like many others, saw the need to better organize and circulate the thousands upon thousands of books in the library. There was an even greater need for a multicampus environment to have the ability to locate library materials on other campuses. This would eliminate the need for a complete duplication of volumes on all three general libraries and the law school.

Players

When planning a large-scale project such as automating libraries on three different campuses, many departments must be notified at the initial planning stages. The players who were called on in the original layout meeting included the Director of Telecommunications, University Librarian, Vice President of Finance, Provost, Director of Facilities Planning, and Manager of Data Center Operation and Network Administration. As the strategy developed into a practical plan, other players became involved. These people consisted of the Director of Academic Computing, the University Microcomputing Support Analyst, and directors of the individual libraries. Figure 1 shows a map of the library computing system.

SYSTEM

Selection

It was decided that a board of particular members should be constituted to review various systems and characteristics. It was felt that the task of selecting such a system was exceptionally involved. Moreover, it was a responsibility that encompassed careful examination and evaluation of currently available systems. Therefore, a Library Automation Committee was created for this purpose. The delegation was appointed to select the system that best accommodated the entire university.

The participants of the committee recognized the significance of their assessment. They devoted a substantial amount of time and energy in exploring and weighing the performance level of many integrated library systems. For example, the members observed assorted vendor demonstrations and visited other university library installations. Furthermore, they understood that their judgments entaileded a major financial investment for the university. Thus, it was essential that the system selected satisfied the present and forecast future requirements of the libraries and its users.

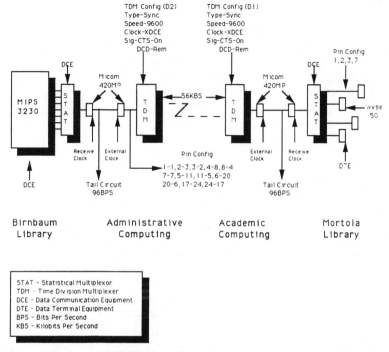

Figure 1. End-to-end INNOPAC configuration.

Criteria

For evaluation purposes, the Library Automation Committee set up a collection of criteria and priorities to help in selecting of a system. The selection was to be gauged on the following: ease of use and operation for both clientele purposes and staff operations; availability of necessary system functions/applications, for example, modules for an online public access catalog, circulation, acquisitions, serials control, and fund accounting; level of system sophistication, for example, system capacity, synthesis of functions, and report generation capacity; expandability of system and potential for future developments and growth; availability and merit of vendor support, both before and after installation; experiences of other libraries currently operating the system; the vendor's financial stability and years in business; and, finally, immediate and all future-related expenditures.

Vendors

The Library Automation Committee focused on five automated library systems. They proceeded to research each system and invite a spokesperson from each company to exhibit his or her system. The systems included: LS/2000 from OCLC Local Systems, Dublin, Ohio; DYNIX from DYNIX, Inc., Provo, Utah; NOTIS from NOTIS, Inc., Chicago, Illinois; PALS from UNISYS, White Plains, New York; and INNOVACQ/INNOPAC from Innovative Interface, Inc., Berkeley, California. INNOVACQ/INNOPAC was the system eventually chosen (see Figure 2).

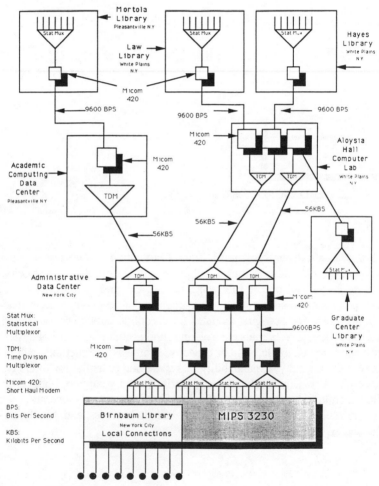

Figure 2. INNOPAC library system.

Funding

Any project of this nature requires a considerable amount of financial support. The initial monies were funded from a grant with two gifts in the amounts of $100,000 each, and a third of $25,000. The total project when completed is estimated to cost in the neighborhood of $650,000. The difference will be subsidized by the university and will be paid with an installment plan.

Installation

The major question that needed to be answered was, "What would be the most cost-effective way to connect all the libraries of the multicampus environment?" Another consideration was to determine on which campus the host server should be located. It was decided that the best way, in our situation, was to connect to the preexisting PACEnet. PACEnet is the university network that already links the campuses by utilizing stat multiplexors, short-haul modems, and high-speed data communication lines (see Figure 3). In the same manner, this new network would be connected via multiplexors and short-haul modems on each campus, linked into PACEnet.

Problems

Unforeseen problems in any major project are always to be expected, and this venture was no exception. One of the first difficulties arose with the data communications multiplexors. The proper clocking speed had to be determined. This brought complications between the time division multiplexors and the statistical division multiplexors .

When choosing to own and set up a system with multivendor equipment, you must also expect finger pointing. More often than not, it seems to be the case that when a problem arises with a multivendor system, practically all companies involved blame the other guy for the dillemma. In this case, during the installation period we were constantly reminded that we did not buy all the items from Innovative Interfaces, and therefore they do not have to support or help us. For example, the same dumb terminals (WYSE-50) if purchased through Innovative would have cost twice the price than regularly discounted vendors. Moreover, it held true for their printers (Okidata), bar code readers, and uninterruptible power supplies (UPS). We found that with a little shopping around we were able to find items with equivalent or better specifications, at a lower price, better quality, and with warranties.

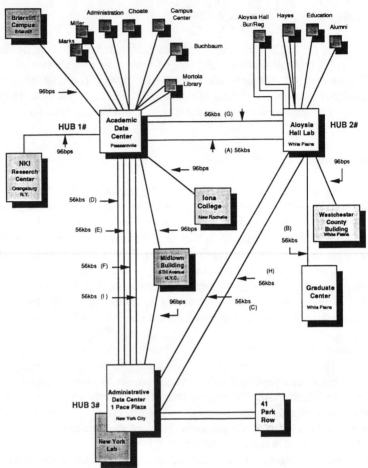

Figure 3. PACENET.

Support

Innovative Interfaces, Inc. has a toll-free technical support line. Most of their technical support staff is very knowledgeable. In addition, they keep notes on a log of every technical call that comes in. Therefore, no matter which technician works on the call, the entire history of the problem does not have to be reiterated. The technician simply calls up and reviews the problem. Moreover, the hold time for a technician is usually not long.

Sometimes, however, there seems to be confusion as to whether certain calls are "library services" or "technical support." In addition, at times, they put a new support staff person on before they are ready to handle the majority of the calls or relatively simple tasks. For example, once a call was placed to change the screen on the print menu; it not only took a week to accomplish this, but it was done wrong.

Although the general feeling of the system is good, there are, of course, some drawbacks. For example, the time difference between New York and California translates into not being able to get library services or general technical support before 12 noon EST or, in other words, after half of our workday is completed, although, emergency services are available from 8 AM EST. However, there have been instances, for example, the Friday after Thanksgiving, when the library was open, yet emergency services were closed for the weekend. This is very difficult for the academic environment to accept as fact, because the system may go down at the worst times, for example, the week of final exams. It is difficult to tell a student who has to do research for a term paper and has come a long way to use the facilities, and cannot because "the system is down." This frustration may lead to many problems.

Maintenance

Hidden costs to many systems exist after the warranty, including maintenance contracts, support, training, and personnel. These costs must be anticipated and budgeted accordingly. It is strongly recommended that the CPU (central processing unit) and the data communication equipment (multiplexors, etc.) be put on a service contract for immediate replacement in the event of failure.

FINAL DISCUSSION

Some original notions and thoughts were looked at differently after the system was actually in use. One of the reasons why INNOVACQ/INNOPAC was chosen was because Innovative would do all the "programming" and so forth. At this time, we feel that relying on Innovative for everything from menu changes, to printer drivers, through UPS drivers is very cumbersome and actually time consuming when someone with little computer knowledge can accomplish the necessary tasks. Hence, we feel it would be more convenient and efficient to have equal control of the complete system, with Innovative still being there in the event of an emergency with little or no computer staff on duty.

Another view that changed after the project began was being able to purchase all the equipment from one vendor—for example, the software, processor, terminals, and printers. The price performance ratio was superior on other brands, with other vendors.

It was also thought that a reference/systems librarian would need to be hired to support such a system. Later it was recognized that such an allocation was not necessary, although a person was required to be trained in a relatively routine matter of backing up the system. After all the quirks and slight errors were out of the system, a hardware/software person was not essential. However, since hardware equipment does break down occasionally, it was decided to leave that to the microcomputing support staff.

FUTURE EXPANSIONS

We hope in the future to connect the INNOVACQ/INNOPAC network to other systems. For example, we envision the library system connected on an Ethernet LAN. We can use the preexisting wiring (unshielded twisted pair) and the Lantronix interfaces already connected into the MIPS (millions of instructions per second) server. In addition, we foresee the system being bridged to the Academic Computing mainframe, that is, the IBM 4381, which has dialup capability. Therefore, anyone with an ID to the mainframe, and either a modem or a terminal connection, can access the library information! Moreover, we have aspirations of linking the system to Westchester County's Electronic Data Processing Database Services (PALS), which Pace has subcontracted for access to over the past few years.

CONCLUSIONS

Overall, the INNOVACQ/INNOPAC system from Innovative Interface, Inc., has been successful at Pace University. After several months of operation, the faculty, staff, and students are very pleased with its ease of operation, extensive range of functions, and quick response time from all the campuses. However, some drawbacks occur in the support and control of the system.

ACKNOWLEDGMENTS

We would like to acknowledge the University President, Dr. Patricia O'Donnell Ewers, the University Librarian, Henry Birnbaum, and the University Director of Academic Computing, Lawrence Kittinger, for their continued support in this project.

Computing at Scripps College: A Case Study

Dorothy H. Hess
Director of Administrative Computing
Scripps College

Nancy Krimmer
Director of Academic Computing
Scripps College

Scripps College is a liberal arts institution serving nearly 600 FTE (full-time equivalent) women whose SAT scores average more than 1150. Scripps is part of a consortium of schools in southern California called the Claremont Colleges. It includes Harvey Mudd College, Claremont McKenna College, Pitzer College, Pomona College and Claremont Graduate School. Students at any of the undergraduate schools can enroll in courses at any of the other schools.

The major emphases of study at Scripps are the humanities and the arts. There are many opportunities for study at other U.S. institutions on an exchange, as well as and also at foreign campuses on four different continents.

Computing at Scripps College is administered separately in the academic and administrative sectors, although there is a current study to combine them administratively. Because there is concentrated study in computer programming and related fields on some of the other Claremont campuses, they are not duplicated on Scripps Campus.

The largest investment in technology on campus has been in administration. where more than 50 staff members use an integrated system.

Scripps has a student computing lab, a faculty lab, and a teaching lab connected through a Novell network. Many of the professors are using personal computers for their research and/or teaching. There is a five-year plan to provide each faculty member with this capability.

ADMINISTRATIVE BACKGROUND

In the 1970s and even into the early 1980s, computing lent itself to centralized operations. This was also the case at the Claremont colleges. There were two DEC-10 machines. (I don't think it is necessary to explain the configuration, since they can be seen in the Digital museum.) They were centrally located so that all the colleges had access.

Scripps was attached via dedicated lines to the Registrar's office, Student Billing and Receivables and Development offices, and Financial services. Only five lines were available to these four offices.

Programs were written in System 1022 and were basically developed by the staff at Pomona College, assisted and operated by a central computing staff. In this scenario, the other colleges basically followed where Pomona led, creating office recording procedures that were very similar. Any requested changes, few as they were, were made by either the staff from Pomona or the central office of computing. Financial Services were all centralized as well.

The Office of Admissions was using an IBM System 6 word processor with a single operator.

In 1983 a task force deemed it financially unsound to continue this process. Scripps, a woman's college, wanted to control its own computing environment. A study was completed by the accounting firm of Coopers & Lybrand to find out what other small campuses were doing and with what resources.

As a result, it was decided that Scripps should purchase, and house locally, its own computing power. It became evident, however, that Scripps could not afford to provide good programming support in-house. The study suggested that the purchase of an "off-the-shelf" administrative package tailored for our institution, would be the most feasible route.

After polling small colleges across the nation, three packages were chosen. One was available on Hewlett-Packard hardware, and the other two on Digital Equipment. The decision, a wise one, to stay with Digital in order to be compatible with the other Claremont campuses narrowed down the choices. Of the remaining two, the one with the strongest, longest track record was POISE, which is currently being developed and distributed by Campus America.

In 1985 a director of Administrative Computing was hired. Renovations of a theater costume room and the purchase of equipment amounted to an investment of $500,000.

The DEC hardware of the era was purchased—a VAX 11-750 with two RA81 disk drives and a TU80 tape drive. This was the greatest interactive machine of its day (see Figure 1).

The entire administrative staff, with a few exceptions, was housed in one building, but the distances were too great to run direct lines from each terminal to the computer room. Three DMZ-32 distribution panels were distributed at centralized points throughout the building, and T1 cables were strung from there to the VAX. Silver satin flat wire ran from these centralized areas to punch-down blocks and from there to each terminal.

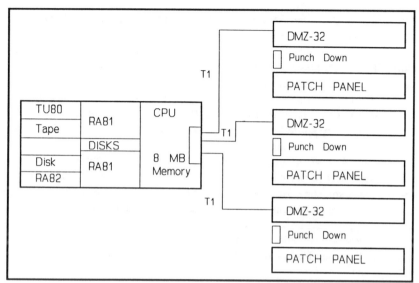

***Figure 1.** VAX 750 configuration.*

VT-100 compatible terminals were distributed to staff members. Twenty-four DEC 100s (read Rainbow) were purchased for word processing. It had been decided that all word processing would be done on the personal computers (Rainbows) and that all database activity and users would be attached to the VAX.

In 1985 secretaries did the word processing. This really meant that instead of "correcto" typewriters, they could now do REMOVE, and CUT and PASTE, and make copies of the same letter to different people.

Use of the database was not nearly as clearly defined. Certainly the few people who had access to the DEC-10 would continue, but there were ideas for additional access.

The basis of the POISE software is DMS, its data management system, on which office modules are based and written. It was decided that Admissions, Student Billing and Receivables, Financial Aid, Development and Alumnae activities, and Registration and records should all participate; so those office modules were purchased.

CONVERSION

In December 1985 an assistant was hired for six months to convert all the DEC-10 data to POISE. Because nothing could be converted from the System-6, Admissions was the first to jump on board. Very little changed in their administration; they thought of the VAX, using POISE, as another System-6. They wanted no changes, even though it could select as many as 26 fields of data instead of only one. They have had a great deal of trouble leaving the old behind. The VAX editor was to be used to create letters to prospects and applicants. This was dissatisfaction number one.

Since there was only one computing center staff person responsible for the conversion of all data from the DEC-10 for all POISE application modules, energies were shifted. (The VAX editor IS a good tool and can DO the job.) Their complaints had to wait.

Financial services, greatly entwined with the other campuses, with a large central staff in place, remained centralized and in fact migrated to an HP-3000 system using BITECH software. They changed their accounting structures to meet new requirements. All the offices that used General Ledger account numbers had to be converted from the DEC-10 to POISE using BI-TECH specifications. This was not an easy task since every office was expecting to be completely converted during the period between December 1985 and June 1986.

Student billing codes were entered into the new system, and end-of-year balances were checked on both systems. Installment billing per Pomona College's program could not be duplicated accurately. There was therefore a problem with aging accounts receivables properly.

Financial aid was being entered into a computer by office staff for the first time in July and being fed into the billing system, which was also picking up registration data for billing purposes.

Gifts to the college from alumnae and friends were converted to POISE but also continued to be double-entered into BITECH on the HP.

All the before-mentioned offices ran parallel systems until the end of the fiscal year in June. By then through some miracle, they were all "functioning" on the VAX.

New applicants accepted for admission to the college now could and would be moved into all systems concurrently—registration, financial aid, billing, housing, and the alumnae file. Their parents became part of the development database.

The 12-month span, from the time when three people were maintaining separate databases, to a time when at least ten people were maintaining seven different parts of databases, became a director's nightmare.

Personnel *within* each office needed to decide what their functions were, and when they needed to occur; persons *between* offices needed to begin to communicate and depend on each other for valid data to be updated in a timely manner. The computing staff was no longer only purchasing and installing equipment. Some of the most important and difficult work being done by the computing staff was developing staff in other offices and educating them, and alerting their supervisors to changing roles and responsibilities. The future had begun.

NETWORKING HARDWARE

A major gift campaign, the largest ever in Scripps history, was to begin, lasting four years. The VAX 750 was too slow. Was it really, or did they just need "their own" computer? The Vice President for Development had attended a conference at which a Macintosh with all the bells and whistles was demonstrated. That's exactly what they needed! Or was it? To some, the new responsibility of integration had never arrived.

An immense task and opportunity presented itself. An analysis of Scripps Computing seemed to suggest that since data were flowing smoothly through the system facilitated by POISE software, there was a distinct possibility that this process should not be interrupted. Indeed why should there be a comparable gift-recording system for +/- 500 donors coexisting with one for 12,000 already in place—with no interface.

There was no time (less than six months) for staff (total of one) to write a program that would handle the cultivation of major donors. But specifications were obtained; the program was designed and mailed to the POISE staff, who completed it in four weeks.

Meanwhile, $100,000 of the "to-be-received" major gifts was designated to develop, and place online, a Microvax II with 8MB of memory and two RD-53 disks networked to the VAX 750. DMS and its compiler BASIC, DECnet, and, of course, VMS now needed to reside on both systems. To facilitate matters, the entire Development and Alumnae applications were moved to the Microvax II with line-printing capability. The system printer on the VAX 750 was shared by both network nodes. Laser printing was available on both systems accessible form either node (see Figure 2).

Scripps staff had begun to see the value of changing roles and duties, so word processing could no longer reside only on personal computers. Part of the task of computing was to create an interface between Mass-11, the word processor of choice now being used on the VAX, and ASCII data from DMS, our database. Correspondence could now contain all kinds of personalized data, pulled from wherever it resided in the database on the VAX.

Integration was becoming more and more important. A new question began to arise. Whose data are they? Where does my job begin and end? Nobody knew, least of all the office directors who had no computing experience. (Enter the computing director.) Someone needs the data that the admissions office is not willing to record. Another office needs data the registrar is not willing to share. The question is how to infiltrate the staff with cooperation!?

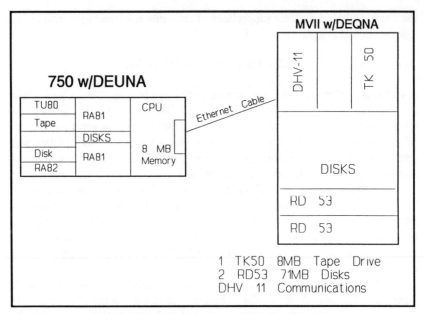

Figure 2. *VAX 750/Microvax II configuration—750 w/Deuna.*

There began a new understanding on the part of computing staff. Once a physical and logical connection is made and functioning, the real networking begins. It suddenly became obvious that the purpose for networking is not to share computing resources but to share data resources and use them wisely. We needed to network the people.

MAJOR UPGRADE

Can I get a terminal? I need to know . . . and she doesn't have time to get it for me. Forty-five people clamoring for networked services where three years ago, there were a lonely five!

POISE is a user-intelligent system. Secretaries began to want to make their own selections from the database so that they would never have to wait. The database administrator in each of the offices was being bombarded by senior staff members for data. The VP of Research and Planning was needing data from everyone.

We share our course schedule with the other colleges on a semester basis so that the students can take courses on any campus. Pomona staff takes the responsibility to "mush" each college's schedule into a "common" file. Each college then retrieves and updates the file for its own use. This continues to be a problem; not in the ASCII data exchange via KERMIT over modem, but with the registrars who have not taken responsibility for their data structures and reliability.

Virtual memory was being reassigned as users' responsibilities changed. More files were being created; longer files were remaining as longitudinal studies were being undertaken. The RD-53s began to get crowded, and the VAX-750 began to groan. It was approaching its fifth birthday. Perhaps it was time to look ahead. It was worth $2,000 on the resale market but was costing more than $13,000 per year in maintenance costs. We were maintaining two CPUs, two VMS, two DECnet, two DMS, two Basic, and two Mass-11 licenses.

What are some alternatives? All our software runs on a VAX; users are familiar with DCL; computing staff are VAX trained.

Is there any reason to create local area networks (LANs) in various offices? Would data be more or less secure, or accessible, if we did? How could it be retrieved by those who need it? Where would the major database reside? Who would bear responsibility for its maintenance?

The other Claremont College campuses were beginning to separate themselves from the old DEC 10, creating their own staffs. They were migrating from System 1022 to System 1032. Should we consider rejoining the Compuserve fold? Every question pointed to a solution in the same direction—stay with what got you here. If it works, don't fix it! Our platforms would stay the same.

I developed a proposal, which senior staff accepted, as the most probable solution (see Figure 3).

	Current	Projected
	VAX(en) 750/MVII	Vax6300
VAX System Hardware	26,664	12,000
Software	14,131	3,400
Application Software	10,000	14,000
Total	50,795	29,400

Figure 3. Yearly maintenance costs.

CURRENT SYSTEM

Change of a technological nature—gigantic change—now became the focus of the Director of Computing. Connecting two CPUs with one 10-foot blue thick wire Ethernet cable began to seem petty when contemplating the future configuration.

The DMZs (distribution panels) were past history. In fact, all communications beyond the new BUS, a BI bus, were handled outside the CPU cabinet.

That famous blue Ethernet cable was now connected to a what, a DELNI, or was it a DEMPR. A thin wire cable then ran to a transceiver that connected to a DEMPR, or was that a DELNI, from where a thin wire, or could we still use a T-1 cable, ran to a what, a Terminal Server. Everything from the CPU to the wiring closet was new technology. From that point, there were no necessary changes in hardware (see Figure 4).

Was it really worth it all! Was the VAX-750 really *that* slow? Maybe we didn't need all this anyway. The answer kept pounding inside my head "Yeah we do, now get started." After all, the operations of the college were not going to diminish. There was going to be a dramatic increase in computing, at least if the information was available.

Optic fiber now connected us over a LANbridge 100 through Harvey Mudd College to the rest of the world. Grover, namesake of the Frank Oz

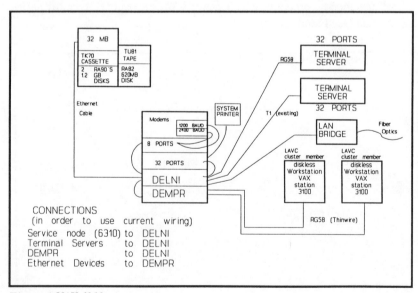

Figure 4. VAX 6310.

character on Sesame Street, a VAX 6310, was installed in late 1989. The terminal servers and other communication equipment were tested and installed over the Christmas holidays.

VMS 5.0 was not a minor upgrade! Now I had to become familiar with LATCP (Local Area Transport Control Program) in order to understand and install the terminal servers. The new SYSMAN Utility is a neat added function, but why did I suddenly need to change my Spoolers.com and Terminals.com. Everything seemed upside-down. Was there really a Christmas that year?

New technology was passing by the MicroVAX. If it were sold, the money could be used to purchase a VAXstation 3100. If we did it within three months, Lotus 1-2-3 would be included. I had just received a memo from the Treasurer—"look into the possibility of loading Lotus on the VAX." The Gods are NOT crazy!

Desktop publishing appeared on campus the same year. Credit for dropping the Mass-11 word processing license on the Microvax was exchanged for WYSIWORD, their DecWindows version, based on DEC's National Advanced Systems (NAS) architecture. What a windfall: for the cost of one VAXstation, we got two stations and two crucial software packages.

Suddenly an LAVC is to be born. What's a Local Area VAX Cluster and why? Two diskless (52Mbyte for caching) VAXstation 3100 workstations would share the VMS system files on the VAX 6310 and share the 2.5 Gbytes of disk storage, all managed from a central point.

What? Something else new from Digital that will solve more problems. MS-DOS services for VMS, no, it's PATHWORKS. It will allow server/client capability and save the $30,000 needed to install a Novell network in the Financial Aid office for multiple Microfaids users.

For years we've been patching and circumventing power shortages and "tan-outs." "The lights work, how come my computer won't work?"

The building is 60 years old—time to upgrade. How does one create an 'intelligent building' within the constraints of the National Registry of History Places! Very carefully.

Figure 5 shows that the plan will be completed by summer of 1992.

THE EVOLUTION OF SCRIPPS COLLEGE ACADEMIC COMPUTING

Prior to 1984, Scripps College's computing needs were met through the rental of four ports on the VAX at Harvey Mudd College. Only a handful of Scripps students ever used the terminal room.

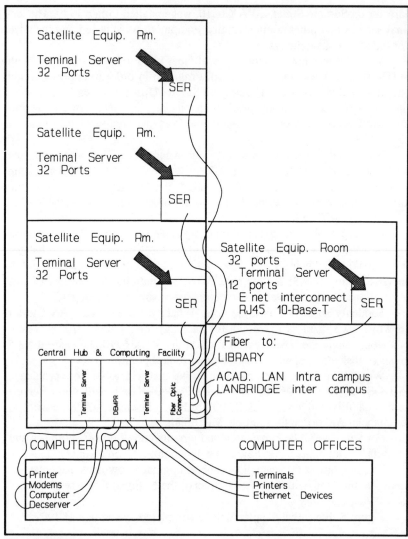

***Figure 5.** The plan to upgrade.*

In 1983-84 the IBM Academic Computing Educational Service (ACES) program placed seven IBM XT computers on loan to the college for a period of one year. At this time, several offices and some faculty members reviewed the XTs for possible purchase and development of a Scripps College Academic Computing Lab.

During the 1984-85 academic year a Keck Foundation Grant provided funds to purchase 18 IBM personal computers (PCs) (8086 CPU two floppy 5 inch disk drives with 256K RAM). Furniture, Okidata printers, and one HP LaserJet and HP color plotter were purchased to create a student microcomputer lab. The on-loan systems from the previous year were purchased and were used by the academic secretarial staff. Three LaserJet printers, and seven OKIDATA 92 dot matrix were bought for the Academic Support secretarial staff.

A goal of induction via word processing (WordStar 3) into the Scripps community was developed and implemented during the first year of the lab. In addition a three-part longitudinal study was created through a combined effort of the Research/Planning office and Academic Computing. This measure consisted of an Observational survey, a Freshman Questionnaire, and an In-Lab User Questionnaire. A requirement that computers be used for ALL papers in first-year English courses was adopted.

As a result of these efforts, seven additional computers and Okidata printers were purchased for use in a small room on the first floor of each dormitory.

By 1987 the VAX terminals were replaced by existing IBM XTs that also functioned as terminals via direct twisted pair connection to Harvey Mudd College.

A year later an Amiga personal computer (non-IBM compatible) was made available for use in fine arts courses.

We purchased an IBM PS 50z the following year and a LaserJet II for an additional lab printer. Needing to compete with rising student computing demands, the Music Department purchased two MAC computers.

By 1990 a Sloan-IBM grant provided funds for a technical classroom and faculty computing lab, which included 13 IBM PS/2 model 30s (286 CPU, 20MB hard disk, a 3 inch floppy and VGA monitors), and three Model 70 PS/2 computers (386 CPU). Two model 70s and one model 30 IBM PS/2 were placed in the faculty lab, and a new classroom was equipped as a technical teaching classroom for the humanities. As stipulated by the Sloan-IBM grant, the equipment is to be used for instructional purposes and workshops, and stipends are to be made available to faculty interested in pursuing the development of computer use within their curriculum.

The Music Department purchased a piano keyboard synthesizer and musical instrument digital interface (MIDI) that they connect to the existing MAC computers and moved the equipment to the new IBM-Sloan technical classroom.

Two additional MACs (MAC IIs) were purchased and placed in the teaching classroom for use primarily in art and psychology.

With the new addition of the second lab, a new network was provided from an educational grant through Novell. Scripps College purchased Ethernet cable and network interface cards for both the Sloan-IBM systems and the existing IBM PCs in the student lab (adapting to use an Ethernet instead of a token-ring for reasons of compatibility and superior performance and future adaptability).

In 1990-91 WordPerfect was adopted as the word processing software for Scripps Academic Computing. The first-year replacement program began, and half of the lab PCs were replaced with IBM-compatible computers (386 25Mhz, 40MB hard drive, dual floppy, 2MB RAM, and VGA display).

An Apple LaserWriter PostScript printer was acquired for use with the MAC computers in the teaching classroom.

Additional storage for the file server was purchased (150MB CORE hard drive).

Currently, a new Novell upgrade has been purchased (in part by a educational program from Novell and Scripps College) and installed. An existing PC (386 with upgraded 150MB internal drive, increasing storage capacity by 80MB—that previously was in the lab) became the file server.

Seven new dorm computers were purchased to replace aging systems (386 25Mhz, 40MB hard drive, dual floppy, 2MB RAM and VGA display) and a few lab system upgrades were necessary for new Windows platform.

A fiber-optic connection to the world of BITNET was recently made using the existing bridge. Electronic mail first introduced to the local Scripps community via Scripps LAN with connections to the worldwide Internet was made possible.

In second phase of upgrade new dorm computers and some lab system components will be purchased. Adoption of windows, consistent with the other Claremont Colleges' student LANs allows for a new ICON driven user interface that is exceedingly simple for students to use.

Additional memory (4MB for each system) and hard drives for any remaining lab computer will be upgraded in response to demands made by software needs.

Planned for 1992 are a fiber connection from our campus library to the database(s) available at Honnold, the central library of the Claremont Colleges, and other available CDs. Long-range plans (1992-95) include the rewiring of all dormitories to provide for data hookups.

About the Contributors

ROBERT ABBOTT is Director of Academic Computing at Bloomsburg University. He is a member of the SSHE Telecommunications Policy committee, the SSHE Academic Computing committee, the Bloomsburg University Academic Computing Advisory committee, and the Administrative Computing Advisory committee.

LAURENCE R. ALVAREZ received his B.S. in Mathematics at the University of the South, Sewanee, Tennessee, his M.A. and Ph.D. in Mathematics at Yale University. He began teaching mathematics at the University of the South in 1964 after a year of teaching at Trinity College. He is currently Professor of Mathematics and Associate Provost at the University of the South.

D. L. ATKIN graduated in Physics and Computer Science at the University of York at which point he became a Systems Programmer working on an early implementation of X.25 on a DECsystem-10. He has been responsible for installing a large VAXcluster system, a campus-wide fibre-optic network, and a number of UNIX workstations and servers. He is currently Chairman of the European Large Site SIG in DECUS (the Digital Equipment User group). His particuloar interests are in automated system and network management.

RICHARD BIALAC is the Chair of the Department of Information Systems and Communications at Georgia College in Milledgeville. Previously, he was chair of a similar department at Xavier University in Cincinnati. He holds a Ph.D. in Information Systems from the University of Cincinnati (1985) and has research interests in database and computer graphics in business. An avid BITNET advocate, he can be reached at RBLIALAC@USCN.

DOUGLAS BIGELOW is Director of Academic Computing at Wesleyan University, where he provides all central computing services for a combined administrative and academic clientele. He is responsible for general computing services and the microcomputer sales and support program, and has designed the computer networks in use at Wesleyan. He is a former Trustee of Bitnet, Inc., and currently serves as a Trustee of the Corporation for Research and Educational Networking. Mr. Bigelow has performed computer and networking consultations for several universities.

ROBERT V. BLYSTONE is a professor of Biology at Trinity University, San Antonio, Texas, where he has taught for 21 years. He teaches courses in Cell and Developmental Biology and serves as the Director of the Electron Microscopy and Visualization Lab. He has served as Department Chair and Chair of the Faculty Senate. Dr. Blystone has been recognized three times for his teaching while at Trinity. His recent research involves computer visualization of growing macrophage cells.

JOHN L. BORDLEY, JR. received his B.S. in Chemistry at Davidson College, and his Ph.D. in Physical Chemistry at Johns Hopkins University. He began teaching general and physical chemistry at the University of the South, Sewanee, Tennessee, in 1970 where he is currently Professor of Chemistry and Director of Academic Computing.

THOMAS W. BURTNETT has been the Director of Academic Computing at Seton Hall University since early 1989. He earned a B.S. from Penn State and an M.S. from Case Western Reserve University. A long-time promoter of networks and their applications, he has held positions in computer services at Penn State, the University of Illinois, and Dickinson College.

CHARLES E. CHULVIK is Director of University Computing Systems and has been involved in computing and data processing in higher education for the past twenty years. He holds a Master of Science degree in Town and Country Planning from the University of Wales and has held positions in the United States and Great Britain. Chulvik has been with the University of Scranton since 1988.

PATRICK CIRIELLO was Supervisor of Networking and Technical Services at Lafayette College where he was responsible for the design and implementation of a campus-wide token-ring network linking all offices, classrooms, and residential rooms. He recently left to join CSC Partners as a consultant.

JEAN F. COPPOLA is the University Microcomputing Support Analyst of Academic Computing for Pace University. Currently, she and her staff handle all microcomputer support, including hardware/software analysis, repair, maintenance, computer virus protection, data recovery, and networks. She is an adjunct instructor in the School of Computer Science and Information Systems. Ms Coppola attended Hofstra University and holds a B.S. in Computer Science. She also holds an M.S. in Computer Science and in Telecommunications both from Pace University. She has lectured on Microcomputer Hardware, Troubleshooting and Maintenance, and on Computer Virus Prevention and Detection. In addition, she has published several papers on building nad analyzing computers, and cellular automata.

MARGARET E. CRAFT, Assistant Director for Special Services, University Library Systems, University of Scranton, oversees the operations of the Media Resources Center as well as the University Archives and Special Collections areas. She is a graduate of Central Michigan University, the University of Michigan, and the University of Scranton. She has been involved in academic and research libraries for over twenty years and has been with the University of Scranton since 1988.

JEROME P. DESANTO is the Assistant Provost for Information Technology and oversees the operations of the University of Scranton's computing systems and campus-wide network of voice, data, and video systems. Formerly the Executive Director of the McDade Technology Center, Desanto has a B.S. and M.B.A. degree from the University of Scranton and has been with the University since 1979.

RICHARD A. DETWEILER is president-elect of Hartwick College in Oneonta, New York. He coauthored his chapter while he was Vice President and Professor of Psychology at Drew University in Madison, New Jersey, where he was responsible for university-wide strategic planning, university/institutional research, and information technology operations. He is a social psychologist with degrees from United States International University (B.A., 1968) and Princeton (M.A., 1972 and Ph.D., 1973). Dr. Detweiler is also known for his spearheading Drew's award-winning "Computer" and "Knowledge Initiatives"—programs that integrated information technology into a liberal arts curriculum.

NANCY ENRIGHT is a faculty member in the English department at Seton Hall University and Director of the Computer Assisted Instruction Center.

ELLEN F. FALDUTO is a member of the University and Institutional Research staff at Drew University in Madison, New Jersey. Since 1986, she has been involved in the planning of Drew's technology initiatives as well as efforts in university-wide planning and research. Ms. Falduto coauthored her chapter while she was a doctoral degree candidate at Seton Hall University. She also has degrees in psychology from Fairleigh Dickinson University (B.A., 1981) and Rensselaer Polytechnic Institute (M.S., 1982). Ms. Falduto's research interests include the psychology of technology implementation.

ALEX FELDMAN received a Ph.D. in Mathematics from the University of Wisconsin-Madison. He has done research in the areas of mathematical logic and theoretical computer science, first at Odyssey Research Associates and then at his present position as Assistant Professor in the Mathematics Department at Boise State University. His interest in networks stems from an interest in fault-tolerant computing as well as experience with installation and education about networks. He has taught courses on network protocols and has provided informal training in many aspects of network use.

JOSEPH L. FLEMING is Director of Computing Services at Denison University. He received his academic training at Albion College and the University of Michigan, and was formerly a faculty member in Physics and Astronomy at Oliet College and Director of Information Systems at Western New Mexico University.

TIMOTHY J. FOLEY is Associate Director of Computing and Consulting Services. He has been at Lehigh for twelve years, starting as Educational Coordinator in the Computing Center. He holds bachelor's and master's degrees in mathematics and a doctorate in educational technology from Lehigh University.

ANN FRENCH is the head of the group responsible for providing documentation (both printed and online) and education about computing for staff and postgraduates at the University of Bristol. She has worked at Bristol since 1975, first as a programmer and advisor, then as a documentor, and became increasingly more involved in education and online information. She implemented a primitive CWIS on a Multics system in 1985.

CARL L. GERBERICH is the Vice President for Information Services at Marist College, Poughkeepsie, New York. He has 40 years of experience in computing and has worked for IBM and General Electric. He received a M.A. in Mathematics from the University of Tennessee and an M.S. and M.Ph. in Systems and Information Sciences from Syracuse University. Gerberich has published articles in the *ACM Journal* and *IEEE Journal of Information Theory*.

LAWRENCE H. GINDLER is the Assistant Director for User Services and Networking at Trinity University, San Antonio, Texas, where he has been for eight years. He is certified in data processing, computer programming, and systems management. Gindler has the responsibility for facilitating faculty and student interaction with computational technology.

BJ GLEASON is an instructor in the Computer Science and Information Systems department at the American University. He is the Chair of the Departmental LAB/LAN Committee and is currently preparing for the new applications and services that will be made available once the fiber optics backbone is installed. His research interests include educational computing, computer architecture, and compiler design. He is also the author of *PBASIC*, a public domain BASIC interpreter for the personal computer.

DENNIS GUSTER is a Professor of Computer Science at St. Cloud State University. His areas of specialization include microcomputers, systems analysis, and networking. Dr. Guster was formerly the Chair of Information and Office Systems at St. Louis Community College at Meramec. He holds degrees from Bemidji State University in Minnesota and the University of Missouri-St. Louis. Dennis gained work experience at the St. Louis Metropolitan Police Department and still does information systems consulting. Dr. Guster's current research interests include user performance characteristics and computer/network performance analysis.

DAVID HEFFNER, Academic Computer Administrator for networking and file servers at Bloomsburg University, has spent over ten years in providing computer services in business and higher education. Having extensive experience as a private consultant in designing implementing computer networks, office automation, and relational databases, he is currently responsible for a network of twelve servers and 180 nodes.

DOROTHY H. HESS began her work in computing ten years ago digitizing working drawings for an architectural firm. In 1983 she moved to higher education as an MIS Specialist at Woodbury University in Los Angeles supporting administrators, using POISE software and serving as VAX Operator. In 1985 she came to Scripps College to convert their data to the newly acquired POISE system. She was promoted to Director of Administrative Computing in 1987. She also serves as System Manager for the VAXen. Having been a founding member of the national POISE Users' Group, she was elected to its first Board of Directors where she currently serves as liaison with Campus America.

LARRY J. HICKERNELL is Head of Media Services, a part of the Media Resources Center of the University of Scranton's library system. In addition, Mr. Hickernell serves as the Assistant Project Manager for IGNET and designed the video portion of the network. He is a graduate of Central Pennsylvania Business School and is currently pursuing his bachelor' degree at the University of Scranton.

NOEL C. HUNTER received a B.A. from Wake Forest University in 1986. He worked as a free-lance programmer, consultant, and musician before returning to Wake Forest in 1989 as the User Support Consultant for the Computer Center. Noel's current responsibilities include management of the student lab network, publication of a monthly newsletter, and training of faculty, students, and staff.

LARRY JONES is currently the Dean of Kent State University's Geauga Campus. Prior to accepting the Deanship, he held several positions in student affairs within the Kent State Regional Campuses. Developing an interest during the late 1970s in the use of microcomputers as productivity tools in administration, Jones began implementing microcomputer and local area network technology at several campuses. He holds the rank of Assistant Professor in Computer Technology. Jones earned his Bachelor of Industrial Engineering Degree at General Motors Institute (GMI), his Master of Education Degree in Student Personnel Administration at Kent State University, and his Doctor of Philosophy Degree in Higher Education Administration and Organizational Development at Kent State.

DAVID KELLEY is the VAX Systems and Network Manager at the University of Hartford, operating their 30 node VAXcluster, and maintaining the campuis-wide fiber-optic network. He is a graduate of the University's Computer Engineering program, and runs a personal computer programming business specializing in student financial aid processing software.

PATRICK KELLY is the Director of Information Systems and Librarian at the University of Limerick, Eire. He is responsible for all information-based systems and services of the university, including the Library, academic computing, educational technology and audio-visual services, telecommunications and networks, administrative computing, and office systems and services.

NANCY KRIMMER is the Director of Academic Computing at Scripps College. A recent graduate, she accepted this position in 1984, to develop the first academic computing facility on campus. In addition to the student PC lab, she has designed a technical classroom used for teaching purposes. Ms. Krimmer also holds workshops for students and faculty on a variety of software applications including: word processing, statistics, graphics, and educational software.

ROBERT LEJEUNE is Director of Academic Computing Services and Faculty Support Center for Computing at St. John's University. He is a graduate of the City College of New York and holds a Ph.D. in Sociology from Columbia University. His main interest is in the use of computers to enhance creativity and productivity in the university.

LES LLOYD is Director of Computing Services at Lafayette College. He received his B.S. in Interdisciplinary Science and his M.B.A. from Rensselaer Polytechnic Institute. He worked several years in industry before joining Drew University in 1985 as Director of Academic Computing and then Lafayette in 1988. Lloyd has edited two works on campus computer networking, *Using Computer Networks on Campus* and *Using Computer Networks on Campus II*. He has led annual conferences on this topic since 1990.

GENE MCGUIRE is an instructor in the Computer Science and Information Systems department at the American University. His research interests include educational computing, hypermedia applications, cognitive issues in computer-mediated communication, and human factors in systems development and implementation. He is member of the faculty Computer Resources Committee where one of the hot topics of the year is the completion of the fiber-optic backbone and the connection of all the existing LANs to this backbone.

JANE MILLYARD has been associated with the University of Kent at Canterbury (UKC) as an administrator since 1963. She is now Head of Information in the Computing Laboratory, with responsibilities in both the Central Computing Service and the Computer Science department. Millyard has an early background in Humanities and is interested in the availability and provision of electronic information systems to the novice computer user. Since 1988, she has been secretary of the Editorial Committee responsible for the implementation of the UKC CWIS.

DR. JOSEPH J. MOELLER, JR., is Vice President for Information Systems at Stevens Institute of Technology. He is responsible for strategic planning and management of the institute's initiatives in computing, networking, information systems, and communications. Dr. Moeller received his B.Eng., M.Eng., and Ph.D. degrees in electrical engineering from Stevens Institute and served as Assistant Professor of Electrical Engineering at Stevens. He has received recognition as an Outstanding Educator of America and an Outstanding Young Man of America. He is also Administrator of the Steering Committee for the New Jersey Intercampus Network, which is linking together all colleges and universities in the state.

LISA NOTARIANNI is the University's Network Services Coordinator and coordinates the delivery of network related services to the University. She attended the Pennsylvania State University and earned an A.S. in Managment of Informational Systems from Lackawanna Junior College.

ROBERT PARRISH is Vice President for Administration and University Treasurer at Bloomsburg University. Having extensive experience in providing administrative computer services in higher education including the current responsibility for the administrative data network, using a UNYSIS 2200/402 mainframe with 174 interactive terminals and networked PC 286 microcomputers, he is responsible for the design and supervision of the telecommunication network, which includes voice, data, and television signals. He also supports the instructional data network with minicomputers, file servers, and hundreds of microcomputers.

MARK RESMER has been the Director of Computing, Media, and Telecommunications Services at Sonoma State University since 1988. He is responsible for planning and implementing of all aspects of information technology on the campus. He has been active in the development of system-wide network policies and services within the California State University, in the development of networked computing facilities which link the K-12 sector and higher education, and in the organization of BESTnet, a multi-national computing organization.

DR. ONKAR P. SHARMA is Professor of Computer Science and Chair of the Division of Computer Science and Mathematics at Marist College, Poughkeepsie, New York. Prior to the current assignment, he served in the Minnesota State University system and the City University of New York. He received his Ph.D. from New York University and his Master's degree from the University of California, Berkeley. Dr. Sharma is author of three books dealing with programming and problem solving.

MICHELE SHOEBRIDGE has held the post of Systems Librarian for three years at Birmingham University. She has responsibility for the Library's housekeeping system (BLCMP's BLS systems) and all the Library's microcomputer applications including a public microcomputer cluster, a CD-ROM network, and an administrative network of over 35 PCs. She has been involved in the university's Working Party on Campus Information Services. She also serves on the JUGL (JANET User Group for Libraries) Committee and the IUIC's (Inter University Information Committee) INFSWG (Information Services Working Group).

RONALD J. SKUTNICK, Assistant Director for Technical Services, University of Scranton Computing Systems, has been with the University of

Scranton for eleven years. He is Project Manager for IGNET. His educational background includes studies at Lackawanna Area Vocational-Technical School and the University of Scranton and his areas of expertise include large systems hardware and operating systems and data communications.

PAUL SMEE has been a senior systems programmer at the University of Bristol since 1980. Before that, he worked for Honeywell, Inc., as a member of the Multics project group. He has long been interested in applications to benefit groups that have not traditionally used computers and is the implementor of the Bristol Info Server.

BRIDGET TOWLER has worked as Systems Librarian in the Brynmor Jones Library at Hull University since 1987. Her current responsibilities include all library automation, ranging from the GEAC systems to personal computer systems and all networked facilities. She has contributed to the development of the Hull Information Service, writing specifications for many of the facilities added during the past four years, including the Information Bulletin Board, the Archives system and the various bibliographic databases. Prior to coming to Hull she was Systems Librarian at Coventry Polytechnic Library where she helped to install the first CLSI LIBS 100 system in the United Kingdom.

THAD WAKEFIELD is a Research Assistant within the Department of Computer Science at St. Cloud State University. His current area of study is data communications/local area networks. He also manages the microcomputer networking laboratory at SCSU.

KEVIN R. WEINER is the Computing Center's Systems Programming Manager. He has been at Lehigh for ten years, starting as Educational Coordinator in the Computing Center. He holds a bachelor's degree in Mathematics and Information Science from Lehigh University.

TOM WHITE is the Data Communications Technician for the University of Richmond. He has a background in Navy Electronics and Navy Nuclear Propulsion. He has worked for various vendors including Timeplex, Datacomm Management Sciences, and Anderson Jacobson. He has 17 years of experience in electronics, 12 of which have been in data communications.

COLIN K. WORK completed a primary degree and diploma in library and information science at University College, Dublin. He began his career in Ireland as a cataloguer in the same university's engineering library. In 1988 he assumed a post in England as software cataloguer at the University of Southampton for the National Information on Software and Services Project. In 1990 he moved to the University's Computing Service where he has been responsible for developing the university's CWIS. Work is a frequent speaker at workshops and conferences on national and local online information.

ROBERT J. YANNOCONE is the Manager of Computing Operations and Network Administration for Academic Computing at Pace University. He has been in the data processing field for twenty-two years with a heavy concentration in data communication for the past ten years. He has been associated with Pace for more than seven years and has been involved in many aspects of data communications, some of which are installation of hardware/software, troubleshooting, lease negotiation, consulting, and designing. He has also been involved in most mediums including the design and installation of multiple campus T1 backbones, token ring local area networks (LANs) and an automated library system, to name a few. Yannocone has been featured in *Computerworld*, "Spotlight-T1," (April, 1987) and *Technological Horizons in Education Journal*, "Economical Modems Help Upgrade Faculty Network at University," (August, 1987).

GORDON YOUNG is Manager of the Information Technology Department at the University of Limerick, Eire. Formerly Systems Manager at the University College at Galway, and Systems Manager at the University of Liverpool, he received his BSc, and C.Eng. from the University of Reading, Mathematices and Computer Science.

Index

Saber Menu System interface, 185
SAS, 2
SASGRAPH, 2
Sassafras Inc, 168
SCANTRON optical mark reader, 2
Science-50, 36
SCOLA, 53
SCOXENIX, 299
Scripps College, 323
SCRIPT, 2
SEEL Telepac, 245
Serial line interface ptotocol
        (SLIP), 134
Seton Hall University, 142
Setonian, The, 143
Sewanee, 148
Sharma, Onkar P., Dr., 98, 341
Shiva:
    EtherGate, 211
    Fastpath, 156, 211
    NetModems, 170
Shoebridge, Michele, 223, 342
Siecor Corporation engineering ser-
        vices, 128
    fiber-optic cable, 128
Silicon Graphics UNIX systems,
        302
Simple Mail Transfer Protocol
        (SMTP),
        18, 19, 94, 163
Simple Network Management Pro-
        tocol (SNMP), 129
Sitelock software, 191
SITfly program, 179
Skutnick, Ronald J., 342
SKYCAM 16, 120
Sloan-IBM grant, 333
Small Business Institute, 106
Smee, Paul, 232, 234, 239, 342
SNN, the Sewanee News Network,
        152
Socrates, 204

Sonoma State University (SSU),
        153, 156
Source Route Bridging, 86
Sparcstation, 31
Spider Systems, 137
Spratt, Brian, 256
SPSS Inc., 2, 56, 152-53
SSU Admissions System, 160
St. Cloud State University (SCSU),
        296
St. Thomas Test Network, 131
Stanford, 100
Stanford University's Mac-IP, 153
Stardent P-3, 31
Starlan Network, 3, 86
Stevens Institute of Technology,
        173
Stratacom frame-relay multiplex-
        ors, 156
Structured query language (SQL),
        161
Studio Works Programs, 142-43
Subnet 14, 216
Subscriber trunk dialing (STD)
        codes, 240
Sun:
    MicroSystems PC-NFS, 133
    SPARCserver 4/330 Entry-level
        Office Server, 234
    workstations, 66, 131
Server, 89
Symantec Antivirus, 187
Synoptics, 118, 129
    1000 LattisNet wiring centers,
        132
SYSMAN Utility, 331
Systat, 152
System 1022, 324
System 1032, 329
System V, 210, 311
System 7, 210
System-6, 325

T-1 circuits, 123, 156
T1 link, 267
Tandy, 149
Tansey, Frank, 160
Tape backup system, 187
Tape drive, 169
TCP/IP, 3
Telegistics, Inc., 46, 86
Terminate-stay-resident (TSR), 21
Texas Higher Education Regional
    Network, 196
TGV:
    MultiNet, 132
    NFS Server, 132
Thick wire or 10base5, 154
Thin wire (10base2), 154
TI 990, 58
Timbuktu, 22, 171
Time domain reflectometer (TDR),
    93
TN3270, 18, 167
Token-ring, 70, 126
Torch XXX, 223
Towler, Bridget, 243, 342
Transfer units, 140
Trinity College, 217
Trinity University, 194
TRW, 130
TU80 tape drive, 324
Turbo:
    C, 104
    C+, 104
    Pascal, 104
TVRO dishes, 139
Twisted pair witing (10baseT), 155
Tymlabs, 151

U.S. Department of Education, 180
U-Matic VCPs, 140
UK:
    IUIC Information Systems
        Working Party 2, 243

Joint Academic Network (JAN-
    ET), 263
ULTRIX, 52, 62
Unisys:
    2200, 12, 15
    mainframe, 297
U6000, 17
United States, 165
University:
    of Birmingham, 223
    of Bristol Info Server 2.02, 237
    of Bristol, 232
    of California, Berkeley, 211
    of Georgia, 58
    of Glasgow, 295
    of Hartford, 66
    of Illinois, 63
    of Kent at Canterbury (UKC),
        255, 313
    of Leeds, 256
    of Limerick, 90
    of Maryland, 103
    of Maryland's MD-DOS/IP
        package, 133
    of Newcastle, 295
    of Reading, 225
    of Richmond, 111
    of Scranton, 116
    of Texas Health Science Center
        at San Antonio, 196
    of the South, 148
    of York, 263, 302
UNIX, 8
UBSD, 258
    vi editor, 263
Unshielded twisted pair (UTP), 157
Ur-prototype Info Server, 234
Usenet news groups, 217, 229
USOC, 127

V.32/V.42bis modems, 170
VGA Monitor, 199, 333